C Recipes

A Problem-Solution Approach

Shirish Chavan

Apress®

C Recipes: A Problem-Solution Approach

Shirish Chavan
Sangli, Maharashtra, India

ISBN-13 (pbk): 978-1-4842-2966-8   ISBN-13 (electronic): 978-1-4842-2967-5
DOI 10.1007/978-1-4842-2967-5

Library of Congress Control Number: 2017950166

Cover image designed by Freepik

Managing Director: Welmoed Spahr
Editorial Director: Todd Green
Acquisitions Editor: Celestin Suresh John
Development Editor: Matthew Moodie
Technical Reviewer: Yogesh Sharma
Coordinating Editor: Prachi Mehta
Copy Editor: Kim Wimpsett
Compositor: SPi Global
Indexer: SPi Global
Artist: SPi Global

Distributed to the book trade worldwide by Springer Science+Business Media New York, 233 Spring Street, 6th Floor, New York, NY 10013. Phone 1-800-SPRINGER, fax (201) 348-4505, e-mail orders-ny@springer-sbm.com, or visit www.springeronline.com. Apress Media, LLC is a California LLC and the sole member (owner) is Springer Science + Business Media Finance Inc (SSBM Finance Inc). SSBM Finance Inc is a **Delaware** corporation.

For information on translations, please e-mail rights@apress.com, or visit www.apress.com/rights-permissions.

Apress titles may be purchased in bulk for academic, corporate, or promotional use. eBook versions and licenses are also available for most titles. For more information, reference our Print and eBook Bulk Sales web page at www.apress.com/bulk-sales.

Any source code or other supplementary material referenced by the author in this book is available to readers on GitHub via the book's product page, located at www.apress.com/978-1-4842-2966-8. For more detailed information, please visit www.apress.com/source-code.

Printed on acid-free paper

This is dedicated to
Honorable Dr. Patangrao Kadam,
Chancellor at Bharati Vidyapeeth University in Pune.

—Shirish Chavan

Contents at a Glance

Contents

About the Author

Shirish Chavan is a software developer, teacher, writer, and orator. He has authored nine books on computers including books on Java, Visual Basic .NET, and desktop publishing (DTP). He has 25 years of experience in various branches of IT. He is mainly interested in cryptography. He is currently working on a book on Python programming and also working on a couple of software projects. He earned his Master of Science degree in theoretical physics from Shivaji University in Kolhapur, India, in 1982. He also teaches computer science and physics at various institutes as a visiting professor.

About the Technical Reviewer

Yogesh Sharma is currently employed as a senior engineer at Mphasis with almost a decade of experience in the development and maintenance of small-scale to enterprise-grade applications. Yogesh earned his bachelor's degree in information technology from VSIT Bombay and is currently experimenting with mobility and NLP technologies with Prof. Yogesh Karunakar. Prior to editing this book, Yogesh reviewed *Beginning Laravel* by Sanjib Sinha (Apress, 2017). He would like to acknowledge his joy for all the support and motivation in his endeavors.

Acknowledgments

Thanks to everyone working at Apress who made this book possible. I am particularly thankful to Mr. Celestin Suresh John, acquisitions editor, and Ms. Prachi Mehta, coordinating editor, for their patience and guidance.

A good number of my techie friends helped me on technical matters in this book. Notable among them are Mr. Ajay Dhande, CEO of Cryptex Technologies in Nagpur (www.cryptextechnologies.com); Prof. Shivajirao Salunkhe and Prof. Manisha Salunkhe of Harsh Computer Institute in Satara; Dr. Vilas Pharande, Principal at Arvind Gavali College of Engineering in Satara (www.agce.sets.edu.in); Prof. Sachin Pratapure and Prof. Vishal Khade at Kalasagar Academy (www.kalasagaracademy.in) in Wai, Satara; Prof. Anant Bodas and Prof. Vikas Dhane at Yashoda College of Engineering in Satara; Prof. Sanjay Adhau of Shrikant Computer Training Center, Amravati (https://www.sctcamravati.com); Dr. Mir Sadique Ali, Principal, P R M I T & R, Amravati (mitra.ac.in); and Mr. Nikhil Kumbhar, CEO of Aphron Infotech in Pune (www.aphroninfotech.in). I am also thankful to Mr. Tushar Soni and Mr. Ajay Sawant, who run the web site Coding Alpha (www.codingalpha.com), and Mr. Neeraj Mishra, who runs the web site The Crazy Programmer (www.thecrazyprogrammer.com), for their valuable help in the making of this book.

Dr. Vijay Bhatkar, eminent computer scientist and father of the Indian supercomputer PARAM 10000, has been a source of inspiration for me. I am grateful to him for inspiring me.

Last but not least, I am always thankful to Mr. Jarron & Mr. John Borges and their active Technical Book Services team in Pune for the prompt supply of books.

Thank you, Sirs and Madams, you all made this book possible. Finally, a note: Pune, Nagpur, and Satara are cities in Maharashtra, India.

Introduction

This book contains good number of C "recipes" for readers at all levels, from beginning to advanced. This book follows a problem-solution approach so that you can quickly find the solution to a desired problem. Every solution comes with suitable code and a brief discussion of that code. An attempt has been made to strike a perfect balance between the theory and practice of C.

C made its first appearance in 1972. For a high-level computer language, it's now at the age of retirement. But despite being 40+ years old, C continues to be strong. C is among the ten most popular computer languages and will remain so for the next 20 years at least. Therefore, any expertise you achieve in C will not be obsolete quickly and will make you productive for years to come. This book will help you solve your problems in C, as well as make you an expert in C.

Who This Book Is For

The book is primarily for working professionals. However, it is also for students, teachers, researchers, code testers, and programmers at all levels, from beginner to advanced. It is expected that you have a working knowledge of C and programming.

How This Book Is Structured

This book consists of 11 chapters. Chapter 1 takes a bird's-eye view of the C language. Chapter 2 deals with control statements. Chapters 3–5 deal with functions, arrays, pointers, and structures. In these chapters you will find the problems faced by working programmers.

Chapter 6 deals with data files and contains a good number of recipes that deal with saving files on disk and retrieving data from saved files. Chapters 7–9 cover topics that fall broadly into the category of data structures. The data structures that have practical utility are covered in these chapters. Chapter 10 covers various cryptographic systems. C and cryptography are a very powerful and inte resting combination. In this chapter, you will experience the power of this combination.

Chapter 11—the last chapter of this book —deals with numerical methods. Computers were invented as number-crunching machines, but with the passage of time, they have emerged as data-processing machines. However, even today, number crunching is one of the most important jobs performed by computers. This chapter offers you good number of recipes that serve as number-crunching utilities.

I sincerely believe this book will be highly useful to a wide spectrum of readers.

CHAPTER 1

■ ■ ■

Welcome to C

C is a procedural programming language. The early history of C is closely parallel to the history of UNIX. This is because C was specifically developed to write the operating system UNIX, which was introduced by Bell Laboratories in 1969 as an alternative to the Multics operating system for the PDP-7 computer. The original version of UNIX was written in assembly language, but programs written in assembly language are less portable than programs written in high-level languages; hence, the people at AT&T decided to rewrite the operating system in a high-level language. This decision was followed by the hunt of a suitable language, but there was no suitable high-level language that would also permit bit-level programming.

During the same period (1970), Kenneth Thompson developed a language for systems programming that was named B after its parent language BCPL (which was developed by Martin Richards in 1967). In 1972, C made its first appearance, as an improved version of B. Developed by Dennis Ritchie, C's name is derived from B (i.e., in the alphabet, the letter *C* follows the letter *B*, and in the name BCPL, the letter *C* follows the letter *B*).

Ritchie, with a group of researchers working at Bell Laboratories, also created a compiler for C. Unlike B, the C language is equipped with an extensive collection of standard types. In 1973, the new version of UNIX was released in which more than 90 percent of the source code of UNIX was rewritten in C, which added to its portability. With the arrival of this new version of UNIX, the computing community realized the power of C. Following the publication of the book *The C Programming Language* in 1978 by Brian Kernighan and Dennis Ritchie, C shot to fame.

In 1983, the American National Standards Institute (ANSI) formed a committee, named X3J11, to create a standard specification of C. In 1989, the standard was ratified as ANSI X3.159-1989, "Programming Language C." This version of C is usually called ANSI C, Standard C, or just C89. In 1990, the ANSI C standard (with a few minor modifications) was adopted by the International Standards Organization (ISO) as ISO/IEC 8999:1990. This version is popularly known as C90. In 1995, C89 was modified, and an international character set was added to it. In 1999, it was further modified and published as ISO 9899:1999. This standard is popularly called C99. In 2000, it was adopted as an ANSI standard.

Electronic supplementary material The online version of this chapter (doi:10.1007/978-1-4842-2967-5_1) contains supplementary material, which is available to authorized users.

© Shirish Chavan 2017
S. Chavan, *C Recipes*, DOI 10.1007/978-1-4842-2967-5_1

Programs, Software, and Operating System

Before proceeding, let me explain the meaning of the term *computer program* (hereafter, simply *program*). Well, a program is nothing but a set of instructions to be fed to a computer so the computer can do some desired work. The relationship between a program and software can be expressed as follows:

program + portability + documentation + maintenance = software

Portability means the ability of a program to run on different platforms (e.g., the Windows platform, UNIX platform, etc.). Documentation means a user's manual and comments inserted in a program. Maintenance means debugging and modifying the program as per the requests of users.

Microsoft Windows is an *operating system*. It consists of a graphical user interface (GUI). *Graphical* means pictorial, and *interface* means middleman, so a GUI is a pictorial middleman between the user and the internal machinery of a computer that assists a user (meaning a computer user). In a hotel, the waiter takes your order, approaches the kitchen, collects the dish ordered by you, and serves you. Similarly, the operating system takes your order, approaches the internal machinery of computer, and then serves you.

Machine Language and Assembly Language

A microprocessor can be aptly described as the brain of a personal computer. This microprocessor is nothing but a single chip. Various microprocessors are available. *Microprocessor* and *central processing unit* (CPU) are synonymous. A microprocessor consists of an important component called an arithmetic and logic unit (ALU), which performs all the computations. A salient feature of an ALU is that it understands only machine language, which in turn consists of only two alphabets, namely, 0 and 1 (by contrast English consists of 26 letters). Here is a typical machine language instruction:

10111100010110

A few decades back, programmers did use machine language to write programs. The then-keyboard consisted of only two keys, captioned 0 and 1. Writing a machine language program and then typing it in a computer was a laborious and tedious job. Then came the assembly languages, which eased the task of programmers. Assembly languages are low-level languages. The following is a typical assembly language statement (which performs a multiplication of two numbers), which is certainly more readable than the machine language instruction given earlier:

MUL X, Y

If a machine language program consists of, say, 50 statements, then the corresponding assembly language program would also consist of approximately 50 statements. As ALU understands only machine language, special software (called an *assembler*) was developed to translate assembly language programs into machine language programs.

Procedural Languages

A typical procedural language is closer to English than assembly language. For example, here is a statement in the procedural language Pascal:

```
If (rollNumber = 147) Then Write ('Entry denied.');
```

The meaning of this statement, which is quite obvious, is as follows: if the value of rollNumber is 147, then display the message "Entry denied." on the screen. To translate a procedural language program into a machine language program, software called a *compiler* is used. Procedural languages are high-level languages.

Programmers use procedural languages in conjunction with the techniques of structured programming. What is structured programming? In a broad sense, the term *structured programming* refers to the movement that transformed the art of programming into a rational science. It all began with a letter by Edsger Dijkstra, "Go To Statement Considered Harmful," published in the March 1968 issue of *Communications of the ACM*. Structured programming rests on the following cornerstones:

- *Modularity*: Instead of writing a one big program, split your program into a number of subprograms or modules.

- *Information hiding*: The interface of a module should exhibit only the least possible information. For example, consider a module that computes the square root of a number. The interface of this module will accept a number and return the square root of that number. The details of this module will remain hidden from the users of this module.

- *Abstraction*: Abstraction is the process of hiding the details in order to facilitate the understanding of a complex system. In a way, abstraction is related to information hiding.

However, as programs grew larger and larger, it became clear that the techniques of structured programming are necessary but not sufficient. Computer scientists then turned to object-oriented programming in order to manage more complex projects.

Object-Oriented Languages

We use computer programs to solve real-life problems. The trouble with the structured paradigm is that using it, you cannot simulate real-life problems on computers conveniently. In a structured paradigm, you use data structures to simulate real-life objects, but these data structures fall far short in simulating real-life objects. Car, house, dog, and tree are the examples of real-life objects, and it is expected that a programming language should be capable of simulating these objects to solve real-life problems. The object-oriented paradigm tackles this problem at its root simply by providing software objects to simulate real-life objects. An object provided by an object-oriented paradigm is an instance of a class and possesses identity, properties, and behavior like real-life objects do. For example, if Bird is a class, then parrot, peacock, sparrow, and eagle are objects or instances of the class Bird. Also, if Mammal is a class, then cat, dog, lion, and tiger are objects or instances of the class Mammal. Compared to the structured paradigm, the object-oriented paradigm is more capable of using existing code. *Code* means a program or its part.

The object-oriented paradigm is as old as the structured paradigm. The movement of the structured paradigm began with Dijkstra's famous letter "Go To Statement Considered Harmful" in 1968, whereas the object-oriented paradigm has its origin in the programming language SIMULA 67, which appeared in 1967. However, the object-oriented capabilities of SIMULA 67 were not very powerful. The first truly object-oriented language was Smalltalk. In fact, the term *object-oriented* was coined through Smalltalk literature. C is not object-oriented language; it is only a procedural language. In 1983 Bjarne Stroustrup added object-oriented capabilities to C and christened this new language as C++, which was the first object-oriented language widely used and respected by the computer industry. Today, the most popular object-oriented language is Java. Object-oriented languages are high-level languages.

Terminology in Computers

In almost all sciences, the terminology is derived from languages like Greek or Latin. Why? If you derive terminology from the English language, then there is a risk that confusion may occur between the technical meaning and the current usage of that term. In computers, however, terminology is derived from English, causing confusion to new learners. English words such as *tree, memory, core, root, folder, file, directory, virus, worm, garbage*, etc., are used as technical terms in the field of computers. You might be unaware that particular term has some technical meaning attached to it apart from its current nontechnical meaning. To avoid confusion, always have a good computer dictionary on your desk. Whenever in doubt, refer to the dictionary.

Compiled and Interpreted Languages

When a computer scientist designs a new programming language, the major problem is the implementation of that language on various platforms. There are two basic methods for implementing a language, as follows:

- *Compilation*: Code in a high-level language is translated into a low-level language. A file is created to store the compiled or translated code. You are then required to execute the compiled code by giving an appropriate command.

- *Interpretation*: Instructions in code are interpreted (executed), one by one, by a virtual machine (or interpreter). No file is created.

These methods are now discussed in detail.

Compilation

In compilation, the source code in a high-level language is translated into the machine language of an actual machine. FORTRAN, Pascal, Ada, PL/1, COBOL, C, and C++ are compiled languages. For example, consider a C program that displays the text "Hello" on the screen. Say hello.c is the file that contains the source code of this program (source code files in C have the extension .c). The C compiler *compiles* (or translates) the source code and produces the executable file hello.exe. The file hello.exe contains instructions in the machine language of the actual machine. You are now required to execute the file hello.exe by giving an appropriate command, and execution of the file hello.exe is not part of the compilation process. The executable file hello.exe that is prepared on the Windows platform can be executed only on the Windows platform. You simply cannot execute this file on the UNIX platform or the Linux platform. However, C compilers for all platforms are available. Hence, you can load the appropriate C compiler on a UNIX or Linux platform, compile the file hello.c to produce the executable file hello.exe, and then execute it on that platform.

The major benefit of compiled languages is that the execution of compiled programs is fast. The major drawback of compiled languages is that executable versions of programs are platform dependent.

Interpretation

In interpretation, a virtual machine is created by adding a desired number of software layers such that the source code in the high-level language is the "machine language code" for this virtual machine. For example, the language BASIC is an interpreted language. Consider a BASIC program that displays the text "Hello" on the screen. Say the source code of this program is stored in the file hello.bas. The source code in hello. bas is fed to the BASIC virtual machine, and instructions in hello.bas are *interpreted* (executed) by the BASIC virtual machine one by one. Also note that programming statements in hello.bas are machine language instructions for the BASIC virtual machine. No new file is created in the interpretation process.

The major benefit of interpreted languages is that programs are platform independent. The major drawback of interpreted languages is that the interpretation (execution) of programs is slow. BASIC, LISP, SNOBOL4, APL, and Java are interpreted languages.

In practice, a pure interpretation, as in the case of BASIC, is seldom used. In almost all interpreted languages (e.g., Java), a combination of compilation and interpretation is used. First, using a compiler, the source code in a high-level language is translated into intermediate-level code. Second, a virtual machine is created such that the intermediate-level code is machine language code for that virtual machine. Intermediate-level code is then fed to a virtual machine for interpretation (execution).

Finally, notice that all scripting languages (e.g., Perl, JavaScript, VBScript, AppleScript, etc.) are pure interpreted languages.

Your First C Program

As a tradition, the first program in a typical C programming book is generally a "Hello, world" program. Let's follow this tradition and create and run (execute) your first program. This program will display the text "Hello, world" on the screen. Type the following text (program) in a C file and save it in the folder C:\Code with the file name hello.c:

```c
#include <stdio.h>
main()
{
  printf("Hello, world\n") ;
  return(0) ;
}
```

Compile and execute this program, and the following line of text appears on the screen:

```
Hello, world
```

A language is called *case-sensitive* if the compiler or interpreter of the language distinguishes between uppercase and lowercase letters. Pascal and BASIC are not case-sensitive languages. C and C++ are case-sensitive languages.

- C is a case-sensitive language, and therefore you should not confuse uppercase and lowercase letters. For example, if you type Main instead of main, it will result in an error.

- Do not confuse the file name and program name. Here, hello.c is the name of the file that contains the source code of the program, whereas hello is the program name.

To explain how this program works (or any other program, for that matter), I need to refer to individual lines of code (LOCs) in this program, and hence, I need to number these lines. Therefore, I have rewritten the program hello with line numbers added to it as comments (these are multiline comments), as shown here. This program produces the same output as the program hello.

```c
/* This program will produce the same output as program hello. Only
difference is that this program contains the comments. Comments are for the
convenience of programmers only. Compiler simply ignores these comments.*/
                                                    /* BL */
#include <stdio.h>                                  /* LOC 1 */
                                                    /* BL    */
main()                                              /* LOC 2 */
{                                                   /* LOC 3 */
  printf("Hello, world\n");                         /* LOC 4 */
  return(0);                                        /* LOC 5 */
}                                                   /* LOC 6 */
```

There are two types of comments in C: multiline comments (also called *block comments*) and single-line comments (also called *line comments*). Single-line comments came from C++ and have been officially incorporated into C since C99.

Now notice the program hello rewritten with single-line comments inserted in it, as shown here. This program produces the same output as the program hello.

```
// This program will produce the same output as program hello. Only
difference is that this
// program contains the comments. Comments are for the convenience of
programmers only.
// Compiler simply ignores these comments.
                                                      // BL
#include <stdio.h>                                    // LOC 1
                                                      // BL
main()                                                // LOC 2
{                                                     // LOC 3
  printf("Hello, world\n");                           // LOC 4
  return(0);                                          // LOC 5
}                                                     // LOC 6
```

Traditionally, C textbooks use only multiline comments and avoid single-line comments. I will follow this convention in this book. In the remaining part of this chapter, I will cover implicit type conversions, explicit type conversions, and the salient features of C.

Salient Features of C

C is a popular language. The following features are responsible for its huge popularity:

- C is a small language. It has only 32 keywords. Hence, it can be learned quickly.

- It has a powerful library of built-in functions. C derives its strength from this library.

- It is a portable language. A C program written for one platform (say, Windows) can be ported to another platform with minor changes (say, Solaris).

- C programs execute fast. Thus, C programs are used where efficiency matters.

- All the constructs required for structured programming are available in C.

- Good number of constructs required for low-level programming are available in C, hence C can be used for systems programming.

- Pointers are available in C, which add to its power.

- The facility of recursion is available in C for solving tricky problems.

- C has the ability to extend itself. Programmers can add the functions coded by them to a library of functions.

- C is almost a strongly typed language.

Implicit Type Conversion

In an assignment statement, the quantity that appears on the right side is called the *r-value*, and the quantity that appears on the left side is called the *l-value*. In every assignment statement, you ensure that the data type of the l-value is the same as that of the r-value. For an example, see the assignment statement given here (assume intN to be the int variable):

```
intN = 350;                    /* L1, now value of intN is 350 */
```

Here, L1 means LOC 1. To save the space, I may use the letter L to denote LOC in code. In LOC 1, the l-value is intN, and the r-value is 350; their data type is the same: int. When the compiler compiles such a statement, it checks the types of both sides of the assignment statement without forgetting. This duty of the compiler is termed *type checking*. What happens if the types of both sides are not the same? Type conversion occurs! In type conversion, the type of the value on the right side is changed to that of the left side before assignment. Type conversions can be classified into two categories.

- Implicit or automatic type conversion (discussed in this section)

- Explicit type conversion (discussed in the next section)

Notice the LOC given here (assume dblN to be the double variable):

```
dblN = 35;                   /* L2, OK, now value of dblN is 35.000000 */
```

In this LOC, the type of dblN is double, and the type of numeric constant 35 is int. Here, the compiler promotes the data type of 35 from int (source type) to double (destination type), and then it assigns the double type constant 35.000000 to dblN. This is known as *implicit type conversion* or *automatic type conversion*. In implicit (or automatic) type conversion, type conversion occurs automatically.

In type conversion, the type of the r-value is called the *source type*, and the type of the l-value is called the *destination type*. If the range of the destination type is wider than the range of the source type, then this type of type conversion is called *widening type conversion*. If the range of the destination type is narrower than the range of source type, then this type of type conversion is called *narrowing type conversion*. The type conversion in LOC 2 is a widening type conversion because a range of double (destination type) is wider than a range of int (source type).

Here is one more example of implicit type conversion (assume intN to be the int variable):

```
intN = 14.85;                 /* L3, OK, now value of intN is 14 */
```

In this LOC, the type of numeric constant 14.85 is double, and the type of inN is int. Here, the compiler demotes the data type of 14.85 from double to int, it truncates and discards its fractional part, and then it assigns the whole-number part, 14, to intN. The type conversion in LOC 3 is a narrowing type conversion.

Here is one more example of implicit type conversion:

```
dblN = 2/4.0;                 /* L4, OK, now value of dblN is 0.500000 */
```

In this LOC, the r-value is an expression that in turn consists of the division of numeric constant 2 by numeric constant 4.0. But the type of numeric constant 2 is int, and the type of numeric constant 4.0 is double. Here, the compiler promotes the type of numeric constant 2 from int to double, and then the division of floating-point numbers 2.0 / 4.0 is performed. The result 0.5 is assigned to dblN.

■ **Note** When different types are mixed in an expression or in an assignment statement, then the compiler performs automatic type conversion while evaluating the expression or performing the assignment. While performing type conversions, the compiler tries its best to prevent the loss of information. But sometimes loss of information is unavoidable.

For example, in LOC 3, there is a loss of information (double type numeric constant 14.85 converted to an int type numeric constant 14). There is no loss of information in widening type conversion, but there is some loss of information in narrowing type conversion. Widening type conversions are always permitted by the compiler happily. Narrowing type conversions are also permitted by the compiler but with reluctance, and sometimes warnings are displayed by the compiler. Type conversions that do not make sense are simply not permitted. Some type conversions are permitted during compile time, but the error is reported during runtime. For example, notice the piece of code given here:

```
double dblN1 = 1.7e+300;              /* LOC K */
float fltN1;                          /* LOC L */
fltN1 = dblN1;                        /* LOC M */
printf("Value of fltN1 %e\n", fltN1); /* LOC N */
```

The compiler compiles this piece of code successfully without any warning. However, when you execute this piece of code, then instead of the expected output, the following lines of text are displayed on the screen:

```
Floating point error: Overflow.
Abnormal program termination
```

The program "crashes" during the execution of LOC M in which narrowing type conversion is attempted. When a program is terminated abruptly during runtime, in programmers' language we say that the program *crashed*.

Different languages allow the mixing of types to different extents. Language that freely allows the mixing of different types without any restriction is called a *weakly typed* language or a language with *weak typing*. A language that does not allow the mixing of different types at all is called a *strongly typed* language or a language with *strong typing*.

■ **Note**   C is almost a strongly typed language.

C's strong type checking is evident in a function call. If a function expects an int type argument and you pass a string of characters to that function as an argument (instead of the int type argument), then the compiler reports an error and halts the compilation of the program, confirming that C is a strongly typed language.

Notice that I used the term *almost* in the previous Note because, to a certain extent, implicit type conversion is allowed in C, which makes C an "almost" strongly typed language, rather than a perfectly strongly typed language.

Explicit Type Conversion

Instead of leaving the type conversion at the mercy of the compiler, you can perform the type conversion explicitly. This operation is called *explicit type conversion, casting,* or *coercion.* The operator used in casting is called *cast.* Notice the LOC given here (assume intN to be an int variable):

```
intN = (int)14.85;              /* L1, OK, casting operation performed */
```

In this LOC, the casting operation is performed on the numeric constant 14.85. An operator cast is nothing but (int). In this operation, the type of 14.85 is changed from double to int, its fractional part is truncated and discarded, and the whole-number part, 14, is returned as a numeric constant of type int, which in turn is assigned to intN. Here is the generic syntax of a casting operation or explicit type conversion:

```
(desiredType)expression
```

Here, desiredType is any valid type such as char, short int, int, long int, float, double, etc. In this syntax, the cast operator is nothing but (desiredType). Notice that parentheses are required and are part of a cast operator. The effect of this casting operation is that the type of expression is changed to desiredType.

In LOC 1, a casting operation is performed on the numeric constant, but it can well be performed on variables. Notice the piece of code given here:

```
int intN;                                                    /* L2 */
double dblN = 3.7;                                           /* L3 */
intN = (int)dblN;                                           /* L4 */
printf("Value of intN is: %d\n", intN);                     /* L5 */
printf("Value of dblN is: %lf\n", dblN);                    /* L6 */
printf("Value of dbln with cast (int) is: %d\n", (int)dblN); /* L7 */
```

This piece of code, after execution, displays the following lines of text on the screen:

```
Value of intN is: 3
Value of dblN is: 3.700000
Value of dbln with cast (int) is: 3
```

In this piece of code, a casting operation is performed on the variable dblN twice, first in LOC 4 and second in LOC 7. Notice that after performing the casting operation on dblN, the value of dblN remains unaffected. Actually, the casting operation is not performed on dblN; the value stored in dblN is retrieved, and then the casting operation is performed on that retrieved value (i.e., on the numeric constant 3.7). No wonder, after performing the casting operation on dblN with operator (int) in LOC 4, the variable dblN has remained unaffected as is evident after execution of LOC 6. The execution of LOC 6 displays the value of dblN to be 3.7. In LOC 7, the argument to the printf() function is not a variable but an expression, as shown here:

```
(int)dblN
```

In this first chapter of this book, I discussed various issues related to the C language. In the remaining chapters of the book, you will see all the C recipes. The purpose of a cookbook is to provide you readymade solutions (i.e., recipes) to your problems and in this book also you will find readymade solutions catering to needs of readers at all levels.

CHAPTER 2

■ ■ ■

Control Statements

This chapter presents recipes that exploit the power of control statements to solve problems. C is rich in control statements. Control statements in C can be broadly classified into three categories, as follows:

- Selection statements
- Iteration statements
- Jump statements

Selection Statements

A selection statement is used to choose one of the several flows of computer control. There are two selection statements: if-else and switch.

Iteration Statements

An iteration statement is used to execute a group of statements repeatedly, a finite number of times. There are three iteration statements: while, do-while, and for.

Jump Statements

There are four jump statements: break, continue, goto, and return. Normally computer control flows linearly from the preceding statement to the next statement in the source code. You use a jump statement when you need to bypass this linear flow and have the computer control jump from one statement to another statement, not necessarily the successive one.

The goto statement is used to jump to another statement within the same function. The continue statement is used only in iteration statements. The break statement is used only in iteration or switch statements. The return statement is used in functions.

© Shirish Chavan 2017
S. Chavan, *C Recipes*, DOI 10.1007/978-1-4842-2967-5_2

2-1. Sum 1 to N Numbers

Problem

You want to develop a program that computes the sum of 1 to N numbers in an interactive manner.

Solution

Write a C program that computes the sum of 1 to N numbers with the following specifications:

- The program uses the for loop to perform the summation of 1 to N numbers. Nothing is sacred about the for loop; you can also use the while loop or the do-while loop, but in these type of programs the for loop is most preferred.

- The program asks the user to enter the number N (0 < N < 30000). If the user enters the number N outside of this range, then the program asks the user to reenter the number.

- When the computed sum is displayed on the screen, the program asks the user whether he or she wants to compute another sum or quit.

The Code

The following is the code of the C program written with these specifications. Type the following C program in a text editor and save it in the folder C:\Code with the file name sum.c:

```
/* This program computes the sum of 1 through N numbers using for statement in an */
/* interactive manner. */                                          /* BL */
                                                                   /* L1 */
#include <stdio.h>                                                 /* BL */
                                                                   /* L2 */
main()                                                             /* L3 */
{                                                                  /* L4 */
  int intN, intCounter, flag;                                      /* L5 */
  unsigned long int ulngSum;                                       /* L6 */
  char ch;                                                         /* BL */
                                                                   /* BL */
  do {                        /* outer do-while loop begins */     /* L7 */
                                                                   /* BL */
    do {                      /* inner do-while loop begins */     /* L8 */
      flag = 0;                                                    /* L9 */
      printf("Enter a number (0 < N < 30000): ");                  /* L10 */
      scanf("%d", &intN);                                          /* L11 */
      if ((intN <=0) || (intN > 30000))                            /* L12 */
        flag = 1;                                                  /* L13 */
    } while (flag);           /* inner do-while loop ends */       /* L14 */
                                                                   /* BL  */
```

```
    ulngSum = 0;                                                      /* L15 */
                                                                      /* BL */
    for (intCounter = 1; intCounter <= intN; intCounter++) {          /* L16 */
     ulngSum = ulngSum + intCounter;                                  /* L17 */
    }                                                                 /* L18 */
                                                                      /* BL */
    printf("Required sum is: %lu\n", ulngSum);                        /* L19 */
    printf("Do you want to continue? (Y/N) : ");                      /* L20 */
       scanf(" %c", &ch);                                             /* L21 */
 } while ((ch == 'y') || (ch == 'Y'));   /* outer do-while loop ends */  /* L22 */
                                                                      /* BL  */
 printf("Thank you.\n");                                              /* L23 */
 return(0);                                                           /* L24 */
}                                                                     /* L25 */
```

Compile and execute this program. A "run" of this program is given here:

```
Enter a number (0 < N < 30000): 10000    ↵
Required sum is: 50005000
Do you want to continue? (Y/N) : y    ↵
Enter a number (0 < N < 30000): 31000    ↵
Enter a number (0 < N < 30000): 25000    ↵
Required sum is: 312512500
Do you want to continue? (Y/N) : n    ↵
Thank you.
```

How It Works

The for loop contained in LOCs 16 to 18 performs the summation of 1 to N numbers. do-while loops with two-level nesting are used in this program. The inner do-while loop keeps the user inside the loop as long as the user fails to enter the number N in the specified range. The outer do-while loop keeps the user inside the loop as long as the user wants to perform the summation again. The inner do-while loop adds robustness to this program. Besides the for loop, you can also use while or do-while loops to perform the summation. To use a while loop to perform summation, replace LOCs 16 to 18 with the following LOCs:

```
intCounter = 0;
while (intCounter < intN) {
   intCounter = intCounter + 1;
   ulngSum = ulngSum + intCounter;
  }
```

To use a do-while loop to perform summation, replace LOCs 16 to 18 with the following LOCs:

```
intCounter = 0;
do {
   intCounter = intCounter + 1;
```

15

```
    ulngSum = ulngSum + intCounter;
  } while (intCounter < 100);
```

Be careful while coding the terminating condition of a loop. An imprudently coded termination condition of a loop is the birthplace of bugs.

Bugs loiter around boundary values.

For example, look at the for loop given here:

```
for (intCounter = 1; intCounter < 100; intCounter++) {
    /*  some code here */
  }
```

At first glance, you may think this for loop performs 100 iterations, but in reality, it performs only 99 iterations. Therefore, be cautious when dealing with boundary values.

An error in a source code is a *bug*. The process of spotting and correcting the error in source code is called *debugging*.

An expert programmer creates programs with the least number of possible bugs and also knows how to debug a program. It is possible to write a small program that is absolutely free from bugs, but professional programs that consists of thousands of LOCs are never free from bugs.

2-2. Compute the Factorial of a Number
Problem

You want to develop a program to compute the factorial of a number.

Solution

The factorial of a positive integer n is denoted by n! and is defined as follows:

```
n! = 1 ×  2 ×  ..... ×  n
```

The factorials of a few numbers are given here:

```
0! = 1                          (by definition)
1! = 1
2! = 1 × 2 = 2
3! = 1 × 2 × 3 = 6
```

Write a C program with the following specifications:

- The program uses a for loop to compute the factorial of N.

- The program asks the user to enter the number N (0 < N <= 12). If the user enters the number N outside of this range, then the program asks the user to reenter the number.

- When the computed sum is displayed on the screen, the program asks the user whether he or she wants to compute another factorial or quit.

The Code

The following is the code of the C program written with these specifications. Type the following C program in a text editor and save it in the folder C:\Code with the file name fact.c:

```
/* This program computes the factorial of number N in an interactive manner. */
                                                           /* BL */
#include <stdio.h>                                         /* L1 */
                                                           /* BL */
main()                                                     /* L2 */
{                                                          /* L3 */
 int intN, intCounter, flag;                               /* L4 */
 unsigned long int ulngFact;                               /* L5 */
 char ch;                                                  /* L6 */
                                                           /* BL */
 do {                    /* outer do-while loop begins */  /* L7 */
                                                           /* BL */
  do {                   /* inner do-while loop begins */  /* L8 */
   flag = 0;                                               /* L9 */
   printf("Enter a number (0 < N <= 12): ");               /* L10 */
   scanf("%d", &intN);                                     /* L11 */
   if ((intN <=0) || (intN > 12))                          /* L12 */
     flag = 1;                                             /* L13 */
  } while (flag);         /* inner do-while loop ends */   /* L14 */
                                                           /* BL  */
 ulngFact = 1;                                             /* L15 */
                                                           /* BL  */
 for (intCounter = 1; intCounter <= intN; intCounter++) {  /* L16 */
  ulngFact = ulngFact * intCounter;                        /* L17 */
 }                                                         /* L18 */
                                                           /* BL  */
 printf("Required factorial is: %lu\n", ulngFact);         /* L19 */
 printf("Do you want to continue? (Y/N) : ");              /* L20 */
    scanf(" %c", &ch);                                     /* L21 */
} while ((ch == 'y') ||(ch == 'Y')); /* outer do-while loop ends */  /* L22 */
                                                           /* BL  */
```

17

```
printf("Thank you.\n");                                    /* L23 */
return(0);                                                  /* L24 */
}                                                           /* L25 */
```

Compile and execute this program. A run of this program is given here:

```
Enter a number (0 < N <= 12): 6    ↵
Required factorial is: 720
Do you want to continue? (Y/N) : y    ↵
Enter a number (0 < N <= 12): 20    ↵
Enter a number (0 < N <= 12): 12    ↵
Required factorial is: 479001600
Do you want to continue? (Y/N) : n    ↵
Thank you.
```

How It Works

The for loop contained in LOCs 16 to 18 computes the factorial of number N. do-while loops with two-level nesting are used in this program. The inner do-while loop keeps the user inside the loop as long as the user fails to enter the number N in the specified range. The outer do-while loop keeps the user inside the loop as long as the user wants to compute the factorial again. The inner do-while loop adds robustness to this program. Besides the for loop, you can also use while or do-while loops to compute the factorial of number N.

2-3. Generate a Fibonacci Sequence
Problem

You want to develop a program to compute the Fibonacci sequence.

Solution

Leonardo Fibonacci (1180 to 1250), also known as Leonardo of Pisa, was an Italian mathematician. He wrote a number of excellent treatises on mathematics, such as *Liber Abaci, Practica Geometriae, Flos*, and *Liber Quadratorum*. The Fibonacci sequence, named after its inventor and mentioned in *Liber Abaci*, begins with 0 and 1, and every successive term is a sum of the two preceding terms. By definition, the first term is 0, and the second term is 1. The first few terms are listed here:

```
First term        By definition      0
Second term       By definition      1
Third term        0 + 1 =            1
Fourth term       1 + 1 =            2
Fifth term        1 + 2 =            3
Sixth term        2 + 3 =            5
```

The terms in the Fibonacci sequence are also called the *Fibonacci numbers*. A possible routine that can generate Fibonacci numbers is given here in pseudocode:

```
declare four int variables a, b, c, and d
a = 0;                              /* by definition */
b = 1;                              /* by definition */
/* ############# loop begins ################ */
print the values of a and b
c = a + b;                          /* compute the next Fibonacci number */
d = b + c;                          /* compute the next Fibonacci number */
a = c;                              /* reset the value of a */
b = d;                              /* reset the value of b */
/* ############# loop ends   ################ */
```

Write a C program with the following specifications:

- The program uses a for loop to compute the Fibonacci numbers.

- The program asks the user to enter the number N (0 < N <= 45). If user enters the number N outside of this range, then the program asks the user to reenter the number. The program then generates N Fibonacci numbers.

- When the computed Fibonacci numbers are displayed on the screen, the program asks the user whether he or she wants to compute another Fibonacci sequence or quit.

The Code

The following is the code of the C program written with these specifications. Type the following text (program) in a C file and save it in the folder C:\Code with the file name fibona.c:

```
/* This program generates N Fibonacci numbers in interactive manner. */
                                                               /* BL */
#include <stdio.h>                                             /* L1 */
                                                               /* BL */
main()                                                         /* L2 */
{                                                              /* L3 */
 int intN, intK, flag;                                         /* L4 */
 long int lngA, lngB, lngC, lngD;                              /* L5 */
 char ch;                                                      /* L6 */
                                                               /* BL */
 do {                    /* outer do-while loop begins */      /* L7 */
                                                               /* BL */
  do {                   /* inner do-while loop begins */      /* L8 */
    flag = 0;                                                  /* L9 */
    printf("Enter a number (0 < N <= 45): ");                  /* L10 */
    scanf("%d", &intN);                                        /* L11 */
```

19

```
    if ((intN <=0) || (intN > 45))              /* L12 */
       flag = 1;                                /* L13 */
    } while (flag);      /* inner do-while loop ends */   /* L14 */
                                                /* BL  */

    lngA = 0;                                   /* L15 */
    lngB = 1;                                   /* L16 */
    printf("Fibonacci Sequence:\n");            /* L17 */
                                                /* BL  */

    for (intK = 1; intK <= intN; intK++) {      /* L18 */
      printf("%d th term is : %ld\n", ((intK * 2) - 1), lngA);   /* L19 */
      if (((intK *2) - 1) == intN) break;       /* L20 */
      printf("%d th term is : %ld\n", (intK * 2), lngB);   /* L21 */
      if ((intK * 2) == intN) break;            /* L22 */
      lngC = lngA + lngB;                       /* L23 */
      lngD = lngB + lngC;                       /* L24 */
      lngA = lngC;                              /* L25 */
      lngB = lngD;                              /* L26 */
    }                                           /* L27 */
                                                /* BL  */

    printf("Do you want to continue? (Y/N) : ");   /* L28 */
       scanf(" %c", &ch);                       /* L29 */
  } while ((ch == 'y') || (ch == 'Y')); /* outer do-while loop ends */   /* L30 */
                                                /* BL  */
  printf("Thank you.\n");                       /* L31 */
  return(0);                                    /* L32 */
}                                               /* L33 */
```

Compile and execute this program. A run of this program is given here:

```
Enter a number (0 < N <= 45): 1    ↵
Fibonacci Sequence:
1 th term is : 0
Do you want to continue? (Y/N) : y    ↵
Enter a number (0 < N <= 45): 50    ↵
Enter a number (0 < N <= 45): 6    ↵
Fibonacci Sequence:
1 th term is : 0
2 th term is : 1
3 th term is : 1
4 th term is : 2
5 th term is : 3
6 th term is : 5
Do you want to continue? (Y/N) : n    ↵
Thank you.
```

How It Works

The for loop contained in LOCs 18 to 27 does most of the work. The code contained in LOCs 23 to 26 computes the Fibonacci numbers. The code contained in LOC 19 and LOC 21 displays the computed Fibonacci numbers on the screen. do-while loops with two-level nesting are used in this program. The inner do-while loop keeps the user inside the loop as long as the user fails to enter the number N in the specified range. The outer do-while loop keeps the user inside the loop as long as the user wants to compute the Fibonacci numbers again. The inner do-while loop adds robustness to this program. Besides the for loop, you can also use while or do-while loops to compute the Fibonacci numbers. The Fibonacci sequence has applications in botany, electrical network theory, searching, and sorting.

2-4. Determine Whether a Given Number Is Prime

Problem

You want to develop a program to determine whether a given number is prime.

Solution

A prime number is a positive whole number that is exactly divisible only by 1 and itself. The first few prime numbers are as follows: 2, 3, 5, 7, 11, 13, 17, 19. All prime numbers are odd numbers except 2. You will develop a program that will determine whether a given number is prime.

When program execution begins, you will be asked to enter a number in the range 2 to 2000000000. Type any integer in this range, and the program will tell you whether that number is prime. Also, enter 0 to terminate the program. Obviously, to find out whether a number N is prime, you must divide it by all numbers from 2 through (N – 1) and check the remainder. Number N is a prime number if the remainder is nonzero in the case of each division; otherwise, it is not a prime number. However, in practice, you will divide the number N by all numbers from 2 through $\sqrt{N}$ (the square root of N) and check the remainder. If N is not exactly divisible by any number from 2 through $\sqrt{N}$, then certainly it is not divisible by any number from 2 through (N – 1).

A routine that will determine whether a given number lngN is prime is given here. Here, isPrime is an int variable; lngN, lngM, and i are long int variables; the value of lngN is 3 or more; and isPrime is set to 1 (to be interpreted as true).

```
isPrime = 1;                    /* L1 */
lngM = ceil(sqrt(lngN));        /* L2 */
for (i = 2; i <= lngM; i++) {   /* L3 */
  if ((lngN % i) == 0) {        /* L4 */
    isPrime = 0;                /* L5 */
    break;                      /* L6 */
  }                             /* L7, if statement ends */
}                               /* L8, for loop ends */
```

In this routine, in LOC 2, by implicit type conversion, the value of lngN is converted into the double type and then fed to sqrt() to compute its square root. The result returned by sqrt() is fed to ceil() to convert it into a nearest whole number on the higher side. The result returned by ceil() is then assigned to lngM after implicit type conversion.

Next, lngN will be divided by all the numbers from 2 through intM. If in all these divisions, the remainder is nonzero, then lngN will be a prime number, otherwise not. This is done in the for loop that spans LOCs 3 to 8. The actual division is performed in LOC 4, and the remainder is checked for its value (whether zero or not). If the remainder is zero, then LOCs 5 and 6 are executed. In LOC 5, the value of the int variable isPrime is set to zero. In LOC 6, a break statement is executed that terminates the for loop. Noting the value of isPrime, the result is displayed on the screen. If isPrime is 1 (true), then lngN is a prime number, and if isPrime is 0 (false), then lngN is not a prime number.

Write a C program with the following specifications:

- The program uses a for loop to check the primeness of a number.

- The program asks the user to enter the number N (2 <= N <= 2000000000) to determine whether that number is prime. If the user enters the number N outside of this range, then the program asks the user to reenter the number. The program then checks the primeness of that number. If the user enters 0, then the program is terminated.

The Code

The following is the code of the C program written with these specifications. Type the following text (program) in a C file and save it in the folder C:\Code with the file name prime.c:

```
/* This program determines whether a given number is prime or not. */
                                                                    /* BL */
                                                                    /* L1 */
#include <stdio.h>                                                  /* L2 */
#include <math.h>                                                   /* BL */
                                                                    /* L3 */
main()                                                              /* L4 */
{                                                                   /* L5 */
  int flag, isPrime;                                                /* L6 */
  long int lngN, lngM, i;                                           /* BL */
                                                                    /* L7 */
  do{                                                               /* BL */
                                                                    /* L8 */
  do {                                                              /* L9 */
    flag = 0;                                                       /* L10 */
    printf("Enter 0 to discontinue.\n");                            /* L11 */
    printf("Enter a number N (2 <= N <= 2000000000)\n");            /* L12 */
    printf("to find whether it is prime or not: ");                /* L13 */
    scanf("%ld", &lngN);                                            /* L14 */
    if (lngN == 0) break;                                           /* L15 */
    if ((lngN < 2) || (lngN > 2000000000))
```

```
      flag = 1;                                              /* L16 */
   } while (flag);                                           /* L17 */
                                                             /* BL  */
   if (lngN == 0) break;                                     /* L18 */
                                                             /* BL  */
   if (lngN == 2) {                                          /* L19 */
     printf("\n2 is a prime number\n\n");                    /* L20 */
     continue;                                               /* L21 */
   }                                                         /* L22 */
                                                             /* BL  */
   isPrime = 1;                                              /* L23 */
   lngM = ceil(sqrt(lngN));                                  /* L24 */
     for (i = 2; i <= lngM; i++) {                           /* L25 */
     if ((lngN % i) == 0) {                                  /* L26 */
        isPrime = 0;                                         /* L27 */
        break;                                               /* L28 */
     }                                                       /* L29 */
   }                                                         /* L30 */
                                                             /* BL  */
   if (isPrime)                                              /* L31 */
     printf("\n%ld is a prime number\n\n", lngN);            /* L32 */
   else                                                      /* L33 */
     printf("\n%ld is not a prime number\n\n", lngN);        /* L34 */
                                                             /* BL  */
 } while (1);                                                /* L35 */
                                                             /* BL  */
printf("\nThank you.\n");                                    /* L36 */
return(0);                                                   /* L37 */
}                                                            /* L38 */
```

Compile and execute this program. A run of this program is given here:

```
Enter 0 to discontinue.
Enter a number in the range (2 <= N <= 2000000000)
to find whether it is prime or not: 17  ↵
17 is a prime number
Enter 0 to discontinue.
Enter a number in the range (2 <= N <= 2000000000)
to find whether it is prime or not: 1999999997  ↵
1999999997 is not a prime number
Enter 0 to discontinue.
Enter a number in the range (2 <= N <= 2000000000)
to find whether it is prime or not: 0  ↵
Thank you.
```

How It Works

The for loop contained in LOCs 25 to 30 does the most of the work of checking the primeness of the number. The code in LOCs 31 to 34 displays the result. do-while loops with two-level nesting are used in this program. The inner do-while loop keeps the user inside the loop as long as the user fails to enter a number N in the specified range. The outer do-while loop keeps the user inside the loop as long as the user wants to checks the primeness of a new number. The inner do-while loop adds robustness to this program. Notice LOC 35, which is reproduced here for your quick reference:

```
} while (1);                                              /* L35 */
```

It seems that this is an infinite loop because no comparison statement is in the parentheses. However, a provision for termination of the loop is made in LOC 18, which is also reproduced here for your quick reference:

```
If (lngN == 0) break;                                     /* L18 */
```

When the value of lngN is zero, the execution of this loop is terminated successfully.

The library functions ceil() and sqrt() are used in LOC 24, which is also reproduced here for your quick reference:

```
lngM = ceil(sqrt(lngN));                                  /* L24 */
```

The library functions ceil() and sqrt() are mathematical functions; that's why I have included the header file math.h in this program through LOC 2. The term sqrt stands for "square root," and the term ceil stands for "ceiling," which in turn means upper limit. Here is the generic syntax of a statement that uses the library function sqrt():

```
dblX = sqrt(dblY);
```

Here, dblY is an expression that evaluates to a constant of the double type, and dblX is a variable of the double type. The function sqrt() computes the square root of dblY and returns the result, which is assigned to the variable dblX.

The function ceil() converts the double value (passed as an argument) into a nearest whole-number value on the higher side and returns the result. Here is the generic syntax of a statement that uses the function ceil():

```
dblX = ceil(dblY);
```

Here, dblY is an expression that evaluates to a constant of type double, and dblX is a double variable.

2-5. Compute the Sine Function

Problem

You want to compute the sine of an angle x using the infinite series expansion.

Solution

You want to compute the sine of an angle x using the infinite series expansion. The formula of the infinite series expansion is given here:

sin x = x - x3/3! + x5/5! - x7/7! + ...

Here, x is in radians, and it takes values in the range -1 <= x <= 1. You can see that the value of successive terms go on, decreasing rapidly. Therefore, it is more than sufficient to include only the first ten terms. If the value of x is 1, then the contribution due to the tenth term is approximately 2E-20, and the contribution due to the 40th term is approximately 1.7E-121.

Write a C program with the following specifications:

- The program uses a for loop to compute the sine of an angle x.

- The program asks the user to enter the angle x (-1 <= x <= 1). If user enters the angle x outside of this range, then the program asks the user to reenter the number.

- When the sine of angle x is displayed on the screen, the program asks the user whether he or she wants to compute the sine of another angle or quit.

The Code

The following is the code of the C program written with these specifications. Type the following text (program) in a C file and save it in the folder C:\Code with the file name sine.c:

```
/* This program computes the sine of an angle where angle X is */
/* in radians and in the range (-1 <= X <= 1). */
                                                        /* BL */
#include <stdio.h>                                      /* L1 */
                                                        /* BL */
main()                                                  /* L2 */
{                                                       /* L3 */
 double dblSine, dblTerm, dblX, dblZ;                   /* L4 */
 int intK, i, flag;                                     /* L5 */
 char ch;                                               /* L6 */
                                                        /* BL */
 do {                   /* outer do-while loop begins */ /* L7 */
                                                        /* BL */
```

```
  do {                    /* inner do-while loop begins */     /* L8  */
    flag = 0;                                                  /* L9  */
    printf("Enter angle in radians (-1 <= X <= 1): ");         /* L10 */
    scanf("%lf", &dblX);                                       /* L11 */
    if ((dblX < -1) || (dblX > 1))                             /* L12 */
       flag = 1;                                               /* L13 */
  } while (flag);         /* inner do-while loop ends */       /* L14 */
                                                               /* BL  */
  dblTerm = dblX;                                              /* L15 */
  dblSine = dblX;                                              /* L16 */
  intK = 1;                                                    /* L17 */
  dblZ = dblX * dblX;                                          /* L18 */
                                                               /* BL  */
  for (i = 1; i <= 10; i++) {                                  /* L19 */
    intK = intK + 2;                                           /* L20 */
    dblTerm = -dblTerm * dblZ /(intK * (intK - 1));            /* L21 */
    dblSine = dblSine + dblTerm;                               /* L22 */
  }                                                            /* L23 */
                                                               /* BL  */
  printf("Sine of %lf is %lf\n", dblX, dblSine);               /* L24 */
  printf("Do you want to continue? (Y/N) : ");                 /* L25 */
    scanf(" %c", &ch);                                         /* L26 */
} while ((ch == 'y') || (ch == 'Y')); /* outer do-while ends */  /* L27 */
                                                               /* BL  */
printf("Thank you.\n");                                        /* L28 */
return(0);                                                     /* L29 */
}                                                              /* L30 */
```

Compile and execute this program. A run of this program is given here:

```
Enter angle in radians (-1 <= X <= 1): 0.5    ⏎
Sine of 0.500000 is 0.479426
Do you want to continue? (Y/N) : y    ⏎
Enter angle in radians (-1 <= X <= 1): 0    ⏎
Sine of 0.000000 is 0.000000
Do you want to continue? (Y/N) : y    ⏎
Enter angle in radians (-1 <= X <= 1): 0.707    ⏎
Sine of 0.707000 is 0.649556
Do you want to continue? (Y/N) : n    ⏎
Thank you.
```

How It Works

The for loop contained in LOCs 19 to 23 computes the sine of an angle x. The code in LOC 24 displays the result. do-while loops with two-level nesting are used in this program. The inner do-while loop keeps the user inside the loop as long as the user fails to enter the angle x in the specified range. The outer do-while loop keeps the user inside the loop as long as the user wants to compute the sine of another angle. The inner do-while loop adds robustness to this program.

2-6. Compute the Cosine Function

Problem

You want to compute the cosine of an angle x using the infinite series expansion.

Solution

You want to compute the cosine of an angle x using the infinite series expansion. The formula of the infinite series expansion is given here:

```
cos x = 1 - x2/2! + x4/4! - x6/6! +...
```

Here, x is in radians, and it takes values in the range -1 <= x <= 1. You can see that the value of successive terms go on, decreasing rapidly. Therefore, it is more than sufficient to include only the first ten terms, as discussed in the preceding recipe.

Write a C program with the following specifications:

- The program uses a for loop to compute the cosine of an angle x.

- The program asks the user to enter the angle x (-1 <= x <= 1). If user enters the angle x outside of this range, then the program asks the user to reenter the number.

- When the cosine of angle x is displayed on the screen, the program asks the user whether he or she wants to compute the cosine of another angle or quit.

The Code

The following is the code of the C program written with these specifications. This time, however, you use a slightly different algorithm for coding compared to the preceding recipe. Type the following text (program) in a C file and save it in the folder C:\Code with the file name cosine.c:

```
/* This program computes the cosine of an angle where angle X is */
/* in radians and in the range (-1 <= X <= 1). */
                                                        /* BL */
#include <stdio.h>                                      /* L1 */
                                                        /* BL */
main()                                                  /* L2 */
{                                                       /* L3 */
 double dblCosine, dblX, dblZ;                          /* L4 */
 int i, j, q, flag, factorial, sign;                    /* L5 */
 char ch;                                               /* L6 */
                                                        /* BL */
 do {                     /* outer do-while loop begins */   /* L7 */
                                                        /* BL */
  do {                    /* inner do-while loop begins */   /* L8 */
```

```
        flag = 0;                                              /* L9  */
        printf("Enter angle in radians (-1 <= X <= 1): ");     /* L10 */
        scanf("%lf", &dblX);                                   /* L11 */
        if ((dblX < -1) || (dblX > 1))                         /* L12 */
            flag = 1;                                          /* L13 */
    } while (flag);          /* inner do-while loop ends */    /* L14 */
                                                               /* BL  */
  dblCosine = 0;                                               /* L15 */
  sign = -1;                                                   /* L16 */
  for (i = 2; i <= 10; i += 2)                                 /* L17 */
      {                                                        /* L18 */
          dblZ = 1;                                            /* L19 */
          factorial = 1;                                       /* L20 */
                                                               /* BL  */
          for (j = 1; j <= i; j++)                             /* L21 */
                                                               /* L22 */
              dblZ = dblZ * dblX;                              /* L23 */
              factorial = factorial * j;                       /* L24 */
                                                               /* L25 */
                                                               /* BL  */
          dblCosine += sign * dblZ / factorial;                /* L26 */
          sign =  - 1 * sign;                                  /* L27 */
      }                                                        /* L28 */
  dblCosine = 1 + dblCosine;                                   /* L29 */
                                                               /* BL  */
  printf("Cosine of %lf is %lf\n", dblX, dblCosine);           /* L30 */
  printf("Do you want to continue? (Y/N) : ");                 /* L31 */
    scanf(" %c", &ch);                                         /* L32 */
  } while ((ch == 'y') || (ch == 'Y')); /* outer do-while ends */ /* L33 */
                                                               /* BL  */
  printf("Thank you.\n");                                      /* L34 */
  return(0);                                                   /* L35 */
}                                                              /* L36 */
```

Compile and execute this program. A run of this program is given here:

```
Enter angle in radians (-1 <= X <= 1): 0.5    ↵
Cosine of 0.500000 is 0.8775826
Do you want to continue? (Y/N) : y    ↵
Enter angle in radians (-1 <= X <= 1): 0    ↵
Cosine of 0.000000 is 1.000000
Do you want to continue? (Y/N) : y    ↵
Enter angle in radians (-1 <= X <= 1): 0.707    ↵
Cosine of 0.707000 is 0.760309
Do you want to continue? (Y/N) : n    ↵
Thank you.
```

How It Works

Two-level nesting of for loops is used to compute the cosine of an angle x. LOC 30 displays the result. do-while loops with two-level nesting are used in this program. The inner do-while loop keeps the user inside the loop as long as the user fails to enter the angle x in the specified range. The outer do-while loop keeps the user inside the loop as long as the user wants to compute the cosine of another angle. The inner do-while loop adds robustness to this program.

2-7. Compute the Roots of Quadratic Equation
Problem

You want to compute the roots of the quadratic equation.

Solution

You want to compute the roots of the quadratic equation $ax2 + bx + c = 0$. These roots are given by the following formulae:

```
(-b + √(b2 - 4ac))/2a          and          (-b - √(b2 - 4ac))/2a
```

Roots can be real or imaginary depending upon the values of a, b, and c. Write a C program with the following specifications:

- The program asks the user to enter the values of a, b, and c, which can be integers or floating-point numbers.

- The program computes the roots and displays the results on the screen using the formulae given earlier.

- When roots of a quadratic equation are displayed on the screen, the program asks the user whether he or she wants to compute the roots of another quadratic equation or quit.

The Code

The following is the code of the C program written with these specifications. Type the following text (program) in a C file and save it in the folder C:\Code with the file name roots.c:

```
/* This program computes the roots of quadratic equation. */
                                                              /* BL */
#include <stdio.h>                                            /* L1 */
#include <math.h>                                             /* L2 */
                                                              /* BL */
main()                                                        /* L3 */
{                                                             /* L4 */
```

29

```
    double dblA, dblB, dblC, dblD, dblRt1, dblRt2;                    /* L5 */
    char ch;                                                         /* L6 */
    do {                    /* do-while loop begins */              /* L7 */
                                                                    /* BL */
    printf("Enter the values of a, b and c : ");                    /* L8 */
    scanf("%lf %lf %lf", &dblA, &dblB, &dblC);                       /* L9 */
                                                                    /* BL */
    dblD = dblB * dblB - 4 * dblA * dblC;                           /* L10 */
    if (dblD == 0)                                                  /* L11 */
    {                                                              /* L12 */
        dblRt1 = ( - dblB) / (2 * dblA);                           /* L13 */
        dblRt2 = dblRt1;                                           /* L14 */
        printf("Roots are real & equal\n");                       /* L15 */
        printf("Root1 = %f, Root2 = %f\n", dblRt1, dblRt2);        /* L16 */
    }                                                              /* L17 */
    else if (dblD > 0)                                             /* L18 */
    {                                                              /* L19 */
        dblRt1 =  - (dblB + sqrt(dblD)) / (2 * dblA);              /* L20 */
        dblRt2 =  - (dblB - sqrt(dblD)) / (2 * dblA);              /* L21 */
        printf("Roots are real & distinct\n");                    /* L22 */
        printf("Root1 = %f, Root2 = %f\n", dblRt1, dblRt2);        /* L23 */
    }                                                              /* L24 */
    else                                                           /* L25 */
    {                                                              /* L26 */
        printf("Roots are imaginary\n");                          /* L27 */
    }                                                              /* L28 */
    printf("Do you want to continue? (Y/N) : ");                  /* L29 */
    scanf(" %c", &ch);                                            /* L30 */
    } while ((ch == 'y') || (ch == 'Y')); /* do-while loop ends */ /* L31 */
    printf("Thank you.\n");                                       /* L32 */
                                                                  /* BL */
    return 0;                                                     /* L33 */
}                                                                 /* L34 */
```

Compile and execute this program. A run of this program is given here:

```
Enter the values of a, b and c : 10   200   -30   ↵
Roots are real and distinct
Root1 = -20.148892,  Root2 = 0.148892
Do you want to continue? (Y/N) : y   ↵
Enter the values of a, b and c : 40   20   15   ↵
Roots are imaginary
Do you want to continue? (Y/N) : n   ↵
Thank you.
```

How It Works

Simple mathematical operations are performed to compute the roots of the quadratic equation. Roots can be real or imaginary depending upon the values of the coefficients a, b, and c. Therefore, provision is made to test whether the roots are real or imaginary. The do-while loop keeps the user inside the loop as long as the user wants to compute the roots of another quadratic equation.

2-8. Compute the Reverse of an Integer
Problem

You want to compute the reverse of an integer.

Solution

You want to compute the reverse of an integer. For example, if a given integer is 12345, then its reverse is 54321, and you want to compute it programatically.
Write a C program with the following specifications:

- The program asks the user to enter an integer N (0 < N <= 30000). If the user enters the integer N outside of this range, then the program asks the user to reenter the integer.

- The program computes the reverse of an integer and displays the results on the screen.

- Then the program asks the user whether he or she wants to compute the reverse of another integer or quit.

The Code

The following is the code of the C program written with these specifications. Type the following text (program) in a C file and save it in the folder C:\Code with the file name reverse.c:

```
/* This program computes the reverse of an integer number. */
                                                              /* BL */
#include <stdio.h>                                            /* L1 */
                                                              /* BL */
main()                                                        /* L2 */
{                                                             /* L3 */
    long int intN, intTemp, intRemainder, intReverse;         /* L4 */
    char ch;                                                  /* L5 */
    do {                      /* outer do-while loop begins */ /* L6 */
      do {                    /* inner do-while loop begins */ /* L7 */
        printf("Enter a number (0 < N <= 30000): ");          /* L8 */
        scanf("%ld", &intN);                                  /* L9 */
```

```
    } while ((intN <= 0) || (intN > 30000));        /* L10 */
      /* inner do-while loop ends */                /* BL  */

    intTemp = intN;                                 /* L11 */
    intReverse = 0;                                 /* L12 */
                                                    /* BL3 */
    while (intTemp > 0)                             /* L14 */
     {                                              /* L15 */
       intRemainder = intTemp % 10;                 /* L16 */
       intReverse = intReverse * 10 + intRemainder; /* L17 */
       intTemp /= 10;                               /* L18 */
     }                                              /* L19 */
                                                    /* BL  */
    printf("The reverse of %ld is %ld.\n", intN, intReverse);  /* L20 */
    printf("Do you want to continue? (Y/N) : ");    /* L21 */
    scanf(" %c", &ch);                              /* L22 */
  } while ((ch == 'y') || (ch == 'Y'));
    /* outer do-while loop ends */                  /* L23 */
  printf("Thank you.\n");                           /* L24 */
                                                    /* BL  */
    return 0;                                       /* L25 */
}                                                   /* L26 */
```

Compile and execute this program. A run of this program is given here:

```
Enter a number (0 < N <= 30000): 12345    ⏎
The reverse of 12345 is 54321.
Do you want to continue? (Y/N): y    ⏎
Enter a number (0 < N <= 30000): 45678    ⏎
Enter a number (0 < N <= 30000): 2593    ⏎
The reverse of 2593 is 3952.
Do you want to continue? (Y/N): n    ⏎
Thank you.
```

How It Works

Simple mathematical operations are performed to compute the reverse of an integer. do-while loops with two-level nesting are used in this program. The inner do-while loop keeps the user inside the loop as long as the user fails to enter the integer N in the specified range. The outer do-while loop keeps the user inside the loop as long as the user wants to compute the reverse of another integer. The inner do-while loop adds robustness to this program.

2-9. Print a Geometrical Pattern Using Nested Loops

Problem

You want to generate and print on-screen the following geometrical pattern using the nested loops (and not using the naïve five `printf()` statements):

```
    1
   212
  32123
 4321234
543212345
```

The order of this pattern is five; i.e., it consists of five lines. You want to generate the pattern of any order from one to nine.

Solution

You can print this pattern programatically using two-level nesting of `for` loops. Write a C program with the following specifications:

- The program asks the user to enter the order of the pattern (1 <= N <= 9). If the user enters an N outside of this range, then the program asks the user to reenter the N.

- The program prints the desired pattern using two-level nesting of `for` loops. However, there will be four `for` loops in this program.

- Then the program asks the user whether he or she wants to print another pattern or quit.

The Code

The following is the code of the C program written with these specifications. Type the following text (program) in a C file and save it in the folder C:\Code with the file name `pattern.c`:

```
/* This program prints the geometrical pattern on the screen. */
                                                                    /* BL */
#include <stdio.h>                                                  /* L1 */
                                                                    /* BL */
main()                                                              /* L2 */
{                                                                   /* L3 */
    int intI, intJ, intK, intL, intOrd;                            /* L4 */
    char ch;                                                        /* L5 */
    do {                    /* do-while loop begins */             /* L6 */
        do {                /* do-while loop begins */             /* L7 */
```

33

```
        printf("Enter the order of pattern (0 < N < 10): ");        /* L8 */
        scanf("%d", &intOrd);                                        /* L9 */
    } while ((intOrd <= 0) || (intOrd >= 10));
    /* do-while loop ends */                                         /* L10 */
                                                                     /* BL */
    for (intI = 1; intI <= intOrd; intI++)                           /* L11 */
    {                                                                /* L12 */
        for (intJ = intOrd; intJ > intI; intJ--)                     /* L13 */
        {                                                            /* L14 */
            printf(" ");                                             /* L15 */
        }                                                            /* L16 */
        for (intK = intI; intK >= 1; intK--)                         /* L17 */
        {                                                            /* L18 */
            printf("%d", intK);                                      /* L19 */
        }                                                            /* L20 */
        for (intL = 2; intL <= intI; intL++)                         /* L21 */
        {                                                            /* L22 */
            printf("%d", intL);                                      /* L23 */
        }                                                            /* L24 */
        printf("\n");                                                /* L25 */
    }                                                                /* L26 */
    printf("Do you want to continue? (Y/N) : ");                     /* L27 */
    scanf(" %c", &ch);                                               /* L28 */
} while ((ch == 'y') || (ch == 'Y')); /* do-while loop ends */       /* L29 */
printf("Thank you\n");                                               /* L30 */
                                                                     /* BL */
    return 0;                                                        /* L31 */
}                                                                    /* L32 */
```

Compile and execute this program. A run of this program is given here:

```
Enter the order of pattern (0 < N < 10): 5   ↵
    1
   212
  32123
 4321234
543212345
Do you want to continue? (Y/N) : n   ↵
Thank you.
```

How It Works

A correct combination of for loops generates the desired pattern. do-while loops with two-level nesting are used in this program. The inner do-while loop keeps the user inside the loop as long as the user fails to enter the integer N in the specified range. The outer do-while loop keeps the user inside the loop as long as the user wants to generate another pattern of a different order. The inner do-while loop adds robustness to this program.

2-10. Generate a Table of Future Value Interest Factors

Problem

You want to generate a table of future value interest factors (FVIFs) and print it on the screen.

Solution

You can generate and print this table programmatically using two-level nesting of for loops. Write a C program with the following specifications:

- The program generates the FVIF table for interest rates varying from 1 percent to 6 percent and for the periods varying from 1 year to 10 years.

- The FVIF values should be accurate up to three decimal points.

The Code

The following is the code of the C program written with these specifications. Type the following text (program) in a C file and save it in the folder C:\Code with the file name interest.c:

```
/* This program computes table of FVIF, Future Value Interest Factors. */
                                                              /* BL */
#include <stdio.h>                                            /* L1 */
#include <math.h>                                             /* L2 */
                                                              /* BL */
#define  MAX_INTEREST  6                                      /* L3 */
#define  MAX_PERIOD   10                                      /* L4 */
                                                              /* BL */
main()                                                        /* L5 */
{                                                             /* L6 */
  int i, interest, years;                                     /* L7 */
  float fvif;                                                 /* L8 */
  printf("\nTable of FVIF (Future Value Interest Factors)."); /* L9 */
  printf("\nRate of interest varies from 1% to 6%.");         /* L10 */
  printf("\nPeriod varies from 1 year to 10 years.");         /* L11 */
  printf("\n\n                    Interest Rate  ");           /* L12 */
  printf("\n\t ------------------------------------------"); /* L13 */
  printf("\nPeriod");                                          /* L14 */
  for (i=1; i<= MAX_INTEREST; i++)                             /* L15 */
    printf("\t  %d%", i);                                      /* L16 */
  printf("\n-------------------------------------------------\n"); /* L17 */
  for(years=1; years <= MAX_PERIOD; years++) {                /* L18 */
```

```
    printf("%d\t", years);                                    /* L19 */
    for(interest=1; interest <= MAX_INTEREST; interest++) {   /* L20 */
        fvif = pow((1+interest*0.01), years);                 /* L21 */
        printf("%6.3f\t", fvif);                              /* L22 */
    }                                                         /* L23 */
    printf("\n");                                             /* L24 */
  }                                                           /* L25 */
  printf("-------------------------------------------------\n");  /* L26 */
  printf("Thank you.\n");                                     /* L27 */
  return 0;                                                   /* L28 */
}                                                             /* L29 */
```

Compile and execute this program. A run of this program is given here:

```
Table of FVIF (Future Value Interest Factors).
Rate of Interest varies from 1% to 6%.
Period varies from 1 year to 10 years.


                         Interest Rate
         ---------------------------------------------
Period     1%      2%      3%      4%      5%      6%
         ---------------------------------------------
1        1.010   1.020   1.030   1.040   1.050   1.060
2        1.020   1.040   1.061   1.082   1.102   1.124
3        1.030   1.061   1.093   1.125   1.158   1.191
4        1.041   1.082   1.126   1.170   1.216   1.262
5        1.051   1.104   1.159   1.217   1.276   1.338
6        1.062   1.126   1.194   1.265   1.340   1.419
7        1.072   1.149   1.230   1.316   1.407   1.504
8        1.083   1.172   1.267   1.369   1.477   1.594
9        1.094   1.195   1.305   1.423   1.551   1.689
10       1.105   1.219   1.344   1.480   1.629   1.791
         ---------------------------------------------
Thank you.
```

How It Works

FVIF tables are useful in calculating the future value of money. The future value (FVn) of the principal amount (P_0) after n years, with a rate of interest (i%) per annum, is given by the following formulae:

$$FV_n = P_0 * (1 + i)n = P_0 * FVIF$$

Here, FVIF = $(1 + i)_n$.

Suppose the principal amount is US$200, the rate of interest is 6 percent per annum, and the period is 8 years; from the previous table you can find that the corresponding FVIF is 1.594 (last column, eighth row). The future value for this amount is given by the following:

$$FV_n = US\$200 * 1.594 = US\$318.80$$

In this program, LOCs 1 to 2 consist of include statements. LOCs 3 to 4 consist of define statements. LOCs 5 to 29 consist of the definition of the main() function. In LOCs 7 to 8, a few variables are declared. LOCs 9 to 11 consist of three printf() statements that print the information about the FVIF table. LOCs 12 to 17 print the heading of the FVIF table. LOCs 18 to 25 consist of nested for loops. The FVIF table is calculated and printed in these nested loops. LOC 26 prints the bottom line of the FVIF table.

CHAPTER 3

■ ■ ■

Functions and Arrays

Besides basic types, C consists of derived types. Figure 3-1 shows a diagrammatic representation of basic types and derived types in C. What brick is to wall, basic type is to derived type. A derived type is built up using one or more basic types as building blocks. Both functions and arrays are derived types in C.

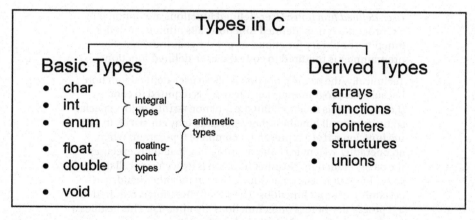

Figure 3-1. *Basic and derived data types in C. Type and data type are synonymous.*

In C, the concept of a function can be explained in a number of ways. Here are some examples:

- A function is a subprogram. It allows you to break a large computing task into smaller ones.

- A function is a piece of code delimited by braces that performs some well-defined task and also returns a value.

- A function is a building block of a program. It is helpful in making existing code reusable.

- A function is also treated as a derived type in C. See Figure 3-1.

- A function is a way to extend the repertoire of the C language.

© Shirish Chavan 2017
S. Chavan, *C Recipes*, DOI 10.1007/978-1-4842-2967-5_3

Every function needs to be coded. Coding a function means writing the programming statements for that function. Functions in C can be classified into three categories: the main() function, library functions, and user-defined functions. These categories are described here in brief:

- *The main() function*: This function is required in a C program. There will be one (and only one) main() function in every C program. When the operating system executes a C program, it actually executes the main() function. The main() function calls library functions and user-defined functions, as per the requirements. The programmer is required to code the main() function.

- *Library functions*: These are also called *system-defined* or *built-in* functions. For example, printf() and scanf() are library functions. Library functions are optional in a C program. But it is virtually impossible to build a useful program that is devoid of library functions. A programmer is not required to code the library functions. Compiler developers code the library functions, compile them, and place them in libraries for you to use.

- *User-defined functions*: User-defined functions are optional in a C program. A user-defined function calls other user-defined functions or library functions, as per the requirements. The programmer is required to code the user-defined functions.

  Technically, the main() function is also a user-defined function because the programmer (i.e., the user) is required to code (i.e., define) this function. But the function main() enjoys special status among all functions that a program may consist of. In fact, the function main() represents a complete C program. When an operating system executes a C program, it actually executes the main() function. No other function is expected to call the main() function. The main() function, on the other hand, can certainly call other functions. The main() function is required in a C program, whereas other functions are optional. This justifies a separate category for the main() function.

- *Array*: An array is a list of items of the same data type and name but different subscripts or indices. Arrays can be one-dimensional or multidimensional. One-dimensional arrays can be represented graphically as lists. Two-dimensional arrays can be represented graphically as tables. Three-dimensional arrays can be represented graphically as blocks or cubes. For four-dimensional and higher arrays, graphical representation is not possible.

3-1. Determine the Value of Pi

Problem

You want to determine the value of the mathematical constant pi.

Solution

Write a C program that determines the value of the mathematical constant pi using the Monte Carlo method, with the following specifications:

- The program asks the user to enter the number of tosses as N ($2 <= N <= 5000$). If the user enters a number N outside of this range, then the program asks the user to reenter the number.

- Every toss will generate a pair of coordinates, x and y, in the range $0 <= x, y <= 1$, which represent a point. It is then tested to see whether the point generated lies within the circle.

- Using the standard formula stated in Figure 3-2, the program computes the value of pi.

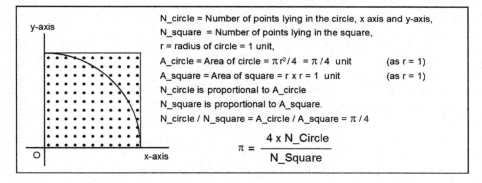

Figure 3-2. *Determination of value of pi using the Monte Carlo method*

The Code

The following is the code of the C program written with these specifications. Type the following C program in a text editor and save it in the folder C:\Code with the file name monte.c:

```
/* This program determines the value of PI using Monte Carlo method. */
                                                          /* BL */
#include <stdio.h>                                        /* L1 */
#include <stdlib.h>                                       /* L2 */
#include <math.h>                                         /* L3 */
```

```
                                                                   /* BL */
main()                                                             /* L4 */
{                                                                  /* L5 */
  int intP, intCircle, intSquare, intToss, intRM, i;               /* L6 */
  float  fltPi, fltX, fltY, fltR;                                  /* L7 */
  char ch;                                                         /* L8 */
  intRM = RAND_MAX;                                                /* L9 */
  do {            /* outer do-while loop begins */                 /* L10 */
      intCircle = 0;                                               /* L11 */
      do {        /* inner do-while loop beginss */                /* L12 */
        printf("Enter the number of tosses (2 <= N <= 5000) : ");  /* L13 */
        scanf("%d", &intToss);                                     /* L14 */
      } while ((intToss < 2) || (intToss > 5000)); /* inner do-wh loop ends */  /* L15 */
      intSquare = intToss;                                         /* L16 */
      for (i = 0; i < intToss; i++) {                              /* L17 */
      intP = rand();                                               /* L18 */
      fltX = ((float)intP)/intRM;                                  /* L19 */
      intP = rand();                                               /* L20 */
      fltY = ((float)intP)/intRM;                                  /* L21 */
      fltR = sqrt((fltX * fltX) + (fltY * fltY));                  /* L22 */
      if (fltR <= 1)                                               /* L23 */
         intCircle = intCircle + 1;                                /* L24 */
      }                                                            /* L25 */
    fltPi = 4 * ((float) intCircle) / intSquare ;                  /* L26 */
    printf("\nThe value of pi is : %f\n", fltPi);                  /* L27 */
   printf("Do you want to continue? (Y/N) : ");                    /* L28 */
      scanf(" %c", &ch);                                           /* L29 */
 } while ((ch == 'y') || (ch == 'Y'));    /* outer do-while loop ends */  /* L30 */
                                                                   /* BL */
 printf("Thank you\n");                                            /* L31 */
 return(0);                                                        /* L32 */
}                                                                  /* L33 */
```

Compile and execute this program. A run of this program is given here:

```
Enter the number of tosses (2 <= N <= 5000) : 500
The value of pi is : 3.112000
Do you want to continue? (Y/N) : y
Enter the number of tosses (2 <= N <= 5000) : 1000
The value of pi is : 3.148000
Do you want to continue? (Y/N) : n
Thank you.
```

How It Works

The accurate value of π (pi) is 3.14159. The most important factor that prevents you from approaching this accurate value is that the random values generated by the C compiler are not truly random. Despite this shortcoming, this program has determined the value of pi with sufficient accuracy. If you use the function srand(), you can input a seed value to this function, and then the random values generated would be more random.

> The city of Monte Carlo is located in Monaco and is famous for gambling and casinos. The Monte Carlo method is based on simple laws of probability and works as follows: Imagine a rectangle of side 2r and a circle of radius r, both concentric with origin 0 of the coordinate system. For simplicity, you consider only one-fourth of these figures in the first quadrant, as shown in Figure 3-2. If you generate a large number of points randomly to be anywhere within the square, then these points will occupy all the available space almost uniformly. In this program, you can generate up to 5,000 points.

In LOCs 18 to 21, a pair of coordinates (fltX and fltY) is created with their values in the range 0 to 1 (boundary values included), and this pair defines a point that lies somewhere in the square (shown in Figure 3-2). The function rand() creates a random integer in the range 0 to RAND_MAX, where RAND_MAX is a compiler-defined constant. In LOC 22, the distance between the origin and the point generated, fltR, is computed. Every point generated adds to the value of intSquare; however, if the value of fltR for that point is equal to or less than 1, then that point also adds to the value of intCircle. In Figure 3-2, the variables intCircle and intSquare are represented by the terms N_Circle and N_Square, respectively.

The for loop spanning LOCs 17 to 25 is iterated intToss times. In LOC 26, the value of π (pi) is computed. In LOC 27, this value is displayed on the screen.

3-2. Pick the Prime Numbers from a List of Numbers
Problem

You want to pick the prime numbers from a list of serial numbers, say, 1 to 1000.

Solution

Write a C program that picks the prime numbers from a list of numbers, 1 to N, using the sieve of Eratosthenes, with the following specifications:

- The program generates a list of numbers from 1 up to N.

- The program deletes the first number in the list, 1, as 1 is not a prime number by definition. The program then deletes the numbers in a list that are multiples of 2, but 2 is not deleted as 2 is a prime number by definition.

- The program then deletes the numbers in a list that are multiples of 3 (as 3 is the next undeleted number after 2), then multiples of 5 (as 5 is the next undeleted number after 3), and then multiples of the next undeleted numbers (up to the square root of N). Finally, you are left with a list of prime numbers.

The Code

The following is the code of the C program written with these specifications. Type the following C program in a text editor and save it in the folder C:\Code with the file name erato.c:

```
/* This program picks the prime numbers from a list of serial numbers with */   /* BL */
/* a range from 1 to 1000. */                                                     /* L1 */
#include <stdio.h>                                                                /* L2 */
#include <math.h>                                                                 /* L3 */
#define SIZE 1000                                                                 /* BL */
                                                                                  /* L4 */
int status[SIZE];                                                                 /* BL */
                                                                                  /* L5 */
void sieve()                                                                      /* L6 */
{                                                                                 /* L7 */
 int i, j, sq;                                                                    /* L8 */
 for(i = 0; i < SIZE; i++) {                                                      /* L9 */
 status[i] = 0;                                                                   /* L10 */
 }                                                                                /* BL */
                                                                                  /* L11 */
 sq = sqrt(SIZE);                                                                 /* BL */
                                                                                  /* L12 */
 for(i=4;i<=SIZE;i+=2) {                                                          /* L13 */
    status[i] = 1;                                                                /* L14 */
 }                                                                                /* BL */
                                                                                  /* L15 */
 for(i = 3; i <= sq; i += 2)                                                      /* L16 */
 {                                                                                /* L17 */
    if(status[i] == 0)                                                            /* L18 */
      {                                                                           /* L19 */
          for(j = 2*i; j <= SIZE; j += i)                                         /* L20 */
             status[j] = 1;                                                       /* L21 */
      }                                                                           /* L22 */
 }                                                                                /* L23 */
 status[1] = 1;                                                                   /* L24 */
}                                                                                 /* BL */
                                                                                  /* L25 */
main()                                                                            /* L26 */
{                                                                                 /* L27 */
 int i, intN;                                                                     /* L28 */
 sieve();                                                                         /* L29 */
 do {                                                                             /* L30 */
   printf("\n\nEnter the number (1 <= N <= 1000) : ");                            /* L31 */
   scanf("%d",&intN);                                                             /* L32 */
 } while ((intN < 1) || (intN > 1000));
```

```
printf("\nFollowing numbers are prime in the range:
                                  1 to %d :\n", intN);    /* L33 */
for (i = 1; i < intN; i++)                               /* L34 */
  if(status[i]==0) printf("%d\t", i);                    /* L35 */
printf("\nThank you.\n");                                /* L36 */
                                                         /* BL  */
return 0;                                                /* L37 */
}                                                        /* L38 */
```

Compile and execute this program. A run of this program is given here:

```
Enter the number (1 <= N <= 1000) :  ↵
Following numbers are prime in the range: 1 to 30 :
2  3  5  7  11  13  17  19  23  29
Thank you.
```

How It Works

How a sieve of Eratosthenes works is simple. This method is particularly useful when you want to compute the first N prime numbers. In this method, nonprime numbers are simply deleted one by one from a list of serial numbers from 1 to N, and finally, you are left only with prime numbers in the list of serial numbers from 1 to N. Figure 3-3 illustrates a sieve of Eratosthenes works.

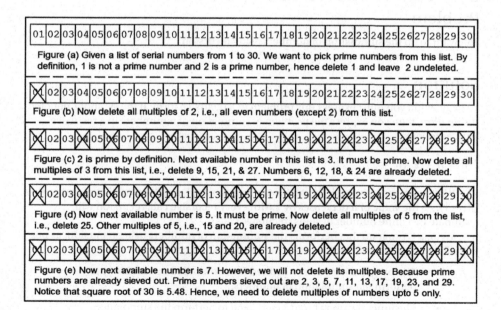

Figure 3-3. *Picking the prime numbers from a list of numbers using a sieve of Eratosthenes*

45

The function sieve() defined in LOCs 5 to 24 does the task of sieving the numbers and picking the prime numbers. An int type array called status of size SIZE is defined in LOC 4, and SIZE is defined to be 1000. All the cells in this array would be filled with either 1s or 0s. These 1 and 0 are status indicators; 0 indicates a prime number, and 1 indicates a nonprime number. For example, cell status[17] would be filled with 0, meaning 17 is prime number; cell status[20] would be filled with 1, meaning 20 is a nonprime number; and so on.

In LOCs 8 and 9, this array is filled with 0s with the help of a for loop. You ignore the first cell in this array, i.e., status[0]. The number 1 is not a prime number by definition; hence, in LOC 23, the program places the integer 1 in the cell status[1]. You know that numbers 2 and 3 are prime numbers and hence leave the status of the corresponding cells unaffected, as zeros are already filled in these cells.

In LOCs 12 to 14, a program deletes all the even numbers in the list (except 2) with the help of a for loop. In reality, the program fills the corresponding cells with status indicator 1. In LOCs 15 to 22, the program deletes the remaining nonprime numbers in the list. In reality, the program fills the corresponding cells with status indicator 1.

In LOC 28, the function sieve() is called, and the array status is filled with required status indicators. When the execution of LOC 28 is complete, the list of prime numbers is already ready in the memory of the machine. LOC 30 asks you to enter the number N in the range of 1 to 1000. In LOCs 34 to 35, the prime numbers in the range of numbers 1 to N are displayed on the screen.

3-3. Sum Numbers Using Recursion

Problem

You want to do the summation of numbers using recursion.

Solution

To begin with, you must express this problem in a recursive form. If the symbol Σ denotes summation, then you express the problem of summation of n numbers in a recursive form as follows:

```
Σ n = n + Σ (n - 1)
```

With every recursive call, the problem of computing Σ n reduces to that of computing Σ (n - 1). As the value of n decreases by 1 with every recursive call, recursion will terminate in a finite number of steps (recursive calls).

Write a C program that performs the summation of numbers using recursion, as per the following specifications:

- The program uses a user-defined function called summation() to perform the summation of numbers.

- The function summation() calls itself to perform the summation.

The Code

The following is the code of the C program written with these specifications. Type the following C program in a text editor and save it in the folder C:\Code with the file name sum2.c:

```
/* This program performs summation of numbers 1 to 4 using recursion. */
                                                            /* BL */
#include <stdio.h>                                          /* L1 */
                                                            /* BL */
int summation (int intM);                                   /* L2 */
                                                            /* BL */
main()                                                      /* L3 */
{                                                           /* L4 */
  int intN = 4, intR;                                       /* L5 */
  intR = summation(intN);                                   /* L6 */
  printf("Sum : 1 + 2 + 3 + 4 = %d\n", intR);               /* L7 */
  return(0);                                                /* L8 */
}                                                           /* L9 */
                                                            /* BL */
int summation(int intM)                                     /* L10 */
{                                                           /* L11 */
 if (intM == 1)                                             /* L12 */
    return 1;                                               /* l13 */
 else                                                       /* L14 */
   return (intM + summation(intM - 1));                     /* L15 */
 }                                                          /* L16 */
```

Compile and execute this program. A run of this program is given here:

```
Sum : 1 + 2 + 3 + 4 = 10
```

How It Works

In this program, LOCs 3 to 9 consist of the definition of the main() function. LOCs 10 to 16 consist of the definition of the summation() function. In LOC 6, a call is made to the function summation(), and integer value 4 is passed to this function as an argument. This is the first call to the function summation(). The value of the argument (i.e., 4) is assigned to the parameter intM, which serves as the local variable inside the function summation(). The function summation() consists of two return statements: if the value of intM is 1, then the value 1 is returned; otherwise, an expression is returned that consists of a function call (see LOC 15). Because the value of intM is 4, LOC 15 is executed, which wants to return the following value:

```
4 + summation(3)
```
                                                            Expression A

47

To compute the value of this expression, the computer once again calls the function summation() with the argument 3. This is the second call to summation(). The values of the local variables in summation() during its first execution are stored in a stack and not thrown away. During the second execution of summation(), the value of intM is 3; hence, once again LOC 15 is executed, which now wants to return the following value:

```
3 + summation (2)                                        Expression B
```

To compute the value of this expression, the computer once again calls the function summation() with the argument 2. This is the third call to summation(). The values of the local variables in summation() during its second execution are stored in a stack and not thrown away. During the third execution of summation(), the value of M is 2; hence, once again, LOC 15 is executed, which now wants to return the following value:

```
2 + summation (1)                                        Expression C
```

To compute the value of this expression, the computer once again calls the function summation() with the argument 1. This is the fourth call to summation(). The values of the local variables in summation() during its third execution are stored in a stack and not thrown away. During the fourth execution of summation(), the value of intM is 1; hence, this time LOC 13 (and not LOC 15) is executed. LOC 13 consists of the return statement; this return statement is executed, and integer value 1 is returned. With the execution of the return statement, the fourth execution of summation() also becomes complete.

Now computer control is transferred back to the third execution of summation(). Recall that while evaluating the expression C—i.e., during the third execution of summation()—a call was made for the fourth execution of summation(). The value returned by the fourth execution of summation() is nothing but simply 1, and this is the value of summation(1). Insert this value in expression C, as follows:

```
2 + summation (1) = 2 + 1 = 3
```

Thus, the value of expression C turns out to be 3. Well, this is the third execution of summation(). The computer executes the return statement and returns the value 3 to complete the execution of LOC 15 as well as the third execution of summation().

Now computer control is transferred back to the second execution of summation(). Recall that while evaluating the expression B (i.e., during the second execution of summation()), a call was made for the third execution of summation(). The value returned by the third execution of summation() is nothing but simply 3, and this is the value of summation(2). Insert this value in expression B, as follows:

```
3 + summation(2) = 3 + 3 = 6
```

Thus, the value of expression B turns out to be 6. Well, this is the second execution of summation(). The computer executes the return statement and returns the value 6 in order to complete the execution of LOC 15 as well as the second execution of summation().

Now computer control is transferred back to the first execution of summation().
Recall that while evaluating the expression A (i.e., during the first execution of
summation()), a call was made for the second execution of summation(). The value
returned by the second execution of summation() is nothing but simply 6, and this is the
value of summation(3). Insert this value in expression A, as follows:

```
4 + summation(3) = 4 + 6 = 10
```

Thus, the value of expression A turns out to be 10. Well, this is the first execution of
summation(). The computer executes the return statement and returns the value 10 to
complete the execution of LOC 15 as well as the first execution of summation(). The call
for the first execution of summation() was made in LOC 6. The value returned by the first
execution of summation(), which is nothing but 10, is now assigned to intR (see LOC 6).
This is the result of the summation of integers 1 to 4. This result is displayed on the screen
after the execution of LOC 7.

3-4. Compute the Fibonacci Sequence Using Recursion
Problem

You want to compute the Fibonacci sequence using recursion.

Solution

Write a C program that computes the Fibonacci sequence using recursion with the
following specifications:

- The program should compute the first N Fibonacci numbers.

- The program consists of a user-defined function called fib(),
  and this function calls itself recursively in order to compute the
  Fibonacci numbers.

- The computed Fibonacci numbers are displayed on the screen.

The Code

The following is the code of the C program written with these specifications. Type the following
C program in a text editor and save it in the folder C:\Code with the file name fibona2.c:

```
/* This program computes Fibonacci sequence using recursion. */
                                                              /* BL */
#include <stdio.h>                                            /* L1 */
                                                              /* BL */
int fib(int);                                                 /* L2 */
                                                              /* BL */
```

49

```
main()                                                      /* L3  */
{                                                           /* L4  */
    int intK, intN;                                         /* L5  */
    do {                                                    /* L6  */
        printf("Enter a suitable number: 1 <= N <= 24: ");  /* L7  */
        scanf("%d", &intN);                                 /* L8  */
    } while (intN < 1 || intN > 24);                        /* L9  */
                                                            /* BL  */
    printf("The first %d Fibonacci numbers are:\n", intN);  /* L10 */
    for (intK = 0; intK < intN; intK++)                     /* L11 */
    {                                                       /* L12 */
        printf("\t%d ", fib(intK));                         /* L13 */
        if (((intK+1) % 6) == 0) printf("\n");              /* L14 */
    }                                                       /* L15 */
    printf("\nThank you.\n");                               /* L16 */
    return 0;                                               /* L17 */
}                                                           /* L18 */
                                                            /* LBL */
int fib(int intP)                                           /* L19 */
{                                                           /* L20 */
    if (intP <= 0)                                          /* L21 */
        return 0;                                           /* L22 */
    else if (intP == 1)                                     /* L23 */
        return 1;                                           /* L24 */
    else                                                    /* L25 */
        return fib(intP - 1) + fib(intP - 2);               /* L26 */
}                                                           /* L27 */
```

Compile and execute this program. A run of this program is given here:

```
Enter a suitable number : 1 <= N <= 24: 12   ↵
The first 12 Fibonacci numbers are:
        0       1       1       2       3       5
        8      13      21      34      55      89
Thank you.
```

How It Works

This program computes the first N Fibonacci numbers. The do-while loop spanning LOCs 6 to 9 accepts the value for number N, and it is assigned to the int type variable intN. The for loop spanning LOCs 11 to 15 computes the N Fibonacci numbers. LOC 13 prints the computed Fibonacci numbers on the screen. LOC 13 also calls the function fib() with an input argument intK. The function fib() is defined in LOCs 19 to 27. In LOC 26, two recursive calls are made to this function; in the first recursive call, the value of the input argument is decreased by 1, and in the second recursive call, the value of the input argument is decreased by 2. In successive recursive calls, the value of the input argument continues decreasing, and when it becomes 0 or 1, the standard values of the first and second Fibonacci numbers are returned, as shown in LOCs 21 to 24.

3-5. Compute the Factorial of a Number Using Recursion

Problem

You want to compute the factorial of a number using recursion.

Solution

Write a C program that computes the factorial of a number using recursion with the following specifications:

- The program asks the user to enter the number N (1 <= N <= 12). If 0 is entered, then the program is discontinued.

- The program defines the function fact(). The program computes the factorial of a number using recursion. It calls the function fact() recursively to make this computation.

- The computed result is displayed on the screen.

The Code

The following is the code of the C program written with these specifications. Type the following C program in a text editor and save it in the folder C:\Code with the file name fact2.c:

```c
/* This program computes factorial of a number using recursion. */
                                                                  /* BL */
#include <stdio.h>                                                /* L1 */
                                                                  /* BL */
unsigned long int fact(int intM);                                 /* L2 */
                                                                  /* BL */
main()                                                            /* L3 */
{                                                                 /* L4 */
  int intN;                                                       /* L5 */
  unsigned long int lngN;                                         /* L6 */
  do {                                                            /* L7 */
     printf("Enter 0 to discontinue\n");                          /* L8 */
     printf("Enter a suitable number: 1 <= N <= 12: ");           /* L9 */
     scanf("%d", &intN);                                          /* L10 */
     if (intN == 0)                                               /* L11 */
        break;                                                    /* L12 */
     lngN = fact(intN);                                           /* L13 */
     printf("%d! = %ld\n", intN, lngN);                           /* L14 */
  } while (1);                                                    /* L15 */
  printf("Thank you.\n");                                         /* L16 */
```

```
    return(0);                                          /* L17 */
  }                                                     /* L18 */
                                                        /* BL  */
unsigned long int fact(int intM)                        /* L19 */
{                                                       /* L20 */
  if (intM == 1)                                        /* L21 */
    return 1;                                           /* L22 */
  else                                                  /* L23 */
    return (intM * fact(intM - 1));                     /* L24 */
}                                                       /* L25 */
```

Compile and execute this program. A run of this program is given here:

```
Enter 0 to discontinue
Enter a suitable number: 1 <= N <= 12: 6     ↵
6! = 720
Enter 0 to discontinue
Enter a suitable number: 1 <= N <= 12: 12    ↵
12! = 479001600
Enter 0 to discontinue
Enter a suitable number: 1 <= N <= 12: 0     ↵
Thank you.
```

How It Works

In LOC 10, the number N entered by the user is accepted by the program and assigned to the variable intN. In LOC 13, the factorial of intN is computed by making a call to the function fact(). The function fact() is defined in LOCs 19 to 25. Inside this function, in LOC 24, the function fact() calls itself recursively. With every call, the value of the input argument is decreased by 1. When the value of the input argument is 1, then the value 1 is returned, as shown in LOCs 21 to 22.

3-6. Search the Largest Element in an Array of Integers
Problem

You want to search the largest element in the array of integers using recursion.

Solution

Write a C program that searches the largest element in the array of integers with the following specifications:

- The program asks the user to enter the size of array N (2 <= N <= 14).
  The program then asks the user to enter the N integers.

- Define a function named largest() that calls itself recursively and computes the largest element in the array of integers.

- The program displays the searched value of the largest element on the screen.

The Code

The following is the code of the C program written with these specifications. Type the following C program in a text editor and save it in the folder C:\Code with the file name maxnum.c:

```
/* This program finds largest element in array of integers. */
                                                              /* BL */
#include <stdio.h>                                            /* L1 */
                                                              /* BL */
int largest(int xList[], int low, int up);                    /* L2 */
                                                              /* BL */
main()                                                        /* L3 */
{                                                             /* L4 */
    int intN, i, myList[15];                                 /* L5 */
    do {                                /* do-while loop begins */ /* L6 */
      printf("Enter the length of array (2 <= N <= 14) : ");  /* L7 */
      scanf("%d", &intN);                                     /* L8 */
    } while ((intN < 2) || (intN > 14)); /* do-while  loop ends */ /* L9 */
    printf("Enter %d Elements : ", intN);                    /* L10 */
    for (i = 0; i < intN; i++)                               /* L11 */
      scanf("%d", &myList[i]);                               /* L12 */
    printf("The largest element in array: %d",
    largest(myList, 0, (intN-1)));                           /* L13 */
    printf("\nThank you.\n");                                /* L14 */
    return 0;                                                /* L15 */
}                                                            /* L16 */
                                                             /* BL  */
int largest(int xList[], int low, int up)                    /* L17 */
{                                                            /* L18 */
    int max;                                                 /* L19 */
    if (low == up)                                           /* L20 */
        return xList[low];                                   /* L21 */
    else                                                     /* L22 */
    {                                                        /* L23 */
        max = largest(xList, low + 1, up);                   /* L24 */
        if (xList[low] >= max)                               /* L25 */
            return xList[low];                               /* L26 */
        else                                                 /* L27 */
            return max;                                      /* L28 */
    }                                                        /* L29 */
}                                                            /* L30 */
```

Compile and execute this program. A run of this program is given here:

```
Enter the length of array (2 <= N <= 14) : 8   ⏎
Enter 8 Elements : 22   13   256   5   74   8   4   926   ⏎
The largest element in array: 926
Thank you.
```

How It Works

LOCs 6 to 9 consist of a do-while loop, and it accepts the length of an array entered by the user. LOCs 11 to 12 consist of a for loop that accepts the elements (which are integers) of the array entered by the user. LOC 13 displays the value of the largest element of the array, and it also makes a call to the function largest(). LOCs 17 to 30 consist of the definition of the function largest(); it searches the largest element of the array by calling itself recursively and then returns this largest element. This returned value by the function largest() is used by LOC 13 to display it on the screen with the help of the function printf().

3-7. Solve the Classic Problem of the Towers of Hanoi

You want to solve the classic problem of the towers of Hanoi using the method of recursion.

Solution

Write a C program that solves the classic problem of the towers of Hanoi using the method of recursion with the following specifications:

- The program asks the user to enter the number of disks n ($1 <= n <= 10$).

- The program defines the function move(), which calls itself recursively to solve the problem.

- The program prints the computed result on the screen.

The Code

The following is the code of the C program written with these specifications. Type the following C program in a text editor and save it in the folder C:\Code with the file name hanoi.c:

```
/* This program solves the classic problem of Towers of Hanoi using the
method of recursion. */
                                                          /* BL */
#include <stdio.h>                                        /* L1 */
                                                          /* BL */
```

```
void move(int N, char chrFrom, char chrTo, char chrTemp);       /* L2 */
                                                                /* BL */
main()                                                          /* L3 */
{                                                               /* L4 */
  int intN;                                                     /* L5 */
  do {                                                          /* L6 */
    printf("\nEnter 0 to discontinue\n");                       /* L7 */
    do {                                                        /* L8 */
      printf("Enter a number (1 <= n <= 10): ");                /* L9 */
      scanf("%d", &intN);                                       /* L10 */
    } while ((intN < 0) || (intN> 10));                         /* L11 */
    if (intN == 0)                                              /* L12 */
      break;                                                    /* L13 */
    move(intN, 'L', 'R', 'C');                                  /* L14 */
  } while (1);                                                  /* L15 */
  printf("Thank you.\n");                                       /* L16 */
  return(0);                                                    /* L17 */
}                                                               /* L18 */
                                                                /* BL */
void move(int N, char chrFrom, char chrTo, char chrTemp)        /* L19 */
{                                                               /* L20 */
  if (N > 0) {                                                  /* L21 */
    move(N-1, chrFrom, chrTemp, chrTo);                         /* L22 */
    printf("Move disk %d from %c to %c\n", N, chrFrom, chrTo );  /* L23 */
    move(N-1, chrTemp, chrTo, chrFrom);                         /* L24 */
  }                                                             /* L25 */
  return;                                                       /* L26 */
}                                                               /* L27 */
```

Compile and execute this program. A run of this program is given here:

```
Enter 0 to discontinue
Enter a number (1 <= n <= 10): 3    ↵
Move disk 1 from L to R
Move disk 2 from L to C
Move disk 1 from R to C
Move disk 3 from L to R
Move disk 1 from C to L
Move disk 2 from C to R
Move disk 1 from L to R

Enter 0 to discontinue
Enter a number (1 <= n <= 10): 0    ↵
Thank you.
```

How It Works

The towers of Hanoi are located in a temple situated in the city of Hanoi, which in turn is located in Asia. The legend goes something like this. There are three poles, as shown in Figure 3-4. Also, there are 64 disks of gold, all of different radii. Each disk has a hole in the center so that disks can be stacked around any of the poles, resulting in the formation of a tower, like a spindle pack of CDs. To begin with, disks are stacked around the left pole in the order of increasing radius from top to bottom (see Figure 3-4; however, the figure shows only four disks). Priests in the temple are trying to move all 64 disks to the right pole. The pole at the center can be used for temporary storage. Their actions are restricted by the following conditions:

- A single disk should be moved at a time.

- A disk removed from a pole cannot be placed on the ground. It must be placed around one of the three poles.

- A larger disk cannot be placed on a smaller disk. You can certainly place a smaller disk on a larger disk.

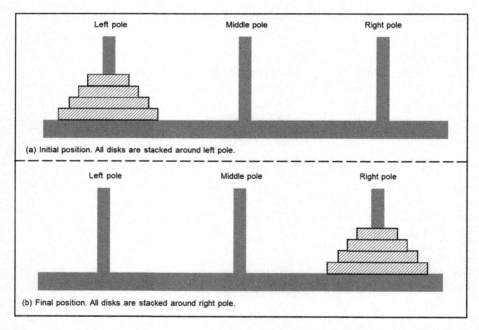

(a) Initial position. All disks are stacked around left pole.

(b) Final position. All disks are stacked around right pole.

Figure 3-4. *Classic problem of the towers of Hanoi can be attempted successfully during recursion*

It is believed that when the task assigned to priests is complete, the world will come to an end. Computer scientists have shown keen interest in this problem, because it shows the utility of recursion, not because they are apprehensive about the possibility of end of world. Using recursion, this problem can be solved by writing a simple program. Yes, you can solve this problem simply by using iterations, and without using recursion, but the program becomes quite complex.

For programming purposes, you can assume that there are n disks stacked around the left pole, where n is an integer variable. Disks are numbered from top to bottom serially with the topmost disk numbered as 1 and the bottommost disk numbered as n. Let's develop a program for shifting n disks from the left pole to the right pole, without violating any of the three conditions stated earlier. The problem can be expressed in recursive form as follows:

1. Move the top $(n - 1)$ disks from the left pole to the center pole using the right pole for temporary storage.

2. Move the nth disk (the largest and hence the bottommost disk) from the left pole to the right pole.

3. Move the $(n - 1)$ disks from the center pole to the right pole using the left pole for temporary storage.

All these three steps appeared—without any distortion—in a recursive function move() that is defined in LOCs 19 to 25. With every recursive call, the value of n decreases by 1, and hence recursion stops after a finite number of calls. Also, $n = 0$ is the stopping condition for this program.

3-8. Solve the Eight Queens Problem
Problem

You want to solve the eight queens problem using backtracking.

Solution

Backtracking is a general-purpose algorithm to find some or all possible solutions to a computing problem. In backtracking, to begin with, all possible candidates (which are likely to succeed) are considered, and then the candidates that are unable to succeed are discarded. Finally, you are left with only those candidates that successfully solve the problem. Here, on a chessboard, eight queens are to be arranged in such a manner that no queen can attack another queen. A successful solution requires that no two queens share the same row, column, or diagonal. Write a C program that solves the eight queens problem using recursion with the following specifications:

•   Define a function called queen(). Two int values are to be passed to this function as input arguments: a row number on a chessboard and the number of queens on the chessboard (which is eight in this case).

- The function queen() calls the function print(), the function place(), and also the function queen() itself recursively.

- The function place() checks the possibility of placing the queens at proposed squares on a chessboard. If everything is OK, it returns 1; otherwise, it returns 0.

- The function print() prints the successful positions of queens on the screen.

The following is the code of the C program written with these specifications. Type the following C program in a text editor and save it in the folder C:\Code with the file name queens.c:

```
/* This program solves the classic 8-queens problem using backtracking. */
                                                                    /* BL */
#include<stdio.h>                                                   /* L1 */
#include<math.h>                                                    /* L2 */
                                                                    /* BL */
void queen(int row, int p);                                         /* L3 */
int chess[8],count;                                                 /* L4 */
                                                                    /* BL */
main()                                                              /* L5 */
{                                                                   /* L6 */
 int p = 8;                                                         /* L7 */
 queen(1,p);                                                        /* L8 */
 return 0;                                                          /* L9 */
}                                                                   /* L10 */
                                                                    /* BL */
void print(int p)                                                   /* L11 */
{                                                                   /* L12 */
 int i,j;                                                           /* L13 */
 char ch;                                                           /* L14 */
 printf("\n\nThis is Solution no. %d:\n\n",++count);                /* L15 */
 for(i=1;i<=p;++i)                                                  /* L16 */
  printf("\t%d",i);                                                 /* L17 */
                                                                    /* BL */
 for(i=1;i<=p;++i)                                                  /* L18 */
 {                                                                  /* L19 */
  printf("\n\n%d",i);                                               /* L20 */
  for(j=1;j<=p;++j)                                                 /* L21 */
  {                                                                 /* L22 */
   if(chess[i]==j)                                                  /* L23 */
    printf("\tQ");                                                  /* L24 */
   else                                                             /* L25 */
    printf("\t-");                                                  /* L26 */
  }                                                                 /* L27 */
}                                                                   /* L28 */
```

```
printf("\n\n\nThere are total 92 solutions for 8-queens problem.");  /* L29 */
printf("\nStrike Enter key to continue : ");                         /* L30 */
scanf("%c", &ch);                                                    /* L31 */
}                                                                    /* L32 */
                                                                     /* BL */
int place(int row,int column)                                        /* L33 */
{                                                                    /* L34 */
 int i;                                                              /* L35 */
 for(i=1;i<=row-1;++i)                                               /* L36 */
 {                                                                   /* L37 */
  if(chess[i]==column)                                               /* L38 */
   return 0;                                                         /* L39 */
  else                                                               /* L40 */
   if(abs(chess[i]-column)==abs(i-row))                              /* L41 */
     return 0;                                                       /* L42 */
 }                                                                   /* L43 */
                                                                     /* BL */
 return 1;                                                           /* L44 */
}                                                                    /* L45 */
                                                                     /* L46 */
void queen(int row,int p)                                            /* L47 */
{                                                                    /* L48 */
 int column;                                                         /* L49 */
 for(column=1;column<=p;++column)                                    /* L50 */
 {                                                                   /* L51 */
  if(place(row,column))                                              /* L52 */
  {                                                                  /* L53 */
   chess[row]=column;                                                /* L54 */
   if(row==p)                                                        /* L55 */
    print(p);                                                        /* L56 */
   else                                                              /* L57 */
    queen(row+1,p);                                                  /* L58 */
  }                                                                  /* L59 */
 }                                                                   /* L60 */
}                                                                    /* L61 */
```

Compile and execute this program. Notice, there are 92 successful solutions to this problem. As execution begins, solution 1 is displayed on the screen, as shown here. Press the Enter key, and then solution 2 appears on the screen. If you are not interested in viewing all 92 solutions, then just press the Enter key and keep it pressed for few seconds. A run of this program is given here:

This is Solution no. 1:

	1	2	3	4	5	6	7	8
1	Q	-	-	-	-	-	-	-
2	-	-	-	-	Q	-	-	-
3	-	-	-	-	-	-	-	Q
4	-	-	-	-	-	Q	-	-
5	-	-	Q	-	-	-	-	-
6	-	-	-	-	-	-	Q	-
7	-	2	-	-	-	-	-	-
8	-	-	-	Q	-	-	-	-

There are total 92 solutions for 8-queens problem.
Strike Enter key to continue:

How It Works

LOCs 5 to 10 define the main() function. In LOC 7, the value of the int variable p is set to 8, because the number of queens on a chessboard is 8. In LOC 8, the function queen() is called. The first argument to queen() is the int value 1, and it indicates row 1. The second argument to queen() is the int variable p, and the value of p is set to the int value 8 (i.e., the number of queens on the chessboard). LOCs 47 to 61 define the function queen(). The function queen() calls the function place() to check whether the placement situation (under consideration) is safe for queens. If everything is OK, then place() returns 1; otherwise, it returns 0. Once a successful situation for the queens is found, then the function queen() calls the function print() to print the successful placement situation on the screen, as shown in LOC 56. In LOC 58, the function queen() calls itself recursively for further investigation of a placement situation, which is under consideration.

3-9. Compute Permutations and Combinations of a Given Set of Objects
Problem

You want to compute the permutations and combinations of a given set of objects.

Solution

Write a C program that computes the permutations and combinations of a given set of objects with the following specifications:

- The program uses the formulae shown in Figure 3-5 and computes permutations and combinations of r objects taken at a time from a total n object.

$$P(n, r) = \frac{n!}{(n - r)!}$$

Figure (a) Formula for permutations of 'r' objects taken at a time from total 'n' objects.

$$C(n, r) = \frac{n!}{(n - r)!\, r!}$$

Figure (b) Formula for combinations of 'r' objects taken at a time from total 'n' objects.

Figure 3-5. *Formulae for permutations and combinations of r objects taken at a time from a total n objects*

- The program displays the computed results on the screen and asks the user whether he or she wants to continue.

The Code

The following is the code of the C program written with these specifications. Type the following C program in a text editor and save it in the folder C:\Code with the file name p&c.c:

```
/* This program computes the permutations and combinations of a given set of
objects. */                                                         /* BL */
#include <stdio.h>                                                  /* L1 */
                                                                    /* BL */
int fact(int);                                                      /* L2 */
int combination(int, int);                                          /* L3 */
int permutation(int, int);                                          /* L4 */
                                                                    /* BL */
int main()                                                          /* L5 */
{                                                                   /* L6 */
    int intN, intR, intC, intP;                                     /* L7 */
    char ch;                                                        /* L8 */
    do {                                                            /* L9 */
      do {                                                          /* L10 */
        printf("Enter the total no. of objects (1 <= n <= 7) :");   /* L11 */
        scanf("%d", &intN);                                         /* L12 */
      } while ((intN < 1) || (intN > 7));                           /* L13 */
                                                                    /* L14 */
      do {                                                          /* L15 */
        printf("Enter the no. of objects to be picked at a time "); /* L16 */
        printf("(1 <= r <= %d) :", intN);                           /* L17 */
        scanf("%d", &intR);                                         /* L18 */
      } while ((intR < 1) || (intR > intN));                        /* L19 */
                                                                    /* BL */
      intC = combination(intN, intR);                               /* L20 */
```

61

```
        intP = permutation(intR, intR);              /* L21 */
                                                      /* BL */
      printf("\nCombinations : %d", intC);            /* L22 */
      printf("\nPermutations : %d", intP);            /* L23 */
      fflush(stdin);                                  /* L24 */
      printf("\nDo you want to continue? (Y/N) : ");  /* L25 */
      scanf("%c", &ch);                               /* L26 */
   } while ((ch == 'Y') || (ch == 'y'));              /* L27 */
   printf("\nThank you.\n");                          /* L28 */
                                                      /* BL */
   return 0;                                          /* L29 */
}                                                     /* L30 */
                                                      /* BL */
int combination(int intN, int intR)                  /* L31 */
{                                                     /* L32 */
   int intC;                                          /* L33 */
   intC = fact(intN) / (fact(intR) * fact(intN - intR)); /* L34 */
   return intC;                                       /* L35 */
}                                                     /* L36 */
                                                      /* BL */
int permutation(int intN, int intR)                  /* L37 */
{                                                     /* L38 */
   int intP;                                          /* L39 */
   intP = fact(intN) / fact(intN - intR);             /* L40 */
   return intP;                                       /* L41 */
}                                                     /* L42 */
                                                      /* BL */
int fact(int intN)                                    /* L43 */
{                                                     /* L44 */
   int i;                                             /* L45 */
   int facto = 1;                                     /* L46 */
   for (i = 1; i <= intN; i++)                        /* L47 */
   {                                                  /* L48 */
      facto = facto * i;                              /* L49 */
   }                                                  /* L50 */
   return facto;                                      /* L51 */
}                                                     /* L52 */
```

Compile and execute this program. A run of this program is given here:

```
Enter the total no. of objects (1 <= n <=) : 7   ↵
Enter the no. of objects to be picked at a time (1 <= r <=) : 4   ↵
Combinations : 35
Permutations : 24
Do you want to continue? (Y/N) : n
Thank you.
```

How It Works

The program consists of two do-while loops. First, the do-while loop spans LOCs 9 to 13. This loop accepts the integer value for *n* (the total number of objects) in the range 1 <= n <= 7. Second, the do-while loop spans LOCs 15 to 19. This loop accepts the integer value for *r* (the number of objects to be taken at a time) in the range 1 <= r <= n. The function combination() is defined in LOCs 31 to 36. The function permutation() is defined in LOCs 37 to 42. The function fact() is defined in LOCs 43 to 52. In LOCs 20 to 21, calls are made to the functions combination() and permutation(). The computed values of combinations and permutations are displayed on the screen in LOCs 22 to 23.

3-10. Perform the Summation of Two Matrices
Problem

You want to perform the summation of two matrices.

Solution

Figure 3-6 illustrates the summation of matrices. Write a C program that performs the summation of two matrices A and B such that A + B = C (C is also a matrix), with the following specifications:

- The program asks the user to enter the order of a matrix (i.e., the number of rows and columns in a matrix).

- The program accepts data for the two matrices A and B. Matrices can be added to or subtracted from one another, provided they have the same number of rows and columns.

- In the program, define three functions: input(), output(), and add(). The function input() accepts the data from the keyboard for matrices A and B. The function output() displays the matrices A, B, and C on the screen. The function add() performs the summation of matrices A and B and fills the values in the matrix C.

Let A, B, and C are matrices of same size. Let A + B = C.

$$A = \begin{bmatrix} a & b & c \\ d & e & f \end{bmatrix} \qquad B = \begin{bmatrix} g & h & i \\ j & k & l \end{bmatrix} \qquad A + B = C = \begin{bmatrix} a+g & b+h & c+i \\ d+j & e+k & f+l \end{bmatrix}$$

Figure 3-6. *Addition of matrices*

The Code

The following is the code of the C program written with these specifications. Type the following C program in a text editor and save it in the folder C:\Code with the file name summat.c:

```
/* This program performs the summation of two matrices. */        /* BL */
#include <stdio.h>                                                /* L1 */
                                                                  /* BL */
void input(int mat[][12], int, int);                              /* L2 */
void output(int mat[][12], int, int);                             /* L3 */
void add(int matA[][12], int matB[][12], int matC[][12], int, int); /* L4 */
                                                                  /* BL */
int main()                                                        /* L5 */
{                                                                 /* L6 */
    int row, col;                                                 /* L7 */
    int A[12][12], B[12][12], C[12][12];                          /* L8 */
                                                                  /* BL */
    do {                                                          /* L9 */
      printf("Enter number of rows (1 <= M <= 12) :");            /* L10 */
      scanf("%d", &row);                                          /* L11 */
    } while ((row < 1) || (row > 12));                            /* L12 */
                                                                  /* BL */
    do {                                                          /* L13 */
      printf("Enter number of columns (0 < N <= 12) :");          /* L14 */
      scanf("%d", &col);                                          /* L15 */
    } while ((col < 1) || (col > 12));                            /* L16 */
                                                                  /* BL */
    printf("\nEnter Data for Matrix A :\n");                      /* L17 */
    input(A, row, col);                                           /* L18 */
    printf("\n");                                                 /* L19 */
    printf("\nMatrix A Entered by you :\n");                      /* L20 */
    output(A, row, col);                                          /* L21 */
                                                                  /* BL */
    printf("\nEnter Data for Matrix B :\n");                      /* L22 */
    input(B, row, col);                                           /* L23 */
    printf("\n");                                                 /* L24 */
    printf("\nMatrix B Entered by you :\n");                      /* L25 */
    output(B, row, col);                                          /* L26 */
                                                                  /* BL */
    add(A, B, C, row, col);                                       /* L27 */
    printf("\nMatirx A + Matrix B = Matrix C. \n");               /* L28 */
    printf("Matrix C :\n");                                       /* L29 */
    output(C, row, col);                                          /* L30 */
    printf("\nThank you. \n");                                    /* L31 */
                                                                  /* BL */
```

```
    return 0;                                                      /* L32 */
}                                                                  /* L33 */
                                                                   /* BL  */
void input(int mat[][12], int row, int col)                       /* L34 */
{                                                                  /* L35 */
    int i, j;                                                      /* L36 */
    for (i = 0; i < row; i++)                                      /* L37 */
    {                                                              /* L38 */
        printf("Enter %d values for row no. %d : ", col, i);       /* L39 */
        for (j = 0; j < col; j++)                                  /* L40 */
            scanf("%d", &mat[i][j]);                               /* L41 */
    }                                                              /* L42 */
}                                                                  /* L43 */
                                                                   /* BL  */
void output(int mat[][12], int row, int col)                      /* L44 */
{                                                                  /* L45 */
    int i, j;                                                      /* L46 */
    for (i = 0; i < row; i++)                                      /* L47 */
    {                                                              /* L48 */
        for (j = 0; j < col; j++)                                  /* L49 */
        {                                                          /* L50 */
            printf("%d\t", mat[i][j]);                             /* L51 */
        }                                                          /* L52 */
        printf("\n");                                              /* L53 */
    }                                                              /* L54 */
}                                                                  /* L55 */
                                                                   /* BL  */
void add(int matA[][12], int matB[][12], int matC[][12], int m, int n) /* L56 */
{                                                                  /* L57 */
    int i, j;                                                      /* L58 */
    for (i = 0; i < m; i++)                                        /* L59 */
    {                                                              /* L60 */
        for (j = 0; j < n; j++)                                    /* L61 */
        {                                                          /* L62 */
            matC[i][j] = matA[i][j] + matB[i][j];                  /* L63 */
        }                                                          /* L64 */
    }                                                              /* L65 */
}                                                                  /* L66 */
```

Compile and execute this program. A run of this program is given here:

```
Enter number of ros (1 <= M <= 12) : 3    ↵
Enter number of columns (0 <= N <= 12) : 5    ↵

Enter Data for Matrix A :
Enter 5 values for row no. 0 : 10 11 12 13 14    ↵
Enter 5 values for row no. 1 : 11 12 13 14 15    ↵
Enter 5 values for row no. 2 : 12 13 14 15 16    ↵
```

```
Matrix A Entered by you :
10   11   12   13   14
11   12   13   14   15
12   13   14   15   16

Enter Data for Matrix B :
Enter 5 values for row no. 0 : 14 15 16 17 18   ↵
Enter 5 values for row no. 1 : 15 16 17 18 19   ↵
Enter 5 values for row no. 2 : 16 17 18 19 20   ↵

Matrix B Entered by you :
14   15   16   17   18
15   16   17   18   19
16   17   18   19   20

Matrix A + Matrix B = Matrix C.
Matrix C :
24   26   28   30   32
26   28   30   32   34
28   30   32   34   36

Thank you.
```

How It Works

The program consists of two do-while loops. First, the do-while loop accepts the integer value for the number of rows, in the range 1 <= M <= 12. Second, the do-while loop accepts the integer value for the number of columns, in the range 1 <= N <= 12. LOCs 18 and 23 make a call to the function input() and accept the data for matrices A and B, respectively. LOCs 21 and 26 make a call to the function output() and display the matrices A and B on the screen, respectively. LOC 27 makes a call to the function add(), performs the summation of matrices A and B, and fills the values in matrix C. LOC 30 makes a call to the function output() and displays the matrix C on the screen. LOCs 34 to 43 define the function input(). LOCs 44 to 55 define the function output(). LOCs 56 to 66 define the function add().

3-11. Compute the Transpose of a Matrix

Problem

You want to compute the transpose of a matrix.

Solution

Write a C program that computes the transpose of matrix A such that the transpose is A = B (B is also a matrix; see Figure 3-7), with the following specifications:

- The program asks the user to enter the order of a matrix (i.e., the number of rows and columns in a matrix).

- The program accepts data for matrix A. It computes the transpose of matrix A and displays the resultant matrix B on the screen.

Let A and B are matrices. Let B is transpose of A.

$$A = \begin{bmatrix} a & b & c \\ d & e & f \end{bmatrix} \qquad \text{Transpose of } A = B = \begin{bmatrix} a & d \\ b & e \\ c & f \end{bmatrix}$$

Figure 3-7. Transpose of a matrix

The Code

The following is the code of the C program written with these specifications. Type the following C program in a text editor and save it in the folder C:\Code with the file name transp.c:

```
/* This program computes transpose of a matrix A. */   /* BL */
                                                        /* L1 */
#include <stdio.h>                                      /* BL */
                                                        /* L2 */
main()                                                  /* L3 */
{                                                       /* L4 */
    int mat[12][12], transpose[12][12];                 /* L5 */
    int i, j, row, col;                                 /* BL */
                                                        /* L6 */
    do{                                                 /* L7 */
      printf("Enter number of rows R (0 < R < 13): ");  /* L8 */
      scanf("%d", &row);                                /* L9 */
    } while ((row < 1) || (row > 12));                  /* BL */
                                                        /* L10 */
    do{                                                 /* L11 */
      printf("Enter number of columns C (0 < C < 13): ");/* L12 */
      scanf("%d", &col);
```

```
    } while ((col < 1) || (col > 12));                      /* L13 */
                                                            /* BL  */
    for (i = 0; i < row; i++)                               /* L14 */
    {                                                       /* L15 */
        printf("Enter %d values for row no. %d : ", col, i); /* L16 */
        for (j = 0; j < col; j++)                           /* L17 */
            scanf("%d", &mat[i][j]);                        /* L18 */
    }                                                       /* L19 */
                                                            /* BL  */
    printf("\nMatrix A:\n");                                /* L20 */
    for (i = 0; i < row; i++)                               /* L21 */
    {                                                       /* L22 */
        for (j = 0; j < col; j++)                           /* L23 */
        {                                                   /* L24 */
            printf("%d\t", mat[i][j]);                      /* L25 */
        }                                                   /* L26 */
        printf("\n");                                       /* L27 */
    }                                                       /* L28 */
                                                            /* BL  */
    for (i = 0; i < row; i++)                               /* L29 */
    {                                                       /* L30 */
        for (j = 0; j < col; j++)                           /* L31 */
        {                                                   /* L32 */
            transpose[j][i] = mat[i][j];                    /* L33 */
        }                                                   /* L34 */
    }                                                       /* L35 */
                                                            /* BL  */
    printf("\nTranspose of matrix A: \n");                  /* L36 */
    for (i = 0; i < col; i++)                               /* L37 */
    {                                                       /* L38 */
        for (j = 0; j < row; j++)                           /* L39 */
        {                                                   /* L40 */
            printf("%d\t", transpose[i][j]);                /* L41 */
        }                                                   /* L42 */
        printf("\n");                                       /* L43 */
    }                                                       /* L44 */
                                                            /* BL  */
    printf("\nThank you.\n");                               /* L45 */
    return 0;                                               /* L46 */
}                                                           /* L47 */
```

Compile and execute this program. A run of this program is given here:

```
Enter number of rows R (0 < R < 13): 2    ↵
Enter number of columns C (0 < C < 13): 3    ↵
Enter 3 values for row no. 0 : 1  2  3    ↵
Enter 3 values for row no. 1 : 4  5  6    ↵
```

```
Matrix A:
1        2        3
4        5        6

Transpose of matrix A:
1        4
2        5
3        6

Thank you.
```

How It Works

The program consists of two do-while loops. First, the do-while loop accepts the integer value for the number of rows for matrix A, in the range 0 < R < 13. Second, the do-while loop accepts the integer value for the number of columns for matrix A, in the range 0 < C < 13. LOCs 14 to 19 consist of a for loop, and it accepts the data for matrix A. LOCs 21 to 28 consist of a for loop, and it displays matrix A on the screen. LOCs 29 to 35 consist of a for loop, and it computes the transpose of matrix A. LOCs 37 to 44 consist of a for loop, and it displays the transpose of matrix A on the screen. Figure 3-7 illustrates the concept of the transpose of a matrix.

3-12. Compute the Product of Matrices
Problem

You want to compute the product of matrices A and B.

Solution

Write a C program that computes the product of matrices A and B such that A × B = C (C is also a matrix; see Figure 3-8), with the following specifications:

- The program asks the user to enter the order of matrix A and the number of columns in matrix B. The program also displays matrices A and B on the screen.

- The program consists of three functions: input(), output(), and product(). The function input() accepts data from the keyboard, the function output() displays the matrices on the screen, and the function product() computes the product of matrices A and B and fills the data values in matrix C.

- The program computes the product of matrices A and B and displays the result on the screen.

> Product of matrices A x B is possible if columns in A are same as rows in B, i.e.,
>
> $$A_{mn} \times B_{np} = C_{np}$$
>
> In order to compute element cij, pick ith row from A and jth column from matrix B and perform the computation as shown below:
>
> $$c_{ij} = a_{i1}b_{1j} + a_{i2}b_{2j} + \dots\dots + a_{ip}b_{pj}$$

Figure 3-8. *The product of matrices A and B, such that A × B = C*

The Code

The following is the code of the C program written with these specifications. Type the following C program in a text editor and save it in the folder C:\Code with the file name promat.c:

```
/* This program computes the product of two matrices A and B. */
                                                                    /* BL */
#include <stdio.h>                                                  /* L1 */
                                                                    /* BL */
void input(int mat[][8], int, int);                                 /* L2 */
void output(int mat[][8], int, int);                                /* L3 */
void product(int matA[][8], int matB[][8], int matC[][8], int, int, int); /* L4 */
                                                                    /* BL */
int main()                                                          /* L5 */
{                                                                   /* L6 */
    int rowA, colA, rowB, colB;                                     /* L7 */
    int matA[8][8], matB[8][8], matC[8][8];                         /* L8 */
                                                                    /* BL */
    printf("This program performs product of matrices A and B (A x B).\n"); /* L9 */
    do{                                                             /* L10 */
      printf("Enter number of rows in matrix A (1 <= M <= 8): ");   /* L11 */
      scanf("%d", &rowA);                                           /* L12 */
    } while ((rowA < 1) || (rowA > 8));                             /* L13 */
                                                                    /* BL */
    do{                                                             /* L14 */
      printf("Enter number of columns in matrix A (1 <= N <= 8): ");/* L15 */
      scanf("%d", &colA);                                           /* L16 */
    } while ((colA < 1) || (colA > 8));                             /* L17 */
                                                                    /* BL  */
    printf("\nNumber of rows in matrix B is equal ");               /* L18 */
    printf("to number of columns in matirx A:\n");                  /* L19 */
    rowB = colA;                                                    /* L20 */
                                                                    /* BL  */
```

```
   do {                                                      /* L21 */
      printf("Enter number of columns in matrix B (1 <= P <= 8): "); /* L22 */
      scanf("%d", &colB);                                    /* L23 */
   } while ((colB < 1) || (colB > 8));                       /* L24 */
                                                             /* BL  */
   printf("\nEnter data for matrix A :\n");                  /* L25 */
   input(matA, rowA, colA);                                  /* L26 */
   printf("\n");                                             /* L27 */
   printf("Matrix A: \n");                                   /* L28 */
   output(matA, rowA, colA);                                 /* L29 */
   printf("\n");                                             /* L30 */
                                                             /* BL  */
   printf("\nEnter data for matrix B :\n");                  /* L31 */
   input(matB, rowB, colB);                                  /* L32 */
   printf("\n");                                             /* L33 */
   printf("Matrix B: \n");                                   /* L34 */
   output(matB, rowB, colB);                                 /* L35 */
   printf("\n");                                             /* L36 */
                                                             /* BL  */
   product(matA, matB, matC, rowA, colA, colB);              /* L37 */
   printf("Matrix C (matrix A x matrix B = matrix C) : \n"); /* L38 */
   output(matC, rowA, colB);                                 /* L39 */
                                                             /* L40 */
   printf("\nThank you.\n");                                 /* L41 */
   return 0;                                                 /* L42 */
}                                                            /* L43 */
                                                             /* BL  */
void input(int mat[][8], int row, int col)                   /* L44 */
{                                                            /* L45 */
   int i, j;                                                 /* L46 */
   for (i = 0; i < row; i++)                                 /* L47 */
   {                                                         /* L48 */
      printf("Enter %d values for row no. %d : ", col, i);   /* L49 */
         for (j = 0; j < col; j++)                           /* L50 */
             scanf("%d", &mat[i][j]);                        /* L51 */
   }                                                         /* L52 */
}                                                            /* L53 */
                                                             /* BL  */
void output(int mat[][8], int row, int col)                  /* L54 */
{                                                            /* L55 */
   int i, j;                                                 /* L56 */
   for (i = 0; i < row; i++)                                 /* L57 */
   {                                                         /* L58 */
      for (j = 0; j < col; j++)                              /* L59 */
      {                                                      /* L60 */
         printf("%d\t", mat[i][j]);                          /* L61 */
      }                                                      /* L62 */
```

71

```
        printf("\n");                                  /* L63 */
    }                                                  /* L64 */
}                                                      /* L65 */
                                                       /* BL  */
void product(int matA[][8], int matB[][8],
int matC[][8], int m1, int n1, int n2)                 /* L66 */
{                                                      /* L67 */
    int i, j, t;                                       /* L68 */
    for (i = 0; i < m1; i++)                           /* L69 */
    {                                                  /* L70 */
      for (j = 0; j < n2; j++)                         /* L71 */
      {                                                /* L72 */
          matC[i][j] = 0;                              /* L73 */
          for (t = 0; t < n1; t++)                     /* L74 */
          {                                            /* L75 */
            matC[i][j] += matA[i][t] * matB[t][j];     /* L76 */
          }                                            /* L77 */
      }                                                /* L78 */
    }                                                  /* L79 */
}                                                      /* L80 */
```

Compile and execute this program. A run of this program is given here:

```
This program performs product of matrices A axnd B (A x B).
Enter number of rows in matrix A: 3    ↵
Enter number of columns in matrix A: 2    ↵

Number of rows in matrix B is equal to number of columns in matrix A:
Enter number of columns in matrix B: 4    ↵

Enter data for matrix A:
Enter 2 values for row no. 0: 1  2    ↵
Enter 2 values for row no. 1: 3  4    ↵
Enter 2 values for row no. 2: 5  6    ↵

Matrix A:
1       2
3       4
5       6

Enter data for matrix B:
Enter 4 values for row no. 0: 1 2 3 4    ↵
Enter 4 values for row no. 1: 5 6 7 8    ↵

Matrix B:
1       2       3       4
5       6       7       8
```

```
Matrix B (matrix A x matrix B = matrix C):
11      14      17      20
23      30      37      44
35      46      57      68
```

Thank you.

How It Works

The program consists of three do-while loops. First, the do-while loop accepts the integer value for the number of rows for matrix A, in the range 1 <= M <= 8. Second, the do-while loop accepts the integer value for the number of columns for matrix A, in the range 1 <= N <= 8. Third, the do-while loop accepts the integer value for the number of columns for matrix B, in the range 1 <= P <= 8. LOCs 26 and 32 make a call to the function input() and accept the data for matrices A and B, respectively. LOCs 29 and 35 make a call to function output() and display matrices A and B on the screen, respectively. LOC 37 makes a call to function product(), performs the product of matrices A and B, and fills the values in matrix C. LOC 39 makes a call to the function output and displays matrix C on the screen. LOCs 44 to 53 define the function input(). LOCs 54 to 65 define the function output(). LOCs 66 to 80 define the function product().

CHAPTER 4

■ ■ ■

Pointers and Arrays

Pointers are one of the most powerful features of the C language. Pointers allow you to create quite efficient programs in C. However, the logic behind these programs can be quite tricky. "In C, there is a strong relationship between pointers and arrays, strong enough that pointers and arrays should be discussed simultaneously," writes Kernighan and Ritchie in their landmark book, *The C Programming Language*. A pointer is considered to be a derived type in C (see Figure 3-1 in Chapter 3). In this chapter, you will enjoy the recipes made using pointers and arrays.

4-1. Retrieve Data from an Array with the int Type Data
Problem

You want to retrieve the data from an int type array using pointers.

Solution

Write a C program that retrieves the values stored in elements of an int type array using pointers, with the following specifications:

- The program consists of an int type array called marks, which is initialized with a few (say, five) suitable int values.

- The program consists of a for loop that retrieves the values stored in the array marks, with the help of a pointer, and displays the retrieved values on the screen.

- The program also retrieves the value of the array name marks.

© Shirish Chavan 2017
S. Chavan, *C Recipes*, DOI 10.1007/978-1-4842-2967-5_4

The Code

The following is the code of the C program written with these specifications. Type the following C program in a text editor and save it in the folder C:\Code with the file name point1.c:

```
/* This program uses a pointer to retrieve the values stored in elements of */
/* 1-dimensional int type array.  */
                                                                    /* BL */
#include <stdio.h>                                                  /* L1 */
                                                                    /* BL */
main()                                                              /* L2 */
{                                                                   /* L3 */
  int marks [] = {72, 56, 50, 80, 92};                              /* L4 */
  int i, *ptr;                                                      /* L5 */
  ptr = &marks[0];                                                  /* L6 */
  for (i = 0; i < 5; i++)                                           /* L7 */
    printf("Element no %d, value: %d\n", i+1, *(ptr+i)) ;           /* L8 */
    printf("Value of array name marks is: %u\n", marks);            /* L9 */
  return(0);                                                        /* L10 */
}                                                                   /* L11 */
```

Compile and execute this program, and the following lines of text appear on the screen:

```
Element no 1, value: 72
Element no 2, value: 56
Element no 3, value: 50
Element no 4, value: 80
Element no 5, value: 92
Value of array name marks is: 65516
```

How It Works

In LOC 4, an int type array named marks is declared and also initialized with the suitable int values. In LOC 5, a pointer-to-int is declared, namely, ptr. In LOC 6, the pointer ptr is made to point to the first element of the array, marks[0]. When the pointer ptr is increased to (ptr + 1), it points to the next element, marks[1], and so on (see Figure 4-1). When ptr is dereferenced using the operator *, it returns the value of the first element, marks[0]. When (ptr + 1) is dereferenced using the operator *, it returns the value of the second element, marks[1], and so on. The for loop spanning LOCs 7 to 8 retrieves the int values stored in the array named marks and displays them on the screen. In LOC 9, the value of the array named marks is displayed on the screen. Note the following points:

- The array named marks has the value 65516, which is nothing but the base address of the array marks. It means, like some pointer, the array named marks is pointing to the memory cell 65516.

- In LOC 6, the pointer ptr is made to point to marks[0]; hence, like the array named marks, it is also pointing to memory cell 65516.

- In this program, you use the pointer variable ptr to retrieve the values in elements or arrays. But as the pointer variable ptr and array named marks are pointing to the same memory cell, it is possible to retrieve the values in elements using the array named marks instead of the pointer variable ptr.

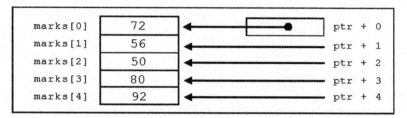

Figure 4-1. *Accessing the elements of the int type array called marks using a pointer-to-int variable called ptr*

4-2. Retrieve Data from an Array Using the Array Name

Problem

You want to retrieve the data from a one-dimensional array using the array name.

Solution

Write a C program that retrieves the values stored in the elements of the one-dimensional array using the array name, with the following specifications:

- The program consists of an int type array named marks, which is initialized with a few (say, five) suitable int values.

- The program consists of a for loop, which retrieves the values stored in the array named marks, using the array name marks and the dereferencing operator *, and displays the retrieved values on the screen.

- The program also retrieves the addresses of the elements of the array marks.

The Code

The following is the code of the C program written with these specifications. Type the following C program in a text editor and save it in the folder C:\Code with the file name point2.c:

```
/* This program uses array name and dereferencing operator * to retrieve the
values stored */
/* in elements of 1-dimensional array. */
                                                           /* BL */
#include <stdio.h>                                         /* L1 */
                                                           /* BL */
main()                                                     /* L2 */
{                                                          /* L3 */
 int marks [] = {72, 56, 50, 80, 92};                     /* L4 */
 int i ;                                                   /* L5 */
 printf("Values stored in array elements.\n");            /* L6 */
 for (i = 0; i < 5; i++)                                   /* L7 */
  printf("Element no. %d, value: %d\n", i+1, *(marks+i));  /* L8 */
                                                           /* BL */
 printf("\nValue of array-name marks: %u\n\n", marks);    /* L9 */
                                                           /* BL */
 printf("Addresses of array elements:\n");                /* L10 */
 for (i = 0; i < 5; i++)                                   /* L11 */
  printf("Address of element marks[%d] : %u\n", i, &marks[i]); /* L12 */
 return(0);                                                /* L13 */
}                                                          /* L14 */
```

Compile and execute this program, and the following lines of text appear on the screen:

```
Values stored in array elements.
Element no. 1, value: 72
Element no. 2, value: 56
Element no. 3, value: 50
Element no. 4, value: 80
Element no. 5, value: 92

Value of array-name marks: 65516

Addresses of array elements:
Address of element marks[0] : 65516
Address of element marks[1] : 65518
Address of element marks[2] : 65520
Address of element marks[3] : 65522
Address of element marks[4] : 65524
```

How It Works

In LOC 4, an int type array named marks is declared and also initialized with suitable int values. The for loop spanning LOCs 7 to 8 retrieves the values stored in the elements of the array marks using the array name and the dereferencing operator *. In LOC 9, the value of the array named marks is displayed on the screen. The for loop spanning LOCs 11 to 12 retrieves and displays on the screen the addresses of the elements of the array marks.

Compare LOC 8 in this program with LOC 8 in the preceding program, point1. You will notice that the expression *(ptr + i) is now replaced with the expression *(marks + i). Notice that there's no need to declare a pointer like ptr because the array named marks can serve the same purpose.

The expression *(marks + i) used in LOC 8 is fully equivalent to the expression marks[i]. In fact, whenever the compiler meets an expression of the form marks[i], the former immediately converts the latter into the form *(marks + i).

■ **Note**   Whenever a compiler meets an expression of the form arrayName[subscript], the former immediately converts the latter into the form *(arrayName + subscript). Therefore, programs that make use of pointers to process arrays are more efficient than their nonpointer counterparts.

You have used an array named marks in lieu of the pointer-to-int variable ptr to retrieve the values stored in the elements of the array marks successfully. This does not mean that the array named marks and the pointer-to-int variable ptr are fully equivalent. Notice the differences between the array name and the pointer variable:

- Since ptr is a variable of type pointer-to-int, you can assign an address of any int variable to it. However, you cannot assign an address of any variable to the array named marks. For example, notice the LOCs given here (assume that n is an int variable):

```
ptr = &n;                    /* OK */
marks = &n;                  /* ERROR */
```

- Since ptr is a variable of type pointer-to-int, you can add (subtract) an integer to (from) it. However, you cannot add (subtract) an integer to (from) the array named marks to change its value. For example, notice the LOCs given here:

```
ptr = ptr + 1;               /* OK */
marks = marks + 1;           /* ERROR */
```

4-3. Retrieve Data from an Array with char and double Type Data

Problem

You want to retrieve data from one-dimensional char and double type arrays.

Solution

Write a C program that retrieves the values stored in elements of one-dimensional char and double type arrays, with the following specifications:

- The program consists of char type array text and a double type array num that are initialized with suitable values.

- The program consists of for loops that retrieve the values stored in these arrays using array names and the dereferencing operator *.

- The program also retrieves the addresses of elements of these arrays.

The Code

The following is the code of the C program written with these specifications. Type the following C program in a text editor and save it in the folder C:\Code with the file name point3.c:

```
/* This program retrieves the data stored in 1-dimensional char and
double type */
/* arrays using the pointers. */                              /* BL */

#include <stdio.h>                                            /* L1 */
                                                              /* BL */
main()                                                        /* L2 */
{                                                             /* L3 */
 char text[] = "Hello";                                       /* L4 */
 double num[] = {2.4, 5.7, 9.1, 4.5, 8.2};                    /* L5 */
 int i ;                                                      /* L6 */
 printf("Values stored in elements of array text.\n");        /* L7 */
 for (i = 0; i < 5; i++)                                      /* L8 */
  printf("Element no. %d, value: %c\n", i+1, *(text+i));      /* L9 */
                                                              /* BL */
 printf("\nValues stored in elements of array num.\n");       /* L10 */
 for (i = 0; i < 5; i++)                                      /* L11 */
  printf("Element no. %d, value: %.1f\n", i+1, *(num+i));     /* L12 */
                                                              /* BL */
 printf("\nValue of array-name text: %u\n\n", text);          /* L13 */
                                                              /* BL */
```

```
printf("Addresses of elements of array text:\n");            /* L14 */
for (i = 0; i < 5; i++)                                       /* L15 */
 printf("Address of element text[%d] : %u\n", i, &text[i]);   /* L16 */
                                                              /* BL  */
printf("\nValue of array-name num: %u\n\n", num);             /* L17 */
                                                              /* BL  */
printf("Addresses of elements of array num:\n");              /* L18 */
for (i = 0; i < 5; i++)                                        /* L19 */
 printf("Address of element num[%d] : %u\n", i, &num[i]);     /* L20 */
                                                              /* BL  */
return(0);                                                    /* L21 */
}                                                             /* L22 */
```

Compile and execute this program, and the following lines of text appear on the screen:

```
Values stored in elements of array text.
Element no. 1, value: H
Element no. 2, value: e
Element no. 3, value: l
Element no. 4, value: l
Element no. 5, value: o

Values stored in elements of array num.
Element no. 1, value: 2.4
Element no. 2, value: 5.7
Element no. 3, value: 9.1
Element no. 4, value: 4.5
Element no. 5, value: 8.2

Value of array-name text: 65520

Addresses of elements of array text:
Address of element text[0] : 65520
Address of element text[1] : 65521
Address of element text[2] : 65522
Address of element text[3] : 65523
Address of element text[4] : 65524

Value of array-name num: 65480

Addresses of elements of array num:
Address of element num[0] : 65480
Address of element num[1] : 65488
Address of element num[2] : 65496
Address of element num[3] : 65504
Address of element num[4] : 65512
```

How It Works

In LOC 4, a char type array called text is created and also initialized with suitable data. In LOC 5, a double type array called num is created and also initialized with suitable data. The for loop spanning LOCs 8 to 9 displays the data stored in array text using the array name. The for loop spanning LOCs 11 to 12 displays the data stored in the array num using the array name. In LOC 13, the value of the array name text is displayed on the screen. The for loop spanning LOCs 15 to 16 displays the addresses of the elements of the array text. In LOC 17, the value of the array name num is displayed on the screen. The for loop spanning LOCs 19 to 20 displays the addresses of the elements of the array num on the screen.

This program is similar to the preceding one. Notice that when 1 is added to text, the resulting expression (text + 1) points to the next element in the text array. The expression (text + i) points to the (i+1)th element in the text array. Also, when 1 is added to num, then the resulting expression (num + 1) points to the next element in the num array. The expression (num + i) points to the (i+1)th element in the num array. An element in the text array occupies one memory cell, whereas an element in the num array occupies eight memory cells.

4-4. Access the Out-of-Bounds Array Elements
Problem

You want to access the out-of-bounds array elements.

Solution

Write a C program that accesses the out-of-bound array elements, with the following specifications:

- The program creates an int type array named num and initializes it with suitable data.

- The program declares two pointers to the int type variables.

- The program accesses the out-of-bound array elements with the help of pointers.

The Code

The following is the code of the C program written with these specifications. Type the following C program in a text editor and save it in the folder C:\Code with the file name point4.c:

```
/* This program accesses array elements which are out of bounds. */
                                                                    /* BL */
#include <stdio.h>                                                  /* L1 */
                                                                    /* BL */
main()                                                              /* L2 */
{                                                                   /* L3 */
  int num[] = {12, 23, 45, 65, 27, 83, 32, 93, 62, 74, 41};         /* L4 */
  int *ipt1, *ipt2;                                                 /* L5 */
                                                                    /* BL */
  ipt1 = &num[5];                                                   /* L6 */
  ipt2 = &num[6];                                                   /* L7 */
                                                                    /* BL */
  printf("Current value of *ipt1: %d\n", *ipt1);                    /* L8 */
  printf("Current value of *ipt2: %d\n", *ipt2);                    /* L9 */
                                                                    /* BL */
  ipt1 = ipt1 - 2;                                                  /* L10 */
  ipt2 = ipt2 + 3;                                                  /* L11 */
                                                                    /* BL  */
  printf("Now current value of *ipt1: %d\n", *ipt1);                /* L12 */
  printf("Now current value of *ipt2: %d\n", *ipt2);                /* L13 */
                                                                    /* BL  */
  ipt1 = ipt1 - 15;                                                 /* L14 */
  ipt2 = ipt2 + 22;                                                 /* L15 */
                                                                    /* BL  */
  printf("Now current value of *ipt1: %d\n", *ipt1);                /* L16 */
  printf("Now current value of *ipt2: %d\n", *ipt2);                /* L17 */
                                                                    /* BL  */
  return(0);                                                        /* L18 */
}                                                                   /* L19 */
```

Compile and execute this program, and the following lines of text appear on the screen:

```
Current value of *ipt1: 83
Current value of *ipt2: 32
Now current value of *ipt1: 65
Now current value of *ipt2: 74
Now current value of *ipt1: -44
Now current value of *ipt2: 12601
```

How It Works

In LOC 4, an int type array named num is created and initialized with suitable data. In LOC 5, two pointers-to-int variables, namely, ipt1 and ipt2, are declared. In LOCs 6 to 7, the directions of ipt1 and ipt2 are set pointing to in-bound elements of the array num. The values of the elements to which ipt1 and ipt2 are pointing are displayed on the screen in LOCs 8 to 9. A similar procedure is repeated in LOCs 10 to 13.

LOCs 14 and 15 are reproduced here for your quick reference:

```
ipt1 = ipt1 - 15;                    /* L14, legal but immoral */
ipt2 = ipt2 + 22;                    /* L15, legal but immoral */
```

In these LOCs, both pointers are made to point to data values that are beyond the range of the array num. In LOCs 16 and 17, the data values referred to by these pointers are retrieved and displayed on the screen. You can compile and execute this program successfully; the compiler will not complain despite that you have retrieved the data values beyond the range of the array num. Therefore, you could call LOCs 14 to 17 legal but immoral. The data values outputted in LOCs 16 and 17 are -44 and 12601. Do not imagine that these integer values are stored at respective locations by the operating system. You cannot make any assumption about the data stored in these locations. Perhaps there is not any data but only executable code. Here, you have just retrieved the data values from out-of-bound locations. What happens if you try to store some arbitrary values at these out-of-bound locations? The program may crash, and the computer may hang.

■ **Caution**   Avoid fiddling with out-of-bound elements of arrays. Such fiddling is justified only as a last measure. If you try to store some arbitrary values at out-of-bound locations, then your program may crash and your computer may hang.

4-5. Store Strings
Problem
You want to store strings.

Solution
Write a C program that stores strings, with the following specifications:

- The program declares a char type array named name and initializes it with a suitable string.

- The program declares a pointer-to-char variable called pname and makes it point to a string in memory.

- The program displays both these strings on the screen.

The Code

The following is the code of the C program written with these specifications. Type the following C program in a text editor and save it in the folder C:\Code with the file name point5.c:

```
/* This program stores the strings using pointer to char and char type
array. */
                                                        /* BL */
#include <stdio.h>                                      /* L1 */
                                                        /* BL */
main()                                                  /* L2 */
{                                                       /* L3 */
 int i;                                                 /* L4 */
 char name[] = "Shirish";                               /* L5 */
 char *pname = "Shirish";                               /* L6 */
                                                        /* BL */
 printf("name: %s\n", name);                            /* L7 */
 printf("pname: %s\n", pname);                          /* L8 */
                                                        /* BL */
 strcpy(name, "Dick");                                  /* L9 */
 pname = "Dick";                                        /* L10 */
                                                        /* BL  */
 printf("name: %s\n", name);                            /* L11 */
 printf("pname: %s\n", pname);                          /* L12 */
                                                        /* BL  */
 printf("name (all eight bytes):  ");                   /* L13 */
 for(i = 0; i < 8; i++) {                               /* L14 */
  printf("%c ", name[i]);                               /* L15 */
 }                                                      /* L16 */
                                                        /* BL  */
 printf("\npname (all eight bytes):  ");                /* L17 */
 for(i = 0; i < 8; i++) {                               /* L18 */
  printf("%c ", *(pname + i));                          /* L19 */
 }                                                      /* L20 */
                                                        /* BL  */
 return(0);                                             /* L21 */
}                                                       /* L22 */
```

Compile and execute this program, and the following lines of text appear on the screen:

```
name: Shirish
pname: Shirish
name: Dick
pname: Dick
name (all eight bytes):  D i c k   s h
pname (all eight bytes):  D i c k   n a m
```

How It Works

In LOC 5, a char type array named name is declared and initialized with a string constant of "Shirish". Figure 4-2 (a) shows what happens at the memory level after the execution of LOC 5. As shown in Figure 4-2 (a), the char type array name is created, which is 8 bytes long, and the string constant "Shirish" is stored in it.

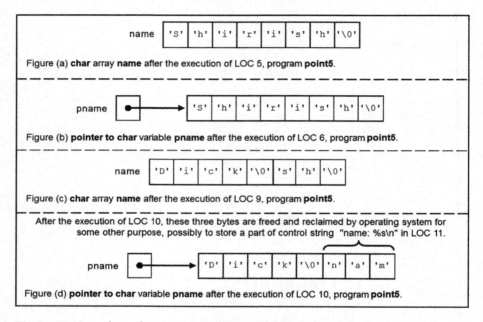

Figure (a) **char** array **name** after the execution of LOC 5, program **point5**.

Figure (b) **pointer to char** variable **pname** after the execution of LOC 6, program **point5**.

Figure (c) **char** array **name** after the execution of LOC 9, program **point5**.

After the execution of LOC 10, these three bytes are freed and reclaimed by operating system for some other purpose, possibly to store a part of control string "name: %s\n" in LOC 11.

Figure (d) **pointer to char** variable **pname** after the execution of LOC 10, program **point5**.

Figure 4-2. *Snapshots of memory during the execution of program point5*

In LOC 6, the pointer-to-char variable pname is declared and is set to point to the first character of the string constant "Shirish". Notice that the string constants created in LOCs 5 and 6 are different. Figure 4-2 (b) shows what happens at the memory level after the execution of LOC 6. As shown in Figure 4-2 (b), a string constant "Shirish" is placed in a memory block that is 8 bytes long, the pointer-to-char variable pname is created, and it is set pointing to the first character of the string constant "Shirish".

In LOCs 7 and 8, the strings associated with name and pname are displayed on the screen.

In LOC 9, the string constant "Dick" is copied to the char array name. Figure 4-2 (c) shows what happens at the memory level after the execution of LOC 9. As shown in Figure 4-2 (c), the string constant "Dick" (which is 5 bytes long) is overwritten on the existing string constant "Shirish" (which is 8 bytes long). Therefore, the last 3 bytes in the array name still contain the old data ('s', 'h', and '\0'). Notice that 8 bytes are reserved for the char array name, and unused bytes will not be reclaimed by the operating system.

In LOC 10, the string constant "Dick" is assigned to pname. Figure 4-2 (d) shows what happens at the memory level after the execution of LOC 10. As shown in Figure 4-2 (d), the string constant "Dick" (which is 5 bytes long) is overwritten on the existing string constant "Shirish" (which is 8 bytes long). The unused 3 bytes in the memory block are reclaimed by the operating system and used for some other purpose. Notice that the last 3 unused bytes now contain the characters 'n', 'a', and 'm'. Possibly these 3 bytes are used by the operating system to store part of the control string "name: %s\n" in LOC 11. Unlike the char array name, the block of bytes pointed to by pname is not a reserved one; hence, unused bytes are immediately reclaimed by the operating system. Notice an example from everyday life. Say there are four passengers sitting on a bench in a local train in Mumbai. One of the passengers walks off. The remaining three passengers change their positions to reclaim the empty space on the bench and sit comfortably.

In LOCs 11 and 12, the string constants associated with name and pname are displayed on the screen. This string is nothing but "Dick".

In LOCs 14 to 16, you use the for loop to display the contents of the 8 bytes reserved for the char array name. In LOCs 18 to 20, you use the for loop to display the contents of the memory block of 8 bytes, which is pointed to by pname.

4-6. Store Strings Without Initialization
Problem

You want to store the strings without initializations.

Solution

Write a C program that stores strings without initializations, with the following specifications:

- The program declares a char type array called name and a pointer-to-char variable called pname. However, no initializations are made.

- The program copies a suitable string to the array name and sets the pointer pname pointing to a suitable string.

- The program displays both strings on the screen.

The Code

The following is the code of the C program written with these specifications. Type the following C program in a text editor and save it in the folder C:\Code with the file name point6.c:

```
/* This program stores the strings using a pointer to char and a char array, */
/* without initializations. */
                                                    /* BL */
#include <stdio.h>                                  /* L1 */
                                                    /* BL */
main()                                              /* L2 */
{                                                   /* L3 */
 int i;                                             /* L4 */
 char name[8] ;                                     /* L5 */
 char *pname ;                                      /* L6 */
                                                    /* BL */
 strcpy(name, "Shirish");                           /* L7 */
 pname = "Shirish";                                 /* L8 */
                                                    /* BL */
 printf("\nname: %s\n", name);                      /* L9 */
 printf("pname: %s\n", pname);                      /* L10 */
                                                    /* BL */
 strcpy(name, "Dick");                              /* L11 */
 pname = "Dick";                                    /* L12 */
                                                    /* BL */
 printf("name: %s\n", name);                        /* L13 */
 printf("pname: %s\n", pname);                      /* L14 */
                                                    /* BL */
 printf("name (all eight bytes):  ");               /* L15 */
 for(i = 0; i < 8; i++) {                           /* L16 */
  printf("%c ", name[i]);                           /* L17 */
 }                                                  /* L18 */
                                                    /* BL */
 printf("\npname (all eight bytes):  ");            /* L19 */
 for(i = 0; i < 8; i++) {                           /* L20 */
  printf("%c ", *(pname + i));                      /* L21 */
 }                                                  /* L22 */
                                                    /* BL */
 return(0);                                         /* L23 */
}                                                   /* L24 */
```

Compile and execute this program, and the following lines of text appear on the screen:

```
name: Shirish
pname: Shirish
name: Dick
pname: Dick
name (all eight bytes):  D i c k   s h
pname (all eight bytes):  D i c k   n a m
```

How It Works

The output of this program is the same as that of the preceding program, and there's no reason why it should not be. However, this time you did not initialize name and pname.

After the execution of LOC 5, a char type array called name is created that is 8 bytes long. It doesn't contain anything; see Figure 4-3 (a). After the execution of LOC 7, the string constant "Shirish" is placed in this array, as shown in Figure 4-3 (a).

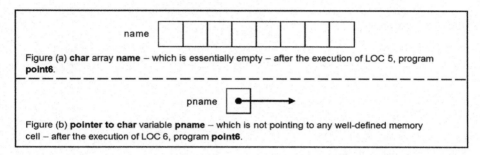

Figure (a) **char** array **name** – which is essentially empty – after the execution of LOC 5, program **point6**.

Figure (b) **pointer to char** variable **pname** – which is not pointing to any well-defined memory cell – after the execution of LOC 6, program **point6**.

Figure 4-3. *Snapshots of memory during the execution of program point6*

After the execution of LOC 6, a pointer-to-char variable called pname is created. As it is not initialized, it contains garbage. This means pname is not pointing to any well-defined memory cell; see Figure 4-3 (b).

In LOC 7, the string constant "Shirish" is copied to the array name. In LOC 8, the pointer pname is made to point to another string constant, "Shirish." After LOC 8, this program works the same as the preceding program.

4-7. Store Strings in an Interactive Session
Problem

You want to store strings in an interactive session.

Solution

Write a C program that stores strings in an interactive session, with the following specifications:

- The program declares a char type array named name and a pointer-to-char variable pname. However, no initializations are made.

- The program accepts two strings from the keyboard. The first string is assigned to the array name. The pointer pname is set pointing to the second string.

- The program displays both strings on the screen.

The Code

The following is the code of the C program written with these specifications. Type the following C program in a text editor and save it in the folder C:\Code with the file name point7.c:

```
/* This program stores the strings using a pointer to char and a char type
array */
/* in an interactive session. */
                                                              /* BL */
#include <stdio.h>                                            /* L1 */
                                                              /* BL */
main()                                                        /* L2 */
{                                                             /* L3 */
 int i;                                                       /* L4 */
 char name[8] ;                                               /* L5 */
 char *pname;                                                 /* L6 */
                                                              /* BL */
 printf("\nEnter name: ");                                    /* L7 */
 scanf(" %[^\n]", name);                                      /* L8 */
 printf("Enter name again: ");                                /* L9 */
 scanf(" %[^\n]", pname);                                     /* L10 */
                                                              /* BL */
 printf("name: %s\n", name);                                  /* L11 */
 printf("pname: %s\n", pname);                                /* L12 */
                                                              /* BL */
 return(0);                                                   /* L13 */
}                                                             /* L14 */
```

Compile and execute this program. A run of this program is given here:

```
Enter name: Shirish      ↵
Enter name again: Shirish      ↵
name: Shirish
pname: Shirish
```

How It Works

In LOC 5, it is specified that the length of the char array should be 8 bytes. Therefore, the name you type as a response to the request "Enter name: " should contain at a maximum seven characters. During compile time, the compiler knows that this string will have a length of 8 bytes.

In LOC 6, a pointer-to-char variable named pname is declared; however, the program is silent about the length of the string to which pname will be pointing. During compile time, the compiler is unaware of the length of this string. Therefore, by default, a typical compiler allows you to enter a string of 127 characters from the keyboard to be assigned to pname. You can also use the malloc() function in this program to allocate memory dynamically for the string to be associated with pname.

In LOCs 11 to 12, these strings are displayed on the screen.

4-8. Retrieve the Addresses of Elements in a Two-Dimensional Array

Problem

You want to retrieve the addresses of the elements in a two-dimensional array.

Solution

Write a C program that retrieves the addresses of the elements in a two-dimensional array, with the following specifications:

- The program declares a two-dimensional int type array called num and initializes it with suitable data.

- The program retrieves and displays on the screen the addresses of the elements using a nested for loop with two-level nesting.

The Code

The following is the code of the C program written with these specifications. Type the following C program in a text editor and save it in the folder C:\Code with the file name point8.c:

```
/* Addresses of all elements of a 2-dimensional array are displayed on the
screen. */
                                                          /* BL */
#include <stdio.h>                                        /* L1 */
                                                          /* BL */
main()                                                    /* L2 */
{                                                         /* L3 */
 int r, c;                                                /* L4 */
 int num[3][2] = {                                        /* L5 */
                  {14, 457},                              /* L6 */
                  {24, 382},                              /* L7 */
                  {72, 624}                               /* L8 */
                 };                                       /* L9 */
                                                          /* BL */
 for(r = 0; r < 3; r++) {                                 /* L10 */
  for(c = 0; c < 2; c++)                                  /* L11 */
   printf("Address of num[%d][%d]: %u \n", r, c, &num[r][c]); /* L12 */
 }                                                        /* L13 */
                                                          /* BL */
 return(0);                                               /* L14 */
}                                                         /* L15 */
```

Compile and execute this program, and the following lines of text appear on the screen:

```
Address of num[0][0]: 65514
Address of num[0][1]: 65516
Address of num[1][0]: 65518
Address of num[1][1]: 65520
Address of num[2][0]: 65522
Address of num[2][1]: 65524
```

How It Works

In LOC 4, two int variables are declared to represent the rows and columns in a two-dimensional array. In LOCs 5 to 9, a two-dimensional int type array named num is declared and also initialized with suitable data. LOCs 10 to 13 consist of two-level nesting of for loops that display on the screen the addresses of all the elements of the array num.

Figure 4-4 shows a diagrammatic representation of the addresses of a two-dimensional array called num. As the structure of memory is like a list, addresses are always stored like a list. The base address of the array num is 65514. Also, notice that the base addresses of 14, 24, and 72 represent the base addresses of the first, second, and third rows of num (see LOCs 6 to 8), which are 65514, 65518, and 65522 respectively.

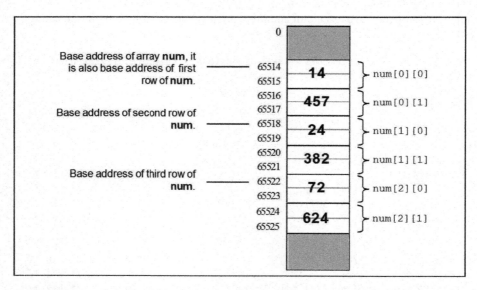

Figure 4-4. *Memory after creation of two-dimensional int array num that consists of three rows and two columns*

4-9. Retrieve the Base Addresses of Rows in a Two-Dimensional Array

Problem

You want to retrieve the base addresses of the rows in a two-dimensional array.

Solution

Write a C program that retrieves the base addresses of rows in a two-dimensional array, with the following specifications:

- The program declares a two-dimensional int type array called num and initializes it with suitable data.

- The program retrieves and displays on the screen the base addresses of the rows of num.

The Code

The following is the code of the C program written with these specifications. Type the following C program in a text editor and save it in the folder C:\Code with the file name point9.c:

```c
/* This program displays the base addresses of rows of a 2-dimensional array
on the screen.   */
                                                            /* BL */
#include <stdio.h>                                          /* L1 */
                                                            /* BL */
main()                                                      /* L2 */
{                                                           /* L3 */
 int r;                                                     /* L4 */
 int num[3][2] = {                                          /* L5 */
                {14, 457},                                  /* L6 */
                {24, 382},                                  /* L7 */
                {72, 624}                                   /* L8 */
            };                                              /* L9 */
                                                            /* BL */
    for(r = 0; r < 3; r++)                                  /* L10 */
      printf("Base address of row %d is: %u \n", r+1, num[r]); /* L11 */
                                                            /* BL */
 return(0);                                                 /* L12 */
}                                                           /* L13 */
```

Compile and execute this program, and the following lines of text appear on the screen:

```
Base address of row 1 is: 65514
Base address of row 2 is: 65518
Base address of row 3 is: 65522
```

How It Works

In LOC 4, the int variable r is declared to represent a row. In LOCs 5 to 9, the two-dimensional array num is declared and also initialized with suitable data. The for loop spanning LOCs 10 to 11 displays the base addresses of the rows of the two-dimensional array num.

Notice that num[r] returns the address of row number (r + 1). You can also assign the value returned by num[i] to the pointer-to-int variable, as follows (let ptrInt be the pointer-to-int variable):

```
ptrInt = num[0];                                                /* L14 */
```

Now ptrInt is pointing to the first element of the first row. You can display the address stored in ptrInt and the value of the element to which ptrInt is pointing using the LOCs given here:

```
printf("Address: %u \n", ptrInt);
printf("Value of element: %d \n", *ptrInt);
```

These LOCs after execution display the following lines of text on the screen:

```
Address: 65514
Value of element: 14
```

In LOC 11, you can apply the address operator & to num[r] as follows:

```
printf("Base address of row %d is: %u \n", r+1, &num[r]);       /* L15 */
```

You can replace LOC 11 in this program with LOC 15 and still compile and execute the program successfully. However, in LOC 14, if you apply the address operator & to num[0] as follows:

```
ptrInt = &num[0];                       /* L16, compiler issues a warning */
```

...and compile LOC 16, then the compiler issues a warning with the following words: "Suspicious pointer conversion." A pointer-related variable contains a lot of information. If you make an assignment in which a pointer-related variable is an r-value and the compiler suspects that all the information in the r-value will not be passed to the l-value, then the compiler issues a warning such as nonportable pointer conversion or suspicious pointer conversion. You are free to ignore the warning, but it is advisable to avoid such coding.

4-10. Retrieve Data from a Two-Dimensional Array

Problem

You want to develop a program that retrieves the values of the elements of a two-dimensional array.

Solution

Write a C program that retrieves the values of the elements of a two-dimensional array, with the following specifications:

- The program creates a two-dimensional int type array named num with the data values filled in it.

- The program uses a pointer to an array to retrieve and display the data stored in num on the screen.

The Code

The following is the code of the C program written with these specifications. Type the following C program in a text editor and save it in the folder C:\Code with the file name point10.c:

```
/* This program uses pointer to array in order to retrieve the values of
elements of */
/* a 2-dimensional array. */
                                                    /* BL */
#include <stdio.h>                                  /* L1 */
                                                    /* BL */
main()                                              /* L2 */
{                                                   /* L3 */
  int num[3][2] = {                                 /* L5 */
                 {14, 457},                         /* L6 */
                 {24, 382},                         /* L7 */
                 {72, 624}                          /* L8 */
               };                                   /* L9 */
  int (*ptrArray) [2];                              /* L10 */
  int row, col, *ptrInt;                            /* L11 */
    for(row = 0; row < 3; row++){                   /* L12 */
    ptrArray = &num[row];                           /* L13 */
    ptrInt = (int *) ptrArray;                      /* L14 */
    for(col = 0; col < 2; col++)                    /* L15 */
     printf("%d    ", *(ptrInt + col));             /* L16 */
    printf("\n");                                   /* L17 */
    }                                               /* L18 */
                                                    /* BL  */
  return(0);                                        /* L19 */
}                                                   /* L20 */
```

Compile and execute this program, and the following lines of text appear on the screen:

```
14    457
24    382
72    624
```

How It Works

In LOCs 5 to 9, the two-dimensional int type array named num is declared, and it is also filled with suitable int values.

You can declare a pointer to an array variable. This pointer points to the base address of the array. In LOC 10, a pointer-to-int array variable called ptrArray is declared. The array in question consists of two elements. Notice that in LOC 10 an array of pointers is not declared, but a pointer to an array is declared. Also, the parentheses around *ptrArray are required. In LOC 11, a pointer-to-int variable called ptrInt is declared.

In LOC 13, the address of the row in num is assigned to ptrArray. It is reproduced here for your quick reference:

```
ptrArray = &num[row];                                    /* L13 */
```

Both ptrArray and ptrInt are pointers, but they are different from one another. ptrArray is a pointer to an array, whereas ptrInt is a pointer-to-int. You want to assign ptrArray to ptrInt because in order to retrieve the values in the elements of the array, you need to dereference ptrInt. But as they are a different type of pointer, you cannot make direct assignment such as given here:

```
ptrInt = ptrArray;              /* Avoid. compiler issues a warning!  */
```

To do such assignment, first you need to cast ptrArray to type int * (i.e., pointer-to-int), and this casting is done in LOC 14, which is reproduced here for your quick reference:

```
ptrInt = (int *) ptrArray;                               /* OK, L14 */
```

Now ptrInt can be dereferenced after adding the appropriate integer values to it. For example, notice the LOCs given here (let intN1 and intN2 be int variables):

```
intN1 = *(ptrInt + 0);          /* now intN1 contains the value 14 */
intN2 = *(ptrInt + 1);          /* now intN2 contains the value 457 */
```

The for loop spanning LOCs 12 to 18 retrieves the int values stored in the two-dimensional array num and displays these values on the screen.

4-11. Retrieve Data from a Two-Dimensional Array Using an Array Name

Problem

You want to retrieve the data stored in a two-dimensional array using an array name.

Solution

Write a C program that retrieves the data stored in a two-dimensional array using an array name, with the following specifications:

- The program creates three two-dimensional arrays called t1, t2, and t3. Then the program fills t1 and t2 with suitable data values.

- The program fills the data values in t3 by adding data values in t1 and t2, using the rules of matrix addition.

- The program retrieves the data values stored in t1, t2, and t3 by dereferencing the array name and displays them on the screen. The program uses different flavors of dereferencing.

The Code

The following is the code of the C program written with these specifications. Type the following C program in a text editor and save it in the folder C:\Code with the file name point11.c:

```
/* This program adds two tables of numbers and enters the results in third
table and then */
/* displays it on the screen using pointers and using three different
approaches. */
                                                      /* BL */
#include <stdio.h>                                    /* L1 */
                                                      /* BL */
main()                                                /* L2 */
{                                                     /* L3 */
  int i, j, *p1, *p2, *p3;                            /* L4 */
  int t1 [][4] = {                                    /* L5 */
                      {12, 14, 16, 18},               /* L6 */
                      {22, 24, 26, 28},               /* L7 */
                      {32, 34, 36, 38}                /* L8 */
               };                                     /* L9 */
  int t2 [3][4] = {                                   /* L10 */
                      {13, 15, 17, 19},               /* L11 */
                      {23, 25, 27, 29},               /* L12 */
                      {33, 35, 37, 39}                /* L13 */
               };                                     /* L14 */
```

97

```
int t3 [3][4];                                              /* L15 */
                                                            /* BL  */
printf("\nTable t3 is computed and displayed:\n\n");        /* L16 */
                                                            /* BL  */
for(i = 0; i < 3; i++) {                                    /* L17 */
 for(j = 0; j < 4; j++) {                                   /* L18 */
   *(t3[i] + j) = *(t1[i] + j) + *(t2[i] + j);              /* L19 */
    printf("%d  ", *(t3[i] + j));                           /* L20 */
 }                                                          /* L21 */
 printf("\n");                                              /* L22 */
}                                                           /* L23 */
                                                            /* BL  */
printf("\n\nTable t3 is computed and displayed again:\n\n");/* L24 */
                                                            /* BL  */
for(i = 0; i < 3; i++) {                                    /* L25 */
 for(j = 0; j < 4; j++) {                                   /* L26 */
  *(*(t3 + i) + j) = *(*(t1 + i) + j) + *(*(t2 + i) + j);   /* L27 */
   printf("%d  ", t3[i][j]);                                /* L28 */
 }                                                          /* L29 */
  printf("\n");                                             /* L30 */
}                                                           /* L31 */
                                                            /* BL  */
p1 = (int *) t1;                                            /* L32 */
p2 = (int *) t2;                                            /* L33 */
p3 = (int *) t3;                                            /* L34 */
printf("\n\nTable t3 is computed and displayed again:\n\n");/* L35 */
                                                            /* BL  */
for(i = 0; i < 3; i++) {                                    /* L36 */
 for(j = 0; j < 4; j++) {                                   /* L37 */
  *(p3 + i * 4 + j) = *(p1 + i * 4 + j) + *(p2 + i * 4 + j);/* L38 */
   printf("%d  ", *(p3 + i * 4 + j));                       /* L39 */
 }                                                          /* L40 */
 printf("\n");                                              /* L41 */
}                                                           /* L42 */
                                                            /* BL  */
 return(0);                                                 /* L43 */
}                                                           /* L44 */
```

Compile and execute this program, and the following lines of text appear on the screen:

```
Table t3 is computed and displayed:
25  29  33  37
45  49  53  57
65  69  73  77
```

Table t3 is computed and displayed again:
```
25  29  33  37
45  49  53  57
65  69  73  77
```

Table t3 is computed and displayed again:
```
25  29  33  37
45  49  53  57
65  69  73  77
```

How It Works

An individual element in a two-dimensional array is retrieved using this expression:

```
arrayName[row][col]                                    Expression A
```

However, whenever the compiler meets an expression of the form arrayName[k], the former immediately converts the latter into the form *(arrayName + k). Assuming that k in this expression is nothing but col in the expression A, you can rewrite the previously given expression as follows:

```
*(arrayName[row] + col)                                Expression B
```

Now again assuming that row in expression B is nothing but k in the expression arrayName[k], you can rewrite the previously given expression as follows:

```
*(*(arrayName + row) + col)                            Expression C
```

Besides these three expressions, one more expression is used for the retrieval of elements, and it is given here:

```
ptr = (int *) arrayName;
*(ptr + row * COL + col)                               Expression D
```

Here, COL is the total number of columns in the two-dimensional array, and ptr is a pointer-to-int variable. Notice that expressions A, B, C, and D are fully equivalent.

This program has used the expressions B, C, and D to retrieve the elements of a two-dimensional array. In the block of code spanning LOCs 17 to 23 you use the expression B to access the elements of the two-dimensional arrays t1, t2, and t3. In the block of code spanning LOCs 25 to 31, you use the expression C to access the elements of the two-dimensional arrays t1, t2, and t3. In the block of code spanning LOCs 36 to 42, you use the expression D to access the elements of the two-dimensional arrays t1, t2, and t3.

4-12. Retrieve Data from an Array Using an Array of Pointers

Problem

You want to retrieve the data from an array using an array of pointers.

Solution

Write a C program that retrieves the data from an array by using an array of pointers, with the following specifications:

- The program declares an int type array called intArray. The program also declares an array of pointers-to-int called ptrArray.

- The program fills suitable data values in the array intArray. The program then sets the pointers in ptrArray pointing to cells in the array intArray.

- The program retrieves the data values stored intArray with the help of ptrArray and displays the retrieved values on the screen.

The Code

The following is the code of the C program written with these specifications. Type the following C program in a text editor and save it in the folder C:\Code with the file name point12.c:

```
/* This program uses an array of pointers-to-int. */
                                                        /* BL */
#include <stdio.h>                                      /* L1 */
                                                        /* BL */
main()                                                  /* L2 */
{                                                       /* L3 */
  int i, intArray[6];                                   /* L4 */
  int *ptrArray[6];                                     /* L5 */
                                                        /* BL */
 for(i = 0; i < 6; i++) {                               /* L6 */
  intArray[i] = (i + 2) * 100;                          /* L7 */
  ptrArray[i] = &intArray[i ];                          /* L8 */
 }                                                      /* L9 */
                                                        /* BL */
 for(i = 0; i < 6; i++)                                 /* L10 */
  printf("intArray[%d], Value: %d, Address: %u\n",      /* L11 */
                      i, *(ptrArray[i]), ptrArray[i]);  /* L12 */
                                                        /* BL  */
  return(0);                                            /* L13 */
}                                                       /* L14 */
```

Compile and execute this program, and the following lines of text appear on the screen:

```
intArray[0], Value: 200, Address: 65514
intArray[1], Value: 300, Address: 65516
intArray[2], Value: 400, Address: 65518
intArray[3], Value: 500, Address: 65520
intArray[4], Value: 600, Address: 65522
intArray[5], Value: 700, Address: 65524
```

How It Works

In LOC 4, you declare an array of integers called intArray. In LOC 5, you declare an array of pointers-to-int called ptrArray. LOCs 6 to 9 consist of a for loop. Inside this loop, all the elements of intArray are filled with values according to an arbitrary formula in LOC 7. In LOC 8, each element in ptrArray is set pointing to the corresponding element in intArray, as shown in Figure 4-5.

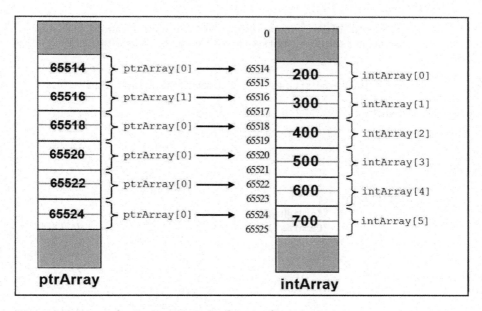

Figure 4-5. *Array of pointers ptrArray and array of integers intArray*

LOCs 10 to 12 consist of another for loop. The body of this for loop consists of only one statement, which is fitted in two LOCs (11 and 12) as it is rather long. This statement sends the output to the screen. This for loop displays on the screen the values stored in the array intArray, as well as the addresses of the cells of intArray.

4-13. Swap Strings Physically

Problem

You want to swap strings physically.

Solution

Write a C program that swaps strings physically, with the following specifications:

- The program creates a two-dimensional array of characters called friends and stores suitable strings in it. The program displays the strings (before swapping) on the screen.

- The program swaps the strings physically using a for loop. After swapping, the program displays the strings on the screen.

The Code

The following is the code of the C program written with these specifications. Type the following C program in a text editor and save it in the folder C:\Code with the file name point13.c:

```
/* This program a swaps the strings in a 2-dimensional array of characters.   */   /* BL */
                                                                                   /* L1 */
#include <stdio.h>                                                                 /* BL */
                                                                                   /* L2 */
main()                                                                             /* L3 */
{                                                                                  /* L4 */
  int i;                                                                           /* L5 */
  char temp;                                                                       /* L6 */
  char friends [5][10] = {                                                         /* L7 */
                    "Kernighan",                                                   /* L8 */
                    "Camarda",                                                     /* L9 */
                    "Ford",                                                        /* L10 */
                    "Nixon",                                                       /* L11 */
                    "Wu"                                                           /* L12 */
                };                                                                 /* BL */
                                                                                   /* L13 */
  printf("Strings before swapping:\n");                                           /* L14 */
  for(i = 0; i < 5; i++)                                                          /* L15 */
   printf("Friend no. %d : %s\n", i+1, friends[i]);                               /* BL */
                                                                                   /* L16 */
  for(i = 0; i < 10; i++) {                                                       /* L17 */
    temp = friends[0][i];                                                          /* L18 */
    friends[0][i] = friends[1][i];                                                 /* L19 */
    friends[1][i] = temp;                                                          /* L20 */
  }                                                                                /* BL */
```

```
printf("\nStrings after swapping:\n");                        /* L21 */
for(i = 0; i < 5; i++)                                        /* L22 */
 printf("Friend no. %d : %s\n", i+1, friends[i]);            /* L23 */
                                                              /* BL  */
return(0);                                                    /* L24 */
}                                                             /* L25 */
```

Compile and execute this program, and the following lines of text appear on the screen:

```
Strings before swapping:
Friend no. 1 : Kernighan
Friend no. 2 : Camarda
Friend no. 3 : Ford
Friend no. 4 : Nixon
Friend no. 5 : Wu

Strings after swapping:
Friend no. 1 : Camarda
Friend no. 2 : Kernighan
Friend no. 3 : Ford
Friend no. 4 : Nixon
Friend no. 5 : Wu
```

How It Works

The block of code spanning LOCs 6 to 12 creates a two-dimensional char array called friends and stores five strings in it, as shown in Figure 4-6. The strings stored in the array friends are as follows:

- "Kernighan"

- "Camarda"

- "Ford"

- "Nixon"

- "Wu"

friends[0]	'K'	'e'	'r'	'n'	'i'	'g'	'h'	'a'	'n'	'\0'
friends[1]	'C'	'a'	'm'	'a'	'r'	'd'	'a'	'\0'		
friends[2]	'F'	'o'	'r'	'd'	'\0'					
friends[3]	'N'	'i'	'x'	'o'	'n'	'\0'				
friends[4]	'W'	'u'	'\0'							

Figure 4-6. *Two-dimensional array friends. Its size is 50 bytes, and 18 bytes are unused in this array, representing a waste of memory.*

The program intends to swap the first two strings, "Kernighan" and "Camarda", so that after the swapping, the first string would be "Camarda" and the second string would be "Kernighan".

The for loop spanning LOCs 14 to 15 displays the strings stored in friends on the screen. The for loop spanning LOCs 16 to 20 swaps the first two strings stored in friends. In this loop, every single character is swapped between the first string and the second string with the help of a char variable called temp in which a character is temporarily stored. Figure 4-7 shows the strings in memory after the swapping. The for loop spanning LOCs 22 to 23 displays the strings on the screen, after swapping.

friends[0]	'C'	'a'	'm'	'a'	'r'	'd'	'a'	'\0'		
friends[1]	'K'	'e'	'r'	'n'	'i'	'g'	'h'	'a'	'n'	'\0'
friends[2]	'F'	'o'	'r'	'd'	'\0'					
friends[3]	'N'	'i'	'x'	'o'	'n'	'\0'				
friends[4]	'W'	'u'	'\0'							

Figure 4-7. Strings stored in friends[0] and friends[1] are swapped. Every character needs to be picked and process individually.

These are the drawbacks of this program:

- The array friends consumes 50 bytes of memory for the storage of strings, out of which 18 bytes of memory are simply wasted.

- During swapping, strings are physically moved, and this physical movement of strings is time-consuming and decreases the performance of the program.

Thus, this program is expensive as it consumes space (i.e., memory) and time (i.e., computing time) in a wasteful manner.

Despite these drawbacks, programmers use this method when the number of strings is small because this program uses very simple logic. The waste mentioned is negligible when the number of strings is not large.

4-14. Swap Strings Logically
Problem
You want to swap strings logically.

Solution
Write a C program that swaps strings logically, with the following specifications:

- The program creates an array of pointers. The program creates the strings in memory. The program sets the pointers (in an array) pointing to the strings, as shown in Figure 4-8.

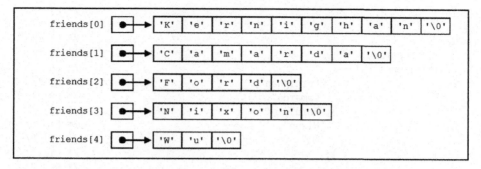

Figure 4-8. *Array of pointers to strings named friends. Compare this arrow with the one shown in Figure 4-6. The wasting of memory is avoided.*

- The program displays the strings (before swapping) on the screen.
  The program swaps the first two strings simply by interchanging the pointers pointing to these strings, as shown in Figure 4-9.

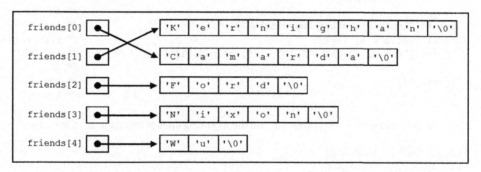

Figure 4-9. *Pointers friends[0] and friends[1] are swapped. Strings are not moved. This process ensures better performance.*

- The program displays the strings (after swapping) on the screen.

The Code

The following is the code of the C program written with these specifications. Type the following C program in a text editor and save it in the folder C:\Code with the file name point14.c:

```
/* This program swaps the strings using an array of pointers to strings. */
                                                              /* BL */
#include <stdio.h>                                            /* L1 */
                                                              /* BL */
```

```
main()                                                   /* L2  */
{                                                        /* L3  */
  int i;                                                 /* L4  */
  char *temporary;                                       /* L5  */
  char *friends [5] = {                                  /* L6  */
                "Kernighan",                             /* L7  */
                "Camarda",                               /* L8  */
                "Ford",                                  /* L9  */
                "Nixon",                                 /* L10 */
                "Wu"                                     /* L11 */
              };                                         /* L12 */
                                                         /* BL  */
  printf("Strings before swapping:\n");                  /* L13 */
  for(i = 0; i < 5; i++)                                 /* L14 */
   printf("Friend no. %d : %s\n", i+1, friends[i]);      /* L15 */
                                                         /* BL  */
  temporary = friends[1];                                /* L16 */
  friends[1] = friends[0];                               /* L17 */
  friends[0] = temporary;                                /* L18 */
                                                         /* BL  */
  printf("\nStrings after swapping:\n");                 /* L19 */
  for(i = 0; i < 5; i++)                                 /* L20 */
   printf("Friend no. %d : %s\n", i+1, friends[i]);      /* L21 */
                                                         /* BL  */
  return(0);                                             /* L22 */
}                                                        /* L23 */
```

Compile and execute this program, and the following lines of text appear on the screen:

```
Strings before swapping:
Friend no. 1 : Kernighan
Friend no. 2 : Camarda
Friend no. 3 : Ford
Friend no. 4 : Nixon
Friend no. 5 : Wu

Strings after swapping:
Friend no. 1 : Camarda
Friend no. 2 : Kernighan
Friend no. 3 : Ford
Friend no. 4 : Nixon
Friend no. 5 : Wu
```

How It Works

The block of code spanning LOCs 6 to 12 creates five strings in memory, creates an array of five pointers called friends, and also sets the pointers in array friends pointing to these strings. Figure 4-8 illustrates the situation after executing LOCs 6 to 12.

The strings stored in memory and pointed to by pointers friends are listed here:

- "Kernighan"

- "Camarda"

- "Ford"

- "Nixon"

- "Wu"

The first pointer in the array of pointers, friends[0], points to the string "Kernighan"; the second pointer in the array of pointers, friends[1], points to string "Camarda"; and so on. The program intends to swap the first two strings, "Kernighan" and "Camarda", so that after the swapping, the first string would be "Camarda" and second string would be "Kernighan". However, unlike in the preceding program point13, where strings were physically moved, in this program strings will not be moved physically; instead, simply the direction of the first two pointers will be interchanged, as shown in Figure 4-9.

The for loop spanning LOCs 14 to 15 displays the strings (before swapping) on the screen. The block of code spanning LOCs 16 to 18 performs the swapping of the first two strings. In LOC 16, the direction of the pointer friends[1] is assigned to the pointer temporary. Now the pointer temporary points to the string "Camarda". In LOC 17, the direction of the pointer friends[0] is assigned to the pointer friends[1]. Now both pointers friends[0] and friends[1] point to the string "Kernighan". In LOC 18, the direction stored in temporary is assigned to the pointer friends[0]. Now the pointer friends[0] points to the string "Camarda". Figure 4-9 illustrates the situation after executing the block of LOCs 16 to 18. Thus, in this program, in reality, strings are not swapped, but pointers are swapped. The for loop spanning LOCs 20 to 21 displays the strings after swapping on the screen.

Here are the benefits of program point14 over the preceding program point13:

- In point13, the char type array named friends has consumed 50 bytes (Figure 4-6). Not all 50 bytes are used. In fact, 18 bytes in this array are unused and represent a wastage of memory. In point14, you use an array of pointers to strings, so now the strings have consumed just 32 bytes (as each one-dimensional char type array is now just enough to accommodate a string, as shown in Figure 4-8). However, in point14, the net savings of memory is less than 18 bytes because five pointers consume 10 bytes, as each pointer needs 2 bytes for storage. Therefore, the net savings of memory is 8 bytes.

- The performance of point14 is better than that of point13. In point13, to swap the first two strings, the for loop spanning LOCs 16 to 20 is iterated ten times, and this loop consists of three statements. Thus, in point13, 30 statements are executed to perform the swapping of strings. In point14, to swap the strings, only three statements (spanning LOCs 16 to 18) are executed.

4-15. Store Strings Interactively

Problem

You want to store the number of strings (say, five) in primary memory in an interactive session.

Solution

Write a C program that stores the five strings (say the names of your friends) in primary memory in an interactive session, with the following specifications:

- The program creates an array of five pointers to strings called friends. The program also creates a char type array named name to store a string entered through the keyboard, temporarily.

- The program uses a for loop to accept the strings entered through the keyboard.

- The program uses the function malloc() to allocate the memory for the storage of strings.

- The program displays the stored strings on the screen.

The Code

The following is the code of the C program written with these specifications. Type the following C program in a text editor and save it in the folder C:\Code with the file name point15.c:

```
/* This program accepts and stores the five strings in an interactive session */
/* using the malloc() function  */
                                                        /* BL */
#include <stdio.h>                                      /* L1 */
#include <stdlib.h>                                     /* L2 */
#include <string.h>                                     /* L3 */
                                                        /* BL */
main()                                                  /* L4 */
{                                                       /* L5 */
 char *friends[5], *ptr, name[30];                      /* L6 */
 int i, length;                                         /* L7 */
                                                        /* BL */
 for(i = 0; i < 5; i++) {                               /* L8 */
  printf("Enter name of friend no. %d: ", i + 1);       /* L9 */
  scanf(" %[^\n]", name);                               /* L10 */
  length = strlen(name);                                /* L11 */
  ptr = (char *) malloc (length + 1);                   /* L12 */
  strcpy(ptr, name);                                    /* L13 */
```

```
  friends[i] = ptr;                              /* L14 */
}                                                /* L15 */
                                                 /* BL  */
printf("\n\nList of friends:\n");                /* L16 */
for(i = 0; i < 5; i++)                           /* L17 */
  printf("Friend no. %d : %s\n", i+1, friends[i]); /* L18 */
                                                 /* BL  */
  return(0);                                     /* L19 */
}                                                /* L20 */
```

Compile and execute this program. A run of this program is given here:

```
Enter name of friend no. 1: Kernighan    ↵
Enter name of friend no. 2: Camarda      ↵
Enter name of friend no. 3: Ford      ↵
Enter name of friend no. 4: Nixon        ↵
Enter name of friend no. 5: Wu        ↵

List of friends:
Friend no. 1 : Kernighan
Friend no. 2 : Camarda
Friend no. 3 : Ford
Friend no. 4 : Nixon
Friend no. 5 : Wu
```

How It Works

In LOC 6, the following happens: an array of pointers to strings is declared called friends, a pointer-to-char is declared called ptr, and a char type array is declared called name.

The for loop spanning LOCs 8 to 15 is responsible for accepting and storing the strings entered through the keyboard. The strings to be entered are the names of five friends; hence, it is assumed that the length of name would be up to 30 characters only.

LOC 10 consists of a call to the scanf() function. It accepts the string of characters typed by the user and assigns it to the char type array called name. Notice that the string is delimited by the newline character ('\n'). After typing the string when the user pressed the Enter key, the typed string (except the newline character) is stored in the char type array called name.

In LOC 11, the length of the string (stored in name) is computed and assigned to the int variable length. LOC 12 consists of a call to the malloc() function.

The function malloc() allocates memory during runtime. It allocates a block of contiguous memory and returns the base address of that block of memory. The generic syntax of a statement that uses the function malloc() is given here:

```
ptrPtr = (dataType *) malloc (size);
```

Here, ptrPtr is a pointer to the dataType variable; dataType is any valid data type such as int, char, float, etc.; and size is an integer (or expression that evaluates to an integer) that indicates the number of bytes required for storage. If required memory cannot be allocated, then the null pointer is returned. The header file <stdlib.h> contains the prototype of the function malloc().

After the execution of LOC 12, a contiguous block of memory of size (length + 1) bytes is allocated, and the pointer ptr is set pointing to it. After execution of LOC 13, the contents of the array name are copied to this allocated block of memory. After execution of LOC 14, the direction of the pointer ptr is assigned to the pointer friends[i]. Therefore, after execution of LOC 14, the pointer friends[i] is pointing to the allocated block of memory mentioned in LOCs 12 and 13. Here, i is the serial number of the string. For the first string, the value of i is 0, for the second string the value of i is 1, and so on.

The for loop spanning LOCs 17 to 18 displays the strings stored in memory on the screen.

4-16. Pass Arguments to a Program from the Command Line

Problem

You want to pass the arguments to a program from a command line.

Solution

Write a C program with the following specifications:

- The program accepts arguments from the command line.

- The program uses pointers to deal with the arguments.

- The program displays the arguments on the screen.

The Code

The following is the code of the C program written with these specifications. Type the following C program in a text editor and save it in the folder C:\Code with the file name point16.c:

```
/* This program uses command-line arguments. */
                                                        /* BL */
#include <stdio.h>                                      /* L1 */
                                                        /* BL */
main(int argc, char *argv[])                            /* L2 */
{                                                       /* L3 */
 int i;                                                 /* L4 */
 printf("Few towns in %s district:\n", argv[1]);        /* L5 */
 for(i = 2; i < argc; i++)                              /* L6 */
```

```
    printf("%s\n", argv[i]);                               /* L7 */
    return(0);                                             /* L8 */
}                                                          /* L9 */
```

Compile and execute this program, and the following line of text appears on the screen.

```
Few towns in (null) district:
```

This program expects arguments, but you have not passed any argument to this program. As a result, this program has displayed somewhat bizarre-looking output.

Now let's execute this program from the command line with arguments. Let's assume that all executable files (such as hello.exe) are stored in the folder C:\Output. Open the Command Prompt window. See to it that folder C:\Output is the current folder. Type the following command:

```
C:\Output> point16 Sangli Miraj Kavathe Tasgav Vita Shirala Kadegav    ↵
```

Now the following lines of text appear on the screen:

```
Few towns in Sangli district:
Miraj
Kavathe
Tasgav
Vita
Shirala
Kadegav
```

How It Works

C has made provisions for command-line arguments. When you intend to pass arguments to a program, the first line of the main() function looks like this:

```
main(int argc, char *argv[])                               /* L2 */
```

In the given LOC, parentheses contain a parameter list. Normally, arguments are passed to a function in a function call. But as the main() function is called by the execution environment, arguments are also passed to the main() function by the execution environment. When program execution begins, the function main() is called with two arguments, namely, argc (argument count) and argv (argument vector). Notice that the same names are used for parameters and arguments. The argument argc indicates the number of arguments being passed to the program, and its data type is int. The argument argv is an array of pointers-to-char that contain the arguments, one per string. The size of argv is (argc + 1). As per convention, argv[0] represents the name of the program being executed. This means the minimum possible value of argc is 1. Also, the Null value is associated with argv[argc]. In other words, argv[argc] is a null pointer. The remaining arguments are true arguments and are passed to the program for processing.

In the case of this program, argc is 8 because we have typed 8 strings, namely, point16, Sangli, Miraj, Kavathe, Tasgav, Vita, Shirala, and Kadegav. These strings are associated with various pointers as follows:

String	Name of pointer to char
"point16"	argv[0]
"Sangli"	argv[1]
"Miraj"	argv[2]
"Kavathe"	argv[3]
"Tasgav"	argv[4]
"Vita"	argv[5]
"Shirala"	argv[6]
"Kadegav"	argv[7]

Also, a null value is associated with the pointer argv[8].

It is responsibility of the execution environment to do the following:

- To count the strings and pass that number as argc to the program

- To build the array argv (which is an array of pointers-to-char), to associate various strings to the appropriate elements in this array as tabulated earlier, and to pass this array to the program

Consider the case when no arguments are passed to the program. In such a case, argc is 1, and the array argv has only two elements, namely, argv[0] and argv[1]. In addition, the pointer argv[0] is associated with the string "point16", and the pointer argv[1] is associated with value null. After the execution of LOC 5, the following line of text is displayed on the screen:

```
Few towns in (null) district:
```

LOC 5 is reproduced here for your quick reference:

```
printf("Few towns in %s district:\n", argv[1]);              /* L5 */
```

The value of argv[1] is null. This value is placed at the conversion specification %s, and you get the output shown earlier. LOCs 6 to 7 consist of a for loop; as the value of argc is 1, the condition (2 < argc) turns out to be false during the first iteration, and not a single iteration of the for loop takes place. Then the program terminates.

Now consider the case when the arguments listed earlier are passed to the program. argv[0] is associated with the string "point16", and argv[8] is associated with the value null. Other elements of argv are associated with the argument strings as tabulated earlier. As the value of argv[1] is "Sangli", after the execution of LOC 5, the following line of text is displayed on the screen:

```
Few towns in Sangli district:
```

As the value of argc is 8, the for loop performs six iterations and displays the names of six towns, one town per iteration.

Since argv is a pointer to an array of pointers, you can dereference it to access the strings associated with it. This means instead of using the expression given here:

```
argv[k];
```

...you can also use the expression given here:

```
*(argv + k)
```

The program point16 was rewritten with this modification and is given here. Type the following text (program) in a C file and save it in the folder C:\Code with the file name point17.c:

```
/* This program also uses command-line arguments. An alternative version. */
                                                    /* BL */
#include <stdio.h>                                  /* L1 */
                                                    /* BL */
main(int argc, char *argv[])                        /* L2 */
{                                                   /* L3 */
 int i;                                             /* L4 */
 printf("Few towns in %s district:\n", *++argv);    /* L5 */
 for(i = 2; i < argc; i++)                          /* L6 */
  printf("%s\n", *++argv);                          /* L7 */
 return(0);                                         /* L8 */
}                                                   /* L9 */
```

Compile and execute this program with or without arguments and you get the same output as with point5.

It produces the same output as the preceding program. Notice the expression *++argv. In this expression, the first integer, 1, is added to the pointer argv (i.e., it is made to point to the next string), and then it is dereferenced using the operator * to retrieve the string to which it is pointing.

4-17. Retrieve Stored Strings Using a Pointer to a Pointer

Problem

You want to retrieve stored strings using a pointer to a pointer.

Solution

Write a C program that retrieves stored strings using a pointer to pointer, with the following specifications:

- The program declares a two-dimensional char type array named cities and initializes it with suitable data (strings).

- The program declares a pointer-to-char variable called ptr and a pointer to pointer-to-char variable ptrPtr. The program retrieves the strings stored in the array cities with the help of the pointer variables ptr and ptrPtr and displays them on the screen.

The Code

The following is the code of the C program written with these specifications. Type the following C program in a text editor and save it in the folder C:\Code with the file name point18.c:

```c
/* This program retrieves the stored strings using a pointer to po inter to
char type array. */                                         /* B1 */

#include <stdio.h>                                           /* L1 */
                                                             /* BL */
main()                                                       /* L2 */
{                                                            /* L3 */
  int i, j;                                                  /* L4 */
  char ch;                                                   /* L5 */
  char cities[5][10] = {                                     /* L6 */
                        "Satara",                            /* L7 */
                        "Sangli",                            /* L8 */
                        "Karad",                             /* L9 */
                        "Pune",                              /* L10 */
                        "Mumbai"                             /* L11 */
                                                             /* L12 */
                       };                                    /* L13 */
  char *ptr, **ptrPtr;                                       /* BL */
                                                             /* L14 */
  ptrPtr = &ptr;                                             /* BL */
                                                             /* L15 */
  for(i=0; i<5; i++) {                                       /* L16 */
  ptr = (char *) cities[i];                                  /* L17 */
  j = 0;                                                     /* BL */
                                                             /* L18 */
  do {                                                       /* L19 */
    ch = *(ptr + j);                                         /* L20 */
    printf("%c", ch);                                        /* L21 */
    j = j + 1;                                               /* L22 */
  } while(ch != '\0');                                       /* BL */
```

```
 printf("\t\t");                        /* L23 */
 j = 0;                                 /* L24 */
                                        /* BL  */
 do {                                   /* L25 */
   ch = *(*ptrPtr + j);                 /* L26 */
   printf("%c", ch);                    /* L27 */
   j = j + 1;                           /* L28 */
 } while(ch != '\0');                   /* L29 */
                                        /* BL  */
 printf("\n");                          /* L30 */
 }                                      /* L31 */
                                        /* BL  */
 return(0);                             /* L32 */
}                                       /* L33 */
```

Compile and execute this program, and the following lines of text appear on the screen:

```
Satara      Satara
Sangli      Sangli
Karad       Karad
Pune        Pune
Mumbai      Mumbai
```

How It Works

In LOC 4, two int variables, i and j, are declared. In LOC 5, a char variable called ch is declared. In LOCs 6 to 12, the two-dimensional char type array called cities is declared and also initialized with suitable strings. In LOC 13, a pointer-to-char variable ptr and a pointer to pointer-to-char variable ptrPtr are declared. Notice the following about this program:

- ch is a char variable.

- ptr is a pointer to a char variable.

- *ptr is a char variable.

- ptrPtr is a pointer to a pointer-to-char variable.

- *ptrPtr is a pointer-to-char variable.

- **ptrPtr is a char variable.

Figure 4-10 shows the diagrammatic representation of the char array cities and the pointers ptr and ptrPtr. Notice the output of this program. You can see two columns, and each column lists the names of cities. The first column is outputted by the do-while loop in LOCs 18 to 22 using *ptr. The second column is outputted by the do-while loop in LOCs 25 to 29 using **ptrPtr. Both do-while loops are placed in a for loop. This for loop performs five iterations, and in each iteration a single line of text is displayed on the screen. Notice LOC 14, which is reproduced here for your quick reference:

```
ptrPtr = &ptr;                         /* L14 */
```

115

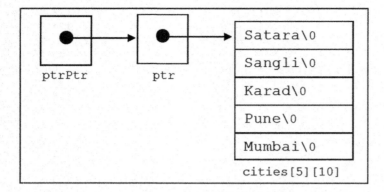

Figure 4-10. *Diagrammatic representation of pointer-to-char variable ptr and pointer-to-char variable ptrPtr. Notice that ptrPtr is pointing to ptr, and ptr is pointing to the first character in the first row of a two-dimensional char type array called cities.*

In LOC 14, the address of ptr is assigned to ptrPtr. As ptrPtr is a pointer to a pointer-to-char, you can assign to it only the address of a pointer-to-char.

Notice LOC 16, which represents the first statement in the body of the for loop and is reproduced here for your quick reference:

```
ptr = (char *) cities[i];                              /* L16 */
```

In LOC 16, the address of the first character in the ith row is assigned to the pointer variable ptr. The address of the ith row is returned by cities[i]. It is cast to (char *) and then assigned to ptr. This casting is necessary because cities[i] is not a pointer to char; it is a pointer to the ith row.

Thus, during the first iteration, LOC 16 assigns the address of the first character of the first row (i.e., the address of 'S' in "Satara") to ptr. During the second iteration, LOC 16 assigns the address of the first character of the second row (i.e., address of 'S' in "Sangli") to ptr, and so on.

Notice LOC 19 in the first do-while loop, which is reproduced here for your quick reference:

```
ch = *(ptr + j);                                       /* L19 */
```

Notice that this is a nested loop. The outer loop is a for loop. Consider the second iteration of the for loop. At the beginning of the second iteration of the for loop, in LOC 16, ptr is set to point to the first character in the second string (and this second string is nothing but "Sangli"). During the first iteration of the do-while loop, (ptr + j) points to the first character in "Sangli" as j is equal to 0. Consequently, LOC 19 retrieves the first character in "Sangli" (it is 'S'), and it is sent to the screen for display in LOC 20. During the second iteration of the do-while loop, (ptr + j) points to the second character in "Sangli" as j is equal to 1. Consequently, LOC 19 retrieves the second character in "Sangli" (it is 'a'), and it is sent to the screen for display in LOC 20. Proceeding in this manner, the complete string "Sangli" is retrieved and displayed on the screen.

Notice LOC 26 in the second do-while loop, which is reproduced here for your quick reference:

```
ch = *(*ptrPtr + j);                                    /* L26 */
```

Notice that this is also a nested loop. The outer loop is a for loop. Consider the second iteration of the for loop. At the beginning of the second iteration of the for loop, in LOC 16, ptr is set to point to the first character in the second string (and this second string is nothing but "Sangli"). Also, ptrPtr always points to ptr. It means during the second iteration of the for loop, *ptrPtr points to the first character in the second string (and this second string is nothing but "Sangli"). During the first iteration of the do-while loop, (*ptrPtr + j) points to the first character in "Sangli" as j is equal to 0. Consequently, LOC 26 retrieves the first character in "Sangli" (it is 'S'), and it is sent to the screen for display in LOC 27. During the second iteration of the do-while loop, (*ptrPtr + j) points to the second character in "Sangli" as j is equal to 1. Consequently, LOC 26 retrieves the second character in "Sangli" (it is 'a'), and it is sent to the screen for display in LOC 27. Proceeding in this manner, the complete string "Sangli" is retrieved and displayed on the screen.

CHAPTER 5

■ ■ ■

Functions and Structures with Pointers

In this chapter, you will explore the capabilities of functions and structures with the help of pointers. You can certainly use functions and structures without pointers. However, with the use of pointers, you need fewer lines of code to perform the same tasks.

5-1. Pass Arguments by Reference to a Function
Problem

You want to pass arguments by reference to a function to set the values of the credit count of members. This credit count is represented by an integer, and it can be set either from the main() function or from a user-defined function.

Solution

Write a C program that passes the arguments by reference, with the following specifications:

- The program creates two integer variables, intCC1 and intCC2, to store the credit counts of members and assigns predetermined values to them. The program also displays these values on the screen.

- The program defines the function changeCreditCount() in which the int variables intCC1 and intCC2 (which represent credit counts) are passed as arguments by reference. In addition to the function main(), the function changeCreditCount() can also set the values of the credit count.

© Shirish Chavan 2017
S. Chavan, *C Recipes*, DOI 10.1007/978-1-4842-2967-5_5

- The program changes the values of credit counts from the function changeCreditCount(). New values of credit counts are displayed on the screen. When the execution of changeCreditCount() is complete and control returns to the main() function, then the program again displays the values of credit counts to verify that the values of credit counts set in changeCreditCount() are intact.

The Code

The following is the code of the C program written with these specifications. Type the following C program in a text editor and save it in the folder C:\Code with the filename ref.c:

```
/* In this programs arguments are passed by reference to set the credit
count. */
                                                          /* BL */
#include <stdio.h>                                        /* L1 */
                                                          /* BL */
void changeCreditCount(int *p1, int *p2);                 /* L2 */
                                                          /* BL */
main()                                                    /* L3 */
{                                                         /* L4 */
 int intCC1 = 15, intCC2 = 20;                            /* L5 */
 printf("Computer-control is in main() function\n");      /* L6 */
 printf("intCC1 = %d and intCC2 = %d\n", intCC1, intCC2); /* L7 */
 changeCreditCount(&intCC1, &intCC2);                     /* L8 */
 printf("Computer-control is back in main() function\n"); /* L9 */
 printf("intCC1 = %d and intCC2 = %d\n", intCC1, intCC2); /* L10 */
 return(0);                                               /* L11 */
}                                                         /* L12 */
                                                          /* BL  */
void changeCreditCount(int *p1, int *p2)                  /* L13 */
{                                                         /* L14 */
  printf("Computer-control is in changeCreditCount() function\n"); /* L15 */
  printf("Initial values of *p1 and *p2: \n");            /* L16 */
  printf("*p1 = %d and *p2 = %d\n", *p1, *p2);            /* L17 */
  *p1 = *p1 * 4;                                          /* L18 */
  *p2 = *p2 * 4;                                          /* L19 */
  printf("Now values of *p1 and *p2 are changed\n");      /* L20 */
  printf("*p1 = %d and *p2 = %d\n", *p1, *p2);            /* L21 */
  return;                                                 /* L22 */
}                                                         /* L23 */
```

Compile and execute this program, and the following lines of text appear on the screen:

```
Computer-control is in main() function
intCC1 = 15 and intCC2 = 20
Computer-control is in changeCreditCount() function
Initial values of *p1 and *p2:
*p1 = 15 and *p2 = 20
Now values of *p1 and *p2 are changed
*p1 = 60 and *p2 = 80
Computer-control is back in main() function
intCC1 = 60 and intCC2 = 80
```

How It Works

When you pass arguments by reference and change the values of parameters in the called function, the values of arguments in the caller function are also changed. You exploit this fact to set the values of credit counts either from the main() function or from a user-defined function.

When you pass arguments by reference, you actually pass pointers to the called function. When you intend to pass arguments by reference, then you need to do the following:

- Prefix each argument in a function call with the address operator & (as in LOC 8).

- Prefix each parameter with the indirection operator * in the function prototype (as in LOC 2) and function definition (as in LOC 13).

LOC 2 consists of the prototype of function changeCreditCount(). In LOC 2, the parameters p1 and p2 are prefixed by the indirection operator * as follows:

```
void changeCreditCount(int *p1, int *p2);        /* L2, passing the arguments
                                                    by reference */
```

The block of code spanning LOCs 13 to 23 consists of the definition of the function changeCreditCount(). Inside the main() function, in LOC 5, two int variables, intCC1 and intCC2, are declared and also initialized with the values 15 and 20, respectively. In LOC 7, the values of intCC1 and intCC2 are displayed on the screen. In LOC 8, the function changeCreditCount() is called. LOC 8 is reproduced here for your quick reference:

```
changeCreditCount(&intCC1, &intCC2);             /* L8, passing the arguments
                                                    by reference */
```

Inside the function changeCreditCount(), the data resides in parameters p1 and p2. Because the arguments are passed by reference, the variables p1 and p2 are nothing but the aliases of the variables intCC1 and intCC2.

In LOC 17, the values of p1 and p2 are displayed on the screen, which are nothing but the current values of intCC1 and intCC2, which in turn are nothing but 15 and 20, respectively. In LOCs 18 and 19, the values of p1 and p2 are updated to 60 and 80, respectively. In LOC 21, the updated values of p1 and p2 (i.e., 60 and 80) are displayed on the screen. LOC 22 consists of the return statement. After execution of LOC 22, the control is returned to the main() function. Next, LOC 9 in the function main() is executed, and after execution of this LOC, the message "Computer-control is back in main() function" is displayed on the screen. In LOC 10, the values of intCC1 and intCC2 (which are now 60 and 80) are displayed on the screen, and then the execution of program is complete. Notice that as variables p1 and p2 in the function changeCreditCount() are nothing but aliases of the variables intCC1 and intCC2 in main(), when the values of p1 and p2 are updated in LOCs 18 and 19, the values of intCC1 and intCC2 in main() are also updated automatically.

5-2. Display Data Stored in Nested Structures
Problem

You want to access the members and embedded members in nested structures and then display the data stored in these structures on the screen. Figure 5-1 shows the data stored in structures, and Figure 5-2 shows the structure diagrammatically.

Table Showing the Biodata of Five Secret Agents				
Name	Roll Number	Age in years	Weight in kg	Joining Date
Dick	1	21	70.6	10/18/2006
Robert	2	22	75.8	8/24/2007
Steve	3	20	53.7	3/19/2006
Richard	4	19	83.1	6/22/2006
Albert	5	18	62.3	7/26/2007

Figure 5-1. Table showing the biodata of five secret agents

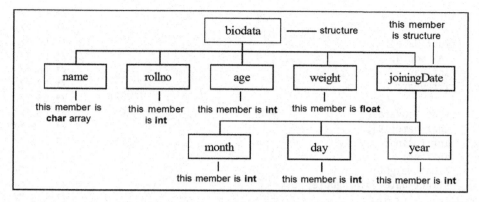

Figure 5-2. *Diagrammatic representation of structure biodata that consists of structure joiningDate as its member. Notice that joiningDate is a structure variable of type struct date.*

Solution

Write a C program that uses pointers to structures to access the members and embedded members in nested structures and then to display the data stored in these structures on the screen, with the following specifications:

- The program creates a structure called date to store the joining dates of members. The program creates the structure biodata to store the biodata of members, and the structure date is also a member of the structure biodata (see Figure 5-1 and Figure 5-2). To save the space, use only the first two records shown in Figure 5-1.

- The program creates two variables of type struct biodata and assigns suitable values to them.

- The program uses pointers to structures to retrieve the data stored in structures and displays this data on the screen.

The Code

The following is the code of the C program written with these specifications. Type the following C program in a text editor and save it in the folder C:\Code with the filename stru1.c:

```
/* In this program pointers to structures are used to access the embedded members in */
/* nested structures. The data in structures is then displayed on the screen. */
                                                              /* BL */
#include <stdio.h>                                            /* L1 */
                                                              /* BL */
```

```
main()                                                          /* L2 */
{                                                               /* L3 */
 struct date {                                                  /* L4 */
   int month;                                                   /* L5 */
   int day;                                                     /* L6 */
   int year;                                                    /* L7 */
 };                                                             /* L8 */
 struct biodata {                                               /* L9 */
   char name[15];                                               /* L10 */
   int rollno;                                                  /* L11 */
   int age;                                                     /* L12 */
   float weight;                                                /* L13 */
   struct date joiningDate;                                     /* L14 */
 };                                                             /* L15 */
struct biodata *ptr1, sa1 = {"Dick", 1, 21, 70.6F, 10, 18, 2006};    /* L16 */
struct biodata *ptr2, sa2 = {"Robert", 2, 22, 75.8F, 8, 24, 2007};   /* L17 */
ptr1 = &sa1;                                                    /* L18 */
ptr2 = &sa2;                                                    /* L19 */
                                                                /* BL */
printf("Biodata of Secret Agent # 1: \n");                     /* L20 */
printf("\tName: %s\n", (*ptr1).name);                          /* L21 */
printf("\tRoll Number: %d\n", (*ptr1).rollno);                 /* L22 */
printf("\tAge: %d years \n", (*ptr1).age);                     /* L23 */
printf("\tWeight: %.1f kg\n", (*ptr1).weight);                 /* L24 */
printf("\tJoining Date: %d/%d/%d\n\n", (*ptr1).joiningDate.month,    /* L25 */
        (*ptr1).joiningDate.day, (*ptr1).joiningDate.year);    /* L26 */
                                                                /* BL */
printf("Biodata of Secret Agent # 2: \n");                     /* L27 */
printf("\tName: %s\n", ptr2->name);                            /* L28 */
printf("\tRoll Number: %d\n", ptr2->rollno);                   /* L29 */
printf("\tAge: %d years \n", ptr2->age);                       /* L30 */
printf("\tWeight: %.1f kg\n", ptr2->weight);                   /* L31 */
printf("\tJoining Date: %d/%d/%d\n", ptr2->joiningDate.month,  /* L32 */
        ptr2->joiningDate.day, ptr2->joiningDate.year);        /* L33 */
                                                                /* BL */
 return(0);                                                     /* L34 */
}                                                               /* L35 */
```

Compile and execute this program, and the following lines of text appear on the screen:

```
Biodata of Secret Agent # 1:
Name: Dick
Roll Number: 1
Age: 21 years
Weight: 70.6 kg
Joining Date: 10/18/2006
Biodata of Secret Agent # 2:
```

```
Name: Robert
Roll Number: 2
Age: 22 years
Weight: 75.8 kg
Joining Date: 8/24/2007
```

How It Works

In LOCs 4 to 8, the structure date is defined. In LOCs 9 to 15, the structure biodata is defined. The structure date is a member of the structure biodata. In LOCs 16 to 17, the variables sa1 and sa2 of type biodata are declared and initialized with suitable values. In the same LOCs (i.e., 16 to 17), the pointers ptr1 and ptr2 to the structure biodata are declared. In LOC 18, the pointer ptr1 is set pointing to the variable sa1. In LOC 19, the pointer ptr2 is set pointing to variable sa2.

In the block of code spanning LOCs 20 to 26, the data assigned to variable sa1 (it is the biodata of Secret Agent #1) is displayed on the screen. LOC 21 displays the name of Secret Agent #1 on the screen, and it is reproduced here for your quick reference:

```
printf("\tName: %s\n", (*ptr1).name);                /* L21 */
```

The construction (*ptr1).name is used to retrieve the string name stored in sa1. Similar constructions are used in the remaining LOCs (i.e., 22 to 26) to retrieve the data stored in sa1. LOCs 25 and 26 represent a single statement, but as it is very long, it is shown on two LOCs. In this statement, the construction (*ptr1).joiningDate.month is used to retrieve the month, the construction (*ptr1).joiningDate.day is used to retrieve the day, and the construction (*ptr1).joiningDate.year is used to retrieve the year of birth of Secret Agent #1.

In the block of code spanning LOCs 27 to 33, the data assigned to variable sa2 (it is the biodata of Secret Agent #2) is displayed on the screen. In this block of code, different constructions are used, compared to the preceding block of code, to retrieve the data stored in variable sa2. LOC 28 displays the name of Secret Agent #2 on the screen, and it is reproduced here for your quick reference:

```
printf("\tName: %s\n", ptr2->name);                  /* L28 */
```

The construction ptr2->name is used to retrieve the string name stored in sa2. Similar constructions are used in the remaining LOCs (i.e., 29 to 33) to retrieve the data stored in sa2. LOCs 32 and 33 represent a single statement, but as it is very long, it is put on two LOCs. In this statement, the construction ptr2->joiningDate.month is used to retrieve the month, the construction ptr2->joiningDate.day is used to retrieve the day, and the construction ptr2->joiningDate.year is used to retrieve the year of birth of Secret Agent #2.

Constructions (*ptr).joiningDate.month and ptr->joiningDate.month can be used in scanf() statements, as shown here:

```
scanf("%d", &agent.joiningDate.month);
scanf("%d", &(*ptr).joiningDate.month);
scanf("%d", &ptr->joiningDate.month);
```

Either of these LOCs, after execution, accepts an integer value from the keyboard and assigns it to agent.joiningDate.month.

Constructions (*ptr).joiningDate.month and ptr->joiningDate.month can also be used in assignment statements, as shown here:

```
agent.joiningDate.month = agent.joiningDate.month + 3;
(*ptr).joiningDate.month = (*ptr).joiningDate.month + 3;
ptr->joiningDate.month = ptr->joiningDate.month + 3;
```

Either of these LOCs, after execution, increases the value of agent.joiningDate. month by 3.

Now here are a few words about the dot operator and the arrow operator.

Dot Operator

In the following code, you assign the suitable values to sa1:

```
strcpy(sa1.name, "Dick");                                    /* L1 */
sa1.rollno = 1;                                              /* L2 */
sa1.age = 21;                                                /* L3 */
sa1.weight = 70.6F;                                          /* L4 */
```

Notice that an individual member of a structure is accessed using the following construction:

```
structureVariableName.memberName
```

The dot (.) that connects structureVariableName to memberName is called a *structure member operator*. The construction given here can be used in a program like an ordinary variable. For example, notice the LOCs given here:

```
sa1.age = sa1.age + 1;                                       /* L5 */
sa1.weight = sa1.weight + 2.3;                               /* L6 */
```

After execution of LOC 5, the value of sa1.age increases by 1 (it changes from 21 to 22). After execution of LOC 6, the value of sa1.weight increases by 2.3 (it changes from 70.6 to 72.9).

Arrow Operator

Notice the piece of code given here:

```
struct biodata {                                             /* L1 */
  char name[15];                                             /* L2 */
  int rollno;                                                /* L3 */
  int age;                                                   /* L4 */
```

```
    float weight;                                              /* L5 */
};                                                             /* L6 */
struct biodata *ptr, agent = {"Dick", 1, 21, 70.6F};          /* L7 */
ptr = &agent;                                                  /* L8 */
printf("Biodata of secret agent:\n");                          /* LL */
printf("Name: %s\n", (*ptr).name);                             /* L9 */
printf("Roll Number: %d\n", (*ptr).rollno);                    /* L10 */
printf("Age: %d years \n", (*ptr).age);                        /* L11 */
printf("Weight: %.1f kg\n\n", (*ptr).weight);                  /* L12 */
```

This piece of code, after execution, displays the following lines of text on the screen:

```
Biodata of secret agent:
Name: Dick
Roll Number: 1
Age: 21 years
Weight: 70.6 kg
```

In this piece of code, the structure biodata is declared in LOCs 1 to 6. In LOC 7, you declare a pointer called ptr to struct biodata and a variable agent of type struct biodata. In LOC 8, the pointer ptr is made to point to the variable agent. In LOCs 9 to 12, you display the biodata of the agent on the screen. Notice how members of the agent are accessed using the pointer ptr. Construction *ptr can be used instead of the variable agent. Hence, the following LOCs are fully equivalent:

```
printf("Name: %s\n", agent.name);
printf("Name: %s\n", (*ptr).name);
```

Either of these LOCs, after execution, will display the following line of text on the screen:

```
Name: Dick
```

Also, notice that in the construction (*ptr).name, parentheses around *ptr are necessary because the precedence of the structure member operator . is higher than *. The construction *ptr.name means *(ptr.name), which is illegal here because name is not pointer, and hence it cannot be dereferenced.

Pointers to structures are used frequently; hence, an alternative notation, called the *arrow operator*, is provided as a shorthand. This arrow operator is ->. For example, the construction given here:

```
ptr->name
```

...is fully equivalent to either of the following constructions:

```
agent.name
(*ptr).name
```

This means the following LOCs are fully equivalent:

```
printf("Name: %s\n", agent.name);
printf("Name: %s\n", (*ptr).name);
printf("Name: %s\n", ptr->name);
```

Either of these LOCs, after execution, will display the following line of text on the screen:

```
Name: Dick
```

Also, the following LOCs are fully equivalent:

```
printf("Roll Number: %d\n", agent.rollno);
printf("Roll Number: %d\n", (*ptr).rollno);
printf("Roll Number: %d\n", ptr->rollno);
```

Either of these LOCs, after execution, will display the following line of text on the screen:

```
Roll Number: 1
```

Also, the following LOCs are fully equivalent:

```
printf("Age: %d years \n", agent.age);
printf("Age: %d years \n", (*ptr).age);
printf("Age: %d years \n", ptr->age);
```

Either of these LOCs, after execution, will display the following line of text on the screen:

```
Age: 21 years
```

Constructions involving pointers can also be used in scanf() statements. Notice the LOCs given here:

```
scanf("%d", &agent.age);
scanf("%d", &(*ptr).age);
scanf("%d", &ptr->age);
```

Either of these LOCs, after execution, accepts the integer value entered through the keyboard and assigns it to agent.age.

Constructions involving pointers can also be used in assignment statements. Notice the LOCs given here:

```
agent.age = agent.age + 5;
(*ptr).age = (*ptr).age + 5;
ptr->age = ptr->age + 5;
```

Either of these LOCs, after execution, increases the value of agent.age by 5.

Also, notice that it is possible to declare the pointer ptr and the variable agent in LOC 6 and drop LOC 7. This means the piece of code spanning LOCs 1 to 7, given earlier, can be replaced with the following piece of code:

```
struct biodata {                                    /* L1 */
  char name[15];                                    /* L2 */
  int rollno;                                       /* L3 */
  int age;                                          /* L4 */
  float weight;                                     /* L5 */
} *ptr, agent = {"Dick", 1, 21, 70.6F};             /* L6 */
```

5-3. Build a Structure Using a Function
Problem

You want to build a structure using a function.

Solution

Write a C program that passes the individual members of a structure to a function so that this function builds a structure using this data and returns it, with the following specifications:

- The program creates a structure called rectangle that in turn consists of two int type members, height and width. The program creates two variables, rect1 and rect2, of type struct rectangle.

- The program creates a function makeIt() that accepts the values of members height and width as input arguments. The program calls the function makeit() and passes suitable values for height and width to it as input arguments. Using these input arguments, the function makeIt() builds and returns the structure rectangle, which is then assigned to variables rect1 and rect2.

- The data stored in rect1 and rect2 is then displayed on the screen.

The Code

The following is the code of the C program written with these specifications. Type the following C program in a text editor and save it in the folder C:\Code with the filename stru2.c:

```
/* This program uses a function which accepts values of individual mmembers
of structure, */
/* builds a structure, and returns it. */
                                                           /* BL */
#include <stdio.h>                                         /* L1 */
                                                           /* BL */
struct rectangle {                                         /* L2 */
 int height;                                               /* L3 */
 int width;                                                /* L4 */
};                                                         /* L5 */
                                                           /* BL */
struct rectangle makeIt(int height, int width);            /* L6 */
                                                           /* BL */
main()                                                     /* L7 */
{                                                          /* L8 */
 struct rectangle rect1, rect2;                            /* L9 */
 rect1 = makeIt(20, 30);                                   /* L10 */
 rect2 = makeIt(40, 80);                                   /* L11 */
                                                           /* BL  */
 printf("Dimensions of rect1: \n");                        /* L12 */
 printf("height: %d\n", rect1.height);                     /* L13 */
 printf("width: %d\n\n", rect1.width);                     /* L14 */
                                                           /* BL */
 printf("Dimensions of rect2: \n");                        /* L15 */
 printf("height: %d\n", rect2.height);                     /* L16 */
 printf("width: %d\n\n", rect2.width);                     /* L17 */
                                                           /* BL  */
 return(0);                                                /* L18 */
}                                                          /* L19 */
                                                           /* BL  */
struct rectangle makeIt(int height, int width)             /* L20 */
{                                                          /* L21 */
  struct rectangle myRectangle;                            /* L22 */
  myRectangle.height = height;                             /* L23 */
  myRectangle.width = width;                               /* L24 */
  return myRectangle;                                      /* L25 */
}                                                          /* L26 */
```

Compile and execute this program, and the following lines of text appear on the screen:

```
Dimensions of rect1:
height: 20
width: 30
Dimensions of rect2:
height: 40
width: 80
```

How It Works

In the block of code spanning LOCs 2 to 5, the structure rectangle is defined. It consists of two int type members, namely, height and width. The values of these two members are passed as arguments to the function makeIt() that builds a rectangle and then returns the structure rectangle. The block of code spanning LOCs 20 to 16 defines the function makeIt(). The parameter names in the function makeIt() were chosen to be same as the member names in the structure (i.e., height and width) to keep the logic simple.

The scope of the structure rectangle is set to be external (it is declared outside of any function) so that it can be accessed from any function. LOC 6 consists of the function prototype. In LOC 9, two variables, rect1 and rect2, of type struct rectangle are declared.

In LOC 10, a call is made to the function makeIt(), and arguments 20 and 30 are provided as values of the parameters height and width. The function makeIt() returns a structure rectangle with its member values set accordingly (i.e., height is 20 and width is 30), and this returned structure is assigned to the variable rect1.

Similarly, in LOC 11, a call is made to the function makeIt() but with different arguments (40 and 80). The structure returned by makeIt() is then assigned to the variable rect2.

LOCs 12 to 17 display the values of members belonging to the structures rect1 and rect2.

5-4. Modify the Data in a Structure by Passing It to a Function

Problem

You want to modify the data in a structure by passing it to a function.

Solution

Write a C program, with the following specifications, that passes a structure to a function as an input argument, and this function resets the data in this structure and returns it:

- The program creates a structure rectangle that in turn consists of two int type members, height and width. The program also creates two variables, rect1 and rect2, of type struct rectangle and initializes these variables with suitable values. The data stored in rect1 and rect2 is displayed on the screen.

- The program creates a function called doubleIt() that accepts the variable of type struct rectangle (i.e., rect1 or rect2) as the input argument, resets the data of this variable, and then returns this variable. Using these returned variables, the variables rect1 and rect2 are reset.

- The reset data stored in rect1 and rect2 is again displayed on the screen.

The Code

The following is the code of the C program written with these specifications. Type the following C program in a text editor and save it in the folder C:\Code with the filename stru3.c:

```
/* This program uses a function which accepts a structure as an input   
argument */                                                               /* BL */
/* and returns a structure after modifying data in it. */                 
                                                                          /* BL */
#include <stdio.h>                                                        /* L1 */
                                                                          /* BL */
struct rectangle {                                                        /* L2 */
 int height;                                                              /* L3 */
 int width;                                                               /* L4 */
};                                                                        /* L5 */
                                                                          /* BL */
struct rectangle doubleIt(struct rectangle ourRect);                      /* L6 */
                                                                          /* BL */
main()                                                                    /* L7 */
{                                                                         /* L8 */
 struct rectangle rect1 = {10, 15}, rect2 = {25, 35};                     /* L9 */
                                                                          /* BL */
 printf("Dimensions of rect1 before modification: \n");                  /* L10 */
 printf("height: %d\n", rect1.height);                                   /* L11 */
 printf("width: %d\n\n", rect1.width);                                   /* L12 */
                                                                          /* BL */
 rect1 = doubleIt(rect1);                                                /* L13 */
                                                                          /* BL */
 printf("Dimensions of rect1 after modification: \n");                   /* L14 */
 printf("height: %d\n", rect1.height);                                   /* L15 */
 printf("width: %d\n\n", rect1.width);                                   /* L16 */
                                                                          /* BL */
 printf("Dimensions of rect2 before modification: \n");                  /* L17 */
 printf("height: %d\n", rect2.height);                                   /* L18 */
 printf("width: %d\n\n", rect2.width);                                   /* L19 */
                                                                          /* BL */
 rect2 = doubleIt(rect2);                                                /* L20 */
                                                                          /* BL */
```

```
printf("Dimensions of rect2 after modification: \n");       /* L21 */
printf("height: %d\n", rect2.height);                        /* L22 */
printf("width: %d\n\n", rect2.width);                        /* L23 */
                                                             /* BL  */
return(0);                                                   /* L24 */
}                                                            /* L25 */
                                                             /* BL  */
struct rectangle doubleIt (struct rectangle ourRect)         /* L26 */
{                                                            /* L27 */
  ourRect.height = 2 * ourRect.height;                       /* L28 */
  ourRect.width = 2 * ourRect.width;                         /* L29 */
  return ourRect;                                            /* L30 */
}                                                            /* L31 */
```

Compile and execute this program, and the following lines of text appear on the screen:

```
Dimensions of rect1 before modification:
height: 10
width: 15
Dimensions of rect1 after modification:
height: 20
width: 30
Dimensions of rect2 before modification:
height: 25
width: 35
Dimensions of rect2 after modification:
height: 50
width: 70
```

How It Works

LOCs 2 to 5 define the structure rectangle. The structure rectangle consists of two int type members, namely, height and width. LOC 6 consists of the prototype of the function doubleIt().

In LOC 9, two variables, rect1 and rect2, of type struct rectangle are declared and also initialized with suitable values. LOCs 10 to 12 display the data stored in rect1. In LOC 13, the function doubleIt() is called. In this function call, the input argument is rect1, and the value returned by doubleIt() is also assigned to rect1. LOCs 26 to 31 define the function doubleIt(). This function accepts a variable of type struct rectangle as an input, doubles the values of its members, and returns the modified value of that variable. LOCs 14 to 16 display the data stored in rect1 after modification.

LOCs 17 to 19 display the values of members of rect2. In LOC 20, function doubleIt() is called. The argument to this function is rect2, and the value returned by this function is assigned to rect2. This function simply doubles the values of members of rect2. LOCs 21 to 23 display the values of members of rect2 after modification by doubleIt().

In this program, the structure rectangle is declared outside of any function so that its scope should be external. The structure rectangle can be accessed from any function.

5-5. Modify the Data in a Structure by Passing a Pointer-to-Structure to a Function

Problem

You want to modify the data in a structure by passing a pointer-to-structure to a function.

Solution

Write a C program that modifies the data in a structure by passing a pointer-to-structure to a function, with the following specifications:

- The program creates a structure called rectangle that in turn consists of two int type members, namely, height and width. The program also creates two variables, rect1 and rect2, of type struct rectangle and initilizes these variables with suitable values. The data stored in rect1 and rect2 is displayed on the screen.

- The program creates a function called doubleIt() that accepts the pointer-to-struct rectangle (say, &rect1) as an input argument and modifies the data in rect1.

- The reset data stored in rect1 is again displayed on the screen. The procedure is then repeated for rect2.

The Code

The following is the code of the C program written with these specifications. Type the following C program in a text editor and save it in the folder C:\Code with the filename stru4.c:

```
/* This program uses a function which accepts a pointer to structure as an
input argument */
/* and modifies data in that structure. */
                                                          /* BL */
#include <stdio.h>                                        /* L1 */
                                                          /* BL */
struct rectangle {                                        /* L2 */
 int height;                                              /* L3 */
 int width;                                               /* L4 */
};                                                        /* L5 */
                                                          /* BL */
```

```
void doubleIt(struct rectangle *ptr);                      /* L6  */
                                                           /* BL */
main()                                                     /* L7  */
{                                                          /* L8  */
  struct rectangle rect1 = {10, 15}, rect2 = {25, 35};     /* L9  */
                                                           /* BL  */
  printf("Dimensions of rect1 before modification: \n");   /* L10 */
  printf("height: %d\n", rect1.height);                    /* L11 */
  printf("width: %d\n\n", rect1.width);                    /* L12 */
                                                           /* BL  */
doubleIt(&rect1);                                          /* L13 */
                                                           /* BL  */
  printf("Dimensions of rect1 after modification: \n");    /* L14 */
  printf("height: %d\n", rect1.height);                    /* L15 */
  printf("width: %d\n\n", rect1.width);                    /* L16 */
                                                           /* BL  */
  printf("Dimensions of rect2 before modification: \n");   /* L17 */
  printf("height: %d\n", rect2.height);                    /* L18 */
  printf("width: %d\n\n", rect2.width);                    /* L19 */
                                                           /* BL  */
doubleIt(&rect2);                                          /* L20 */
                                                           /* BL  */
  printf("Dimensions of rect2 after modification: \n");    /* L21 */
  printf("height: %d\n", rect2.height);                    /* L22 */
  printf("width: %d\n\n", rect2.width);                    /* L23 */
                                                           /* BL  */
 return(0);                                                /* L24 */
}                                                          /* L25 */
                                                           /* BL  */
void doubleIt (struct rectangle *ptr)                      /* L26 */
{                                                          /* L27 */
  ptr->height = 2 * ptr->height;                           /* L28 */
  ptr->width = 2 * ptr->width;                             /* L29 */
  return;                                                  /* L30 */
}                                                          /* L31 */
```

Compile and execute this program, and the following lines of text appear on the screen:

```
Dimensions of rect1 before modification:
height: 10
width: 15
Dimensions of rect1 after modification:
height: 20
width: 30
Dimensions of rect2 before modification:
height: 25
width: 35
```

```
Dimensions of rect2 after modification:
height: 50
width: 70
```

How It Works

LOCs 2 to 5 define the structure `rectangle`. The structure `rectangle` consists of two `int` type members, namely, `height` and `width`. The structure `rectangle` is declared outside of any function so that its scope is `external`. The structure `rectangle` can be accessed from any function. LOC 6 consists of the prototype of the function `doubleIt()`. This function accepts a pointer-to-`struct rectangle` as an input and then doubles the values of the members of the structure, namely, `height` and `width`. This function does not return any value, and its return type is `void`.

In LOC 9, two variables, `rect1` and `rect2`, of type `struct rectangle` are declared and are also initialized with suitable initializers. LOCs 10 to 12 display the values of the members of `rect1`. In LOC 13, the function `doubleIt()` is called. The argument to this function is `&rect1`. This function simply doubles the values of members of `rect1`. LOCs 14 to 16 display the values of members of `rect1` after modification by `doubleIt()`.

LOCs 17 to 19 display the values of members of `rect2`. In LOC 20, function `doubleIt()` is called. The argument to this function is `&rect2`. This function simply doubles the values of the members of `rect2`. LOCs 21 to 23 display the values of members of `rect2` after modification by `doubleIt()`.

LOCs 26 to 31 consist of the definition of the function `doubleIt()`.

5-6. Store and Retrieve Data Using an Array of Structures

Problem

You want to store and retrieve data using an array of structures.

Solution

Write a C program that stores and retrieves the data using an array of structures, with the following specifications:

- The program declares a structure, namely, `biodata`. The program creates an array, namely, `agents` of type `struct biodata`.

- The program fills the elements of the array `agents` with suitable data, in batch mode. Figure 5-1 shows the data stored in this array. To save the space, use only the first two records shown in Figure 5-1.

- The program displays the data filled in the elements of the array on the screen.

The Code

The following is the code of the C program written with these specifications. Type the following C program in a text editor and save it in the folder C:\Code with the filename stru5.c:

```
/* In this program an array of structures is used. */
                                                        /* BL */
#include <stdio.h>                                      /* L1 */
                                                        /* BL */
main()                                                  /* L2 */
{                                                       /* L3 */
  struct biodata {                                      /* L4 */
    char name[15];                                      /* L5 */
    int rollno;                                         /* L6 */
    int age;                                            /* L7 */
    float weight;                                       /* L8 */
  } ;                                                   /* L9 */
                                                        /* BL */
  struct biodata agents[2];                             /* L10 */
                                                        /* Bl */
  strcpy(agents[0].name, "Dick");                       /* L11 */
  agents[0].rollno = 1;                                 /* L12 */
  agents[0].age = 21;                                   /* L13 */
  agents[0].weight = 70.6F;                             /* L14 */
                                                        /* BL */
  strcpy(agents[1].name, "Robert");                     /* L15 */
  agents[1].rollno = 2;                                 /* L16 */
  agents[1].age = 22;                                   /* L17 */
  agents[1].weight = 75.8F;                             /* L18 */
                                                        /* BL */
  printf("Biodata of Secret Agent # 1: \n");            /* L19 */
  printf("\tName: %s\n", agents[0].name);               /* L20 */
  printf("\tRoll Number: %d\n", agents[0].rollno);      /* L21 */
  printf("\tAge: %d years \n", agents[0].age);          /* L22 */
  printf("\tWeight: %.1f kg\n\n", agents[0].weight);    /* L23 */
                                                        /* BL */
  printf("Biodata of Secret Agent # 2: \n");            /* L24 */
  printf("\tName: %s\n", agents[1].name);               /* L25 */
  printf("\tRoll Number: %d\n", agents[1].rollno);      /* L26 */
  printf("\tAge: %d years \n", agents[1].age);          /* L27 */
  printf("\tWeight: %.1f kg\n", agents[1].weight);      /* L28 */
                                                        /* BL */
  return(0);                                            /* L29 */
}                                                       /* L30 */
```

Compile and execute this program, and the following lines of text appear on the screen:

```
Biodata of Secret Agent # 1:
Name: Dick
Roll Number: 1
Age: 21 years
Weight: 70.6 kg
Biodata of Secret Agent # 2:
Name: Robert
Roll Number: 2
Age: 22 years
Weight: 75.8 kg
```

How It Works

In LOCs 4 to 9, the structure biodata is created. In LOC 10, an array of structures called agents is created of type struct biodata. This array consists of only two elements: agents[0] and agents[1].

- agents[0] is meant for storing the first record shown in Figure 5-1.

- agents[1] is meant for storing the second record shown in Figure 5-1.

In LOCs 11 to 14, the first element of the array, agents[0], is filled with data. In LOCs 15 to 18, the second element of the array, agents[1], is filled with data.

The individual structure member in an array element is accessed using the construction shown here:

```
arrayElementName.memberName
```

Here, the dot (.) is a *structure member operator*. For example, the member age in the first array element agents[0] can be accessed using the construction given here:

```
agents[0].age
```

In LOCs 19 to 23, the data filled in agents[0] is displayed on the screen. In LOCs 24 to 28, the data filled in agents[1] is displayed on the screen.

In this program, you assign the values to individual members of array elements. Can you initialize array elements? Certainly! You can do so. Notice the piece of code given here:

```
struct biodata {                                              /* L1 */
  char name[15];                                              /* L2 */
  int rollno;                                                 /* L3 */
  int age;                                                    /* L4 */
  float weight;                                               /* L5 */
} ;                                                           /* L6 */
                                                              /* BL */
```

```
struct biodata agents[2] =                              /* L7 */
                        {                               /* L8 */
                            {"Dick", 1, 21, 70.6F},     /* L9 */
                            {"Robert", 2, 22, 75.8F}    /* L10 */
                        };                              /* L11 */
```

In this piece of code, you declare an array called agents that consists of two elements and initialize these elements using the data contained in the first two records shown in Figure 5-1 as initializers. Replace LOCs 10 to 18 in the program stru6 with LOCs 7 to 11 in the piece of code given earlier, and the program works equally well.

5-7. Store and Retrieve Data Using an Array of Structures in Interactive Mode

Problem

You want store and retrieve data using an array of structures in interactive mode.

Solution

Write a C program that stores and retrieves data using an array of structures, with the following specifications:

- The program declares a structure, namely, biodata. The program creates an array called agents of type struct biodata.

- The program fills the elements of the array agents with suitable data in interactive mode. Figure 5-1 shows the data to be stored in this array.

- The program displays the data filled in the elements of the array on the screen.

The Code

The following is the code of the C program written with these specifications. Type the following C program in a text editor and save it in the folder C:\Code with the filename stru6.c:

```
/* An interactive program that makes use of array of structures. */
                                                        /* BL */
#include <stdio.h>                                      /* L1 */
                                                        /* BL */
main()                                                  /* L2 */
{                                                       /* L3 */
    int i;                                              /* L4 */
    struct biodata {                                    /* L5 */
```

```
        char name[15];                                         /* L6  */
        int rollno;                                            /* L7  */
        int age;                                               /* L8  */
        float weight;                                          /* L9  */
    } ;                                                        /* L10 */
                                                               /* BL  */
struct biodata agents[5];                                      /* L11 */
                                                               /* BL  */
for(i = 0; i < 5; i++) {                                       /* L12 */
    printf("\nEnter Biodata of Secret Agent # %d: \n", i+1);   /* L13 */
    printf("Name: ");                                          /* L14 */
    scanf("%s", &agents[i].name);                              /* L15 */
    printf("Roll Number: ");                                   /* L16 */
    scanf("%d", &agents[i].rollno);                            /* L17 */
    printf("Age: ");                                           /* L18 */
    scanf("%d", &agents[i].age);                               /* L19 */
    printf("Weight: ");                                        /* L20 */
    scanf("%f", &agents[i].weight);                            /* L21 */
}                                                              /* L22 */
                                                               /* BL  */
printf("\nNow data entered by you will ");                     /* L23 */
printf("be displayed on the screen.\n\n");                     /* L24 */
for(i = 0; i < 5; i++) {                                       /* L25 */
    printf("Biodata of Secret Agent # %d: \n", i+1);           /* L26 */
    printf("\tName: %s\n", agents[i].name);                    /* L27 */
    printf("\tRoll Number: %d\n", agents[i].rollno);           /* L28 */
    printf("\tAge: %d years \n", agents[i].age);               /* L29 */
    printf("\tWeight: %.1f kg\n\n", agents[i].weight);         /* L30 */
}                                                              /* L31 */
                                                               /* BL  */
    return(0);                                                 /* L32 */
}                                                              /* L33 */
                                                               /* BL  */
linkfloat()                                                    /* L34 */
{                                                              /* L35 */
    float number = 10, *pointer;                               /* L36 */
    pointer = &number;                                         /* L37 */
    number = *pointer;                                         /* L38 */
    return(0);                                                 /* L39 */
}                                                              /* L40 */
```

Compile and execute this program. A run of this program is given here:

```
Enter Biodata of Secret Agent # 1:
Name: Dick      ↵
Roll Number: 1       ↵
Age: 21      ↵
Weight: 70.6      ↵
```

```
Enter Biodata of Secret Agent # 2:
Name: Robert      ↵
Roll Number: 2       ↵
Age: 22    ↵
Weight: 75.8     ↵
Enter Biodata of Secret Agent # 3:
Name: Steve    ↵
Roll Number: 3    ↵
Age: 20    ↵
Weight: 53.7     ↵
Enter Biodata of Secret Agent # 4:
Name: Richard    ↵
Roll Number: 4       ↵
Age: 19    ↵
Weight: 83.1     ↵
Enter Biodata of Secret Agent # 5:
Name: Albert    ↵
Roll Number: 5    ↵
Age: 18    ↵
Weight: 62.3      ↵

Now data entered by you will be displayed on the screen.
Biodata of Secret Agent # 1:
Name: Dick
Roll Number: 1
Age: 21 years
Weight: 70.6 kg
Biodata of Secret Agent # 2:
Name: Robert
Roll Number: 2
Age: 22 years
Weight: 75.8 kg
Biodata of Secret Agent # 3:
Name: Steve
Roll Number: 3
Age: 20 years
Weight: 53.7 kg
Biodata of Secret Agent # 4:
Name: Richard
Roll Number: 4
Age: 19 years
Weight: 83.1 kg
Biodata of Secret Agent # 5:
Name: Albert
Roll Number: 5
Age: 18 years
Weight: 62.3 kg
```

How It Works

In LOCs 5 to 10, the structure biodata is created. In LOC 11, an array called agents is created of type struct biodata. LOCs 12 to 22 consist of a for loop that performs five iterations and accepts data from the user through the keyboard to be filled in the array. The user enters the data of the five secret agents from Figure 5-1. In a single iteration, the data of a single secret agent is accepted and filled in a corresponding element of the array.

In LOCs 23 to 31, the data of the five secret agents that is stored in the array agents is displayed on the screen. LOCs 25 to 31 consists of a for loop that performs five iterations and displays the data of five secret agents stored in the array agents. In a single iteration, the data of a single secret agent is displayed on the screen.

Notice the benefit of using an array of structures instead of individual variables. Now you can use a for loop to handle the input as well as the output.

Also, notice that this program is short despite that it handles the biodata of five secret agents compared to the earlier program, which handled the biodata of only two secret agents.

The piece of code contained in LOCs 34 to 40 is the definition of the function linkfloat(). If you don't include this function, then during runtime the program crashes and the following message appears on the screen: "Floating point formats not linked. Abnormal program termination." The program crashes when the scanf() function is about to accept the floating-point value for weight for the first member. To prevent the abnormal termination of this program, you are required to include this function somewhere in the program, preferably at the end of the program. There's no need to call this function.

5-8. Invoke a Function Using a Pointer-to-Function
Problem

You want to invoke a function using a pointer-to-function.

Solution

Write a C program that invokes a function using a pointer-to-function, with the following specifications:

- The program declares the pointer-to-function ptrFunc.

- The program declares two functions, sum() and add(). These functions perform the addition of numbers. The return type of these functions is int.

- The program invokes the functions sum() and add() using the pointer-to-function ptrFunc.

The Code

The following is the code of the C program written with these specifications. Type the following C program in a text editor and save it in the folder C:\Code with the filename point19.c:

```
/* This program uses a pointer-to-function to invoke functions.  */   /* BL */
#include <stdio.h>                                                     /* L1 */
                                                                       /* BL */
int sum (double n1, double n2);                                        /* L2 */
int add(int m1, int m2);                                               /* L3 */
                                                                       /* BL */
main()                                                                 /* L4 */
{                                                                      /* L5 */
  int r;                                                               /* L6 */
  int (*ptrFunc)();                                                    /* L7 */
                                                                       /* BL */
  ptrFunc = sum;                                                       /* L8 */
  r = (*ptrFunc)(2.3, 4.5);                                            /* L9 */
  printf("(int)(2.3 + 4.5) = %d\n", r);                                /* L10 */
                                                                       /* BL */
  ptrFunc = add;                                                       /* L11 */
  r = (*ptrFunc)(10, 15);                                              /* L12 */
  printf("10 + 15 = %d\n", r);                                         /* L13 */
                                                                       /* BL */
  return(0);                                                           /* L14 */
}                                                                      /* L15 */
                                                                       /* BL */
int sum(double j1, double j2)                                          /* L16 */
{                                                                      /* L17 */
 int result;                                                           /* L18 */
 result = (int)(j1 + j2);                                              /* L19 */
 return(result);                                                       /* L20 */
}                                                                      /* L21 */
                                                                       /* BL */
int add(int k1, int k2)                                                /* L22 */
{                                                                      /* L23 */
 return(k1 + k2);                                                      /* L24 */
}                                                                      /* L25 */
```

Compile and execute this program, and the following lines of text appear on the screen:

```
(int) (2.3 + 4.5) = 6
10 + 15 = 25
```

143

How It Works

In LOC 2, the prototype of the function sum() is declared. The return type of sum() is int, and it has two parameters of type double. In LOC 3, the prototype of the function add() is declared. The return type of add() is int, and it has two parameters of type int. In LOC 6, an int variable r is declared to store the values returned by the functions sum() and add() temporarily. In LOC 7, a pointer-to-function ptrFunc is declared (the return type of this function must be int).

In LOC 8, the pointer ptrFunc is made to point to the function sum(). In LOC 9, the function sum() is called using the pointer ptrFunc and two double type arguments (2.3 and 4.5) are passed to the function sum(). Also, the value returned by sum() is assigned to the variable r. In LOC 10, the value of r is displayed on the screen.

In LOC 11, the pointer ptrFunc is made to point to the function add(). In LOC 12, the function add() is called using the pointer ptrFunc, and two int type arguments (10 and 15) are passed to the function add(). Also, the value returned by add() is assigned to the variable r. In LOC 13, the value of r is displayed on the screen.

LOCs 16 to 21 consist of the definition of the function sum(). In this function, two double type arguments are added, the result is subjected to a cast operation in order to change its type to int, and then the result is returned.

LOCs 22 to 25 consist of the definition of the function add(). In this function two int type arguments are added, and the result is returned.

If you find the logic of this program difficult to understand, then consider another program, point20, that is easier to understand.

First, notice the following generic syntax:

(a)   Declaring a pointer to a function

(b)   Setting that pointer pointing to a function

(c)   Calling that function using the pointer

Here is the generic syntax:

```
returnType functionName (parameterList);              /* L1 */
returnType (*pointerToFunction)();                    /* L2 */
pointerToFunction = functionName;                     /* L3 */
(*pointerToFunction)(argumentList);                   /* L4 */
pointerToFunction(argumentList);                      /* L5 */
```

In this block of code, LOC 1 consists of the prototype of the function functionName(), and LOC 2 consists of the declaration of the pointer-to-function named pointerToFunction. Generally, LOC 1 is placed outside the main() function, whereas LOCs 2 to 4 are placed inside the main() function. Notice that returnType mentioned in LOCs 1 and 2 must be the same. The parentheses shown in LOCs 1 and 2 are required and cannot be omitted. In LOC 3, the address of functionName is assigned to pointerToFunction. In LOC 4, the function functionName() is called using the pointer pointerToFunction. In LOC 5 also, the function functionName() is called using the pointer pointerToFunction. But the syntax given in LOC 4 is standard and is more preferred.

Type the following C program in a text editor and save it in the folder C:\Code with the filename point20.c:

```
/* This program uses a pointer-to-function to invoke a function.  */
                                                        /* BL */
#include <stdio.h>                                      /* L1 */
                                                        /* BL */
void welcome(void);                                     /* L2 */
                                                        /* BL */
main()                                                  /* L3 */
{                                                       /* L4 */
  void (*ptrFunc)();                                    /* L5 */
  ptrFunc = welcome;                                    /* L6 */
  (*ptrFunc)();                                         /* L7 */
  return(0);                                            /* L8 */
}                                                       /* L9 */
                                                        /* BL */
void welcome(void)                                      /* L10 */
{                                                       /* L11 */
 printf("Welcome boys and girls.\n");                   /* L12 */
 return;                                                /* L13 */
}                                                       /* L14 */
```

Compile and execute this program, and the following line of text appears on the screen:

```
Welcome boys and girls.
```

In this program, in LOC 2, the prototype for the function welcome() is declared. The return type of welcome() is void. In LOC 5, a pointer-to-function named ptrFunc is declared. Notice the term void in LOC 5, which indicates that this pointer can point to only that function whose return type is void. In LOC 6, the pointer ptrFunc is set pointing to the function welcome().

■ **Note** LOC 6 exploits the following fact: the value of the function name is nothing but the address of the function definition stored in memory.

In LOC 7, the function welcome() is invoked (i.e., called) using the pointer ptrFunc. Notice that ptrFunc is a pointer, whereas *ptrFunc is a function.

5-9. Implement a Text-Based Menu System

Problem

You want to implement a text-based menu system using a pointer-to-function.

Solution

Write a C program that implements a text-based menu system using a pointer-to-function, with the following specifications:

- The program declares an array of pointers-to-functions called funcPtr. In this program, Edit-menu is to be implemented and consists of four menu items: Cut, Copy, Paste, and Delete.

- The program declares four functions: cut(), copy(), paste(), and delete(). These functions are called when the corresponding menu item is activated by the user.

The Code

The following is the code of the C program written with these specifications. Type the following C program in a text editor and save it in the folder C:\Code with the filename point21.c:

```
/* This program uses a pointer-to-function to implement text based menu system.  */
                                                            /* BL */
#include <stdio.h>                                          /* L1 */
                                                            /* BL */
void cut (int intCut);                                      /* L2 */
void copy (int intCopy);                                    /* L3 */
void paste (int intPaste);                                  /* L4 */
void delete (int intDelete) ;                               /* L5 */
                                                            /* BL */
main()                                                      /* L6 */
{                                                           /* L7 */
   void (*funcPtr[4])(int) = {cut, copy, paste, delete};    /* L8 */
   int intChoice;                                           /* L9 */
   printf("\nEdit Menu: Enter your choices (0, 1, 2, or 3).\n");  /* L10 */
   printf("Please do not enter any other number
except 0, 1, 2, or 3 to \n");                               /* L11 */
   printf("avoid abnormal termination of program.\n");      /* L12 */
   printf("Enter 0 to activate menu-item Cut.\n");          /* L13 */
   printf("Enter 1 to activate menu-item Copy.\n");         /* L14 */
   printf("Enter 2 to activate menu-item Paste.\n");        /* L15 */
   printf("Enter 3 to activate menu-item Delete.\n");       /* L16 */
```

146

```
    scanf("%d", &intChoice);                        /* L17 */
    (*funcPtr[intChoice])(intChoice);               /* L18 */
    printf("Thank you.\n");                         /* L19 */
    return(0);                                       /* L20 */
}                                                    /* L21 */
                                                     /* BL  */
void cut (int intCut)                                /* L22 */
{                                                    /* L23 */
  printf("You entered %d.\n", intCut);              /* L24 */
  printf("Menu-item Cut is activated.\n");          /* L25 */
}                                                    /* L26 */
                                                     /* BL  */
void copy (int intCopy)                              /* L27 */
{                                                    /* L28 */
  printf("You entered %d.\n", intCopy);             /* L29 */
  printf("Menu-item Copy is activated.\n");         /* L30 */
}                                                    /* L31 */
                                                     /* BL  */
void paste (int intPaste)                            /* L32 */
{                                                    /* L33 */
  printf("You entered %d.\n", intPaste);            /* L34 */
  printf("Menu-item Paste is activated.\n");        /* L35 */
}                                                    /* L36 */
                                                     /* BL  */
void delete (int intDelete)                          /* L37 */
{                                                    /* L38 */
  printf("You entered %d.\n", intDelete);           /* L39 */
  printf("Menu-item Delete is activated.\n");       /* L40 */
}                                                    /* L41 */
```

Compile and execute this program. A run of this program is given here:

```
Edit Menu: Enter your choices (0, 1, 2, or 3).
Please do not enter any other number except 0, 1, 2, or 3 to
avoid abnormal termination of program.
Enter 0 to activate menu-item Cut.
Enter 1 to activate menu-item Copy.
Enter 2 to activate menu-item Paste.
Enter 3 to activate menu-item Delete.
2     ⏎
You entered 2.
Menu-item Paste is activated.
Thank you.
```

How It Works

In LOCs 2 to 5, the prototypes of functions cut(), copy(), paste(), and delete() are declared. In LOC 8, an array of pointers called funcPtr is declared and consists of four elements, and it is also initialized. The pointers in the array funcPtr are made to point toward the functions cut(), copy(), paste(), and delete(), and serially (i.e., pointer funcPtr[0] is pointing toward the function cut(), etc.). In LOCs 10 to 16, the user is advised to enter an integer in the range 0 to 3 to activate the corresponding menu item in Edit-menu. The choice entered by the user is stored in the int variable intChoice. In LOC 18, the corresponding function is called using the appropriate pointer in the array funcPtr. LOCs 22 to 16 consist of the definition of the function cut(). LOCs 27 to 31 consist of the definition of the function copy(). LOCs 32 to 36 consist of the definition of the function paste(). LOCs 37 to 41 consist of the definition of the function delete().

CHAPTER 6

Data Files

A *file* is a collection of data that is named and saved in the secondary storage (like on a disk or tape). The contents of a file can be retrieved and modified as per the requirements of the storage.

Every piece of data that is loaded in the primary or secondary memory of a computer is not a file. It is only when you save that data on the disk and name it suitably that the collection of data assumes the status of a file. Why use files? Read on. Primary memory is volatile; when you switch off the computer, everything that is stored in primary memory is lost. Therefore, it is necessary to save the data on the secondary storage (because the secondary storage is not volatile). It is also necessary to offer some suitable name to that collection of data so anyone can refer to that collection of data unambiguously. When you do this (i.e., save the collection of data on the secondary storage and name it), you get a file. A file is also called a *disk file* in order to distinguish it from a device file.

6-1. Read a Text File Character by Character
Problem
You want to read a text file character by character.

Solution
Write a C program that reads a text file character by character, with the following specifications:

- The program opens and reads an existing text file called `test.txt` that is stored in the default folder of `C:\Compiler`.

- The program uses the function `fgetc()` to read a character from a file and uses the function `putchar()` to display the character on the screen.

Create a small text file, named `test.txt`, with the following contents:

```
Welcome to C programming.
Thank you.
```

© Shirish Chavan 2017
S. Chavan, *C Recipes*, DOI 10.1007/978-1-4842-2967-5_6

Place the compiler in the folder C:\Compiler. Place the text file test.txt in this folder. This is the folder from which the compiler gets launched every time you start it because the main program file of the compiler rests in this folder.

The Code

The following is the code of the C program written with these specifications. Type the following C program in a text editor and save it in the folder C:\Code with the file name files1.c:

```
/* This program reads the contents of the text file test.txt and displays */
/* these contents on the screen.  */
                                                     /* BL */
#include <stdio.h>                                   /* L1 */
                                                     /* BL */
main()                                               /* L2 */
{                                                    /* L3 */
 int num;                                            /* L4 */
 FILE *fptr;                                         /* L5 */
 fptr = fopen("test.txt", "r");                      /* L6 */
 num = fgetc(fptr);                                  /* L7 */
                                                     /* BL */
 while(num != EOF) {                                 /* L8 */
  putchar(num);                                      /* L9 */
  num = fgetc(fptr);                                 /* L10 */
 }                                                   /* L11 */
                                                     /* BL */
 fclose(fptr);                                       /* L12 */
 return(0);                                          /* L13 */
}                                                    /* L14 */
```

Compile and execute this program, and the following lines of text appear on the screen:

```
Welcome to C programming.
Thank you.
```

How It Works

Now let's see how this program works. In LOC 4, an int variable called num is declared. In LOC 5, a pointer to the FILE variable fptr is declared. FILE is a derived type. To use this type (i.e., FILE) effectively, you are not required to know its composition or internal details. LOC 5 is reproduced here for your quick reference:

```
FILE *fptr;                                          /* L5 */
```

After reading LOC 5, you should be expecting the following LOCs to follow LOC 5:

```
FILE var;                                                      /*  LOC A */
fptr = &var;                                                   /*  LOC B */
```

In LOC A, a FILE variable named var is declared, and in LOC B, the address of var is assigned to fptr. After all, this is the generic procedure of using the pointers in C. Contrary to your expectations, instead of LOCs A and B, LOC 6 follows LOC 5, which is reproduced here for your quick reference:

```
fptr = fopen("test.txt", "r");                                 /*  L6 */
```

By and large, LOC 6 performs, among other things, everything that LOCs A and B are supposed to perform. In LOC 6, a call is made to the function fopen(), which is used to "open" a file. Before using any file in a program, you are required to open it using the function fopen().

The function fopen() creates an anonymous variable of type FILE, sets a pointer pointing to that variable, and then returns the pointer that is assigned to fptr. The function fopen() also creates a special pointer and sets it pointing to the first character in the file test.txt; this is not the usual pointer in C but just a "marker" that always points to the next character in the file to be read. To avoid confusion, I will call this special pointer a *marker*. When the first character in the file is read, the marker is automatically made to point to the second character in the file. When the second character in the file is read, the marker is automatically made to point to the third character in the file. And so on.

Also note that this "marker" is not an official term in C language. When the marker points to the first character in a file, then according to standard terminology in the C language, you can say that the file is positioned to the first character of the file. When the marker points to the second character in a file, then according to standard terminology in the C language, you say that the file is positioned to the second character of the file. And so on.

■ **Note**   Whenever a file is opened using the function fopen(), the file is positioned to the first character of the file.

Notice that two arguments are passed to the function fopen(), and both these arguments are strings.

The first argument represents the file name: "test.txt".

The second argument represents the mode: "r".

The first argument represents the name of a file to be opened. The second argument represents the mode in which a file will be opened. The mode "r" indicates that this file will be opened for reading only. You just cannot modify the contents of this file. The generic syntax of a statement that uses the function fopen() is given here:

```
fptr = fopen(filename, "mode")
```

Here, fptr is the pointer to the FILE variable, the file name is an expression that evaluates to a string constant that consists of the name of a file (with or without the path) to be opened, and "mode" is a string constant that consists of one of the file-opening modes. The function fopen( ) creates an anonymous variable of type FILE, associates the file being opened with this variable, and then returns a pointer to FILE pointing to this anonymous variable, which, in turn, is assigned to the pointer variable fptr. If file opening fails (i.e., a file cannot be opened), then fopen( ) returns a NULL pointer. Also, once a file is opened, thereafter it is referred to using the pointer variable fptr. If a file name is devoid of a path, then it is assumed that the file rests in the default folder, which is C:\Compiler.

After the execution of LOC 6, the file test.txt opens successfully. Hereafter, you will not use the file name test.txt to refer to this file; instead, you will use the pointer variable fptr to refer to this file. Also, the marker is now set pointing to the first character in the file test.txt. This means the file is positioned to the first character of the file.

In LOC 7, the first character in the file test.txt is read, and its ASCII value is assigned to the int variable num. The contents of the file test.txt are reproduced here for your quick reference:

```
Welcome to C programming.
Thank you.
```

Notice that the first character in the file is 'W' and its ASCII value is 87. LOC 7 is reproduced here for your quick reference:

```
num = fgetc(fptr);                                        /* L7 */
```

LOC 7 consists of a call to the function fgetc( ). This function reads a character from the file represented by fptr and returns its ASCII value, which, in turn, is assigned to the int variable num. As the marker is pointing to the first character in the file (it is 'W'), fgetc( ) reads it and returns its ASCII value (it is 87), which, in turn, is assigned to num. Also, the marker is now advanced so as to point to the second character in the file, i.e., 'e'. All this takes place as LOC 7 executes.

The generic syntax of a statement that uses the function fgetc( ) is given here:

```
intN = fgetc(fptr);
```

Here, intN is an int variable, and fptr is a pointer to the FILE variable. The function fgetc( ) reads the character pointed to by the marker, from the file specified by fptr. After reading the character, fgetc( ) returns its ASCII value, which is assigned to the int variable intN and sets the marker pointing to the next character. If fgetc( ) encounters an end-of-file-character (which is the character ^Z whose ASCII value is 26, pronounced as "Control-Z"), then instead of returning its ASCII value 26, it returns the value of the symbolic constant EOF, which is the int value -1. EOF stands for "end of file." However, apart from the end-of-file situation, this value is also returned by some functions when an error occurs. It is a symbolic constant defined in the file <stdio.h> as follows:

```
#define EOF (-1)                          /* End of file indicator */
```

EOF represents an int value -1. Do not think that the value of EOF is stored at the end of file. Actually, it is not. Character ^Z is stored at the end of file to mark the end of a text file.

You must have noticed that the function fgetc() works like the function getchar() that you use to read a character from the keyboard. However, the function getchar() doesn't expect any argument, whereas the function fgetc() expects a pointer to the FILE variable as an argument.

C also offers the function getc() that is identical to the function fgetc(); the only difference is that the function getc() is implemented as a macro, whereas the function fgetc() is implemented as a function.

LOCs 8 to 11 consist of a while loop. The rest of the file is read in this loop. LOC 8 consists of a continuation condition of a loop, and it is reproduced here for your quick reference:

```
while(num != EOF) {                                           /* L8 */
```

You can read the expression in parentheses (which represents a continuation condition of a loop) because while num is not equal to EOF, looping is permitted. In other words, LOC 8 tells you that looping is permitted as long as the value of num is not equal to -1. However, looping terminates once num becomes equal to -1. For now, the value of num is 87; hence, looping is permitted. Now the first iteration begins. The body of this while loop consists of only LOCs 9 and 10. Notice LOC 9, which is reproduced here for your quick reference:

```
putchar(num);                                                 /* L9 */
```

The function putchar() converts the int value 87 stored in num to the corresponding char constant 'W' and sends this char constant to the screen for display. LOC 10 is same as LOC 7 and is reproduced here for your quick reference:

```
num = fgetc(fptr);                                            /* L10 */
```

I have already discussed how LOC 7 works. Before the execution of LOC 10, the marker was pointing to the second character in the file, i.e., 'e'. After the execution of LOC 10, the ASCII value of 'e' (which is 101) is assigned to num, and the marker is advanced so as to point to the next (third) character in the file.

LOCs 9 and 10 are executed repeatedly as many times as there are characters in a file. This loop performs 37 iterations as there are 26 characters in the first line and 11 characters in the second line, including the newline character at the end of each line. Consider the 37th iteration of the loop. In LOC 9, the character constant newline (ASCII value 10) is sent to the screen for display. This is the last character in the second line and also the last useful (useful from the point of view of the user of the file) character in the file. In LOC 10, the end-of-file character ^Z is read by fgetc(); however, its ASCII value 26 is not returned by fgetc(). Instead, a special value -1 (the value of the symbolic constant EOF) is returned by fgetc(), and it is assigned to num. At the beginning of the 38th iteration, the continuation condition (num != EOF) turns out to be false, and iteration is not permitted. Then the next LOC, which follows the while loop, is executed. This next LOC is LOC 12, which is reproduced here for your quick reference:

```
fclose(fptr);                                                 /* L12 */
```

153

The function `fclose()` is used to close a file. It is advisable that an opened file should be closed when it is no longer needed in a program. Think of the function `fclose()` as a counterpart of the function `fopen()`. The function `fclose()` accepts only one argument; this argument is a pointer to the `FILE` variable and then closes the file specified by that pointer to the `FILE` variable. It returns the value 0 if the operation (of closing the file) is successful and returns the value EOF (i.e., -1) if the operation fails. After the execution of LOC 12, the file specified by `fptr` (which is `test.txt`) is closed. The generic syntax of a statement that uses the function `fclose()` is given here:

```
intN = fclose(pointer_to_FILE_variable);
```

Here, `pointer_to_FILE_variable` is a pointer to the `FILE` variable, and `intN` is an `int` type variable. The value returned by `fclose()`, which is either 0 (if the operation is successful) or -1 (if the operation fails), is stored in `intN`.

The program terminates after the execution of LOC 12.

Finally, notice that even if you don't close a file, it is closed automatically when the program is terminated. However, it is advisable to close a file when it is no longer needed in a program because of these reasons:

- There is an upper limit on the number of files that can remain open at a time.

- When a file is closed, some housekeeping actions are performed by the programming environment that are badly needed.

- Some memory is freed.

6-2. Handle Errors When File Opening Fails
Problem

You want to handle the situation safely when file opening fails.

Solution

Write a C program that safely handles the situation when file opening fails, with the following specifications:

- The program opens the text file `satara.txt` that is placed in the folder `C:\Code`. The program checks whether the file opening is successful with the help of the function `feof()`. If file opening fails, then the program ensures a safe exit and avoids crashing.

- The program reads the file, displays its contents on the screen, and then closes the file. If file closing fails, the program reports it.

In the preceding recipe, I did not take into account the possibility that file opening (and therefore file closing) can fail. If file closing fails, then sometimes you can ignore it, because when a program is terminated, all open files are closed automatically. But if file opening fails, then the program will certainly not work as per your expectations. Therefore, it is absolutely necessary in a program to check whether file opening is successful. Also, it is advisable to check whether file closing is successful.

Create a small text file, named `satara.txt`, with the following contents:

```
Satara is surrounded by mountains.
Satara was capital of Maratha empire for many years.
```

Place this text file in the folder `C:\Code`.

The Code

The following is the code of the C program written with these specifications. Type the following C program in a text editor and save it in the folder `C:\Code` with the file name `files2.c`:

```
/* This program reads the contents of a text file and displays these
contents on the screen. */
/* File-opening and file-closing is checked for success. File is placed in the */
/* desired folder. Function feof() is used to detect the end of file. */
                                                              /* BL */
#include <stdio.h>                                            /* L1 */
                                                              /* BL */
main()                                                        /* L2 */
{                                                             /* L3 */
 int num, k = 0;                                              /* L4 */
 FILE *fptr;                                                  /* L5 */
 fptr = fopen("C:\\Code\\satara.txt", "r");                  /* L6 */
 if (fptr != NULL) {                                          /* L7 */
  puts("File satara.txt is opened successfully");            /* L8 */
  puts("Contents of file satara.txt:");                      /* L9 */
  num = fgetc(fptr);                                          /* L10 */
                                                              /* BL  */
  while(!feof(fptr)) {                                        /* L11 */
    putchar(num);                                             /* L12 */
    num = fgetc(fptr);                                        /* L13 */
  }                                                           /* l14 */
                                                              /* BL  */
  k = fclose(fptr);                                           /* L15 */
  if(k == -1)                                                 /* L16 */
    puts("File-closing failed");                             /* L17 */
  else                                                        /* L18 */
    puts("File satara.txt is closed successfully");          /* L19 */
 }                                                            /* L20 */
 else                                                         /* L21 */
  puts("File-opening failed");                               /* L22 */
 return(0);                                                   /* L23 */
}                                                             /* L24 */
```

Compile and execute this program, and the following lines of text appear on the screen:

```
File satara.txt is opened successfully
Contents of file satara.txt:
Satara is surrounded by mountains.
Satara was capital of Maratha empire for many years.
File satara.txt is closed successfully
```

How It Works

EOF is a value (-1) that is returned when the end of file occurs. EOF stands for "end of file." In addition to an end-of-file situation, this value is also returned by some functions when an error occurs. To differentiate between these two causes of a returned EOF, two functions are available in C: feof( ) and ferror( ). The generic syntax of a statement that uses the function feof( ) is given here:

```
intN = feof(fptr);
```

Here, intN is an int variable, and fptr is a pointer to the FILE variable. This function returns a nonzero (true) value when the end of file has occurred on the file specified by fptr; otherwise, it returns a zero (false) value.

Also, the generic syntax of a statement that uses the function ferror( ) is given here:

```
intN = ferror(fptr);
```

Here, intN is an int variable, and fptr is a pointer to FILE variable. This function returns a nonzero (true) value if an error has occurred on the file specified by fptr; otherwise, it returns a zero (false) value.

Notice LOC 6, which is reproduced here for your quick reference:

```
fptr = fopen("C:\\Code\\satara.txt", "r");                      /* L6 */
```

The name of file to be opened, with the path, is given here:

```
C:\Code\satara.txt
```

In LOC 6, instead of a single backslash, a double backslash is used in the string file name because it (the double backslash) is an escape sequence.

Notice LOC 7, which is reproduced here for your quick reference:

```
if (fptr != NULL) {                                             /* L7 */
```

In this LOC, the value of fptr is checked. Only if the file opening is successful is the code block spanning LOCs 8 to 19 executed; otherwise, LOC 22 is executed, which displays the following message on the screen:

```
File-opening failed
```

In LOC 15, the value returned by fclose() is assigned to an int variable named k. If the file closing fails, then the value of -1 is assigned to the int variable k, and in that case the following message appears on the screen:

```
File-closing failed
```

However, failure messages did not appear in the output of this program because both operations (file opening and file closing) were successful.

Notice LOC 11, which is reproduced here for your quick reference:

```
while(!feof(fptr)) {                                           /* L11 */
```

The function feof() returns a nonzero (true) value when the end of file occurs; otherwise, it returns a zero (false) value. Notice the logical negation operator ! prefixed to feof(). As a result, iterations are discontinued after the occurrence of the end of file. You can read LOC 11 as follows: while not the end of file, iterations are permitted.

6-3. Write to a Text File in Batch Mode
Problem
You want to write to a text file in a batch mode.

Solution
Write a C program that writes to a text file in batch mode, with the following specifications:

- The program writes to a file using the function fputs().

- The program creates a text file, namely, kolkata.txt, in a folder called C:\Code and writes the following couple of lines to it:

      Kolkata is very big city.
      It is also very nice city.

The Code
The following is the code of the C program written with these specifications. Type the following C program in a text editor and save it in the folder C:\Code with the file name files3.c:

```
/* This program creates a text file kolkata.txt using the function fputs(). */
                                                               /* BL */
#include <stdio.h>                                             /* L1 */
                                                               /* BL */
main()                                                         /* L2 */
```

157

```
{                                                           /* L3 */
 int k = 0;                                                 /* L4 */
 FILE *fptr;                                                /* L5 */
 fptr = fopen("C:\\Code\\kolkata.txt", "w");                /* L6 */
 if (fptr != NULL) {                                        /* L7 */
  puts("File kolkata.txt is opened successfully.");         /* L8 */
  fputs("Kolkata is very big city.\n", fptr);               /* L9 */
  fputs("It is also very nice city.\n", fptr);              /* L10 */
  k = fclose(fptr);                                         /* L11 */
  if(k == -1)                                               /* L12 */
    puts("File-closing failed");                            /* L13 */
  if(k == 0)                                                /* L14 */
    puts("File is closed successfully.");                   /* L15 */
 }                                                          /* L16 */
 else                                                       /* L17 */
  puts("File-opening failed");                              /* L18 */
 return(0);                                                 /* L19 */
}                                                           /* L20 */
```

Compile and execute this program, and the following lines of text appear on the screen:

```
File kolkata.txt is opened successfully.
File is closed successfully.
```

Open the file kolkata.txt, just created, in a suitable text editor and verify that its contents are as expected.

How It Works

Notice LOC 6, which is reproduced here for your quick reference:

```
fptr = fopen("C:\\Code\\kolkata.txt", "w");                 /* L6 */
```

Here, the file name is "C:\\Code\\kolkata.txt", and the mode is "w". As you are going to write to a file, file-opening mode must be "w". This means a file named kolkata.txt will be opened for writing in the specified folder C:\Code. Notice LOCs 9 and 10, which are reproduced here for your quick reference:

```
fputs("Kolkata is very big city.\n", fptr);                 /* L9 */
fputs("It is also very nice city.\n", fptr);                /* L10 */
```

For the sake of clarity, I have used two statements; otherwise, a single statement is sufficient. Either LOC consists of a call to the function fputs(), which is used for writing a string to a file. How this function works closely resembles the function puts(), which is used to display a string on the screen. However, there are three main differences between how these functions work, as follows:

- The function puts() writes (displays) an argument string on the screen. The function fputs() writes an argument string to a file.

- The function puts() expects only one argument, and it is string. The function fputs() expects two arguments: a string and a pointer to the FILE variable.

- The function puts() replaces the string-terminating character '\0' in the string with the newline character '\n' before displaying that string on the screen. The function fputs() simply throws away the string-terminating character '\0' and writes the remaining string to the file.

Notice the generic syntax of a statement that uses the function fputs() given here:

```
intN = fputs(string, fptr);
```

Here, intN is an int variable, the string is an expression that evaluates to a string constant, and fptr is a pointer to the FILE variable; the string constant is written to a file specified by fptr. If the operation succeeds, then a nonnegative value is returned by this function; otherwise, EOF is returned. In LOCs 9 and 10, I have preferred to ignore the value returned by this function. However, in a professional program, you should catch the returned value and see whether the operation is successful. Write errors are common while writing to disk.

In LOC 9, the string "Kolkata is very big city.\n" is written to a file specified by fptr (i.e., kolkata.txt).

■ **Note**   When you read a file, the marker is advanced accordingly so that it always points to the next character to be read. Similarly, when you write to a file, the marker is advanced accordingly so that it always points to the location in the file where the next character will be written.

Before the execution of LOC 9, the file positions to the first character of the file. The string "Kolkata is very big city.\n" consists of 26 characters. After the execution of LOC 9, the file positions to the 27th character of the file.

In LOC 10, the string "It is also very nice city.\n" is written to the file. This string consists of 27 characters. Therefore, after the execution of LOC 10, the file positions to the 54th character of the file.

Finally, notice that when a string is written to a file using the function fputs(), then the character '\0', which is a string-terminating character, is not written to the file, nor it is replaced by '\n' as in the case of puts().

6-4. Write to a Text File in Interactive Mode

Problem

You want to write to a text file in interactive mode.

Solution

Write a C program that writes to a text file in interactive mode, with the following specifications:

- The program writes to a file using the function fputs().

- The program creates the text files in an interactive manner. It accepts the name and text of the file in an interactive manner.

The Code

The following is the code of the C program written with these specifications. Type the following C program in a text editor and save it in the folder C:\Code with the file name files4.c:

```
/* This program creates a text file in an interactive session
using the function fputs(). */
                                                             /* BL */

#include <stdio.h>                                           /* L1 */
#include <string.h>                                          /* L2 */
                                                             /* BL */
main()                                                       /* L3 */
{                                                            /* L4 */
 int k = 0, n = 0;                                           /* L5 */
 char filename[40], temp[15], store[80];                     /* L6 */
 FILE *fptr;                                                 /* L7 */
 printf("Enter filename (AAAAAAA.AAA) extension optional: "); /* L8 */
 scanf("%s", temp);                                          /* L9 */
 strcpy(filename, "C:\\Code\\");                             /* L10 */
 strcat(filename, temp);                                     /* L11 */
 fptr = fopen(filename, "w");                                /* L12 */
 if (fptr != NULL) {                                         /* L13 */
  printf("File %s is opened successfully.\n", filename);     /* L14 */
  puts("Enter the lines of text to store in the file.");     /* L15 */
  puts("Strike Enter key twice to end the line-entry-session."); /* L16 */
  fflush(stdin);                                             /* L17 */
  gets(store);                                               /* L18 */
  n = strlen(store);                                         /* L19 */
                                                             /* BL */
  while(n != 0){                                             /* L20 */
   fputs(store, fptr);                                       /* L21 */
   fputs("\n", fptr);                                        /* L22 */
```

```
    gets(store);                                    /* L23 */
    n = strlen(store);                              /* L24 */
  }                                                 /* L25 */
                                                    /* BL  */
  k = fclose(fptr);                                 /* L26 */
  if(k == -1)                                       /* L27 */
    puts("File-closing failed");                    /* L28 */
  if(k == 0)                                        /* L29 */
    puts("File is closed successfully.");           /* L30 */
}                                                   /* L31 */
else                                                /* L32 */
 puts("File-opening failed");                       /* L33 */
 return(0);                                         /* L34 */
}                                                   /* L35 */
```

Compile and execute this program. A couple of runs of this program are given here. Here is the first run:

```
Enter filename (AAAAAAA.AAA) extension optional: Mumbai.txt    ↵
File C:\Code\Mumbai.txt is opened successfully.
Enter the lines of text to store in the file.
Strike Enter key twice to end the line-entry-session.
Mumbai is capital of Maharashtra.    ↵
Mumbai is financial capital of India.    ↵
↵
File is closed successfully.
```

Here is the second run:

```
Enter filename (AAAAAAA.AAA) extension optional: wai    ↵
File C:\Code\wai is opened successfully.
Enter the lines of text to store in the file.
Strike Enter key twice to end the line-entry-session.
Wai is a small town in Satara district.    ↵
There are good number of temples in Wai.    ↵
↵
File is closed successfully.
```

How It Works

Now let's discuss how this program works with reference to the second run. In LOC 6, three char arrays are declared, namely, filename, temp, and store. The file name you entered ("wai") is stored in the array temp, to which the path is added, and then the file name with the path "C:\\Code\\wai" is stored in the array file name. Notice LOC 11, which is reproduced here for your quick reference:

```
strcat(filename, temp);                             /* L11 */
```

In LOC 11, the function strcat() is called. This function is used for concatenating the strings. Before the execution of LOC 11, filename and temp contains the following strings:

- File name: "C:\\Code\\"

- Temp: "wai"

After the execution of LOC 11, filename and temp contains the following strings:

File name: "C:\\Code\\wai"
Temp: "wai"

Notice that the string stored in temp is appended to the string stored in the file name. The generic syntax of a statement that uses the function strcat() is given here:

```
storage = strcat(destination, source);
```

Here, storage is a pointer-to-char variable, the destination is a char array (or pointer-to-char variable), and the source is an expression that evaluates to a string constant. The string constant in source is appended to the string constant in the destination, and a copy of the resulting string constant is stored in the destination and returned. The returned value is generally ignored, and I have chosen to ignore it in LOC 11.

Next, notice LOC 17, which is reproduced here for your quick reference:

```
fflush(stdin);                                              /* L17 */
```

The function fflush() is used to flush out the stray characters loitering in the passage between the keyboard and the central processing unit (technically speaking, in the input buffer). You enter the file name wai and then press the Enter key. The file name entered is read and assigned to temp by the programming environment, but the Enter key stroke (i.e., newline character) remains in the passage (between the keyboard and the CPU), and it needs to be flushed out. This flushing is performed by the function fflush() in LOC 17.

Next, notice LOCs 18 and 19, which are reproduced here for your quick reference:

```
gets(store);                                               /* L18 */
n = strlen(store);                                         /* L19 */
```

The function gets() in LOC 18 reads the first string typed, which is "Wai is a small town in Satara district.", and places it in the char array store. In LOC 19, the function strlen() computes and returns the length of this string (which is 39), which is assigned to the int variable n.

Next, the while loop begins. Notice LOC 20, the first LOC of the while loop, which is reproduced here for your quick reference:

```
while(n != 0) {                                            /* L20 */
```

Notice the continuation condition of the while loop. Looping is permitted only if n is not equal to zero. Now the value of n is 39; hence, iteration is permitted. The first iteration begins. Notice LOCs 21 and 22, which are reproduced here for your quick reference:

```
fputs(store, fptr);                                        /* L21 */
fputs("\n", fptr);                                         /* L22 */
```

Both LOCs call the function fputs() that, in turn, writes an argument string to the file specified by the pointer to the FILE variable fptr. LOC 21 writes the string stored in the store to the file specified by fptr. LOC 22 writes the string "\n" to the file specified by fptr. In LOC 22, you are appending the newline character to the string manually. If you don't do this, then retrieving the strings (from a file) using the function fgets() becomes difficult as the function fgets() assumes that strings stored in a file are terminated with newline characters.

Next, LOCs 23 and 24 are executed, which are the same as LOCs 18 and 19. In LOC 23, the second string typed, which is "There are good number of temples in Wai.", is read by the function gets() and is stored in the store. In LOC 24, its length is computed, which is 40, and is returned by the function strlen(), which in turn is assigned to the int variable n.

As execution of the first iteration is complete, computer control goes to LOC 20, the first LOC of the while loop. As the value of n is 40 and not zero, the second iteration is permitted. In LOC 21, the string stored in store, which is "There are good number of temples in Wai.", is written to the file specified by fptr. In LOC 22, the newline character is written to the file specified by fptr.

Next, LOCs 23 and 24 are executed. In LOC 23, the third string typed, which is the null string because you pressed the Enter key at the beginning of the line, is read by the function fgets(). In LOC 24, the length of the null string, which is the zero, is returned by the function strlen(), which in turn is assigned to the int variable n.

As execution of the second iteration is complete, computer control goes to LOC 20, the first LOC of the while loop. As the value of n is zero, the third iteration is not permitted. Computer control then goes to LOC 26, in which the file specified by fptr is closed.

6-5. Read a Text File String by String
Problem

You want to read a text file string by string.

Solution

Write a C program that reads a text file string by string, with the following specifications:

- The program reads the text file kolkata.txt using the function fgets() and then displays the text in the file on the screen using the function printf().

- The program checks for successful file opening and file closing.

The Code

The following is the code of the C program written with these specifications. Type the following C program in a text editor and save it in the folder C:\Code with the file name files5.c:

```
/* This program reads the file kolkata.txt using the function fgets(). */
                                                          /* BL */
#include <stdio.h>                                        /* L1 */
                                                          /* BL */
```

```
main()                                                    /* L2 */
{                                                         /* L3 */
 int k = 0;                                               /* L4 */
 char *cptr;                                              /* L5 */
 char store[80];                                          /* L6 */
 FILE *fptr;                                              /* L7 */
 fptr = fopen("C:\\Code\\kolkata.txt", "r");             /* L8 */
 if (fptr != NULL) {                                      /* L9 */
  puts("File kolkata.txt is opened successfully.");      /* L10 */
  puts("Contents of this file:");                        /* L11 */
  cptr = fgets(store, 80, fptr);                          /* L12 */
                                                          /* BL */
  while (cptr != NULL) {                                  /* L13 */
   printf("%s", store);                                   /* L14 */
   cptr = fgets(store, 80, fptr);                         /* L15 */
  }                                                       /* L16 */
                                                          /* BL */
  k = fclose(fptr);                                       /* L17 */
  if(k == -1)                                             /* L18 */
     puts("File-closing failed");                         /* L19 */
  if(k == 0)                                              /* L20 */
     puts("\nFile is closed successfully.");              /* L21 */
 }                                                        /* L22 */
 else                                                     /* L23 */
  puts("File-opening failed");                            /* L24 */
 return(0);                                               /* L25 */
}                                                         /* L26 */
```

Compile and execute this program, and the following lines of text appear on the screen:

```
File kolkata.txt is opened successfully.
Contents of this file:
Kolkata is very big city.
It is also very nice city.
File is closed successfully.
```

How It Works

Think of the function fgets() as the counterpart of the function fputs(). The function fgets() is used for reading the strings from a file. The generic syntax of a statement that uses the function fgets() is given here:

```
cptr = fgets(storage, n, fptr);
```

Here, cptr is a pointer-to-char variable, storage is a char type array, n is an expression that evaluates to an integer constant, and fptr is a pointer to the FILE variable. The function fgets() reads a string from the file specified by fptr and stores that string in the array storage. At most (n - 1) characters are read by fgets(), and the string stored in storage is always terminated with '\0'. Then the function fgets() returns a pointer to char pointing to the first character in array storage when the string-reading operation is successful; otherwise, it returns NULL. Also, notice that the function fgets() reads a string starting at the current location (pointed to by the marker), up to and including the first newline character it encounters, unless it reaches an EOF or has read (n - 1) characters before that point. It then appends the '\0' character (string-terminating character) to that string before storing it in storage.

In LOC 5, a pointer-to-char variable called cptr is declared. In LOC 6, the char array store is declared. In LOC 8, the file kolkata.txt is opened for reading, and it is associated with a pointer to the FILE variable fptr. Notice LOC 12, which is reproduced here for your quick reference:

```
cptr = fgets(store, 80, fptr);                                    /* L12 */
```

In LOC 12, the following tasks are performed:

- The first string stored in the file specified by fptr is read, and it is placed in the char array called store. Notice that this string is "Kolkata is very big city."

- The marker is advanced so as to point to the next string available in the file specified by fptr.

- The function fgets() returns a pointer to char pointing to the first character in the char array store, which is assigned to cptr. You need this value only to detect the end of file. When the end of file occurs, fgets() returns NULL.

The second argument to fgets() in LOC 12 is the integer value 80. It indicates that fgets() will read at most 79 characters when called (80 - 1). This means if a string stored in a file consists of more than 79 characters, then the remaining characters will not be read. In the next call to fgets(), it will start reading the next string.

Next, there is a while loop in LOCs 13 to 16, which is reproduced here for your quick reference:

```
while (cptr != NULL) {                                            /* L13 */
  printf("%s", store);                                            /* L14 */
  cptr = fgets(store, 80, fptr);                                  /* L15 */
}                                                                 /* L16 */
```

In LOC 13, the value stored in cptr is tested for its equivalence with NULL in order to detect the occurrence of the end of file. In LOC 14, the string stored in the char array store (which is "Kolkata is very big city.") is displayed on the screen. Notice that this is the first iteration of the while loop. In LOC 15 (which is the same as LOC 12), the next string in the file (which is "It is also very nice city.") is read and stored in the char array store. Also, the pointer to the first character of store is returned, which is assigned to cptr. As execution of first iteration is complete, computer control goes to LOC 13 again.

Next, LOC 13 is executed. No NULL value is still assigned to cptr; hence, the second iteration is permitted. Next, LOC 14 is executed in which the string stored in store (which is "It is also very nice city.") is displayed on the screen. Next, LOC 15 is executed in which fgets() tries to read the next string (third string) in the file. But as this file (kolkata.txt) consists of only two strings, this reading operation fails, and fgets() returns a NULL value, which is assigned to cptr. As the execution of the second iteration is complete, computer control goes to LOC 13 again.

Next, LOC 13 is executed. As a NULL value is assigned to cptr, the third iteration is not permitted, and execution of the loop terminates. Next, computer control passes to LOC 17 in which the file specified by fptr is closed.

6-6. Write to a Text File Character by Character
Problem
You want to write to a text file character by character.

Solution
Write a C program that writes to a text file character by character, with the following specifications:

- The program opens the text file jaipur.txt in write mode.

- The program writes to this file in interactive mode using the function fputc().

The Code
The following is the code of the C program written with these specifications. Type the following C program in a text editor and save it in the folder C:\Code with the file name files6.c:

```
/* This program creates a text file in an interactive session using the
function fputc(). */
                                                        /* BL */
#include <stdio.h>                                      /* L1 */
                                                        /* BL */
main()                                                  /* L2 */
{                                                       /* L3 */
  int k = 0, n = 0;                                     /* L4 */
  FILE *fptr;                                           /* L5 */
  fptr = fopen("C:\\Code\\jaipur.txt", "w");            /* L6 */
  if (fptr != NULL) {                                   /* L7 */
    puts("File jaipur.txt is opened successfully.");    /* L8 */
    puts("Enter text to be written to file. Enter * to"); /* L9 */
    puts("terminate the text-entry-session.");          /* L10 */
    n = getchar();                                      /* L11 */
                                                        /* BL */
```

```
  while(n != '*'){                                        /* L12 */
   fputc(n, fptr);                                        /* L13 */
   n = getchar();                                         /* L14 */
  }                                                       /* L15 */
                                                          /* BL  */
  k = fclose(fptr);                                       /* L16 */
  if(k == -1)                                             /* L17 */
    puts("File-closing failed");                          /* L18 */
  if(k == 0)                                              /* L19 */
    puts("File is closed successfully.");                 /* L20 */
 }                                                        /* L21 */
 else                                                     /* L22 */
  puts("File-opening failed");                            /* L23 */
 return(0);                                               /* L24 */
}                                                         /* L25 */
```

Compile and execute this program. A run of this program is given here:

```
File jaipur.txt is opened successfully.
Enter text to be written to file. Enter * to
terminate the text-entry-session.
Jaipur is capital of Rajsthan.   ⏎
Jaipur is famous for historical Hawamahal.   ⏎
*  ⏎
File is closed successfully.
```

How It Works

You have typed two lines of text to be written to the file jaipur.txt. When you type a character, it is not processed by the CPU. Characters typed stand in a queue. It is only when you press the Enter key that these characters (standing in a queue) are processed by the CPU, one by one. First, type the following line of text and press Enter:

```
Jaipur is capital of Rajsthan.
```

Notice LOC 11, which is reproduced here for your quick reference:

```
n = getchar();                                           /* L11 */
```

The function getchar() reads the first character in the line of text, which is 'J', and returns its ASCII value (it is 74), which is assigned to the int variable n.

Next, the execution of the while loop begins, which spans LOCs 12 to 15. LOC 12 is reproduced here for your quick reference:

```
while(n != '*') {                                        /* L12 */
```

Notice the continuation condition of the `while` loop in LOC 12. This loop iterates as long as n is not equal to character '*'. (Or more correctly, it iterates as long as n is not equal to 64, the ASCII value of '*'. As n is equal to 74 and not equal to 64, iteration is permitted.) Now the first iteration begins.

Next, LOC 13 is executed, which is reproduced here for your quick reference:

```
fputc(n, fptr);                                                          /* L13 */
```

The function `fputc()` writes the character, whose ASCII value is stored in the `int` variable n, in the file specified by `fptr`. As the ASCII value of 'J' is stored in n, the character 'J' is written to the file specified by `fptr` (i.e., to the file `jaipur.txt`).

The generic syntax of a statement that uses the function `fputc()` is given here:

```
intN = fputc (n, fptr);
```

Here, `intN` is an `int` variable, n is an expression that evaluates to an integer value, and `fptr` is a pointer to the `FILE` variable. The function `fputc()` writes the character, whose ASCII value is n, to the file specified by `fptr`. The function `fputc()` returns the value of `EOF` if the operation fails and returns the value of n if operation is successful.

C also offers the function `putc()`, which is identical to the function `fputc()`; the only difference is that the function `putc()` is implemented as a macro, whereas the function `fputc()` is implemented as a function.

Next, LOC 14 is executed, which is same as LOC 11. In LOC 14, the next character in the line of text is read, which is 'a', and its ASCII value (97) is assigned to variable n. As execution of the first iteration is complete, computer control goes to LOC 12 again. As the value of n is not equal to 64 (ASCII value of *), the second iteration is permitted, and so on. In this manner, the characters in the line of text are written to the file. When the character is *, then the continuation condition in LOC 12 fails, and further iterations are not permitted.

In this program, you use the character * as a terminating character. What if * is part of the text? Ideally, the terminating character should not be a printable character. You can use ^Z (Control-Z) as a terminating character, which can be passed to the program simply by pressing the function key F6.

6-7. Write Integers to a Text File
Problem
You want to write the integers to a text file.

Solution
Write a C program that writes the integers to the text file `numbers.dat`, with the following specifications:

- The program uses the function `fprintf()` to write to the file.
- The program writes integer values to the file.

The Code

The following is the code of the C program written with these specifications. Type the following C program in a text editor and save it in the folder C:\Code with the file name files7.c:

```
/* This program writes data to a file using the function fprintf() */
                                                               /* BL */
#include <stdio.h>                                             /* L1 */
                                                               /* BL */
main()                                                         /* L2 */
{                                                              /* L3 */
 int i, k = 0;                                                 /* L4 */
 FILE *fptr;                                                   /* L5 */
 fptr = fopen("C:\\Code\\numbers.dat", "w");                   /* L6 */
 if (fptr != NULL) {                                           /* L7 */
  puts("File numbers.dat is opened successfully.");            /* L8 */
                                                               /* BL */
  for(i = 0; i < 10; i++)                                      /* L9 */
    fprintf(fptr, "%d ", i+1);                                 /* L10 */
                                                               /* BL */
  puts("Data written to file numbers.dat successfully.");      /* L11 */
                                                               /* BL */
  k = fclose(fptr);                                            /* L12 */
  if(k == -1)                                                  /* L13 */
    puts("File-closing failed");                               /* L14 */
  if(k == 0)                                                   /* L15 */
    puts("File is closed successfully.");                      /* L16 */
 }                                                             /* L17 */
 else                                                          /* L18 */
  puts("File-opening failed");                                 /* L19 */
 return(0);                                                    /* L20 */
}                                                              /* L21 */
```

Compile and execute this program, and the following lines of text appear on the screen:

```
File numbers.dat is opened successfully.
Data written to file numbers.dat successfully.
File is closed successfully.
```

Open the file numbers.dat in a suitable text editor and verify that its contents are as follows:

```
1  2  3  4  5  6  7  8  9  10
```

How It Works

In the preceding recipes you used the functions `fputc()` and `fputs()` to write the characters and strings to a file, respectively. But if you want to write the data of other data types (e.g., `int`, `float`, etc.) to a file, then you need to use the function `fprintf()`.

■ **Note** Using the function `fprintf()`, you can write the data items of different data types to a file in a single statement. Also, `fprintf()` can be used to write the formatted data to a file. `fprintf()` writes the data to a file in text format.

LOCs 9 and 10 consist of a `for` loop, and in this loop data is written to the file `numbers.dat`. These LOCs are reproduced here for your quick reference:

```
for(i = 0; i < 10; i++)                                    /* L9 */
  fprintf(fptr, "%d ", i+1);                               /* L10 */
```

This `for` loop iterates ten times and writes ten numbers to the file, one number per iteration. The numbers are actually written to the file in LOC 10, in which a call is made to the function `fprintf()`. You should also note that the `fprintf()` function always writes the data to a file in character format (or text format).

The function `fprintf()` works like the function `printf()`. There are two main differences, however, as follows:

- The function `printf()` sends the data to the screen for display, whereas the function `fprintf()` sends the data to the file for writing it in that file.

- Like the function `printf()`, the function `fprintf()` also expects the control string and a comma-separated list of arguments. However, the function `fprintf()` expects one more argument compared to the function `printf()`. This extra argument is a pointer to the `FILE` variable (i.e., `fptr`), and this must be a first argument.

Before proceeding, notice the generic syntax of a statement that uses the function `fprintf()` given here:

```
intN = fprintf(fptr, "control string", arg1, arg2, ..., argN);
```

Here, `intN` is an `int` variable, `fptr` is a pointer to the `FILE` variable, `"control string"` is a control string that appears in the `printf()` function, and `arg1`, `arg2`, ..., `argN` is a comma-separated list that appears in the `printf()` function. The values of arguments are inserted in the control string (to replace the corresponding conversion specifications), and the resulting string is written to the file specified by `fptr`. The function `fprintf()` returns an `int` value that indicates the number of characters written to the file if operation is successful; otherwise, it returns `EOF`. For example, except for the tenth iteration of the `for` loop, the `fprintf()` function in LOC 10 returns 2 (one digit + one space), and in the tenth iteration it returns 3 (two digits + one space).

6-8. Write Structures to a Text File

Problem

You want to write the structures to a text file.

Solution

Write a C program that writes the structures to the text file agents.dat, with the following specifications:

- The program opens the file agents.dat in write mode.

- The program accepts the data for structures (shown in Figure 6-1) in interactive mode.

Table Showing the Biodata of Five Secret Agents				
	Name	Roll Number	Age in years	Weight in kg
First record	Dick	1	21	70.6
Second record	Robert	2	22	75.8
Third record	Steve	3	20	53.7
Fourth record	Richard	4	19	83.1
Fifth record	Albert	5	18	62.3

Note: Individual row in this table is termed as record. This table consists of five records.

Figure 6-1. *Table showing the biodata of five secret agents*

- The program uses the function fprintf() to write the structures to the file.

The Code

The following is the code of the C program written with these specifications. Type the following C program in a text editor and save it in the folder C:\Code with the file name files8.c:

```
/* This program writes a structure to a file using the function fprintf() */
                                                                  /* BL */
#include <stdio.h>                                                /* L1 */
                                                                  /* BL */
main()                                                            /* L2 */
{                                                                 /* L3 */
```

171

```
int k = 0;                                                          /* L4 */
char flag = 'y';                                                    /* L5 */
FILE *fptr;                                                         /* L6 */
struct biodata{                                                     /* L7 */
 char name[15];                                                     /* L8 */
 int rollno;                                                        /* L9 */
 int age;                                                           /* L10 */
 float weight;                                                      /* L11 */
};                                                                  /* L12 */
struct biodata sa;                                                  /* L13 */
fptr = fopen("C:\\Code\\agents.dat", "w");                          /* L14 */
if (fptr != NULL) {                                                 /* L15 */
 printf("File agents.dat is opened successfully.\n");              /* L16 */
                                                                    /* BL */
 while(flag == 'y'){                                                /* L17 */
  printf("Enter name, roll no, age, and weight of agent: ");       /* L18 */
  scanf("%s %d %d %f", sa.name,                                     /* L19 */
                          &sa.rollno,                               /* L20 */
                          &sa.age,                                  /* L21 */
                          &sa.weight);                              /* L22 */
  fprintf(fptr, "%s %d %d %.1f", sa.name,                           /* L23 */
                                   sa.rollno,                       /* L24 */
                                   sa.age,                          /* L25 */
                                   sa.weight);                      /* L26 */
  fflush(stdin);                                                    /* L27 */
  printf("Any more records(y/n): ");                                /* L28 */
  scanf(" %c", &flag);                                              /* L29 */
 }                                                                  /* L30 */
                                                                    /* Bl */
 k = fclose(fptr);                                                  /* L31 */
 if(k == -1)                                                        /* L32 */
   puts("File-closing failed");                                     /* L33 */
 if(k == 0)                                                         /* L34 */
   puts("File is closed successfully.");                            /* L35 */
}                                                                   /* L36 */
else                                                                /* L37 */
 puts("File-opening failed");                                       /* L38 */
return(0);                                                          /* L39 */
}                                                                   /* L40 */
```

Compile and execute this program. A run of this program is given here:

```
File agents.dat is opened successfully.
Enter name, roll no, age, and weight of agent: Dick  1  21  70.6    ↵
Any more records (y/n): y    ↵
Enter name, roll no, age, and weight of agent: Robert  2  22  75.8    ↵
Any more records (y/n): y    ↵
```

```
Enter name, roll no, age, and weight of agent: Steve  3  20  53.7      ↵
Any more records (y/n): y    ↵
Enter name, roll no, age, and weight of agent: Richard  4  19  83.1      ↵
Any more records (y/n): y    ↵
Enter name, roll no, age, and weight of agent: Albert  5  18  62.3      ↵
Any more records (y/n): n    ↵
File is closed successfully.
```

Open the file agents.dat in a suitable text editor and verify that its contents are as shown here:

```
Dick 1 21 70.6Robert 2 22 75.8Steve 3 20 53.7Richard 4 19 83.1Albert 5 18 62.3
```

How It Works

In this recipe, you use the function fprintf() to write the biodata of five secret agents shown in Figure 6-1 to a file. LOCs 7 to 12 consist of the declaration of the structure biodata. In LOC 13, the variable sa of type struct biodata is declared. The data of a secret member typed in through the keyboard is saved in this variable before writing it to the file. LOCs 17 to 30 consist of a while loop in which the main activity (i.e., accepting the data typed through keyboard and writing it to the file) takes place. Notice the continuation condition of the loop in LOC 17, which is reproduced here for your quick reference:

```
while(flag == 'y'){                                        /* L17 */
```

Iterations are permitted while the value of the char variable flag is 'y'. As the value of the char variable flag is already 'y' (see LOC 5), the first iteration of the loop begins. LOCs 19 to 22 consist of a scanf statement. It is a single statement, but as the statement is long, it is split into four LOCs for better readability. The data of Dick typed (i.e., Dick 1 21 70.6) is read by this scanf statement and assigned to the variable sa.

LOCs 23 to 26 consist of the fprintf statement. Like the preceding statement, this is also a single statement but split into four LOCs for better readability. In this statement, the data stored in the variable sa is written to the file specified by fptr. In LOC 27, the function fflush() is called to flush out the newline character loitering in the passage between the keyboard and the CPU. In addition, a single space is prefixed to the conversion specification %c in LOC 29 to deal with this unwanted newline character. In fact, one of the provisions is enough to deal with this unwanted newline character:

- Provision of LOC 27

- Single space prefixed to %c in LOC 29

In LOC 29, the character typed (either 'y' or 'n') as a reply to the question "Any more records (y/n)" is read and assigned to the char variable flag. If your reply is 'y', then further iterations of the while loop are permitted; otherwise, iterations are discontinued.

6-9. Read Integers Stored in a Text File

Problem

You want to read the integers stored in a text file.

Solution

Write a C program that reads the integers stored in a text file, with the following specifications:

- The program opens the file numbers.dat in reading mode. In this file, the integer values are already stored.

- The program reads the file numbers.dat using the function fscanf() and displays its contents on the screen.

The Code

The following is the code of the C program written with these specifications. Type the following C program in a text editor and save it in the folder C:\Code with the file name files9.c:

```
/* This program reads a file using the function fscanf() */
                                                              /* BL */
#include <stdio.h>                                            /* L1 */
                                                              /* BL */
main()                                                        /* L2 */
{                                                             /* L3 */
  int m = 0, n, k = 0;                                        /* L4 */
  FILE *fptr;                                                 /* L5 */
  fptr = fopen("C:\\Code\\numbers.dat", "r");                 /* L6 */
  if (fptr != NULL) {                                         /* L7 */
   puts("File numbers.dat is opened successfully.");          /* L8 */
   puts("Contents of file numbers.dat:");                     /* L9 */
   m = fscanf(fptr, "%d", &n);                                /* L10 */
                                                              /* BL */
   while(m != EOF){                                           /* L11 */
    printf("%d ", n);                                         /* L12 */
    m = fscanf(fptr, "%d", &n);                               /* L13 */
   }                                                          /* L14 */
                                                              /* BL */
   printf("\n");                                              /* L15 */
   k = fclose(fptr);                                          /* L16 */
   if(k == -1)                                                /* L17 */
     puts("File-closing failed");                             /* L18 */
   if(k == 0)                                                 /* L19 */
```

```
    puts("File is closed successfully.");                    /* L20 */
}                                                            /* L21 */
else                                                         /* L22 */
 puts("File-opening failed");                                /* L23 */
 return(0);                                                  /* L24 */
}                                                            /* L25 */
```

Compile and execute this program, and the following lines of text appear on the screen:

```
File numbers.dat is opened successfully.
Contents of file numbers.dat:
1 2 3 4 5 6 7 8 9 10
File is closed successfully.
```

How It Works

Think of the function fscanf() as the counterpart of the function fprintf(). How the function fscanf() works is analogous to that of the function scanf(). There are two main differences in how these functions work, however, as follows:

- The function scanf() reads the data coming from the keyboard, whereas the function fscanf() reads the data stored in a file.

- Like the function scanf(), the function fscanf() also expects the control string and a comma-separated list of arguments. However, the function fscanf() expects one more argument compared to the function scanf(). This extra argument is a pointer to the FILE variable (i.e., fptr), and this must be a first argument.

Before proceeding, notice the generic syntax of a statement that uses the function fscanf() given here:

```
intN = fscanf(fptr, "control string", arg1, arg2, ..., argN);
```

Here, intN is an int variable; fptr is a pointer to the FILE variable; "control string" is a control string that appears in the scanf() function; and arg1, arg2, ..., argN is a comma-separated list of arguments that appears in the scanf() function. The values of the data items read from a file are assigned to respective arguments. This function returns an int value, which is the number of successful field conversions if the reading operation is successful; otherwise, it returns EOF.

Now let's discuss how this program works. Notice LOC 10, which is reproduced here, for your quick reference:

```
m = fscanf(fptr, "%d", &n);                                  /* L10 */
```

The function fscanf() in LOC 10 reads the first integer stored in the file specified by fptr and assigns this integer to the int variable n. The first integer stored in the file specified by fptr is 1, and this value is assigned to n. Also, one field conversion is successfully read; hence, value 1 is returned, which is assigned to the int variable m.

Next, there is a while loop spanning LOCs 11 to 14. LOC 11 contains the continuation condition of the while loop, which is reproduced here for your quick reference:

```
while(m != EOF){                                      /* L11 */
```

As the value of m is now 1 and not EOF, iteration is permitted, and the first iteration begins. Next, LOC 12 is executed, which is reproduced here for your quick reference:

```
printf("%d ", n);                                     /* L12 */
```

In LOC 12, the value stored in the int variable n, which is 1, is displayed on the screen. Next, LOC 13 is executed, which is the same as LOC 10. In LOC 13, the next int value stored in the file, which is 2, is read and assigned to the int variable n. Next, as the execution of the first iteration is complete, computer control goes to LOC 11. As the value of m is now 2 and not EOF, the second iteration begins, and so on. Proceeding in this manner, the complete file is read.

When all the int values stored in the file are read and fscanf() tries to read the next int value (which is nonexistent), then the reading operation fails, and the function fscanf() returns the EOF value, which is assigned to m, and then the iterations are terminated.

6-10. Read Structures Stored in a Text File

Problem

You want to read the structures stored in a text file.

Solution

Write a C program that reads the structures stored in a text file, with the following specifications:

- The program opens the file agents.dat in reading mode. This file consists of the structures and biodata of five secret agents.

- The program reads the file agents.dat using the function fscanf() and displays its contents on the screen.

The Code

The following is the code of the C program written with these specifications. Type the following C program in a text editor and save it in the folder C:\Code with the file name files10.c:

```
/* This program reads the records stored in a file using the function
fscanf(). */
                                                      /* BL */
#include <stdio.h>                                    /* L1 */
                                                      /* BL */
```

```
main()                                                      /* L2  */
{                                                           /* L3  */
 int k = 0, m = 0;                                          /* L4  */
 FILE *fptr;                                                /* L6  */
 struct biodata{                                            /* L7  */
  char name[15];                                            /* L8  */
  int rollno;                                               /* L9  */
  int age;                                                  /* L10 */
  float weight;                                             /* L11 */
 };                                                         /* L12 */
 struct biodata sa;                                         /* L13 */
 fptr = fopen("C:\\Code\\agents.dat", "r");                 /* L14 */
 if (fptr != NULL) {                                        /* L15 */
  printf("File agents.dat is opened successfully.\n");      /* L16 */
  m = fscanf(fptr, "%s %d %d %f", sa.name,                  /* L19 */
                                  &sa.rollno,               /* L20 */
                                  &sa.age,                  /* L21 */
                                  &sa.weight);              /* L22 */
                                                            /* BL  */
  while(m != EOF){                                          /* L23 */
    printf("Name: %s, Roll no: %d, Age: %d, Weight: %.1f\n",/* L24 */
           sa.name, sa.rollno,sa.age, sa.weight);           /* L25 */
    m = fscanf(fptr, "%s %d %d %f", sa.name,                /* L26 */
                                    &sa.rollno,             /* L27 */
                                    &sa.age,                /* L28 */
                                    &sa.weight);            /* L29 */
  }                                                         /* L30 */
                                                            /* BL  */
  k = fclose(fptr);                                         /* L31 */
  if(k == -1)                                               /* L32 */
    puts("File-closing failed");                            /* L33 */
  if(k == 0)                                                /* L34 */
    puts("File is closed successfully.");                   /* L35 */
 }                                                          /* L36 */
 else                                                       /* L37 */
  puts("File-opening failed");                              /* L38 */
 return(0);                                                 /* L39 */
}                                                           /* L40 */
```

Compile and execute this program, and the following lines of text appear on the screen:

```
File agents.dat is opened successfully.
Name: Dick, Roll no: 1, Age: 21, Weight: 70.6
Name: Robert, Roll no: 2, Age: 22, Weight: 75.8
Name: Steve, Roll no: 3, Age: 20, Weight: 53.7
Name: Richard, Roll no: 4, Age: 19, Weight: 83.1
Name: Albert, Roll no: 5, Age: 18, Weight: 62.3
File is closed successfully.
```

How It Works

Now let's discuss how this program works. Notice LOCs 19 to 22, which contain a single fscanf statement, but because the statement is long, it is split into four LOCs for better readability. These LOCs are reproduced here for your quick reference:

```
m = fscanf(fptr, "%s %d %d %f", sa.name,          /* L19 */
                        &sa.rollno,                /* L20 */
                        &sa.age,                   /* L21 */
                        &sa.weight);               /* L22 */
```

This statement, after execution, reads the data of Dick (i.e., Dick 1 21 70.6) stored in the file specified by fptr and assigns that data to the variable sa. As four conversion specifications are read successfully, the function fscanf() returns the int value 4, which is assigned to the int variable m.

Next, there is a while loop spanning LOCs 23 to 30. LOC 23 contains the continuation condition of the while loop; it is reproduced here for your quick reference:

```
while(m != EOF){                                   /* L23 */
```

As the value of m is now 4 and not EOF, the first iteration begins. Next, the printf statement is executed, which spans LOCs 24 and 25, which are reproduced here for your quick reference:

```
printf("Name: %s, Roll no: %d, Age: %d, Weight: %.1f\n",   /* L24 */
            sa.name, sa.rollno,sa.age, sa.weight);          /* L25 */
```

The data items stored in the variable sa (i.e., the data of Dick) are displayed on the screen in LOCs 24 and 25. Next, the fscanf statement is executed, which spans LOCs 26 to 29. This statement is precisely the same as the statement spanning LOCs 19 to 22. It reads the data of the second secret agent (i.e., the data of Robert) stored in the file and assigns that data to the variable sa. Proceeding in this manner, the complete file is read. When the complete file is read and the function fscanf() tries to read the further data, which simply doesn't exist, then the reading operation fails and the EOF value is returned by this function, which is assigned to the int variable m. Then the iterations are terminated.

6-11. Write Integers to a Binary File

Problem

You want to write the integers to a binary file.

Solution

Write a C program that writes the integers to a binary file, with the following specifications:

- The program opens the binary file num.dat in writing mode and creates an array of integers.

- The program writes the integers to the file num.dat using the function fwrite().

The Code

The following is the code of the C program written with these specifications. Type the following C program in a text editor and save it in the folder C:\Code with the file name files11.c:

```c
/* This program writes an array of int values to a binary file using the
function fwrite(). */
                                                        /* BL */
#include <stdio.h>                                      /* L1 */
                                                        /* BL */
main()                                                  /* L2 */
{                                                       /* L3 */
 int i, k, m, a[20];                                    /* L4 */
 FILE *fptr;                                            /* L5 */
                                                        /* BL */
 for(i = 0; i < 20; i++)                                /* L6 */
  a[i] = 30000 + i;                                     /* L7 */
                                                        /* BL */
 fptr = fopen("C:\\Code\\num.dat", "wb");               /* L8 */
 if (fptr != NULL) {                                    /* L9 */
  puts("File num.dat is opened successfully.");         /* L10 */
  m = fwrite(a, sizeof(int), 10, fptr);                 /* L11 */
  if (m == 10)                                          /* L12 */
    puts("Data written to the file successfully.");     /* L13 */
  k = fclose(fptr);                                     /* L14 */
  if(k == -1)                                           /* L15 */
    puts("File-closing failed");                        /* L16 */
  if(k == 0)                                            /* L17 */
   puts("File is closed successfully.");                /* L18 */
 }                                                      /* L19 */
```

```
else                                              /* L20 */
  puts("File-opening failed");                    /* L21 */
                                                  /* BL  */
return(0);                                         /* L22 */
}                                                 /* L23 */
```

Compile and execute this program, and the following lines of text appear on the screen:

```
File num.dat is opened successfully.
Data written to the file successfully.
File is closed successfully.
```

This program has written the ten integer values (30000, 30001, 30002, 30003, 30004, 30005, 30006, 30007, 30008, 30009) to the binary file num.dat.

Open the file num.dat in a suitable text editor, and you will find that its contents are as follows:

```
0u1u2u3u4u5u6u7u8u9u
```

The contents are unreadable (at least meaningless, if not readable) as the file is binary. You can read the contents of this file using the function fread(). The size of this file is 20 bytes as ten int values are stored in it (10×2 bytes = 20 bytes). A similar text file would end up consuming 50 bytes (10×5 bytes).

How It Works

The function fwrite() is used to write the data to a file in binary format. The function fwrite() is particularly suitable for writing an array to a file in binary format. The file must be opened in binary mode, if the function used for file writing is fwrite(). When you use the function fwrite() instead of the function fprintf(), there are two possible benefits: there is saving of storage space, in general, and the fwrite statement is less complex than the fprintf statement.

The generic syntax of a statement that uses the function fwrite() for writing an array to a file is given here:

```
m = fwrite(arrayName, sizeof(dataType), n, fptr);
```

Here, m is an int variable, arrayName is the name of the array to be written to a file, dataType is the data type of the array, n is the number of elements in the array to be written to the file, and fptr is a pointer to the FILE variable. The function fwrite() writes the n elements of the array arrayName to the file specified by fptr and returns a number that indicates the number of array elements successfully written. If the writing operation fails, then a zero value is returned. The returned value is generally ignored in small programs, but in professional programs it is collected and inspected to find out whether the writing operation was successful.

In LOCs 6 and 7, the int array a is populated with suitable values ranging from 30000 to 30019.

Next, consider LOC 8, which is reproduced here for your quick reference:

```
fptr = fopen("C:\\Code\\num.dat", "wb");                    /* L8 */
```

Notice that the file-opening mode is "wb". It means the file num.dat is opened for writing in binary mode. Next, consider LOC 11, which is reproduced here for your quick reference:

```
m = fwrite(a, sizeof(int), 10, fptr);                       /* L11 */
```

Notice that four arguments are passed to fwrite(). The first argument, a, is the name of the array to be written to the file; the second argument indicates the size of the array element (it is 2 bytes); the third argument, 10, indicates the number of elements of the array to be written to a file; and the fourth argument, fptr, specifies the file to which the array a is to be written. As the size of int is 2, you can replace the the second argument simply with 2. Also, the array a consists of 20 elements, but here we have chosen to write only 10 elements of this array to a file (see the third argument; it is 10). LOC 11, after execution, writes the first ten elements of the array a to the file specified by fptr and returns an int value 10, which is assigned to m. Notice the comfort of writing a complete array in a single statement to a file.

6-12. Write Structures to a Binary File
Problem
You want to write structures to a binary file.

Solution
Write a C program that writes structures to a binary file, with the following specifications:

- The program opens the binary file agents2.dat in writing mode.
- The program writes the structures to agents2.dat using the function fwrite().

The Code
The following is the code of the C program written with these specifications. Type the following C program in a text editor and save it in the folder C:\Code with the file name files12.c:

```
/* This program writes structures to a binary file using the function fwrite(). */
                                                            /* BL */
#include <stdio.h>                                          /* L1 */
                                                            /* BL */
```

```
main()                                                      /* L2 */
{                                                           /* L3 */
 int k = 0;                                                 /* L4 */
 char flag = 'y';                                           /* L5 */
 FILE *fptr;                                                /* L6 */
 struct biodata {                                           /* L7 */
  char name[15];                                            /* L8 */
  int rollno;                                               /* L9 */
  int age;                                                  /* L10 */
  float weight;                                             /* L11 */
 };                                                         /* L12 */
 struct biodata sa;                                         /* L13 */
 fptr = fopen("C:\\Code\\agents2.dat", "wb");               /* L14 */
 if (fptr != NULL) {                                        /* L15 */
  printf("File agents2.dat is opened successfully.\n");     /* L16 */
                                                            /* BL  */
  while(flag == 'y'){                                       /* L17 */
   printf("Enter name, roll no, age, and weight of agent: "); /* L18 */
   scanf("%s %d %d %f", sa.name,                            /* L19 */
                        &sa.rollno,                         /* L20 */
                        &sa.age,                            /* L21 */
                        &sa.weight);                        /* L22 */
   fwrite(&sa, sizeof(sa), 1, fptr);                        /* L23 */
   fflush(stdin);                                           /* L24 */
   printf("Any more records(y/n): ");                       /* L25 */
   scanf(" %c", &flag);                                     /* L26 */
  }                                                         /* L27 */
                                                            /* Bl  */
  k = fclose(fptr);                                         /* L28 */
  if(k == -1)                                               /* L29 */
    puts("File-closing failed");                            /* L30 */
  if(k == 0)                                                /* L31 */
    puts("File is closed successfully.");                   /* L32 */
 }                                                          /* L33 */
 else                                                       /* L34 */
  puts("File-opening failed");                              /* L35 */
 return(0);                                                 /* L36 */
}                                                           /* L37 */
```

Compile and execute this program. A run of this program is given here:

```
File agents2.dat is opened successfully.
Enter name, roll no, age, and weight of agent: Dick  1  21  70.6   ⏎
Any more records(y/n): y     ⏎
Enter name, roll no, age, and weight of agent: Robert  2  22  75.8   ⏎
Any more records(y/n): y     ⏎
Enter name, roll no, age, and weight of agent: Steve  3  20  53.7    ⏎
Any more records(y/n): y     ⏎
```

```
Enter name, roll no, age, and weight of agent: Richard  4   19   83.1     ↵
Any more records(y/n): y   ↵
Enter name, roll no, age, and weight of agent: Albert   5   18   62.3     ↵
Any more records(y/n): n   ↵
File is closed successfully.
```

Open the file agents2.dat in a suitable text editor, and you will find that its contents are as follows:

```
Dick   Å
```

The contents are unreadable (at least meaningless, if not readable) as the file is binary. You can read the contents of this file using the function fread(). Also, compare these contents with the contents of the text file agents.dat, which was written using the function fprintf(), given here:

```
Dick 1 21 70.6Robert 2 22 75.8Steve 3 20 53.7Richard 4 19 83.1Albert 5 18 62.3
```

How It Works

The generic syntax of a statement that uses the function fwrite() for writing a single variable to a file is given here:

```
m = fwrite(&var, sizeof(var), 1, fptr);
```

Here, m is an int variable, var is a variable of any data type, and & is an address operator. The third argument, 1, indicates that the value of only one object is to be written to a file (here var is the object), and fptr is a pointer to the FILE variable. The function fwrite() writes the value of the variable var to a file specified by fptr and returns the int value 1 if the operation is successful; otherwise, it returns zero. The returned value is generally ignored in small programs, and it is ignored in the next program.

This program is a remake of the program files8. The only differences are the following:

- Instead of opening a file in text mode, here it is opened in binary mode.

- Instead of using the function fprintf() for writing the data to a file, the function fwrite() is used.

Notice LOC 14, which is reproduced here for your quick reference:

```
fptr = fopen("C:\\Code\\agents2.dat", "wb");                    /* L14 */
```

In LOC 14, you can see that file-opening mode is "wb". It means the file agents2.dat is opened for writing in binary mode. Notice LOC 23, which is reproduced here for your quick reference:

```
fwrite(&sa, sizeof(sa), 1, fptr);                              /* L23 */
```

This LOC, after execution, writes the data stored in the variable sa to the file specified by fptr. The third argument, 1, indicates that only one object is to be written to a file (here sa is an object).

6-13. Read Integers Written to a Binary File
Problem

You want to read the integers written to a binary file.

Solution

Write a C program that reads the integers written to a binary file, with the following specifications:

- The program opens the binary file num.dat in reading mode.

- The program reads the integers written to the file using the function fread().

The Code

The following is the code of the C program written with these specifications. Type the following C program in a text editor and save it in the folder C:\Code with the file name files13.c:

```
/* This program reads the binary file num.dat using the function fread() */
                                                               /* BL */
#include <stdio.h>                                             /* L1 */
                                                               /* BL */
main()                                                         /* L2 */
{                                                              /* L3 */
 int i, k;                                                     /* L4 */
 int a[10];                                                    /* L5 */
 FILE *fptr;                                                   /* L6 */
                                                               /* BL */
fptr = fopen("C:\\Code\\num.dat", "rb");                       /* L7 */
if (fptr != NULL) {                                            /* L8 */
 puts("File num.dat is opened successfully.");                /* L9 */
                                                               /* L10 */
fread(a, sizeof(int), 10, fptr);                               /* L11 */
```

```
                                                        /* BL  */
puts("Contents of file num.dat:");                      /* L12 */
                                                        /* BL  */
for(i = 0; i < 10; i++)                                 /* L13 */
printf("%d\n", a[i]);                                   /* L14 */
                                                        /* BL  */
k = fclose(fptr);                                       /* L15 */
 if(k == -1)                                            /* L16 */
   puts("File-closing failed");                         /* L17 */
 if(k == 0)                                             /* L18 */
  puts("File is closed successfully.");                 /* L19 */
}                                                       /* L20 */
else                                                    /* L21 */
 puts("File-opening failed");                           /* L22 */
                                                        /* BL  */
 return(0);                                             /* L23 */
}                                                       /* L24 */
```

Compile and execute this program, and the following lines of text appear on the screen:

```
File num.dat is opened successfully.
Contents of file num.dat:
30000
30001
30002
30003
30004
30005
30006
30007
30008
30009
File is closed successfully.
```

How It Works

Think of the function fread() as a counterpart of the function fwrite(). It is used to read binary files. The generic syntax of a statement that uses the function fread() for reading an array stored in a file is given here:

```
m = fread(arrayName, sizeof(dataType), n, fptr);
```

Here, m is an int variable, arrayName is the name of the array in which the values read will be stored, dataType is the data type of an array (e.g., int, float, etc.), n is the number of values to be read, and fptr is a pointer to FILE that specifies the file to be read. The function fread() reads the n values of the data type dataType from the file specified by fptr, stores them in the array arrayName, and returns a number that indicates the

185

number of values read. If the reading operation is quite successful, then the value n is returned. If the reading operation fails and no value is read, then zero is returned. In small programs, the returned value is generally ignored.

Consider LOC 7, which is reproduced here for your quick reference:

```
fptr = fopen("C:\\Code\\num.dat", "rb");                          /* L7 */
```

Notice that file-opening mode is "rb". It means the file num.dat is opened for reading in binary mode. Next, notice LOC 11, which is reproduced here for your quick reference:

```
fread(a, sizeof(int), 10, fptr);                                  /* L11 */
```

In this LOC, the function fread() reads the ten int values stored in the file specified by fptr and then stores these values in the first ten elements of the array a. (Why ten? The third argument says so, and why int? The second argument says so.) Notice the comfort of reading a complete array in a single statement.

Values stored in the array a are then displayed on the screen using the for loop that spans LOCs 13 and 14, reproduced here for your quick reference:

```
for(i = 0; i < 10; i++)                                           /* L13 */
printf("%d\n", a[i]);                                             /* L14 */
```

This for loop performs ten iterations and displays the values stored in the ten elements of array a.

6-14. Read Structures Written to a Binary File
Problem

You want to read the structures written to a binary file.

Solution

Write a C program that reads the structures written to the binary file, with the following specifications:

- The program opens the binary file agents2.dat in reading mode.

- The program reads the structures written to the file using the function fread().

The Code

The following is the code of the C program written with these specifications. Type the following C program in a text editor and save it in the folder C:\Code with the file name files14.c:

```
/* This program reads the structures stored in the binary file agents2.dat */
/* using the function fread() */
                                                                /* BL */
#include <stdio.h>                                              /* L1 */
                                                                /* BL */
main()                                                          /* L2 */
{                                                               /* L3 */
 int k = 0, m = 0;                                              /* L4 */
 FILE *fptr;                                                    /* L5 */
 struct biodata{                                               /* L6 */
  char name[15];                                               /* L7 */
  int rollno;                                                  /* L8 */
  int age;                                                     /* L9 */
  float weight;                                                /* L10 */
 };                                                            /* L11 */
 struct biodata sa;                                            /* L12 */
 fptr = fopen("C:\\Code\\agents2.dat", "rb");                  /* L13 */
 if (fptr != NULL) {                                           /* L14 */
  printf("File agents2.dat is opened successfully.\n");        /* L15 */
  m = fread(&sa, sizeof(sa), 1, fptr);                         /* L16 */
                                                                /* BL  */
  while(m != 0){                                               /* L17 */
   printf("Name: %s, Roll no: %d, Age: %d, Weight: %.1f\n",    /* L18 */
              sa.name, sa.rollno,sa.age, sa.weight);           /* L19 */
   m = fread(&sa, sizeof(sa), 1, fptr);                        /* L20 */
  }                                                            /* L21 */
                                                                /* BL  */
  k = fclose(fptr);                                            /* L22 */
  if(k == -1)                                                  /* L23 */
    puts("File-closing failed");                               /* L24 */
  if(k == 0)                                                   /* L25 */
    puts("File is closed successfully.");                      /* L26 */
 }                                                             /* L27 */
 else                                                          /* L28 */
  puts("File-opening failed");                                 /* L29 */
 return(0);                                                    /* L30 */
}                                                              /* L31 */
```

Compile and execute this program, and the following lines of text appear on the screen:

```
File agents2.dat is opened successfully.
Name: Dick, Roll no: 1, Age: 21, Weight: 70.6
Name: Robert, Roll no: 2, Age: 22, Weight: 75.8
Name: Steve, Roll no: 3, Age: 20, Weight: 53.7
Name: Richard, Roll no: 4, Age: 19, Weight: 83.1
Name: Albert, Roll no: 5, Age: 18, Weight: 62.3
File is closed successfully.
```

How It Works

This program is a remake of the program files10 with the following differences:

- In this program, file-opening mode is "rb" (i.e., the file agents2. dat will be opened for reading in binary mode).

- The function fread() is used instead of the function fscanf() to read the file.

Now let's discuss how this program works. Notice LOC 16, which is reproduced here for your quick reference:

```
m = fread(&sa, sizeof(sa), 1, fptr);                        /* L16 */
```

This LOC, after execution, reads the data of Dick stored in the file specified by fptr and stores that data in the variable sa. The second argument indicates the size of the variable sa. The third argument indicates that only one object (here data that will be stored in the variable sa is the object) is to be read from the file. The fourth argument indicates that the file to be read is specified by fptr. As one object is successfully read, the integer value 1 is returned by this function, which is assigned to m. You are interested in the returned value so that you can detect the end of file. When the end of file occurs, then no object can be read, and fread() returns zero.

Next, there is a while loop that spans LOCs 17 to 21. Notice LOC 17, which is reproduced here for your quick reference:

```
while(m != 0){                                              /* L17 */
```

Notice the continuation condition that says iterations are permitted, while m is not equal to zero. As the value of m is now 1, the first iteration is permitted. Now the first iteration begins. Next, the printf statement spanning LOCs 18 to 19 is executed. This is a single statement, but it is put onto two LOCs because it is long. This printf statement displays the data of Dick on the screen. Next, LOC 20 is executed, which is the same as LOC 16. LOC 20, after execution, reads the data of Robert from the file and stores it in the variable sa. This is how the data of successive members is read from the file. When the end of file occurs and fread() tries to read from the file, then the reading operation fails and zero is returned (m becomes equal to zero), which terminates the execution of the loop.

6-15. Rename a File

Problem

You want to rename a file.

Solution

Write a C program that renames the file kolkata.txt as city.dat.

The Code

The following is the code of the C program written with these specifications. Type the following C program in a text editor and save it in the folder C:\Code with the file name files15.c:

```
/* This program changes the name of file kolkata.txt to city.dat. */
                                                              /* BL */
#include <stdio.h>                                            /* L1 */
                                                              /* BL */
main()                                                        /* L2 */
{                                                             /* L3 */
  int m;                                                      /* L4 */
  m = rename("C:\\Code\\kolkata.txt", "C:\\Code\\city.dat");  /* L5 */
  if (m == 0)                                                 /* L6 */
    puts("Operation of renaming a file is successful.");      /* L7 */
  if (m != 0)                                                 /* L8 */
    puts("Operation of renaming a file failed.");             /* L9 */
  return(0);                                                  /* L10 */
}                                                             /* L11 */
```

Compile and execute this program, and the following line of text appears on the screen:

```
Operation of renaming a file is successful.
```

Open the file city.dat in a suitable text editor and verify that its contents are as shown here:

```
Kolkata is very big city.
It is also very nice city.
```

How It Works

In C, you can rename a file using the function rename(). Also, you can delete a file using the function remove(). The generic syntax of a statement that uses the function rename() is as follows:

```
n = rename(oldFilename, newFilename);
```

Here, oldFilename and newFilename are expressions that evaluate to the string constants, which in turn consist of the old file name and new file name, respectively; n is an int variable. The function rename() changes the name of the file from oldFilename to newFilename and returns an integer value, which is assigned to n. If the operation of renaming is successful, then the zero value is returned; otherwise, a nonzero value is returned.

In this program, the file kolkata.txt is renamed as city.dat in LOC 5. LOC 5 is reproduced here for your quick reference:

```
m = rename("C:\\Code\\kolkata.txt", "C:\\Code\\city.dat");        /* L5 */
```

The first argument to the function rename() is an old file name, and the second argument to the function rename() is a new file name.

6-16. Delete a File

Problem

You want to delete a file.

Solution

Write a C program that deletes the file city.dat.

The Code

The following is the code of the C program written with these specifications. Type the following C program in a text editor and save it in the folder C:\Code with the file name files16.c:

```
/* This program deletes the file city.dat. */
                                                          /* BL */
#include <stdio.h>                                        /* L1 */
                                                          /* BL */
main()                                                    /* L2 */
{                                                         /* L3 */
 int m;                                                   /* L4 */
 m = remove("C:\\Code\\city.dat");                        /* L5 */
```

```
    if (m == 0)                                                    /* L6 */
      puts("Operation of deletion of file is successful.");        /* L7 */
    if (m != 0)                                                    /* L8 */
      puts("Operation of deletion of file failed.");               /* L9 */
     return(0);                                                    /* L10 */
}                                                                  /* L11 */
```

Compile and execute this program, and the following line of text appears on the screen:

```
Operation of deletion of file is successful.
```

The file city.dat is now deleted, and you can verify it by suitable means.

How It Works

The function remove() is used to delete (i.e., remove) a file. The generic syntax of a statement that uses the function remove() is as follows:

```
n = remove(filename) ;
```

Here, filename is an expression that evaluates to a string constant that consists of the name of the file to be deleted, and n is an int variable. The function remove() deletes the file name and returns an integer value that is assigned to n. If the operation of deleting a file is successful, then a zero value is returned; otherwise, a nonzero value is returned.

LOC 5 deletes the file city.dat. LOC 5 is reproduced here for your quick reference:

```
m = remove("C:\\Code\\city.dat");                                 /* L5 */
```

The only argument to the function remove() is the name of the file to be deleted with the path.

6-17. Copy a Text File
Problem

You want to copy a text file.

Solution

Write a C program that creates a copy of the text file satara.txt with the file name town.dat.

The Code

The following is the code of the C program written with these specifications. Type the following C program in a text editor and save it in the folder C:\Code with the file name files17.c:

```
/* This program creates a copy of the text file satara.txt
with the filename town.dat. */
                                                              /* BL */
#include <stdio.h>                                            /* L1 */
                                                              /* BL */
main()                                                        /* L2 */
{                                                             /* L3 */
 FILE *fptrSource, *fptrTarget;                               /* L4 */
 int m, n, p;                                                 /* L5 */
                                                              /* BL */
fptrSource = fopen("C:\\Code\\satara.txt", "r");              /* L6 */
if(fptrSource == NULL){                                       /* L7 */
 puts("Source-file-opening failed");                          /* L8 */
 exit(1);                                                     /* L9 */
}                                                             /* L10 */
puts("Source-file satara.txt opened successfully");          /* L11 */
                                                              /* BL */
fptrTarget = fopen("C:\\Code\\town.dat", "w");                /* L12 */
if(fptrTarget == NULL){                                       /* L13 */
 puts("Target-file-opening failed");                          /* L14 */
 exit(2);                                                     /* L15 */
}                                                             /* L16 */
puts("Target-file town.dat opened successfully");            /* L17 */
                                                              /* BL */
m = fgetc(fptrSource);                                        /* L18 */
                                                              /* BL */
while(m != EOF){                                              /* L19 */
 fputc(m, fptrTarget);                                        /* L20 */
 m = fgetc(fptrSource);                                       /* L21 */
}                                                             /* L22 */
                                                              /* BL */
puts("File copied successfully");                            /* L23 */
                                                              /* BL */
n = fclose(fptrSource);                                       /* L24 */
if(n == -1)                                                   /* L25 */
 puts("Source-file-closing failed");                          /* L26 */
if(n == 0)                                                    /* L27 */
 puts("Source-file closed successfully");                     /* L28 */
                                                              /* BL */
p = fclose(fptrTarget);                                       /* L29 */
if(p == -1)                                                   /* L30 */
 puts("Target-file-closing failed");                          /* L31 */
```

```
  if(p == 0)                                            /* L32 */
    puts("Target-file closed successfully");            /* L33 */
                                                        /* BL  */
  return(0);                                             /* L34 */
}                                                        /* L35 */
```

Compile and execute this program, and the following lines of text appear
on the screen:

```
Source-file satara.txt opened successfully
Target-file town.dat opened successfully
File copied successfully
Source-file closed successfully
Target-file closed successfully
```

Open the file town.dat in a suitable text editor and ensure that its contents are as
shown here:

```
Satara is surrounded by mountains.
Satara was capital of Maratha empire for many years.
```

This confirms that the newly created file town.dat is an exact replica of the file
satara.txt.

How It Works

The generic steps involved in the process of creating a copy of a text file are as follows:

1. Open the source file for reading in text mode.

2. Open the target file for writing in text mode.

3. Read a character in the source file and write it to the target file.

4. Repeat the step 3 until the end of source file occurs.

5. Close the files.

The source file satara.txt is opened in LOC 6. If file opening fails, then LOCs 8 and
9 are executed. Of particular interest is LOC 9, which causes the program to terminate,
and it is reproduced here for your quick reference:

```
exit(1);                                                 /* L9 */
```

The function exit() causes the program to terminate. It is like an emergency exit.
The generic syntax of a statement that uses the function exit() is given here:

```
exit(n);
```

Here, n is an expression that evaluates to an integer constant. If the value of n is zero, then it indicates the normal termination of a program. If the value of n is nonzero, then it indicates the abnormal termination of a program. This indication is meant for the caller program. Before the termination of the program, the function exit() performs the following tasks:

- Flushes out the input and output buffers

- Closes all the open files

In LOC 9, you pass a nonzero argument to the function exit() indicating the abnormal termination of the program. Now notice LOC 15, which is reproduced here for your quick reference:

```
exit(2);                                                              /* L15 */
```

This time you have also passed a nonzero argument to the function exit() to indicate the abnormal termination of the program. But this time you have chosen another nonzero value, 2. Now the caller program is able to know the precise cause of program termination. The caller program inspects the argument; if it is 1, then it concludes that the program terminated because the source file opening failed, and if it is 2, then it concludes that the program terminated because the target file opening failed. Here the caller program is the function main().

The functions fgetc() and fputc() are used in this program to read a character from a file and to write a character to a file, respectively.

6-18. Copy a Binary File
Problem
You want to copy a binary file.

Solution
Write a C program that creates a copy of the binary file hello.exe with the file name world.exe. Also, ensure that the executable file hello.exe is available in the folder C:\ Output. This file displays the text "hello, world" on the screen after execution, and it is the executable version of the ubiquitous hello program coded by Brian Kernighan.

The Code
The following is the code of the C program written with these specifications. Type the following C program in a text editor and save it in the folder C:\Code with the file name files18.c:

```
/* This program creates a copy of the binary file hello.exe named as world.exe. */
                                                                      /* BL */
#include <stdio.h>                                                    /* L1 */
                                                                      /* BL */
```

```
main()                                                  /* L2  */
{                                                       /* L3  */
 FILE *fptrSource, *fptrTarget;                         /* L4  */
 int m, n, p;                                           /* L5  */
                                                        /* BL  */
 fptrSource = fopen("C:\\Output\\hello.exe", "rb");     /* L6  */
 if(fptrSource == NULL){                                /* L7  */
  puts("Source-file-opening failed");                   /* L8  */
  exit(1);                                              /* L9  */
 }                                                      /* L10 */
 puts("Source-file Hello.exe opened successfully");     /* L11 */
                                                        /* BL  */
 fptrTarget = fopen("C:\\Output\\world.exe", "wb");     /* L12 */
 if(fptrTarget == NULL){                                /* L13 */
  puts("Target-file-opening failed");                   /* L14 */
  exit(2);                                              /* L15 */
 }                                                      /* L16 */
 puts("Target-file World.exe opened successfully");     /* L17 */
                                                        /* BL  */
 m = fgetc(fptrSource);                                 /* L18 */
                                                        /* BL  */
 while(m != EOF){                                       /* L19 */
  fputc(m, fptrTarget);                                 /* L20 */
  m = fgetc(fptrSource);                                /* L21 */
 }                                                      /* L22 */
                                                        /* BL  */
 puts("File copied successfully");                      /* L23 */
                                                        /* BL  */
 n = fclose(fptrSource);                                /* L24 */
 if(n == -1)                                            /* L25 */
  puts("Source-file-closing failed");                   /* L26 */
 if(n == 0)                                             /* L27 */
  puts("Source-file closed successfully");              /* L28 */
                                                        /* BL  */
 p = fclose(fptrTarget);                                /* L29 */
 if(p == -1)                                            /* L30 */
  puts("Target-file-closing failed");                   /* L31 */
 if(p == 0)                                             /* L32 */
  puts("Target-file closed successfully");              /* L33 */
                                                        /* BL  */
 return(0);                                             /* L34 */
}                                                       /* L35 */
```

Compile and execute this program, and the following lines of text appear on the screen:

```
Source-file Hello.exe opened successfully
Target-file World.exe opened successfully
File copied successfully
Source-file closed successfully
Target-file closed successfully
```

Using a suitable Command Prompt window, execute the file world.exe and ensure that the following output is displayed on the screen:

```
hello, world
```

This confirms that the file world.exe is an exact replica of the file hello.exe.

How It Works

This program is a remake of the program files17. The program files17 creates a copy of the text file, whereas this program (i.e., files18) creates a copy of the binary file. The only differences are the following:

- In the program files17, the source file (satara.txt) is opened for reading in text mode, whereas in the program files18, the source file (hello.exe) is opened for reading in binary mode.

- In the program files17, the target file (town.dat) is opened for writing in text mode, whereas in the program files18, the target file (world.exe) is opened for writing in binary mode.

LOCs 6 and 12 are reproduced here for your quick reference:

```
fptrSource = fopen("C:\\Output\\hello.exe", "rb");          /* L6 */
fptrTarget = fopen("C:\\Output\\world.exe", "wb");          /* L12 */
```

The first argument to the function fopen() is the name of the file to be opened with the path, and the second argument is the mode in which the file is to be opened. You can see that the opening mode for the file hello.exe is "reading and binary," and the opening mode for the file world.exe is "writing and binary."

6-19. Write to a File and Then Read from That File

Problem

You want to write to a file and also to read that file.

Solution

Write a C program that writes to a file and also reads that file, with the following specifications:

- The program opens the text file pune.txt in writing mode. The program writes some text to this file.

- The program rewinds the file pune.txt using the function rewind().

- The program reads the file pune.txt and displays the text on the screen.

The Code

The following is the code of the C program written with these specifications. Type the following C program in a text editor and save it in the folder C:\Code with the file name files19.c:

```
/* This program performs write and read operations on a file. */
                                                                /* BL */
#include <stdio.h>                                              /* L1 */
                                                                /* BL */
main()                                                          /* L2 */
{                                                               /* L3 */
 FILE *fptr;                                                    /* L4 */
 char store[80];                                                /* L5 */
 int k;                                                         /* L6 */
 fptr = fopen("C:\\Code\\pune.txt", "w+");                      /* L7 */
                                                                /* BL */
 if(fptr != NULL){                                              /* L8 */
  puts("File pune.txt opened successfully");                   /* L9 */
  fputs("Pune is very nice city.", fptr);                      /* L10 */
  puts("Text written to file pune.txt successfully");          /* L11 */
  rewind(fptr);                                                 /* L12 */
  fgets(store, 80, fptr);                                       /* L13 */
  puts("Contents of file pune.txt:");                          /* L14 */
  puts(store);                                                  /* L15 */
  k = fclose(fptr);                                             /* L16 */
  if(k == -1)                                                   /* L17 */
   puts("File-closing failed");                                /* L18 */
  if(k == 0)                                                    /* L19 */
   puts("File closed successfully");                           /* L20 */
 }                                                              /* L21 */
```

```
    else                                                    /* L22 */
      puts("File-opening failed");                          /* L23 */
                                                            /* BL  */
    return(0);                                               /* L24 */
}                                                           /* L25 */
```

Compile and execute this program, and the following lines of text appear on the screen:

```
File pune.txt opened successfully
Text written into file pune.txt successfully
Contents of file pune.txt:
Pune is very nice city.
File closed successfully.
```

How It Works

Hitherto, in every program, you have either written to a file or read a file. However, in this program, you have written to a file, and then the same file is read. This can be done in number of ways. Let's note couple of methods of doing so.

For the first method, follow these steps:

1. Open a file in "w" mode using the function fopen().

2. Write to the file the desired data.

3. Close the file using the function fclose().

4. Open the file again in "r" mode using the function fopen().

5. Read the file.

6. Close the file using the function fclose().

For the second method (used in program files19), follow these steps:

1. Open a file in "w+" mode using the function fopen().

2. Write to the file the desired data.

3. Rewind the file using the function rewind(). To rewind the file means to position the file to its first character.

4. Read the file.

5. Close the file using the function fclose().

When you open a file using the function fopen(), then the file is always positioned to its first character (i.e., the marker is pointing to the first character of the file). As you read the file (or write to the file), then the marker marches ahead accordingly. In the second method, in step 3, you have rewound the file using the function rewind(). This step is necessary because when you write to the file in step 2, then the marker is pointing to the (n + 1)th byte of the file provided that you have written n characters to the file. However, before you read the file, the latter must be positioned to its first character. This can be done simply by closing the file and then opening it again. Alternatively, this can be done simply by calling the function rewind(), which positions the file to its first character.

Notice the simplified syntax of a statement that uses the function rewind() given here:

```
rewind(fptr);
```

Here, fptr is a pointer to the FILE variable. The function rewind() rewinds the file specified by fptr.

In LOC 10 a string is written to the file pune.txt. In LOC 12 the file is rewound using the function rewind(). After the execution of LOC 12, the file is positioned to its first character. In LOC 13, a file is read, and the contents of the file (which are nothing but a single string) are stored in the char array store. In LOC 15, the string stored in store is displayed on the screen.

6-20. Position a Text File to a Desired Character
Problem

You want to position a text file to a desired character in that file.

Solution

Write a C program that positions a text file to a desired character in that file, with the following specifications:

- The program opens the text file pune.txt in reading mode.

- The program uses the function ftell() to find out the current position of the file. Also, the program uses the function fseek() to position the file to the desired character in that file.

- The program positions the file to various desired characters in the file using the functions fseek() and ftell().

The Code

The following is the code of the C program written with these specifications. Type the following C program in a text editor and save it in the folder C:\Code with the file name files20.c:

```
/* This program postions the file to desired characters in that file using */
/* the functions fseek() and ftell(). */
                                                        /* BL */
#include <stdio.h>                                      /* L1 */
                                                        /* BL */
main()                                                  /* L2 */
{                                                       /* L3 */
```

```
FILE *fptr;                                                     /* L4 */
int m, n, k, p;                                                 /* L5 */
fptr = fopen("C:\\Code\\pune.txt", "r");                        /* L6 */
                                                                /* BL */
if(fptr != NULL){                                               /* L7 */
 puts("File pune.txt opened successfully");                     /* L8 */
 puts("Let n denotes current file position");                   /* L9 */
 n = ftell(fptr);                                               /* L10 */
 printf("Now value of n is %d\n", n);                           /* L11 */
 printf("Let us read a single character and it is: ");          /* L12 */
 m = fgetc(fptr);                                               /* L13 */
 putchar(m);                                                    /* L14 */
 printf("\n");                                                  /* L15 */
 n = ftell(fptr);                                               /* L16 */
 printf("Now value of n is %d\n", n);                           /* L17 */
 fseek(fptr, 8, 0);                                             /* L18 */
 puts("Statement \"fseek(fptr, 8, 0);\" executed");             /* L19 */
 n = ftell(fptr);                                               /* L20 */
 printf("Now value of n is %d\n", n);                           /* L21 */
 fseek(fptr, 3, 1);                                             /* L22 */
 puts("Statement \"fseek(fptr, 3, 1);\" executed");             /* L23 */
 n = ftell(fptr);                                               /* L24 */
 printf("Now value of n is %d\n", n);                           /* L25 */
 fseek(fptr, -5, 1);                                            /* L26 */
 puts("Statement \"fseek(fptr, -5, 1);\" executed");            /* L27 */
 n = ftell(fptr);                                               /* L28 */
 printf("Now value of n is %d\n", n);                           /* L29 */
 fseek(fptr, -3, 2);                                            /* L30 */
 puts("Statement \"fseek(fptr, -3, 2);\" executed");            /* L31 */
 n = ftell(fptr);                                               /* l32 */
 printf("Now value of n is %d\n", n);                           /* L33 */
 fseek(fptr, 0, 2);                                             /* L34 */
 puts("Statement \"fseek(fptr, 0, 2);\" executed");             /* L35 */
 n = ftell(fptr);                                               /* L36 */
 printf("Now value of n is %d\n", n);                           /* L37 */
 puts("Now let us perform a read operation");                   /* L38 */
 m = fgetc(fptr);                                               /* L39 */
 printf("Value read is %d\n", m);                               /* L40 */
 n = ftell(fptr);                                               /* L41 */
 printf("Now value of n is still %d\n", n);                     /* L42 */
 fseek(fptr, 0, 0);                                             /* L43 */
 puts("Statement \"fseek(fptr, 0, 0);\" executed");             /* L44 */
 n = ftell(fptr);                                               /* L45 */
 printf("Now value of n is %d\n", n);                           /* L46 */
 puts("That's all.");                                           /* L47 */
                                                                /* BL */
 k = fclose(fptr);                                              /* L48 */
 if(k == -1)                                                    /* L49 */
```

```
  puts("File-closing failed");                    /* L50 */
 if(k == 0)                                        /* L51 */
  puts("File closed successfully.");               /* L52 */
}                                                  /* L53 */
 else                                              /* L54 */
  puts("File-opening failed");                     /* L55 */
                                                   /* BL  */
return(0);                                         /* L56 */
}                                                  /* L57 */
```

Compile and execute this program, and the following lines of text appear on the screen:

```
File pune.txt opened successfully
Let n denotes current file position
Now value of n is 0
Let us read a single character and it is: P
Now value of n is 1
Statement "fseek (fptr, 8, 0);" executed
Now value of n is 8
Statement "fseek (fptr, 3, 1);" executed
Now value of n is 11
Statement "fseek (fptr, -5, 1);" executed
Now value of n is 6
Statement "fseek (fptr, -3, 2);" executed
Now value of n is 20
Statement "fseek (fptr, 0, 2);" executed
Now value of n is 23
Now let us perform a read operation
Value read is -1
Now value of n is still 23
Statement "fseek (fptr, 0, 0);" executed
Now value of n is 0
That's all.
```

How It Works

The function fseek() is used to position a file to the desired character of that file. The function ftell() is used to retrieve the current position of a file. Notice LOC 6, which is reproduced here for your quick reference:

```
fptr = fopen("C:\\Code\\pune.txt", "r");                    /* L6 */
```

After the execution of LOC 6, the file pune.txt opens in "r" mode. Also, the file is positioned to the first character of the file (i.e., 'P'), as shown in Figure 6-2 (a). Whenever you open a file using the function fopen(), the file is always positioned to the first character of the file.

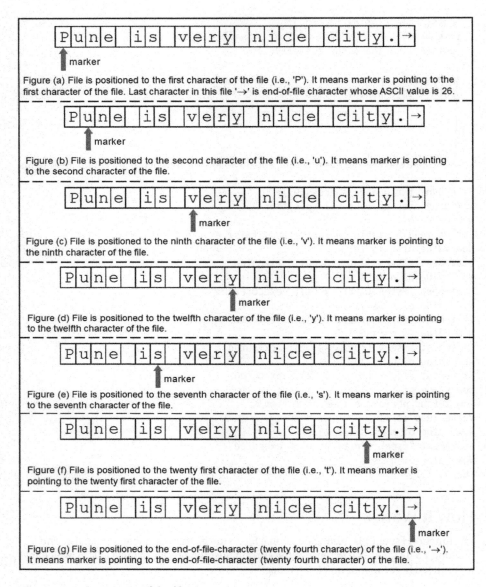

Figure 6-2. *Positioning of the file*

You can retrieve the current position of a file using the function `ftell()`. Notice LOC 10, which is reproduced here for your quick reference:

```
n = ftell(fptr);                                              /* L10 */
```

In LOC 10, the function ftell() returns the long int value 0 (the index of the first character in the file, i.e., 'P'), which is assigned to the long int variable n. Notice that characters in the file are indexed beginning with zero, which is akin to elements in an array. It means the index of the first character 'P' is 0, the index of the second character 'u' is 1, the index of the third character 'n' is 2, and so on.

Notice the generic syntax of a statement that uses the function ftell() given here:

```
n = ftell(fptr);
```

Here, n is a long int variable, and fptr is a pointer to the FILE variable. The function ftell() returns a long int value, which indicates the position of a file specified by fptr.

A character is read using the function fgetc(). Notice LOC 13, which is reproduced here for your quick reference:

```
m = fgetc(fptr);                                            /* L13 */
```

In LOC 13, the function fgetc() reads the character 'P' and returns its ASCII value (it is 80), which is assigned to the int variable m. After the execution of LOC 13, the file is positioned to the second character of the file (i.e., 'u'), as shown in Figure 6-2 (b). LOC 16 is same as LOC 10, and it is reproduced here for your quick reference:

```
n = ftell(fptr);                                            /* L16 */
```

In LOC 16, the function ftell() returns the long int value 1 (the index of the second character of the file, i.e., 'u'), which is assigned to the long int variable n. In LOC 18, the file is positioned to the ninth character in the file (i.e., 'v'), as shown in Figure 6-2 (c). LOC 18 is reproduced here for your quick reference:

```
    fseek(fptr, 8, 0);                                      /* L18 */
```

Because indexing begins with zero, the index of 'v' is 8, and it appears as the second argument in the function call in LOC 18. The first argument in this function call is fptr, a pointer to the FILE variable, and it indicates the file to be positioned. The third argument in this function call is the integer value 0, and it indicates that the counting of characters is to be made from the beginning of the file.

Notice the generic syntax of a statement that uses the function fseek() given here:

```
p = fseek(fptr, offset, origin);
```

Here, p is an int variable, fptr is a pointer to the FILE variable, offset is an expression that evaluates to a long int value, and origin is one of the three values 0, 1, or 2. offset indicates the character offset counted from the origin; when origin is 0, then offset is counted from the beginning of the file (as in the case of LOC 18). When origin is 1, then offset is counted from the current position of the file (i.e., the current position of the character pointed to by the marker). When origin is 2, then offset is counted from the end of the file. The function fseek() positions the file as specified by the arguments and then returns 0 if the operation of positioning the file is successful; otherwise, it returns a nonzero value.

In LOC 20, once again, the current position of the file is retrieved. It is precisely the same as LOC 13 or LOC 16. In LOC 20, the function ftell() returns the long int value 8 (the index of the ninth character of the file, i.e., 'v'), which is assigned to the long int variable n.

In LOC 22, the file is positioned to the character 'y' (in the word "very"), as shown in Figure 6-2 (d). LOC 22 is reproduced here for your quick reference:

```
fseek(fptr, 3, 1);                                                      /* L22 */
```

In this function call, origin (the third argument) is 1, which means the counting of characters is to be made from the current position of the file (i.e., 'v'). Also, offset (the second argument) is 3. Thus, the third character from 'v' is 'y', and hence the file is positioned to 'y'.

In LOC 24, once again, the current position of the file is retrieved, and in this case the value of n is 11 because 'y' is the 12th character of the file.

In LOC 26, the file is positioned to the character 's' (in the word "is"), as shown in Figure 6-2 (e). LOC 26 is reproduced here for your quick reference:

```
fseek(fptr, -5, 1);                                                     /* L26 */
```

Notice that in this function call origin (the third argument) is 1; it means the counting of characters is to be made from the current position of the file (i.e., 'y'). Also, offset (the second argument) is -5. Notice that offset is a negative value, it means counting is to be made in the reverse direction, i.e., to the beginning of file. Thus, the fifth character from 'y' in the reverse direction is 's' (in the word "is"), and hence the file is positioned to 's'.

In LOC 28, once again, the current position of the file is retrieved, and in this case the value of n is 6 because 's' is the seventh character of the file.

In LOC 30, the file is positioned to the character 't' (in the word "city"), as shown in Figure 6-2 (f). LOC 30 is reproduced here for your quick reference:

```
fseek(fptr, -3, 2);                                                     /* L30 */
```

Notice that in this function call origin (the third argument) is 2; this means the counting of characters is to be made from the end of the file (i.e., from the end-of-file character). Also, offset (the second argument) is -3. As offset is a negative value, counting is to be made in the reverse direction, i.e., to the beginning of file. Thus, the third character from the end-of-file-character in the reverse direction is 't', and hence the file is positioned to 't'. In this case, you can imagine that the index of the end-of-file character is 0, the index of the period (.) is -1, the index of 'y' is -2, and the index of 't' is -3.

Also, notice that when origin is 0, then offset must be zero or a positive number. When origin is 2, then offset must be zero or negative number. When origin is 1, then offset can be a positive or negative number.

In LOC 32, once again, the current position of the file is retrieved, and in this case the value of n is 20 because 't' is the 21st character of the file.

In LOC 34, the file is positioned to the end-of-file character, as shown in Figure 6-2 (g). LOC 34 is reproduced here for your quick reference:

```
fseek(fptr, 0, 2);                                    /* L34 */
```

In LOC 36, once again, the current position of the file is retrieved, and in this case the value of n is 23 because the end-of-file character is the 24th character of the file.

In LOC 39, a read operation is performed. LOC 39 is reproduced here for your quick reference:

```
m = fgetc(fptr);                                      /* L39 */
```

Now instead of the ASCII value of the end-of-file character, a special value EOF (its value is -1) is returned by the function fgetc(), which is assigned to m. You inspect the value of m after every read operation to find out whether the end of file has occurred.

LOC 40 displays the value of m on the screen, and it is -1.

Whenever a read operation is performed using the function fgetc(), then the marker is advanced to the next character automatically. But after the execution of LOC 39, the marker is not advanced because the marker is already pointing to the end-of-file character, and it simply cannot be advanced. This is verified in LOC 41, which is reproduced here for your quick reference:

```
n = ftell(fptr);                                      /* L41 */
```

In LOC 41, the value of n turns out to be 23, as expected.

In LOC 43, the file is positioned to the first character of the file, as shown in Figure 6-2 (a). LOC 43 is reproduced here for your quick reference:

```
fseek(fptr, 0, 0);                                    /* L43 */
```

In LOC 45, once again, the current position of the file is retrieved, and in this case the value of n is 0 as expected.

Instead of LOC 43, you can use the LOC given here to position the file to the first character of the file:

```
rewind();                                  /* Equivalent to L43 */
```

Imagine that after LOC 45, the following LOC is executed:

```
fseek(fptr, 30, 0);                    /* Imagine this LOC after L45 */
```

After execution of the LOC shown, the file is positioned to the 31st character of the file. But the file doesn't contain 31 characters. The index of the last character (end-of-file character) in the file is 23. Hence, this LOC should be considered erratic even though you can compile and execute this LOC successfully.

■■ **Note**   Never make the marker point to a character that is not part of the file.

6-21. Read from the Device File Keyboard

Problem

You want to read from the device file keyboard.

Solution

Write a C program with the following specifications:

- The program implements the keyboard using a pointer to the
  FILE constant stdin.

- The program reads the data from the keyboard and displays it on
  the screen.

The Code

The following is the code of the C program written with these specifications. Type the
following C program in a text editor and save it in the folder C:\Code with the file name
files21.c:

```
/* This program reads the device-file "keyboard" and displays */
/* the contents of this file on the screen. */
                                                            /* BL */
#include <stdio.h>                                          /* L1 */
                                                            /* BL */
main()                                                      /* L2 */
{                                                           /* L3 */
 char text[500];                                            /* L4 */
 int m, n = 0, p;                                           /* L5 */
 puts("Type the text. The text you type form the contents"); /* L6 */
 puts("of the device-file keyboard. Strike the function");  /* L7 */
 puts("key F6 to signify the end of this file.");           /* L8 */
                                                            /* BL */
 m = fgetc(stdin);                                          /* L9 */
                                                            /* BL */
 while(m != EOF){                                           /* L10 */
  text[n] = m;                                              /* L11 */
  n = n + 1;                                                /* L12 */
  m = fgetc(stdin);                                         /* L13 */
 }                                                          /* L14 */
```

```
puts("Contents of device file \"keyboard\":");      /* BL  */
                                                     /* L15 */
                                                     /* BL  */
for(p = 0; p < n; p++)                               /* L16 */
  putchar(text[p]);                                  /* L17 */
                                                     /* BL  */
  return(0);                                         /* L18 */
}                                                    /* L19 */
```

Compile and execute this program.

```
Type the text. The text you type form the contents
of device file keyboard. Strike the function key
F6 to signify the end of this file.
Chavan's Street Principle # 1      ↵
Never stand behind donkey or truck.      ↵
Donkey will kick you.      ↵
Truck will reverse and crush you.      ↵
<F6>  ↵
Contents of device file "keyboard":
Chavan's Street Principle # 1
Never stand behind donkey or truck.
Donkey will kick you.
Truck will reverse and crush you.
```

How It Works

According to C, a *file* is a transmitter or receiver of a stream of characters/bytes to or from the CPU, respectively.

In an interactive program, when you type the text, the keyboard transmits a stream of characters to the central processing unit. Hence, the keyboard fits well in C's model of a file. When program sends the output to the monitor for display, the monitor receives a stream of characters from the central processing unit. Hence, the monitor also fits well in C's model of a file. As a generic term, *device file* is used to refer to a keyboard file or a monitor file.

When you read a file or write to a file, you need a pointer to the FILE variable (like fptr used in the preceding programs). Are there any predefined pointers to FILE variables (like fptr) for the device files' keyboard and monitor? Yes, there are pointers to FILE constants (instead of variables) predefined for device files, as listed in Table 6-1.

Table 6-1. *Predefined Pointers to FILE Constants for Device Files*

Pointer to FILE Constants	Device File
stdin	Keyboard
stdout	Monitor
stderr	Monitor

Both stdout and stderr specify the same device file, i.e., monitor; but these constants are used in different contexts. To display the normal text on the monitor, you use the constant stdout, whereas to display the error messages on the monitor (e.g., the file opening failed), you use the constant stderr.

In LOC 4, you declare a char type array called text, which can accommodate 500 characters. Next, consider LOC 9, which is reproduced here for your quick reference:

```
m = fgetc(stdin);                                        /* L9 */
```

This LOC, after execution, reads a character from the file specified by the pointer to the FILE constant stdin (i.e., keyboard) and returns its ASCII value, which is assigned to m. You type three lines of text, and the first line of text is given here:

```
Chavan's Street Principle # 1
```

All these characters are transmitted to the CPU only after pressing the Enter key. After the execution of LOC 9, the first character in this line of text (it is 'C') is read by the function fgetc(), and its ASCII value (it is 67) is returned, which is assigned to variable m.

Next, there is the while loop, which spans LOCs 10 to 14. LOC 10 is reproduced here for your quick reference:

```
while(m != EOF){                                         /* L10 */
```

The continuation condition of the while loop in LOC 10 states that iterations of the while loop are permitted, while m is not equal to EOF. As the value of m is 67 and not EOF, the first iteration is permitted. Next, LOC 11 is executed, which is reproduced here for your quick reference:

```
text[n] = m;                                             /* L11 */
```

In this LOC, the ASCII value of m (which is 67) is assigned to the first element of the array text. (Why the first element? The value of n is 0, which serves as the index of the array text.) As text is a char array, the character 'C' (as its ASCII value is 67) is stored in the first element of text. In LOC 12, the value of n is increased by 1, which serves as the index of the array text. Next, LOC 13 is executed, which is the same as LOC 9. In LOC 13, the next character available in the line of text (it is 'h') is read by the function fgetc(), and so on. When you strike the function key F6, then character Control-Z (its ASCII value is 26) is sent by the keyboard to the CPU. When the function fgetc() reads this character, then instead of returning its ASCII value, it returns the value EOF, and then iterations of the while loop are terminated.

Next, the for loop in LOCs 16 to 17 is executed, which displays the contents of the char array text on the screen.

6-22. Write Text to the Device File Monitor
Problem
You want to write text to the device file monitor.

Solution
Write a C program with the following specifications:

- The program implements the monitor using a pointer to the FILE constant stdout and also a pointer to the FILE constant stderr.

- The program reads the text from the text file satara.txt and writes it to the device file monitor (stdout).

- If the file opening or closing fails, then the program writes the error message to the device file monitor (stderr).

The Code
The following is the code of the C program written with these specifications. Type the following C program in a text editor and save it in the folder C:\Code with the file name files22.c:

```
/* This program reads the disk-file satara.txt and writes those */
/* contents to the device-file "monitor." */
                                                              /* BL */
#include <stdio.h>                                            /* L1 */
                                                              /* BL */
main()                                                        /* L2 */
{                                                             /* L3 */
 int m, k;                                                    /* L4 */
 FILE *fptr;                                                  /* L5 */
 fptr = fopen("C:\\Code\\satara.txt", "r");                   /* L6 */
 if (fptr != NULL){                                           /* L7 */
  puts("Disk-file kolkata.txt opened successfully.");         /* L8 */
  puts("`Its contents are now written to device file monitor:"); /* L9 */
  m = fgetc(fptr);                                            /* L10 */
                                                              /* BL */
  while(m != EOF){                                            /* L11 */
   fputc(m, stdout);                                          /* L12 */
   m = fgetc(fptr);                                           /* L13 */
  }                                                           /* L14 */
                                                              /* BL */
  k = fclose(fptr);                                           /* L15 */
  if(k == -1)                                                 /* L16 */
   fprintf(stderr, "Disk-file closing failed\n");             /* L17 */
```

```
if(k == 0)                                              /* L18 */
    puts("Disk-file closed successfully.");             /* L19 */
}                                                       /* L20 */
else                                                    /* L21 */
    fprintf(stderr, "Disk-file opening failed\n");      /* L22 */
                                                        /* BL  */
return(0);                                              /* L23 */
}                                                       /* L24 */
```

Compile and execute this program, and the following lines of text appear on the screen:

```
Disk-file satara.txt opened successfully.
Its contents are now written to device file monitor:
Satara is surrounded by mountains.
Satara was capital of Maratha empire for many years.
Disk-file closed successfully.
```

How It Works

In LOC 6, the disk file satara.txt is opened for reading. Next, consider LOC 10, which is reproduced here for your quick reference:

```
m = fgetc(fptr);                                        /* L10 */
```

In this LOC, the function fgetc() reads the first character in the file specified by fptr (it is 'S'), and its ASCII value (it is 83) is assigned to the int variable m. Next, there is a while loop that spans LOCs 11 to 14. LOC 11 is reproduced here for your quick reference:

```
while(m != EOF){                                        /* L11 */
```

LOC 11 includes the continuation condition of the while loop, which states that iterations of the while loop are permitted, while m is not equal to EOF. As the value of m is 83, and not EOF, the first iteration of the while loop is permitted. Next, LOC 12 is executed, which is reproduced here for your quick reference:

```
fputc(m, stdout);                                       /* L12 */
```

In LOC 12, the function fputc() writes the character (whose ASCII value is stored in m) to the file specified by the pointer to the FILE constant stdout, and this file is the monitor. Thus, after the execution of LOC 12, the character 'S' is displayed on the screen.

Next, LOC 13 is executed, which is the same as LOC 10. In this LOC, the function fgetc() reads the second character from the file specified by fptr, and so on. Proceeding in this manner, all the readable characters in the file are displayed on the screen.

6-23. Read Text from the Device File Keyboard and Write It to the Device File Monitor

Problem

You want to read the text from the device file keyboard and write it to the device file monitor.

Solution

Write a C program with the following specifications:

- The program implements the keyboard using a pointer to the FILE constant stdin.

- The program implements the monitor using a pointer to the FILE constant stdout.

- The program reads the text from the keyboard and writes it to the monitor.

The Code

The following is the code of the C program written with these specifications. Type the following C program in a text editor and save it in the folder C:\Code with the file name files23.c:

```
/* This program reads the device-file keyboard and writes those */
/* contents to the device-file monitor. */
                                                        /* BL */
#include <stdio.h>                                      /* L1 */
                                                        /* BL */
main()                                                  /* L2 */
{                                                       /* L3 */
 char text[500];                                        /* L4 */
 int m, n = 0, p;                                       /* L5 */
 puts("Type the text. The text you type form the contents");  /* L6 */
 puts("of the device-file keyboard. Strike the function");    /* L7 */
 puts("key F6 to signify the end of this file.");       /* L8 */
                                                        /* BL */
 m = fgetc(stdin);                                      /* L9 */
                                                        /* BL */
 while(m != EOF){                                       /* L10 */
  text[n] = m;                                          /* L11 */
  n = n + 1;                                            /* L12 */
  m = fgetc(stdin);                                     /* L13 */
 }                                                      /* L14 */
                                                        /* BL */
```

211

```
puts("Contents of the device-file keyboard are now");     /* L15 */
puts("written to the device-file monitor.");              /* L16 */
                                                          /* BL  */
for(p = 0; p < n; p++)                                     /* L17 */
  fputc(text[p], stdout);                                 /* L18 */
                                                          /* BL  */
  return(0);                                               /* L19 */
}                                                          /* L20 */
```

Compile and execute this program, and the following lines of text appear on the screen:

```
Type the text. The text you type form the contents
of the device-file keyboard. Strike the function
key F6 to signify the end of this file.
I am a born writer.      ↵
I inherited the art of writing from my country.     ↵
<F6>   ↵
Contents of the device-file keyboard are now
written into the device-file monitor.
I am a born writer.
I inherited the art of writing from my mother.
```

How It Works

During the execution of the program, the text typed by the user of the program is stored in the array text. The block of code spanning LOCs 9 to 14 reads the text from the device file keyboard and stores it in the array text. The block of code in LOCs 17 to 18 writes the text stored in the array text to the device file monitor.

CHAPTER 7

Self-Referential Structures

A self-referential structure is a structure in which one of its members is a pointer to the structure itself. The generic syntax of a self-referential structure is given here:

```
struct tag {
  member1;
  member2;
  - - - -
  struct tag *next;
};
```

Here, next is a pointer variable pointing to the structure struct tag itself. Notice the example of the self-referential structure given here:

```
struct members {
  char name[20];
  struct members *next;
};
```

7-1. Generate Lists of Numbers in an Interactive Manner
Problem

You want to generate a list of numbers in an interactive manner.

Solution

Write a C program that generates a list of numbers, with the following specifications:

- The program determines the size of the list in an interactive manner; i.e., the size of the list is not prefixed.

- The program uses the function `calloc()` to allocate the memory dynamically, which is required for the lists.

- Lists are filled with the numbers generated using a simple ad hoc formula.

The Code

The following is the code of the C program written with these specifications. Type the following C program in a text editor and save it in the folder C:\Code with the file name srs1.c:

```
/* This program uses function calloc() for dynamic allocation of memory. */

#include <stdio.h>                                                /* L1 */
                                                                  /* BL */
main()                                                            /* L2 */
{                                                                 /* L3 */
 int n, i, j;                                                     /* L4 */
 int *ptr, *list[10];                                             /* L5 */
 printf("Enter an integer as size of list (1 <= n <= 20): ");     /* L6 */
 scanf("%d", &n);                                                 /* L7 */
  for(i = 0; i < 10; i++) {                                       /* L8 */
   list[i] = (int *) calloc(n, sizeof(int));                      /* L9 */
   for(j = 0; j < n; j++)                                         /* L10 */
     *(list[i] + j) = i + j + 10;                                 /* L11 */
  }                                                               /* L12 */
                                                                  /* BL */
  printf("Displaying the values of items in list\n");             /* L13 */
   for(i = 0; i < 10; i++) {                                      /* L14 */
    printf("List[%d]: ", i);                                      /* L15 */
    for(j = 0; j < n; j++) {                                      /* L16 */
     printf("%d ", *(list[i] + j));                               /* L17 */
    }                                                             /* L18 */
   printf("\n");                                                  /* L19 */
  }                                                               /* L20 */
                                                                  /* BL */
  return(0);                                                      /* L21 */
}                                                                 /* L22 */
```

Compile and execute this program. A run of this program is given here:

```
Enter an integer as size of list (1 <= n <= 20): 20    ↵
Displaying the values of items in list
List[0]: 10 11 12 13 14 15 16 17 18 19 20 21 22 23 24 25 26 27 28 29
List[1]: 11 12 13 14 15 16 17 18 19 20 21 22 23 24 25 26 27 28 29 30
List[2]: 12 13 14 15 16 17 18 19 20 21 22 23 24 25 26 27 28 29 30 31
List[3]: 13 14 15 16 17 18 19 20 21 22 23 24 25 26 27 28 29 30 31 32
List[4]: 14 15 16 17 18 19 20 21 22 23 24 25 26 27 28 29 30 31 32 33
List[5]: 15 16 17 18 19 20 21 22 23 24 25 26 27 28 29 30 31 32 33 34
List[6]: 16 17 18 19 20 21 22 23 24 25 26 27 28 29 30 31 32 33 34 35
List[7]: 17 18 19 20 21 22 23 24 25 26 27 28 29 30 31 32 33 34 35 36
List[8]: 18 19 20 21 22 23 24 25 26 27 28 29 30 31 32 33 34 35 36 37
List[9]: 19 20 21 22 23 24 25 26 27 28 29 30 31 32 33 34 35 36 37 38
```

How It Works

The function calloc() is used for allocating memory dynamically for arrays. You can also use the function malloc() for allocating memory dynamically for arrays. But calloc() is more convenient for arrays. Unlike malloc(), the calloc() function initializes the entire allocated memory to a null character value ('\0'). Like malloc(), the calloc() function also returns a pointer to void, which points to the first byte of the allocated memory block. The generic syntax of a statement that uses the function calloc() is given here:

```
ptr = (dataType *) calloc (n, size);
```

Here, ptr is a pointer to the dataType variable; dataType is any valid data type such as int, char, float, etc.; size is an integer (or expression that evaluates to an integer) that indicates the number of bytes required for an object (e.g., if the type of array is int, then size is 2); and n is an integer (or expression that evaluates to an integer) that indicates the number of objects (e.g., if the array consists of ten elements, then n is 10). This function allocates a contiguous block of memory whose size in bytes is at least n × size. If the required memory cannot be allocated, then a NULL pointer is returned.

In LOC 5, you declare an array of pointers-to-int that consists of ten elements and is called list. This means you have ten pointers-to-int at your disposal, and you can refer to any one of them using the symbol list[i]. To every pointer, you are going to attach a list of n int type values, and the value of n will be entered by the user at runtime. LOC 7 accepts the value entered for n. LOCs 8 to 12 consist of nested for loops. In LOC 9, you allocate the memory dynamically. LOC 9 is reproduced here for your quick reference:

```
list[i] = (int *) calloc(n, sizeof(int));                           /* L9 */
```

This LOC, after execution, reserves n blocks of memory (each block consists of 2 bytes, which is the size of int) and returns a pointer that is cast to type (int *), and then it is assigned to list[i]. Now you can assign a list of n int values to the int pointer list[i]. And certainly you have assigned a list of n int values to list[i] in LOCs 10 to 11, which consist of the inner for loop that performs n iterations. Assignments are made in LOC 11, and as you can see, arbitrary values are assigned to list[i].

The values assigned to the list are displayed on the screen in LOCs 14 to 20, which consist of nested for loops.

7-2. Create a Linked List Using Anonymous Variables
Problem
You want to create a linked list using anonymous variables.

Solution
Write a C program that creates a linked list, with the following specifications:

- The program uses the anonymous variables, which are created using the function malloc().

- The program creates a structure named members. The char type array named name is a member of this structure. Suitable values are assigned to name, and these names are displayed on the screen.

The Code
The following is the code of the C program written with these specifications. Type the following C program in a text editor and save it in the folder C:\Code with the file name srs2.c:

```
/* This program implements a simple linear linked list. */
/* Function malloc() is used to create the components of list. */
                                                              /* BL */
#include <stdio.h>                                            /* L1 */
#include <stdlib.h>                                           /* L2 */
#include <string.h>                                           /* L3 */
                                                              /* BL */
struct members {                                              /* L4 */
  char name[20];                                              /* L5 */
  struct members *next;                                       /* L6 */
};                                                            /* L7 */
                                                              /* BL */
typedef struct members node;                                  /* L8 */
                                                              /* BL */
void display(node *start);                                    /* L9 */
                                                              /* BL */
main()                                                        /* L10 */
{                                                             /* L11 */
  node *start;                                                /* L12 */
                                                              /* BL */
```

216

```
start = (node *) malloc(sizeof(node));              /* L13 */
strcpy(start->name, "lina");                        /* L14 */
start->next = (node *) malloc(sizeof(node));        /* L15 */
strcpy(start->next->name, "mina");                  /* L16 */
start->next->next = (node *) malloc(sizeof(node));  /* L17 */
strcpy(start->next->next->name, "bina");            /* L18 */
start->next->next->next = (node *) malloc(sizeof(node));  /* L19 */
strcpy(start->next->next->next->name, "tina");      /* L20 */
start->next->next->next->next = NULL;               /* L21 */
                                                    /* BL  */
printf("Names of all the members:\n");              /* L22 */
display(start);                                     /* L23 */
                                                    /* BL  */
  return(0);                                        /* L24 */
}                                                   /* L25 */
                                                    /* BL  */
void display(node *start)                           /* L26 */
{                                                   /* L27 */
 int flag = 1;                                      /* L28 */
                                                    /* BL  */
 do {                                               /* L29 */
   printf("%s\n", start->name);                     /* L30 */
   if(start->next == NULL)                          /* L31 */
     flag = 0;                                      /* L32 */
   start = start->next;                             /* L33 */
 } while (flag);                                    /* L34 */
                                                    /* BL  */
 return;                                            /* L35 */
}                                                   /* L36 */
```

Compile and execute this program, and the following lines of text appear on the screen:

```
Names of all the members:
lina
mina
bina
tina
```

How It Works

First, notice the salient features of this program:

- The declaration of structure members is placed outside the function main() so that its scope is extern and any function can access it without trouble.

- Using typedef, the type named struct members is changed to node as shorter names are more convenient to pronounce and write.

Notice the block of code spanning LOCs 13 to 21. Figure 7-1 illustrates how these LOCs work; the figure consists of nine diagrams, with one diagram per LOC. The salient feature of this program is that variables of type node used here are anonymous and created with the help of the dynamic memory allocation function malloc(). This is the way linked lists are created and processed. You will rarely find the named variables in the programs creating and processing linked lists.

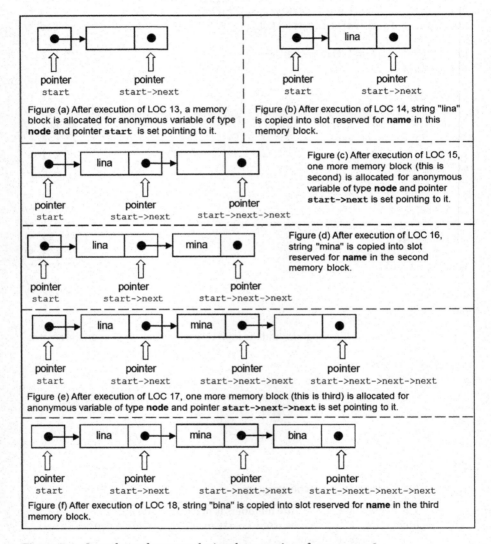

Figure (a) After execution of LOC 13, a memory block is allocated for anonymous variable of type **node** and pointer start is set pointing to it.

Figure (b) After execution of LOC 14, string "lina" is copied into slot reserved for **name** in this memory block.

Figure (c) After execution of LOC 15, one more memory block (this is second) is allocated for anonymous variable of type **node** and pointer start->next is set pointing to it.

Figure (d) After execution of LOC 16, string "mina" is copied into slot reserved for **name** in the second memory block.

Figure (e) After execution of LOC 17, one more memory block (this is third) is allocated for anonymous variable of type **node** and pointer start->next->next is set pointing to it.

Figure (f) After execution of LOC 18, string "bina" is copied into slot reserved for **name** in the third memory block.

Figure 7-1. *Snapshots of memory during the execution of program srs2*

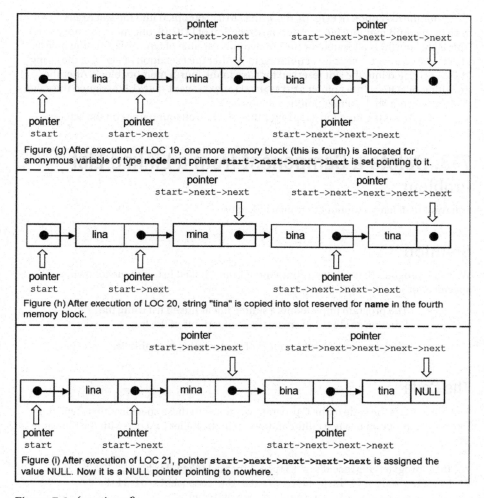

Figure (g) After execution of LOC 19, one more memory block (this is fourth) is allocated for anonymous variable of type **node** and pointer **start->next->next->next** is set pointing to it.

Figure (h) After execution of LOC 20, string "tina" is copied into slot reserved for **name** in the fourth memory block.

Figure (i) After execution of LOC 21, pointer **start->next->next->next->next** is assigned the value NULL. Now it is a NULL pointer pointing to nowhere.

Figure 7-1. (*continued*)

After the execution of LOC 13, a memory block is allocated for the anonymous variable of type node, and the pointer start is set pointing to it. After the execution of LOC 14, the string "lina" is copied into a slot reserved for name in that memory block. After the execution of LOC 15, one more memory block (this is the second) is allocated for the anonymous variable of type node, and the pointer start->next is set pointing to it. After the execution of LOC 16, the string "mina" is copied into the slot reserved for name in the second memory block. After the execution of LOC 17, one more memory block (this is the third) is allocated for the anonymous variable of type node, and the pointer start->next->next is set pointing to it.

After the execution of LOC 18, the string "bina" is copied into the slot reserved for name in the third memory block. After the execution of LOC 19, one more memory block (this is the fourth) is allocated for the anonymous variable of type node, and the pointer start->next->next->next is set pointing to it. After the execution of LOC 20, the string "tina" is copied into the slot reserved for name in the fourth memory block. After the execution of LOC 21, the pointer start->next->next->next->next is assigned the value NULL. Now it is a NULL pointer pointing to nowhere.

LOC 23 calls the function display() that displays all four names on the screen.

7-3. Delete a Component from a Linked List
Problem

You want to delete a component from a linked list.

Solution

Write a C program that deletes a component from a linked list, with the following specifications:

- The program implements a simple linear linked list using the function malloc() to create the components of the list.

- The program deletes a couple of components from this list.

The Code

The following is the code of the C program written with these specifications. Type the following C program in a text editor and save it in the folder C:\Code with the file name srs3.c:

```
/* This program implements a simple linear linked list. */   /* BL */
/* Function malloc() is used to create the components of list. */
/* Couple of components in the list are deleted. */
                                                              /* BL */
#include <stdio.h>                                            /* L1 */
#include <stdlib.h>                                           /* L2 */
#include <string.h>                                           /* L3 */
                                                              /* BL */
struct members {                                              /* L4 */
  char name[20];                                              /* L5 */
  struct members *next;                                       /* L6 */
};                                                            /* L7 */
                                                              /* BL */
typedef struct members node;                                  /* L8 */
                                                              /* BL */
void display(node *start);                                    /* L9 */
                                                              /* BL */
```

```
main()                                                          /* L10 */
{                                                               /* L11 */
  node *start, *temp = NULL;                                    /* L12 */
                                                                /* BL  */
  start = (node *) malloc(sizeof(node));                        /* L13 */
  strcpy(start->name, "lina");                                  /* L14 */
  start->next = (node *) malloc(sizeof(node));                  /* L15 */
  strcpy(start->next->name, "mina");                            /* L16 */
  start->next->next = (node *) malloc(sizeof(node));            /* L17 */
  strcpy(start->next->next->name, "bina");                      /* L18 */
  start->next->next->next = (node *) malloc(sizeof(node));      /* L19 */
  strcpy(start->next->next->next->name, "tina");                /* L20 */
  start->next->next->next->next = NULL;                         /* L21 */
                                                                /* BL  */
  printf("Names of all the members:\n");                        /* L22 */
  display(start);                                               /* L23 */
                                                                /* BL  */
  printf("\nDeleting first component - lina\n");                /* L24 */
  temp = start->next;                                           /* L25 */
  free(start);                                                  /* L26 */
  start = temp;                                                 /* L27 */
  temp = NULL;                                                  /* L28 */
  display(start);                                               /* L29 */
                                                                /* BL  */
  printf("\nDeleting non-first component - bina\n");            /* L30 */
  temp = start->next->next;                                     /* L31 */
  free(start->next);                                            /* L32 */
  start->next = temp;                                           /* L33 */
  temp = NULL;                                                  /* L34 */
  display(start);                                               /* L35 */
                                                                /* BL  */
  return(0);                                                    /* L36 */
}                                                               /* L37 */
                                                                /* BL  */
void display(node *start)                                       /* L38 */
{                                                               /* L39 */
 int flag = 1;                                                  /* L40 */
                                                                /* BL  */
 do {                                                           /* L41 */
   printf("%s\n", start->name);                                 /* L42 */
   if(start->next == NULL)                                      /* L43 */
     flag = 0;                                                  /* L44 */
   start = start->next;                                         /* L45 */
 } while (flag);                                                /* L46 */
                                                                /* BL  */
 return;                                                        /* L47 */
}                                                               /* L48 */
```

221

Compile and execute this program, and the following lines of text appear on the screen:

```
Names of all the members:
lina
mina
bina
tina
Deleting first component - lina
mina
bina
tina
Deleting non-first component - bina
mina
tina
```

How It Works

It is a salient feature of a linked list that you can insert and delete components from it easily. In an array, the deletion or insertion of an element is a troublesome task. Figure 7-2 illustrates how a component can be deleted from a list. The procedure involved in deleting the first component in a list slightly differs from that of another component in a list.

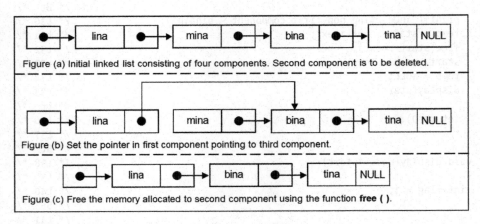

Figure (a) Initial linked list consisting of four components. Second component is to be deleted.

Figure (b) Set the pointer in first component pointing to third component.

Figure (c) Free the memory allocated to second component using the function **free ( )**.

Figure 7-2. *Generic procedure of deleting a component in a linked list*

In LOCs 13 to 21, a linked list is created that consists of four components, as shown in Figure 7-2 (a). In LOCs 25 to 28, the first component (lina) is deleted from the list. In LOCs 31 to 34, the (now) second component (bina) is deleted from the list. Figure 7-3 illustrates the process of removing the first component (lina) from the list. Figure 7-4 illustrates the process of removing the now second component (bina) from the list.

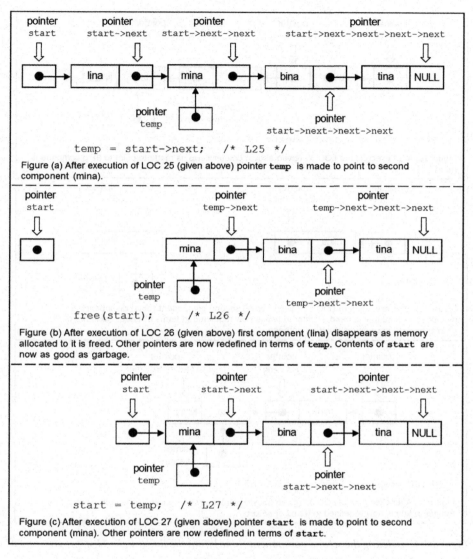

```
temp = start->next;    /* L25 */
```

Figure (a) After execution of LOC 25 (given above) pointer **temp** is made to point to second component (mina).

```
free(start);    /* L26 */
```

Figure (b) After execution of LOC 26 (given above) first component (lina) disappears as memory allocated to it is freed. Other pointers are now redefined in terms of **temp**. Contents of **start** are now as good as garbage.

```
start = temp;    /* L27 */
```

Figure (c) After execution of LOC 27 (given above) pointer **start** is made to point to second component (mina). Other pointers are now redefined in terms of **start**.

Figure 7-3. *Deleting the first component from the linear linked list, program srs3*

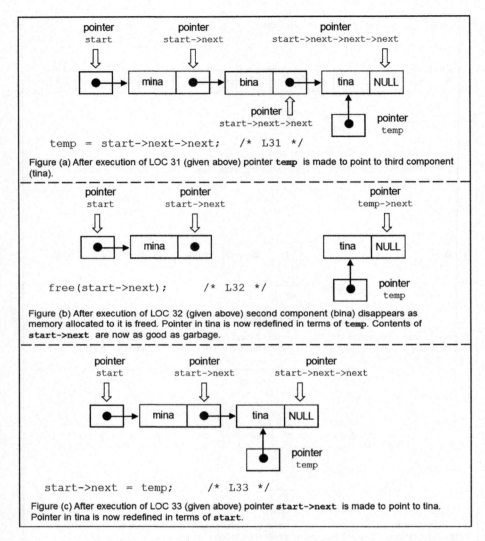

Figure 7-4. *Deleting the second component (bina) from the linear linked list, program srs3*

First, consider the removal of the first component (lina) from the list. LOCs 25 to 28 are reproduced here for your quick reference:

```
temp = start->next;                    /* L25 */
free(start);                           /* L26 */
start = temp;                          /* L27 */
temp = NULL;                           /* L28 */
```

In LOC 25, the pointer temp is made to point to the second component (mina), as shown in Figure 7-3 (a). In LOC 26, the memory allocated to the first component (lina) is freed. As a result, the first component is destroyed, as shown in Figure 7-3 (b). Now the contents of the pointer start are as good as garbage. In LOC 27, the pointer start is made to point to the (now) first component (mina), as shown in Figure 7-3 (c). The process of deletion is now complete. But the pointer temp is still pointing to the first component. A purist may object to this situation. Therefore, to pacify the purists, the pointer temp is assigned a NULL value in LOC 28. But in professional programs, you will not find LOC 28, because it is a useless burden on the performance of the program. If temp is pointing to the list, you should just ignore it.

Now consider the removal of the (now) second component (bina) from the list. LOCs 31 to 34 are reproduced here for your quick reference:

```
temp = start->next->next;                                      /* L31 */
free(start->next);                                             /* L32 */
start->next = temp;                                            /* L33 */
temp = NULL;                                                   /* L34 */
```

In LOC 31, the pointer temp is made to point to the third and last component (tina), as shown in Figure 7-4 (a). In LOC 32, the memory allocated to the second component (bina) is freed; as a result, the second component (bina) is destroyed, as shown in Figure 7-4 (b). Now the contents of the pointer in the first component (mina) are as good as garbage. In LOC 33, the pointer in the first component (mina) is made to point to the second and last component (tina), as shown in Figure 7-4 (c). Now the process of deletion is complete. But to pacify the purists, I have assigned a NULL value to temp in LOC 34. While developing professional programs, you will not use LOC 34 as it is useless burden on the performance of the program.

7-4. Insert a Component into a Linked List
Problem

You want to insert a component in a linked list.

Solution

Write a C program that inserts a component in a linked list, with the following specifications:

- The program implements a simple linear linked list using the function malloc() to create the components of the list.

- The program inserts a couple of components in this list.

The Code

The following is the code of the C program written with these specifications. Type the following C program in a text editor and save it in the folder C:\Code with the file name srs4.c:

```
/* This program implements a simple linear linked list using the function
malloc(). */
/* Couple of components are inserted in the list after creating it. */
                                                              /* BL */
#include <stdio.h>                                            /* L1 */
#include <stdlib.h>                                           /* L2 */
#include <string.h>                                           /* L3 */
                                                              /* BL */
struct members {                                             /* L4 */
  char name[20];                                              /* L5 */
  struct members *next;                                       /* L6 */
};                                                            /* L7 */
                                                              /* BL */
typedef struct members node;                                 /* L8 */
                                                              /* BL */
void display(node *start);                                   /* L9 */
                                                              /* BL */
main()                                                       /* L10 */
{                                                            /* L11 */
  node *start, *temp;                                        /* L12 */
                                                              /* BL  */
  start = (node *) malloc(sizeof(node));                     /* L13 */
  strcpy(start->name, "lina");                               /* L14 */
  start->next = (node *) malloc(sizeof(node));               /* L15 */
  strcpy(start->next->name, "mina");                         /* L16 */
  start->next->next = (node *) malloc(sizeof(node));         /* L17 */
  strcpy(start->next->next->name, "bina");                   /* L18 */
  start->next->next->next = NULL;                            /* L19 */
                                                              /* BL  */
  printf("Names of all the members:\n");                     /* L20 */
  display(start);                                            /* L21 */
                                                              /* BL  */
  printf("\nInserting sita at first position\n");            /* L22 */
  temp = (node *) malloc(sizeof(node));                      /* L23 */
  strcpy(temp->name, "sita");                                /* L24 */
  temp->next = start;                                        /* L25 */
  start = temp;                                              /* L26 */
  display(start);                                            /* L27 */
                                                              /* BL  */
  printf("\nInserting tina between lina and mina\n");        /* L28 */
  temp = (node *) malloc(sizeof(node));                      /* L29 */
  strcpy(temp->name, "tina");                                /* L30 */
```

```
   temp->next = start->next->next;                    /* L31 */
   start->next->next = temp;                          /* L32 */
   display(start);                                    /* L33 */
                                                      /* BL  */
   return(0);                                         /* L34 */
}                                                     /* L35 */
                                                      /* BL  */
void display(node *start)                             /* L36 */
{                                                     /* L37 */
 int flag = 1;                                        /* L38 */
                                                      /* BL  */
 do {                                                 /* L39 */
   printf("%s\n", start->name);                       /* L40 */
   if(start->next == NULL)                            /* L41 */
     flag = 0;                                        /* L42 */
   start = start->next;                               /* L43 */
 } while (flag);                                      /* L44 */
                                                      /* BL  */
 return;                                              /* L45 */
}                                                     /* L46 */
```

Compile and execute this program, and the following lines of text appear on the screen:

```
Names of all the members:
lina
mina
bina
Inserting sita at first position
sita
lina
mina
bina
Inserting tina between lina and mina
sita
lina
tina
mina
bina
```

How It Works

The procedure of inserting a component at the beginning of the list slightly differs from that of inserting a component elsewhere in the list. This program has dealt with both of these cases. Figure 7-5 illustrates the generic procedure of inserting a new component in a linear linked list.

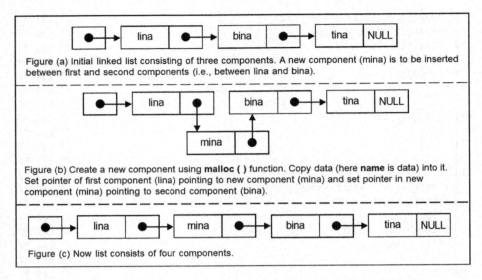

Figure (a) Initial linked list consisting of three components. A new component (mina) is to be inserted between first and second components (i.e., between lina and bina).

Figure (b) Create a new component using **malloc ( )** function. Copy data (here **name** is data) into it. Set pointer of first component (lina) pointing to new component (mina) and set pointer in new component (mina) pointing to second component (bina).

Figure (c) Now list consists of four components.

Figure 7-5. *Generic procedure of inserting a new component in a linear linked list*

A new component (sita) is inserted in the list at the beginning of the list in LOCs 23 to 26. Figure 7-6 illustrates this process. A new component (tina) is inserted in the list between the components lina and mina in LOCs 29 to 32, as illustrated in Figure 7-7.

Consider the block of code spanning LOCs 23 to 26. After the execution of LOC 23, a memory block is allocated for the anonymous variable of type node, and the pointer temp is set pointing to it, as shown in Figure 7-6 (a). After the execution of LOC 24, the string "sita" is copied into the slot reserved for name in this newly allocated memory block, as shown in Figure 7-6 (b). After the execution of LOC 25, the pointer temp->next is set pointing to the first component (lina) in the list, as shown in Figure 7-6 (c). After the execution of LOC 26, the pointer start is set pointing to the newly created component sita, as shown in Figure 7-6 (d). The pointer temp is still pointing to the component sita. A NULL value may be assigned to the pointer temp, but this affects the performance of the program slightly. It is advisable to ignore the pointer temp rather than assigning a NULL value to it.

Now consider the block of code spanning LOCs 29 to 32. After the execution of LOC 29, a memory block is allocated for the anonymous variable of type node, and the pointer temp is set pointing to it, as shown in Figure 7-7 (a). After the execution of LOC 30, a string "tina" is copied into a slot reserved for name in this newly allocated memory block, as shown in Figure 7-7 (b). After the execution of LOC 31, the pointer temp->next is set pointing to the third component (mina) in the list, as shown in Figure 7-7 (c). After the execution of LOC 32, the pointer start->next->next is set pointing to the newly created component tina, as shown in Figure 7-7 (d). The pointer temp is still pointing to the component tina. A NULL value may be assigned to the pointer temp, but this affects the performance of the program slightly (i.e., the execution time increases). It is advisable to ignore the pointer temp rather than assigning a NULL value to it.

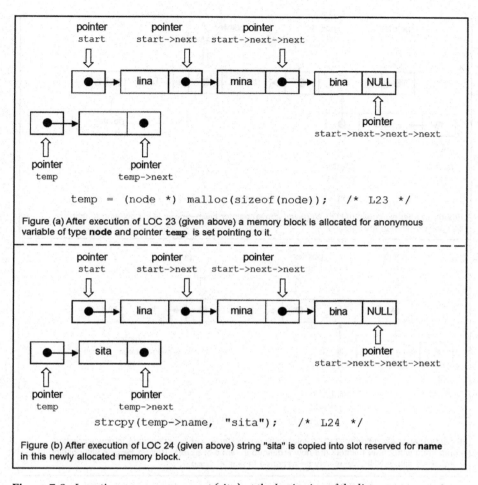

Figure (a) After execution of LOC 23 (given above) a memory block is allocated for anonymous variable of type **node** and pointer `temp` is set pointing to it.

Figure (b) After execution of LOC 24 (given above) string "sita" is copied into slot reserved for **name** in this newly allocated memory block.

Figure 7-6. *Inserting a new component (sita) at the beginning of the list, program srs4*

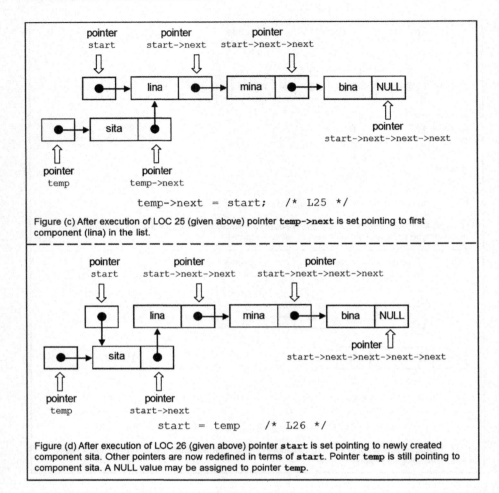

temp->next = start;   /* L25 */

Figure (c) After execution of LOC 25 (given above) pointer **temp->next** is set pointing to first component (lina) in the list.

start = temp   /* L26 */

Figure (d) After execution of LOC 26 (given above) pointer **start** is set pointing to newly created component sita. Other pointers are now redefined in terms of **start**. Pointer **temp** is still pointing to component sita. A NULL value may be assigned to pointer **temp**.

Figure 7-6. (*continued*)

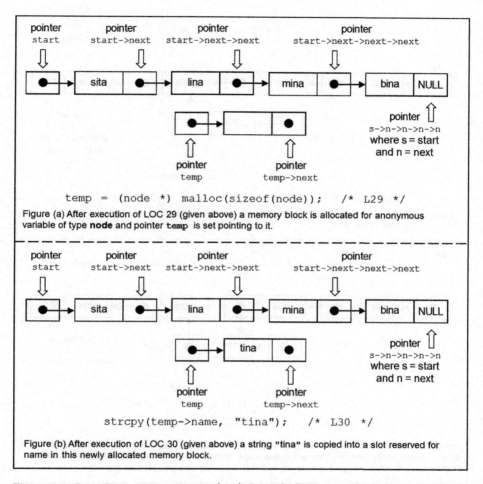

```
temp = (node *) malloc(sizeof(node));   /* L29 */
```

Figure (a) After execution of LOC 29 (given above) a memory block is allocated for anonymous variable of type **node** and pointer **temp** is set pointing to it.

```
strcpy(temp->name, "tina");   /* L30 */
```

Figure (b) After execution of LOC 30 (given above) a string "tina" is copied into a slot reserved for name in this newly allocated memory block.

Figure 7-7. *Inserting a new component (sita) not at the beginning of the list, program srs4*

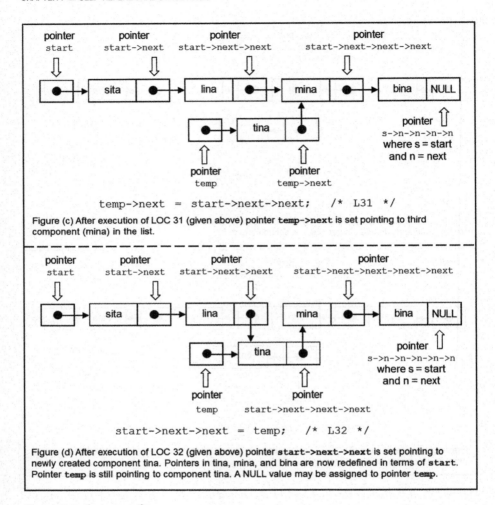

```
temp->next = start->next->next;    /* L31 */
```

Figure (c) After execution of LOC 31 (given above) pointer **temp->next** is set pointing to third
component (mina) in the list.

```
start->next->next = temp;    /* L32 */
```

Figure (d) After execution of LOC 32 (given above) pointer **start->next->next** is set pointing to
newly created component tina. Pointers in tina, mina, and bina are now redefined in terms of **start**.
Pointer **temp** is still pointing to component tina. A NULL value may be assigned to pointer **temp**.

Figure 7-7. (*continued*)

7-5. Create a Linked List in an Interactive Session

Problem

You want to create a linked list in an interactive session.

Solution

Write a C program that creates a linked list in an interactive session, with the following specifications:

- The program implements a simple linear linked list using the function malloc() to create the components of the list.

- The program accepts the data for the components entered by the user during the execution of the program and then displays this data on the screen.

The Code

The following is the code of the C program written with these specifications. Type the following C program in a text editor and save it in the folder C:\Code with the file name srs5.c:

```
/* This program implements a simple linear linked list. */     /* BL */
/* Components of list are created in interactive session. */
                                                               /* BL */
#include <stdio.h>                                             /* L1 */
#include <stdlib.h>                                            /* L2 */
#include <string.h>                                            /* L3 */
                                                               /* BL */
struct members {                                               /* L4 */
  char name[20];                                               /* L5 */
  struct members *next;                                        /* L6 */
};                                                             /* L7 */
                                                               /* BL */
typedef struct members node;                                   /* L8 */
                                                               /* BL */
void display(node *start);                                     /* L9 */
void create(node *start);                                      /* L10 */
                                                               /* BL */
main()                                                         /* L11 */
{                                                              /* L12 */
  node *start, *temp;                                          /* L13 */
                                                               /* BL */
  start = (node *) malloc(sizeof(node));                       /* L14 */
  temp = start;                                                /* L15 */
  create(start);                                               /* L16 */
                                                               /* BL */
  start = temp;                                                /* L17 */
  printf("\nNames of all the members:\n");                     /* L18 */
  display(start);                                              /* L19 */
                                                               /* BL */
  return(0);                                                   /* L20 */
}                                                              /* L21 */
```

233

```
void display(node *start)                                    /* BL  */
{                                                            /* L22 */
 int flag = 1;                                               /* L23 */
                                                             /* L24 */
                                                             /* BL  */
 do {                                                        /* L25 */
   printf("%s\n", start->name);                              /* L26 */
   if(start->next == NULL)                                   /* L27 */
     flag = 0;                                               /* L28 */
   start = start->next;                                      /* L29 */
 } while (flag);                                             /* L30 */
                                                             /* BL  */
 return;                                                     /* L31 */
}                                                            /* L32 */
                                                             /* BL  */
void create(node *start)                                     /* L33 */
{                                                            /* L34 */
 int flag = 1;                                               /* L35 */
 char ch;                                                    /* L36 */
 printf("Enter name: ");                                     /* L37 */
                                                             /* BL  */
 do {                                                        /* L38 */
   scanf(" %[^\n]", start->name);                            /* L39 */
   printf("Any more name? (y/n): ");                         /* L40 */
   scanf(" %c", &ch);                                        /* L41 */
   if(ch == 'n'){                                            /* L42 */
     flag = 0;                                               /* L43 */
     start->next = NULL;                                     /* L44 */
   }                                                         /* L45 */
   else {                                                    /* L46 */
     start->next = (node *) malloc(sizeof(node));            /* L47 */
     start = start->next;                                    /* L48 */
     printf("Enter name: ");                                 /* L49 */
   }                                                         /* L50 */
 } while (flag);                                             /* L51 */
                                                             /* BL  */
 return;                                                     /* L52 */
}                                                            /* L53 */
```

Compile and execute this program. A run of this program is given here:

```
Enter name: lina      ⏎
Any more name? (y/n): y    ⏎
Enter name: mina      ⏎
Any more name? (y/n): y    ⏎
Enter name: bina      ⏎
Any more name? (y/n): y    ⏎
```

```
Enter name: tina      ↵
Any more name? (y/n): n      ↵
Names of all the members:
lina
mina
bina
tina
```

How It Works

This is an interactive program. Professional programs that process linked lists are necessarily interactive programs. In an interactive program, the number of components a list will have is not known at compile time. Therefore, a do-while loop is used in this program, which contains the basic statements to create a new component and fill data in it. After creating a component, a user will be asked whether he or she wants to create one more component. If the user says no, then the loop is terminated; otherwise, it iterates.

As the program starts, LOC 13 is executed in which two pointer variables, start and temp, are declared of type pointer to node. In LOC 14, a memory block is allocated for the anonymous variable of type node, and the pointer start is set pointing to it, as shown in Figure 7-1 (a).

In LOC 15, the value of start is assigned to temp. This step has nothing to do with the creation of components. In LOC 15, the value of start in temp is preserved so that this preserved value can be used while making a call to the function display() in LOC 19.

In LOC 16, a call is made to the function create(). Notice the definition of the function create() given in LOCs 33 to 53. In LOCs 35 and 36 two variables are declared. In LOC 37, you are asked to enter the name for the first component. I have entered the name lina in the run given earlier. Then the do-while loop begins, and LOC 39 is executed. LOC 39 consists of a scanf() function that accepts the name entered through the keyboard for the first component and copies it into the slot reserved for name in the memory block allocated for the first component, as shown in Figure 7-1 (b). Then LOC 40 asks the user a question: Any more items? (y/n). To this question, the user replies yes by typing y. This letter is assigned to the char variable ch in LOC 41.

Then there is the if-else statement spanning LOCs 42 to 50. If the user types n as a response to the previously mentioned question, then LOCs 43 and 44 are executed, or if the user types y instead of n, LOCs 47 to 49 are executed. As the user has typed y, LOCs 47 to 49 are executed. In LOC 47, a memory block is allocated for the anonymous variable of type node, and the pointer start->next is set pointing to it, as shown in Figure 7-1 (c). In LOC 48, the pointer start is set to point to the second component in the list. The pointer in the second component is now redefined as start->next. LOC 48 resets the value of start in every iteration. Because of LOC 48, you will not find long chains like start->next->next->next->next in this program. Figure 7-1 (a) shows the snapshot of memory after the execution of LOC 48. In LOC 49, the user is asked to enter the name for the second component. The user has typed the name mina for the second component in the run given earlier.

Now the second iteration of the loop begins. Next, LOC 39 is executed in which the name typed by the user (mina) is copied into the slot reserved for name in the second component. In LOC 40, the user is asked the question: Any more items? (y/n). To this question, the user has replied yes by typing y. Consequently, computer control jumps to LOC 47 in which a memory block is allocated for the third component of the list, and the pointer start->next (which is the pointer in the second component) is made to point to this third component, as shown in Figure 7-8 (b). After the execution of LOC 48, the pointer start is made to point to the third component in the list, as shown in Figure 7-8 (c). The pointer in the third component is now redefined as start->next. In LOC 49, the user is asked to enter the name for the third component. The user has typed the name bina for the third component in the run given earlier.

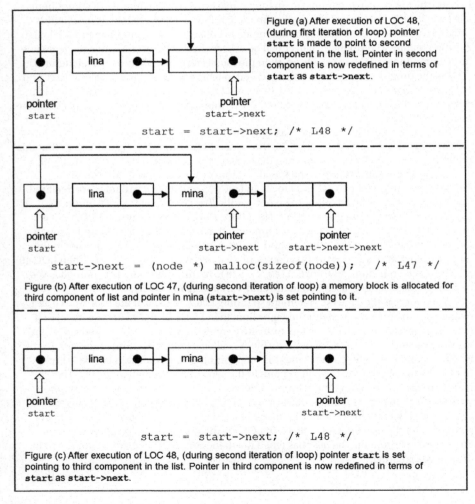

Figure (a) After execution of LOC 48, (during first iteration of loop) pointer **start** is made to point to second component in the list. Pointer in second component is now redefined in terms of **start** as **start->next**.

```
start = start->next; /* L48 */
```

```
start->next = (node *) malloc(sizeof(node)); /* L47 */
```

Figure (b) After execution of LOC 47, (during second iteration of loop) a memory block is allocated for third component of list and pointer in mina (**start->next**) is set pointing to it.

```
start = start->next; /* L48 */
```

Figure (c) After execution of LOC 48, (during second iteration of loop) pointer **start** is set pointing to third component in the list. Pointer in third component is now redefined in terms of **start** as **start->next**.

Figure 7-8. *Snapshots of memory, program srs5*

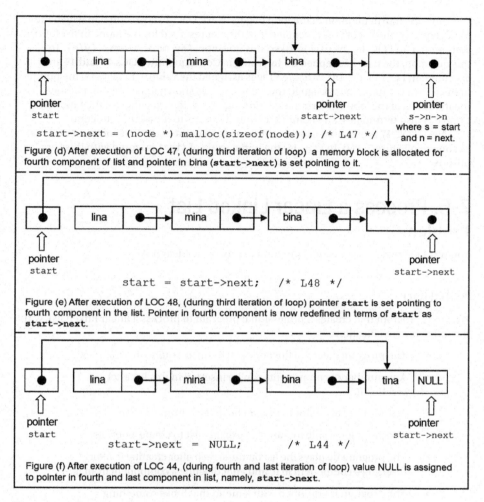

start->next = (node *) malloc(sizeof(node)); /* L47 */

where s = start
and n = next.

Figure (d) After execution of LOC 47, (during third iteration of loop) a memory block is allocated for fourth component of list and pointer in bina (**start->next**) is set pointing to it.

start = start->next;   /* L48 */

Figure (e) After execution of LOC 48, (during third iteration of loop) pointer **start** is set pointing to fourth component in the list. Pointer in fourth component is now redefined in terms of **start** as **start->next**.

start->next = NULL;   /* L44 */

Figure (f) After execution of LOC 44, (during fourth and last iteration of loop) value NULL is assigned to pointer in fourth and last component in list, namely, **start->next**.

Figure 7-8. (*continued*)

Now the third iteration of the loop begins. Next, LOC 39 is executed, in which the name typed by user (bina) is copied into the slot reserved for the name in the third component. In LOC 40, the user is asked this question: Any more items? (y/n). To this question, the user has replied yes by typing y. Consequently, computer control jumps to LOC 47, in which a memory block is allocated for the fourth component of the list, and the pointer start->next (which is the pointer in the third component) is made to point to this fourth component, as shown in Figure 7-8 (d).

After the execution of LOC 48, the pointer start is made to point to the fourth component in the list, as shown in the Figure 7-8 (e). The pointer in the fourth component is now redefined as start->next. In LOC 49, the user is asked to enter the name for the third component. The user has typed the name tina for the fourth component in the run given earlier.

Now the fourth iteration of the loop begins. Next, LOC 39 is executed in which the name typed by the user (tina) is copied into the slot reserved for the name in the fourth component. In LOC 40, the user is asked this question: Any more items? (y/n). To this question, the user has replied no by typing n. Consequently, LOCs 43 and 44 are executed. In LOC 43, the int variable flag is assigned the value 0. In LOC 44, the pointer in the fourth component is assigned the value NULL, as shown in Figure 7-8 (f). Now the iterations of the loop are terminated. Consequently, the execution of the function create() also terminates, and computer control returns to the main() function.

Next, LOC 17 is executed. Now start is made to point to the first component, lina, as shown in Figure 7-1 (i). In LOC 15, the initial value of start is stored with this very purpose.

7-6. Process a Linear Linked List
Problem

You want to create a professional program to process a linear linked list.

Solution

Write a C program that creates a professional program to process a linear linked list, with the following specifications:

- The program creates a linear linked list in an interactive manner.

- Any number of components can be inserted in this list after creating it.

- Any number of components can be deleted from this list.

- The program is able to purge an existing list to create a new list.

- The program displays the list on the screen after creating it, after inserting a component in it, and after deleting a component from it.

- The program is equipped with a menu that looks something like this:

  - Select the desired operation.

  - Enter 1 to create a new linked list.

  - Enter 2 to insert a component in the list.

  - Enter 3 to delete a component from the list.

  - Enter 4 to end the session.

  - Now enter a number (1, 2, 3, or 4).

- When the execution of the program begins, this menu appears on the screen. The user is required to enter a suitable number (1, 2, 3, or 4) to indicate his or her choice. Ideally, the user should enter 1 and then create the suitable list. When the list is created, it is displayed on the screen, and the user is taken back to this menu. Now the user can enter 2 to insert a new component in the list. Also, the user can enter 3 to delete a component from the list. The user can also enter 1 to create a new list. In such a case, an existing list is destroyed. Finally, the user can enter 4 to terminate the execution of the program.

The Code

The following is the code of the C program written with these specifications. Type the following C program in a text editor and save it in the folder C:\Code with the file name srs6.c:

```
/* This program implements a simple linear linked list with professional
quality. */
                                                        /* BL */
#include <stdio.h>                                      /* L1 */
#include <stdlib.h>                                     /* L2 */
#include <string.h>                                     /* L3 */
                                                        /* BL */
struct members {                                        /* L4 */
  char name[20];                                        /* L5 */
  struct members *next;                                 /* L6 */
};                                                      /* L7 */
                                                        /* BL */
typedef struct members node;                            /* L8 */
                                                        /* BL */
int menu(void);                                         /* L9 */
void create(node *start);                               /* L10 */
void display(node *start);                              /* L11 */
node *insert(node *start);                              /* L12 */
node *delete(node *start);                              /* L13 */
node *location(node *start, char target[]);            /* L14 */
                                                        /* BL  */
main()                                                  /* L15 */
{                                                       /* L16 */
  node *start = NULL, *temp;                            /* L17 */
  int selection;                                        /* L18 */
                                                        /* BL  */
  do {                                                  /* L19 */
    selection = menu();                                 /* L20 */
    switch(selection) {                                 /* L21 */
                                                        /* BL  */
```

```
        case 1:                                                          /* L22 */
          start = (node *) malloc(sizeof (node));                        /* L23 */
          temp = start;                                                  /* L24 */
          create(start);                                                 /* L25 */
          start = temp;                                                  /* L26 */
          display(start);                                                /* L27 */
          continue;                                                      /* L28 */
                                                                         /* BL  */
        case 2:                                                          /* L29 */
         if (start == NULL) {                                            /* L30 */
            printf("\nList is empty! Select the option 1.\n");           /* L31 */
            continue;                                                    /* L32 */
         }                                                               /* L33 */
         start = insert(start);                                          /* L34 */
         display(start);                                                 /* L35 */
         continue;                                                       /* L36 */
                                                                         /* BL  */
        case 3:                                                          /* L37 */
          if (start == NULL) {                                           /* L38 */
            printf("\nList is empty! Select the option 1.\n");           /* L39 */
            continue;                                                    /* L40 */
          }                                                              /* L41 */
          start = delete(start);                                         /* L42 */
          display(start);                                                /* L43 */
          continue;                                                      /* L44 */
                                                                         /* BL  */
        default:                                                         /* L45 */
          printf("\nEnd of session.\n");                                 /* L46 */
        }                                                                /* L47 */
    }while(selection != 4);                                              /* L48 */
                                                                         /* BL  */
   return(0);                                                            /* L49 */
}                                                                        /* L50 */
                                                                         /* BL  */
int menu(void)                                                           /* L51 */
{                                                                        /* L52 */
 int selection;                                                          /* L53 */
 do {                                                                    /* L54 */
   printf("\nSelect the desired operation:\n");                          /* L55 */
   printf("Enter 1 to create a new linked list\n");                      /* L56 */
   printf("Enter 2 to insert a component in the list\n");                /* L57 */
   printf("Enter 3 to delete a component from the list\n");              /* L58 */
   printf("Enter 4 to end the session.\n");                              /* L59 */
   printf("\nNow enter a number(1, 2, 3, or 4): ");                      /* L60 */
   scanf("%d", &selection);                                              /* L61 */
   if((selection < 1) || (selection > 4))                                /* L62 */
     printf("Invalid Number! Please try again.\n");                      /* L63 */
```

```
  }while((selection < 1) || (selection > 4));    /* L64 */
  return(selection);                             /* L65 */
}                                                /* L66 */
                                                 /* BL  */
void create(node *start)                         /* L67 */
{                                                /* L68 */
 int flag = 1;                                   /* L69 */
 char ch;                                        /* L70 */
 printf("Enter name: ");                         /* L71 */
                                                 /* BL  */
  do {                                           /* L72 */
    scanf(" %[^\n]", start->name);               /* L73 */
    printf("Any more name?(y/n): ");             /* L74 */
    scanf(" %c", &ch);                           /* L75 */
    if(ch == 'n'){                               /* L76 */
      flag = 0;                                  /* L77 */
      start->next = NULL;                        /* L78 */
    }                                            /* L79 */
    else {                                       /* L80 */
      start->next = (node *) malloc(sizeof(node)); /* L81 */
      start = start->next;                       /* L82 */
      printf("Enter name: ");                    /* L83 */
    }                                            /* L84 */
  } while (flag);                                /* L85 */
                                                 /* BL  */
  return;                                        /* L86 */
}                                                /* L87 */
                                                 /* BL  */
void display(node *start)                        /* L88 */
{                                                /* L89 */
 int flag = 1;                                   /* L90 */
 if (start == NULL){                             /* L91 */
    printf("\nList is empty! Select the option 1.\n"); /* L92 */
    return;                                      /* L93 */
 }                                               /* L94 */
 printf("\nNames of all the members in the list:\n"); /* L95 */
                                                 /* BL  */
  do {                                           /* L96 */
    printf("%s\n", start->name);                 /* L97 */
    if(start->next == NULL)                      /* L98 */
      flag = 0;                                  /* L99 */
    start = start->next;                         /* L100 */
  } while (flag);                                /* L101 */
                                                 /* BL  */
  return;                                        /* L102 */
}                                                /* L103 */
                                                 /* BL  */
```

```
node *insert(node *start)                                    /* L104 */
{                                                            /* L105 */
 int flag = 1;                                               /* L106 */
 node *new, *before, *tmp;                                   /* L107 */
 char newName[20];                                           /* L108 */
 char target[20];                                            /* L109 */
                                                             /* L110 */
 printf("Enter name to be inserted: ");                      /* L111 */
 scanf(" %[^\n]", newName);                                  /* L112 */
 printf("Before which name to place? Type \"last\" if last: ");  /* L113 */
 scanf(" %[^\n]", target);                                   /* L114 */
                                                             /* Bl   */
 if(strcmp(target, "last") == 0) {                           /* L115 */
  tmp = start;                                               /* L116 */
                                                             /* BL   */
  do{                                                        /* L117 */
     start = start->next;                                    /* L118 */
     if(start->next == NULL){                                /* L119 */
     new = (node *)malloc(sizeof(node));                     /* L120 */
     strcpy(new->name, newName);                             /* L121 */
     start->next = new;                                      /* L122 */
     new->next = NULL;                                       /* L123 */
     flag = 0;                                               /* L124 */
     }                                                       /* L125 */
  }while(flag);                                              /* L126 */
                                                             /* BL   */
  start = tmp;                                               /* L127 */
  return(start);                                             /* L128 */
 }                                                           /* L129 */
                                                             /* BL   */
 if(strcmp(start->name, target) == 0) {                      /* L130 */
  new = (node *)malloc(sizeof(node));                        /* L131 */
  strcpy(new->name, newName);                                /* L132 */
  new->next = start;                                         /* L133 */
  start = new;                                               /* L134 */
 }                                                           /* L135 */
 else {                                                      /* L136 */
  before = location(start, target);                          /* L137 */
  if (before == NULL)                                        /* L138 */
    printf("\nInvalid entry! Please try again\n");           /* L139 */
  else {                                                     /* L140 */
    new = (node *)malloc(sizeof(node));                      /* L141 */
    strcpy(new->name, newName);                              /* L142 */
    new->next = before->next;                                /* L143 */
    before->next = new;                                      /* L144 */
  }                                                          /* L145 */
 }                                                           /* L146 */
```

```
  return(start);                                          /* L147 */
}                                                         /* L148 */
                                                          /* BL   */
node *delete(node *start)                                 /* L149 */
{                                                         /* L150 */
 node *before, *tmp;                                      /* L151 */
 char target[20];                                         /* L152 */
                                                          /* BL   */
 printf("\nEnter name to be deleted: ");                  /* L153 */
 scanf(" %[^\n]", target);                                /* L154 */
                                                          /* BL   */
 if(strcmp(start->name, target) == 0)                     /* L155 */
    if(start->next == NULL){                              /* L156 */
      free(start);                                        /* L157 */
      start = NULL;                                       /* L158 */
    }                                                     /* L159 */
    else                                                  /* L160 */
   {                                                      /* L161 */
     tmp = start->next;                                   /* L162 */
     free(start);                                         /* L163 */
     start = tmp;                                         /* L164 */
   }                                                      /* L165 */
 else {                                                   /* L166 */
  before = location(start, target);                       /* L167 */
  if(before == NULL)                                      /* L168 */
    printf("\nInvalid entry. Please try again.\n");       /* L169 */
  else {                                                  /* L170 */
    tmp = before->next->next;                             /* L171 */
    free(before->next);                                   /* L172 */
    before->next = tmp;                                   /* L173 */
  }                                                       /* L174 */
 }                                                        /* L175 */
 return(start);                                           /* L176 */
}                                                         /* L177 */
                                                          /* BL   */
node *location(node *start, char target[])                /* L178 */
{                                                         /* L179 */
 int flag = 1;                                            /* L180 */
 if(strcmp(start->next->name, target) == 0)               /* L181 */
   return(start);                                         /* L182 */
 else if(start->next == NULL)                             /* L183 */
     return(NULL);                                        /* L184 */
 else {                                                   /* L185 */
                                                          /* BL   */
  do{                                                     /* L186 */
    start = start->next;                                  /* L187 */
    if(strcmp(start->next->name, target) == 0)            /* L188 */
     return(start);                                       /* L189 */
```

```
    if(start->next == NULL){                                    /* L190 */
      flag = 0;                                                 /* L191 */
      printf("Invalid entry. Please try again.\n");             /* L192 */
    }                                                           /* L193 */
  }while(flag);                                                 /* L194 */
                                                                /* BL   */
  }                                                             /* L195 */
  return(NULL);                                                 /* L196 */
}                                                               /* L197 */
```

Compile and execute this program. A run of this program is given here:

```
Select the desired operation:
Enter 1 to create a new linked list
Enter 2 to insert a component in the list
Enter 3 to delete a component from the list
Enter 4 to end the session.
Now enter a number (1, 2, 3, or 4): 1    ↵
Enter name: lina    ↵
Any more name?(y/n): y    ↵
Enter name: mina    ↵
Any more name?(y/n): y    ↵
Enter name: bina    ↵
Any more name?(y/n): y    ↵
Enter name: tina    ↵
Any more name?(y/n): n    ↵
Names of all the members in the list:
lina
mina
bina
tina
Select the desired operation:
Enter 1 to create a new linked list
Enter 2 to insert a component in the list
Enter 3 to delete a component from the list
Enter 4 to end the session.
Now enter a number (1, 2, 3, or 4): 2    ↵
Enter name to be inserted: sita    ↵
Before which name to place? Type "last" if last: lina    ↵
Names of all the members in the list:
sita
lina
mina
bina
tina
```

```
Select the desired operation:
Enter 1 to create a new linked list
Enter 2 to insert a component in the list
Enter 3 to delete a component from the list
Enter 4 to end the session.
Now enter a number (1, 2, 3, or 4): 2      ↵
Enter name to be inserted: gita     ↵
Before which name to place? Type "last" if last: bina     ↵
Names of all the members in the list:
sita
lina
mina
gita
bina
tina
Select the desired operation:
Enter 1 to create a new linked list
Enter 2 to insert a component in the list
Enter 3 to delete a component from the list
Enter 4 to end the session.
Now enter a number (1, 2, 3, or 4): 2      ↵
Enter name to be inserted: rita     ↵
Before which name to place? Type "last" if last: last      ↵
Names of all the members in the list:
sita
lina
mina
gita
bina
tina
rita
Select the desired operation:
Enter 1 to create a new linked list
Enter 2 to insert a component in the list
Enter 3 to delete a component from the list
Enter 4 to end the session.
Now enter a number (1, 2, 3, or 4): 3      ↵
Enter name to be deleted: sita     ↵
Names of all the members in the list:
lina
mina
gita
bina
tina
rita
```

```
Select the desired operation:
Enter 1 to create a new linked list
Enter 2 to insert a component in the list
Enter 3 to delete a component from the list
Enter 4 to end the session.
Now enter a number (1, 2, 3, or 4): 3      ↲
Enter name to be deleted: rita     ↲
Names of all the members in the list:
lina
mina
gita
bina
tina
Select the desired operation:
Enter 1 to create a new linked list
Enter 2 to insert a component in the list
Enter 3 to delete a component from the list
Enter 4 to end the session.
Now enter a number (1, 2, 3, or 4): 3      ↲
Enter name to be deleted: mina      ↲
Names of all the members in the list:
lina
gita
bina
tina
Select the desired operation:
Enter 1 to create a new linked list
Enter 2 to insert a component in the list
Enter 3 to delete a component from the list
Enter 4 to end the session.
Now enter a number (1, 2, 3, or 4): 1      ↲
Enter name: dick     ↲
Any more name?(y/n): y      ↲
Enter name: tom     ↲
Any more name?(y/n): y      ↲
Enter name: harry      ↲
Any more name?(y/n): n      ↲
Names of all the members in the list:
dick
tom
harry
Select the desired operation:
Enter 1 to create a new linked list
Enter 2 to insert a component in the list
Enter 3 to delete a component from the list
Enter 4 to end the session.
```

```
Now enter a number (1, 2, 3, or 4): 3      ↵
Enter name to be deleted: tom     ↵
Names of all the members in the list:
dick
harry
Select the desired operation:
Enter 1 to create a new linked list
Enter 2 to insert a component in the list
Enter 3 to delete a component from the list
Enter 4 to end the session.
Now enter a number (1, 2, 3, or 4): 3      ↵
Enter name to be deleted: dick      ↵
Names of all the members in the list:
harry
Select the desired operation:
Enter 1 to create a new linked list
Enter 2 to insert a component in the list
Enter 3 to delete a component from the list
Enter 4 to end the session.
Now enter a number (1, 2, 3, or 4): 3      ↵
Enter name to be deleted: harry      ↵
List is empty! Select the option 1.
Select the desired operation:
Enter 1 to create a new linked list
Enter 2 to insert a component in the list
Enter 3 to delete a component from the list
Enter 4 to end the session.
Now enter a number (1, 2, 3, or 4): 4      ↵
End of session.
```

How It Works

This program consists of six user-defined functions. This is how they work:

- menu(): This function displays the menu. It takes no argument and returns an int value. It is defined in LOCs 51 to 66.

- create(): This function creates a linked list. It expects the pointer start as an argument. It returns no value. It is defined in LOCs 67 to 87.

- display(): This function displays the components in the linked list on the screen. It is defined in LOCs 88 to 103.

- `insert()`: This function inserts a new component in a linked list. It expects the pointer `start` (which is a pointer to the first component in the list) as an argument. After making the successful insertion, it returns the pointer `start` (it is modified after insertion, if the insertion is made at the beginning of the list). It is defined in LOCs 104 to 148. LOCs 116 to 128 handle the case in which a new component is to be inserted last. LOCs 131 to 134 handle the case in which a new component is to be inserted at the beginning of the list. LOCs 137 to 147 handle the case in which a new component is to be inserted elsewhere. In this last case (i.e., insertion elsewhere), a call is made to the function `location()`, which returns a pointer to a component before the target component.

- `delete()`: This function deletes a component in the linked list. It is defined in LOCs 149 to 177. It expects the pointer `start` (which is a pointer to the first component in the list) as an argument. After making the successful deletion, it returns the pointer `start` (it is modified after deletion, if the first component in the list is deleted). LOCs 156 to 165 handle the case in which a first component in the list is to be deleted. In this case, two subcases arise: (a) when the list contains only one component and (b) when the list contains two or more components. LOCs 157 to 158 handle the first subcase, and LOCs 162 to 164 handle the second subcase. LOCs 167 to 174 handle the case in which a nonfirst component in the list is to be deleted. In this piece of code, (a) a call is made to the function `location()` in the LOC 167, (b) LOCs 168 to 169 handle the case in which an invalid entry is made, and (c) LOCs 171 to 173 handle the case in which the successful deletion of the nonfirst component is to be made.

- `location()`: This function is called by the functions `insert()` and `delete()`. It expects the pointer `start` (which is a pointer to the first component in the list) and a `char` string (which consists of the name of the component, such as `lina`, `mina`, etc.) as arguments. It returns a pointer to node. It is defined in LOCs 178 to 197. If the name of the (n + 1)th component is passed to this function as an argument, then it returns a pointer to the nth component. For example, if the string `"mina"` is passed as an argument, then it returns a pointer to the component `lina`. The name of the first component is never passed to this function as an argument.

7-7. Create a Linear Linked List with Forward and Backward Traversing

Problem

You want to create a linked list with forward and backward traversing.

Solution

Write a C program that creates a linked list with forward and backward traversing, with the following specifications:

- The program implements a linear linked list and fills the components of the list with suitable data.

- The program consists of two functions, namely, showforward() and showbackward(); these functions display the data in the components on the screen using forward and backward traversing, respectively.

The Code

The following is the code of the C program written with these specifications. Type the following C program in a text editor and save it in the folder C:\Code with the file name srs7.c:

```
/* This program implements a linear linked list with forward */
/* and backward traversing. */
                                                          /* BL */
#include <stdio.h>                                        /* L1 */
#include <string.h>                                       /* L2 */
                                                          /* BL */
struct members {                                          /* L3 */
  char name[20];                                          /* L4 */
  struct members *forward, *backward;                     /* L5 */
};                                                        /* L6 */
                                                          /* BL */
typedef struct members node;                              /* L7 */
                                                          /* BL */
void showforward(node *start);                            /* L8 */
void showbackward(node *end);                             /* L9 */
                                                          /* BL */
main()                                                    /* L10 */
{                                                         /* L11 */
  node m1, m2, m3, *start, *end;                          /* L12 */
                                                          /* BL */
```

```
  strcpy(m1.name, "lina");                                    /* L13 */
  strcpy(m2.name, "mina");                                    /* L14 */
  strcpy(m3.name, "bina");                                    /* L15 */
                                                              /* BL  */
  start = &m1;                                                /* L16 */
  start->forward = &m2;                                       /* L17 */
  start->forward->forward = &m3;                              /* L18 */
  start->forward->forward->forward = NULL;                    /* L19 */
                                                              /* BL  */
  end = &m3;                                                  /* L20 */
  end->backward = &m2;                                        /* L21 */
  end->backward->backward = &m1;                              /* L22 */
  end->backward->backward->backward = NULL;                   /* L23 */
                                                              /* BL  */
  printf("Names of members (forward traversing):\n");         /* L24 */
  showforward(start);                                         /* L25 */
  printf("\nNames of members (backward traversing):\n");      /* L26 */
  showbackward(end);                                          /* BL  */
  return(0);                                                  /* L27 */
}                                                             /* L28 */
                                                              /* BL  */
void showforward(node *start)                                 /* L29 */
{                                                             /* L30 */
 int flag = 1;                                                /* L31 */
                                                              /* BL  */
 do {                                                         /* L32 */
   printf("%s\n", start->name);                               /* L33 */
   if(start->forward == NULL)                                 /* L34 */
     flag = 0;                                                /* L35 */
   start = start->forward;                                    /* L36 */
  } while (flag);                                             /* L37 */
                                                              /* BL  */
 return;                                                      /* L38 */
}                                                             /* L39 */
                                                              /* BL  */
void showbackward(node *end)                                  /* L40 */
{                                                             /* L41 */
 int flag = 1;                                                /* L42 */
                                                              /* BL  */
 do {                                                         /* L43 */
   printf("%s\n", end->name);                                 /* L44 */
   if(end->backward == NULL)                                  /* L45 */
     flag = 0;                                                /* L46 */
   end = end->backward;                                       /* L47 */
  } while (flag);                                             /* L48 */
                                                              /* BL  */
 return;                                                      /* L49 */
}                                                             /* L50 */
```

Compile and execute this program, and the following lines of text appear on the screen:

```
Names of members (forward traversing):
lina
mina
bina
Names of members (backward traversing):
bina
mina
lina
```

How It Works

In this program, a linear linked list is implemented with the provision of forward and backward traversing. Figure 7-9 shows a typical linear linked list with forward and backward traversing.

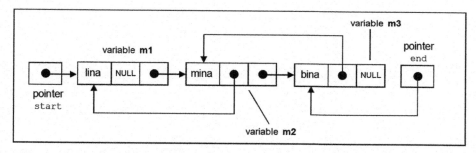

Figure 7-9. *A linear linked list with forward and backward traversing, program srs7*

In this program, the structure member consists of two pointers to the parent type (see LOC 6): forward (which is the same as the next pointer in the preceding programs) and backward. Also, in the program, two pointers to node are declared, namely, start and end. The pointer start is associated with the pointer forward, and the pointer end is associated with the pointer backward. The logic behind traversing the components in the list is the same as in the preceding programs. For forward traversing, you start with the pointer start and then march ahead with the help of the pointer forward in each component. For backward traversing, you start with the pointer end and then march backward with the help of the pointer backward in each component. The function showforward() displays the names of members using forward traversing, and the function showbackward() displays the names of members using backward traversing. It is possible to write a single function for both types of traversing, but to keep the things simple, I have gone for two separate functions.

CHAPTER 8

Stacks and Queues

A *stack* is an abstract data structure. Specifically, a stack is a list of elements in which you can insert the elements and also delete the elements from it. This list is open at one end and closed at the other end. The operations of insertion and deletion can be done only from the open end. A stack is also called a last in first out (LIFO) data structure. A stack of dishes in a cafeteria is an example of LIFO. In this stack, the waiter places (inserts) the dishes at the top of the stack, and customers take (delete) the dishes from the top of the stack.

The operations of inserting and deleting elements from the stack are called *pushing* and *popping* in technical jargon, respectively.

Note   The term *push* indicates the insertion of an element into a stack. The term *pop* indicates the deletion of an element from a stack.

Stacks can be implemented in terms of arrays and linked lists. Some of the applications of stacks are listed here:

- Conversion of an algebraic expression from one form to another. Generally, the forms are infix expression, prefix expression, and postfix expression.

- Evaluation of an algebraic expression.

- Storage of variables when a function is called.

- Reversal of a string.

A queue is also an abstract data structure somewhat analogous to a stack. However, unlike a stack, a queue is open at both ends. One end is called the *front end*, and other end is called the *rear end*. Insertion is done at the rear end, and deletion is done at the front end. A queue is also known as a first in first out (FIFO) data structure. A circular queue is a special type of queue in which the front end is joined to the rear end.

© Shirish Chavan 2017
S. Chavan, *C Recipes*, DOI 10.1007/978-1-4842-2967-5_8

A queue can be implemented in terms of arrays and linked lists. Queues are used in the following cases:

- In printing machines, to print the files standing in a queue

- To access the files from a secondary storage system

- In an operating system, for scheduling jobs waiting for their turn

- In a ticket reservation system that consists of multiple reservation counters at different locations

- While implementing a breadth-first traversal of a graph

8-1. Implement a Stack as an Array
Problem

You want to implement a stack as an array.

Solution

Write a C program that implements a stack as an array, with the following specifications:

- The program defines four functions: stackMenu(), displayStack(), popItem(), and pushItem(). The purpose of stackMenu() is to display a menu on the screen that offers choices for users. The purpose of displayStack() is to display the elements stored in a stack on the screen. The purpose of popItem() is to pop the element from the stack. The purpose of pushItem() is to push the item into the stack.

- The elements to be pushed into the stack are int type data values. The maximum capacity of this stack is eight elements only.

- A stack is an array of int values.

The Code

The following is the code of the C program written with these specifications. Type the following C program in a text editor and save it in the folder C:\Code with the file name stack1.c:

```
/* This program implements a stack in terms of array. */
                                                        /* BL */
# include <stdio.h>                                     /* L1 */
# include <stdlib.h>                                    /* L2 */
# define STACKSIZE 8                                    /* L3 */
                                                        /* BL */
```

```
int stack[STACKSIZE];                                              /* L4 */
int intTop = 0;                                                    /* L5 */
int stackMenu(void);                                               /* L6 */
void displayStack(void);                                           /* L7 */
void popItem(void);                                                /* L8 */
void pushItem(void);                                               /* L9 */
                                                                   /* BL */
void main()                                                        /* L10 */
{                                                                  /* L11 */
  int intChoice;                                                   /* L12 */
  do {                       /* do-while statement begins */       /* L13 */
    intChoice = stackMenu();                                       /* L14 */
    switch(intChoice) {      /* switch statement begins */         /* L15 */
      case 1:                                                      /* L16 */
        pushItem();                                                /* L17 */
        break;                                                     /* L18 */
      case 2:                                                      /* L19 */
        popItem();                                                 /* L20 */
        break;                                                     /* L21 */
      case 3:                                                      /* L22 */
        displayStack();                                            /* L23 */
        break;                                                     /* L24 */
      case 4:                                                      /* L25 */
        exit(0);                                                   /* L26 */
    }                        /* switch statement ends */           /* L27 */
    fflush(stdin);                                                 /* L28 */
  } while(1);                /* do-while statement begins */        /* L29 */
}                                                                  /* L30 */
                                                                   /* BL  */
int stackMenu()                                                    /* L31 */
{                                                                  /* L32 */
  int intChoice;                                                   /* L33 */
  printf("\n\n Enter 1 to Push an Element onto Stack. ");          /* L34 */
  printf("\n Enter 2 to Pop an Element from Stack. ");             /* L35 */
  printf("\n Enter 3 to Displays the Stack on the Screen.");       /* L36 */
  printf("\n Enter 4 to Stop the Execution of Program.");          /* L37 */
  printf("\n Enter your choice (0 <= N <= 4): ");                  /* L38 */
  scanf("%d", &intChoice);                                         /* L39 */
  return intChoice;                                                /* L40 */
}                                                                  /* L41 */
                                                                   /* BL*/
void displayStack()                                                /* L42 */
{                                                                  /* L43 */
  int j;                                                           /* L44 */
  if(intTop == 0) {                                                /* L45 */
    printf("\n\nStack is Exhausted.");                             /* L46 */
    return;                                                        /* L47 */
  }                                                                /* L48 */
```

```
  else {                                                  /* L49 */
    printf("\n\nElements in stack:");                     /* L50 */
    for(j=intTop-1; j > -1; j--)                          /* L51 */
    printf("\n%d", stack[j]);                             /* L52 */
  }                                                       /* L53 */
}                                                         /* L54 */
                                                          /* BL  */
void popItem()                                            /* L55 */
{                                                         /* L56 */
  if(intTop == 0) {                                       /* L57 */
    printf("\n\nStack is Exhausted.");                    /* L58 */
    return;                                               /* L59 */
  }                                                       /* L60 */
  else                                                    /* L61 */
    printf("\n\nPopped Element: %d ", stack[--intTop]);   /* L62 */
}                                                         /* L63 */
                                                          /* BL  */
void pushItem()                                           /* L64 */
{                                                         /* L65 */
  int intData;                                            /* L66 */
  if(intTop == STACKSIZE) {                               /* L67 */
    printf("\n\nStack is Completely Filled.");            /* L68 */
    return;                                               /* L69 */
  }                                                       /* L70 */
  else {                                                  /* L71 */
    printf("\n\nEnter Element K (0 <= K <= 30000) : ");   /* L72 */
    scanf("%d", &intData);                                /* L73 */
    stack[intTop] = intData;                              /* L74 */
    intTop = intTop + 1;                                  /* L75 */
    printf("\n\nElement Pushed into the stack");          /* L76 */
  }                                                       /* L77 */
}                                                         /* L78 */
```

Compile and execute this program. A run of this program is given here:

```
Enter 1 to Push an Element into Stack.
Enter 2 to Pop an Element from Stack.
Enter 3 to Display the Stack on the Screen.
Enter 4 to Stop the Execution of the Program.
Enter your choice (0 <= N <= 4): 1    ↵

Enter Element K (0 <= N < 30000): 2468    ↵

Enter 1 to Push an Element into Stack.
Enter 2 to Pop an Element from Stack.
Enter 3 to Display the Stack on the Screen.
Enter 4 to Stop the Execution of the Program.
Enter your choice (0 <= N <= 4): 1    ↵
```

```
Enter Element K (0 <= N < 30000): 3200   ↵

Enter 1 to Push an Element into Stack.
Enter 2 to Pop an Element from Stack.
Enter 3 to Display the Stack on the Screen.
Enter 4 to Stop the Execution of the Program.
Enter your choice (0 <= N <= 4): 1   ↵

Enter Element K (0 <= N < 30000): 4555   ↵

Enter 1 to Push an Element into Stack.
Enter 2 to Pop an Element from Stack.
Enter 3 to Display the Stack on the Screen.
Enter 4 to Stop the Execution of the Program.
Enter your choice (0 <= N <= 4): 3   ↵

Elements in Stack:
4555
3200
2468

Enter 1 to Push an Element into Stack.
Enter 2 to Pop an Element from Stack.
Enter 3 to Display the Stack on the Screen.
Enter 4 to Stop the Execution of the Program.
Enter your choice (0 <= N <= 4): 2   ↵

Popped Element: 4555

Enter 1 to Push an Element into Stack.
Enter 2 to Pop an Element from Stack.
Enter 3 to Display the Stack on the Screen.
Enter 4 to Stop the Execution of the Program.
Enter your choice (0 <= N <= 4): 3   ↵

Elements in Stack:
3200
2468

Enter 1 to Push an Element into Stack.
Enter 2 to Pop an Element from Stack.
Enter 3 to Display the Stack on the Screen.
Enter 4 to Stop the Execution of the Program.
Enter your choice (0 <= N <= 4): 4   ↵
```

How It Works

This program defines four functions: stackMenu(), displayStack(), popItem(), and pushItem(). LOCs 31 to 41 define the function stackMenu(). LOCs 42 to 54 define the function displayStack(). LOCs 55 to 63 define the function popItem(). LOCs 64 to 78 define the function pushItem(). The array stack and variable intTop are placed outside of any function so that their scope should be global. Almost all the code in the main() function is placed in a do-while loop so that these LOCs can be executed repeatedly with convenience. In LOC 14, a call is made to the function stackMenu(). This function displays the menu before the user and asks him or her to enter a choice. The choices are as follows: enter 1 to push an element into a stack, enter 2 to pop an item from a stack, enter 3 to display the stack on the screen, and enter 4 to stop the execution of the program. The choice entered by the user is returned by the stackMenu() function, and it is assigned to the int variable intChoice. LOCs 15 to 27 consist of a switch statement. The value stored in intChoice is passed to this switch statement. Depending upon the value of intChoice, the switch statement calls the concerned function. For choice 1, the function pushItem() is called. For choice 2, the function popItem() is called. For choice 3, the function displayStack() is called. For choice 4, the function exit() is called that terminates the execution of the program.

8-2. Implement a Stack as a Linked List
Problem

You want to implement a stack as a linked list.

Solution

Write a C program that implements a stack as a linked list, with the following specifications:

- The program defines five functions: getnode(), stackMenu(), displayStack(), popItem(), and pushItem(). The purpose of stackMenu() is to display a menu on the screen that offers choices for users. The purpose of displayStack() is to display the elements stored in a stack on the screen. The purpose of popItem() is to pop the element from the stack. The purpose of pushItem() is to push the item into the stack.

- The elements to be pushed into the stack are int type data values. The maximum capacity of this stack is eight elements only.

- Implement the stack as a linked list of int values.

The Code

The following is the code of the C program written with these specifications. Type the following C program in a text editor and save it in the folder C:\Code with the file name stack2.c:

```
/* This program implements a stack in terms of a linked list. */
                                                            /* BL */
# include <stdio.h>                                         /* L1 */
# include <stdlib.h>                                        /* L2 */
                                                            /* BL */
struct intStack                                             /* L3 */
{                                                           /* L4 */
  int element;                                              /* L5 */
  struct intStack *next;                                    /* L6 */
};                                                          /* L7 */
typedef struct intStack node;                               /* L8 */
node *begin=NULL;                                           /* L9 */
node *top = NULL;                                           /* L10 */
                                                            /* BL */
node* getnode()                                             /* L11 */
{                                                           /* L12 */
  node *temporary;                                          /* L13 */
  temporary=(node *) malloc( sizeof(node)) ;                /* L14 */
  printf("\nEnter Element (0 <= N <= 30000): ");            /* L15 */
  scanf("%d", &temporary -> element);                       /* L16 */
  temporary -> next = NULL;                                 /* L17 */
  return temporary;                                         /* L18 */
}                                                           /* L19 */
                                                            /* BL  */
void pushItem(node *newnode)                                /* L20 */
{                                                           /* L21 */
  node *temporary;                                          /* L22 */
  if( newnode == NULL ) {                                   /* L23 */
    printf("\nThe Stack is Completely Fillled");            /* L24 */
    return;                                                 /* L25 */
  }                                                         /* L26 */
  if(begin == NULL) {                                       /* L27 */
     begin = newnode;                                       /* L28 */
     top = newnode;                                         /* L29 */
  }                                                         /* L30 */
  else {                                                    /* L31 */
    temporary = begin;                                      /* L32 */
    while( temporary -> next != NULL)                       /* L33 */
      temporary = temporary -> next;                        /* L34 */
    temporary -> next = newnode;                            /* L35 */
    top = newnode;                                          /* L36 */
  }                                                         /* L37 */
```

```
  printf("\nElement is pushed into the Stack");      /* L38 */
}                                                     /* L39 */
                                                      /* BL */
void popItem()                                        /* L40 */
{                                                     /* L41 */
  node *temporary;                                    /* L42 */
  if(top == NULL) {                                   /* L43 */
    printf("\nStack is Exhausted");                   /* L44 */
    return;                                           /* L45 */
  }                                                   /* L46 */
  temporary = begin;                                  /* L47 */
  if( begin -> next == NULL) {                        /* L48 */
    printf("\nPopped Element is: %d ", top -> element); /* L49 */
    begin = NULL;                                     /* L50 */
    free(top);                                        /* L51 */
    top = NULL;                                       /* L52 */
  }                                                   /* L53 */
  else {                                              /* L54 */
    while(temporary -> next != top) {                 /* L55 */
      temporary = temporary -> next;                  /* L56 */
    }                                                 /* L57 */
    temporary -> next = NULL;                         /* L58 */
    printf("\n Popped Element is: %d ", top -> element); /* L58 */
    free(top);                                        /* L59 */
    top = temporary;                                  /* L60 */
  }                                                   /* L61 */
}                                                     /* L62 */
                                                      /* BL */
void displayStack()                                   /* L63 */
{                                                     /* L64 */
  node *temporary;                                    /* L65 */
  if(top == NULL) {                                   /* L66 */
    printf("\nStack is Exhausted ");                  /* L67 */
  }                                                   /* L68 */
  else {                                              /* L69 */
    temporary = begin;                                /* L70 */
    printf("\nElements in the stack : ");             /* L71 */
    printf("\nLeft-Most Element Represents Bottom  :  "); /* L72 */
    printf("Right-Most Element Represents Top \n\n"); /* L73 */
    printf("%d", temporary -> element);               /* L74 */
    while(temporary != top) {                         /* L75 */
      temporary = temporary -> next;                  /* L76 */
      printf("\t%d ", temporary -> element);          /* L77 */
    }                                                 /* L78 */
  }                                                   /* L79 */
}                                                     /* L80 */
                                                      /* BL */
int stackMenu()                                       /* L81 */
{                                                     /* L82 */
```

```
    int intChoice;                                               /* L83 */
    printf("\n\nEnter 1 to Push an Element into Stack. ");        /* L84 */
    printf("\nEnter 2 to Pop an Element from Stack. ");           /* L85 */
    printf("\nEnter 3 to Displays the Stack on the Screen.");     /* L86 */
    printf("\nEnter 4 to Stop the Execution of Program.");        /* L87 */
    printf("\nEnter your choice (0 <= N <= 4): ");                /* L88 */
    scanf("%d", &intChoice);                                      /* L89 */
    return intChoice;                                            /* L90 */
}                                                                /* L91 */
                                                                 /* BL */
void main()                                                      /* L92 */
{                                                                /* L93 */
  int intChoice;                                                 /* L94 */
  node *newnode;                                                 /* L95 */
  do {                                                           /* L96 */
    intChoice = stackMenu();                                     /* L97 */
    switch(intChoice) {                                          /* L98 */
      case 1:                                                    /* L99 */
        newnode = getnode();                                     /* L100 */
        pushItem(newnode);                                       /* L101 */
        break;                                                   /* L102 */
      case 2:                                                    /* L103 */
        popItem();                                               /* L104 */
        break;                                                   /* L105 */
      case 3:                                                    /* L106 */
        displayStack();                                          /* L107 */
        break;                                                   /* L108 */
      case 4:                                                    /* L109 */
        exit(0);                                                 /* L110 */
    }                                                            /* L111 */
    fflush(stdin);                                               /* L112 */
  } while( 1 );                                                  /* L113 */
}                                                                /* L114 */
```

Compile and execute this program. A run of this program is given here:

```
Enter 1 to Push an Element into the Stack.
Enter 2 to Pop an Element from the Stack.
Enter 3 to Display the Stack on the Screen.
Enter 4 to Stop the Execution of the Program.
Enter your choice (0 <= N <= 4): 1    ↵

Enter Element (0 <= K <= 30000): 222    ↵

Element is pushed into the Stack.

Enter 1 to Push an Element into the Stack.
Enter 2 to Pop an Element from the Stack.
```

```
Enter 3 to Display the Stack on the Screen.
Enter 4 to Stop the Execution of the Program.
Enter your choice (0 <= N <= 4): 1    ↵

Enter Element (0 <= K <= 30000): 333    ↵

Element is pushed into the Stack.

Enter 1 to Push an Element into the Stack.
Enter 2 to Pop an Element from the Stack.
Enter 3 to Display the Stack on the Screen.
Enter 4 to Stop the Execution of the Program.
Enter your choice (0 <= N <= 4): 1    ↵

Enter Element (0 <= K <= 30000): 444    ↵

Element is pushed into the Stack.

Enter 1 to Push an Element into the Stack.
Enter 2 to Pop an Element from the Stack.
Enter 3 to Display the Stack on the Screen.
Enter 4 to Stop the Execution of the Program.
Enter your choice (0 <= N <= 4): 3    ↵

Elements in the stack:
Left-Most Element Represents Bottom : Right-Most Element Represents Top

222     333     444

Enter 1 to Push an Element into the Stack.
Enter 2 to Pop an Element from the Stack.
Enter 3 to Display the Stack on the Screen.
Enter 4 to Stop the Execution of the Program.
Enter your choice (0 <= N <= 4): 2    ↵

Popped Element is: 444

Enter 1 to Push an Element into the Stack.
Enter 2 to Pop an Element from the Stack.
Enter 3 to Display the Stack on the Screen.
Enter 4 to Stop the Execution of the Program.
Enter your choice (0 <= N <= 4): 3    ↵

Elements in the stack:
Left-Most Element Represents Bottom : Right-Most Element Represents Top

222     333

Enter 1 to Push an Element into the Stack.
```

```
Enter 2 to Pop an Element from the Stack.
Enter 3 to Display the Stack on the Screen.
Enter 4 to Stop the Execution of the Program.
Enter your choice (0 <= N <= 4): 4  ↵
```

How It Works

This program defines five functions: getnode(), stackMenu(), displayStack(), popItem(), and pushItem(). LOCs 11 to 19 define the function getnode(). LOCs 20 to 39 define the function pushItem(). LOCs 40 to 62 define the function popItem(). LOCs 63 to 80 define the function displayStack(). LOCs 81 to 91 define the function stackMenu(). LOCs 92 to 114 define the main() function. Almost all the code in the main() function is placed in a do-while loop so that these LOCs can be executed repeatedly with convenience. When a user pushes an element onto the stack, the function pushItem() is called. When a user pops an element from the stack, the function popItem() is called. When a user wants to display the stack on the screen, the function displayStack() is called.

In LOC 97, a call is made to the function stackMenu(). This function displays the menu before the user and asks him or her to enter a choice. The choices are as follows: enter 1 to push an element into a stack, enter 2 to pop an item from a stack, enter 3 to display the stack on the screen, and enter 4 to stop the execution of the program. The choice entered by the user is returned by the stackMenu() function, and it is assigned to the int variable intChoice.

LOCs 98 to 111 consist of a switch statement. The value stored in intChoice is passed to this switch statement. Depending upon the value of intChoice, the switch statement calls the concerned function. For choice 1, the function pushItem() is called. For choice 2, the function popItem() is called. For choice 3, the function displayStack() is called. For choice 4, the function exit() is called that terminates the execution of the program.

8-3. Convert an Infix Expression to a Postfix Expression

Problem

You want to convert an infix expression into a postfix expression.

Solution

Write a C program that converts an infix expression into a postfix expression, with the following specifications:

- The program defines three functions: lowPriority(), pushOpr(), and popOpr(). The function lowPriority() assigns the appropriate priority value to every operator in an infix equation. The function pushOpr() is invoked after pushing an operator into the stack. The function popOpr() is to be invoked after popping an operator from the stack.

- It is assumed that only one of the following operators is used in an expression: +, -, *, /, %, ^, and (.

The Code

The following is the code of the C program written with these specifications. Type the following C program in a text editor and save it in the folder C:\Code with the file name stack3.c:

```
/* This program converts an infix expression into a postfix expression. */
                                                          /* BL */
# include <stdio.h>                                       /* L1 */
# include <string.h>                                      /* L2 */
                                                          /* BL */
char postfixExp[60];                                      /* L3 */
char infixExp[60];                                        /* L4 */
char operatorStack[60];                                   /* L5 */
int i=0, j=0, intTop=0;                                   /* L6 */
                                                          /* BL */
int lowPriority(char opr, char oprStack)                  /* L7 */
{                                                         /* L8 */
  int k, p1, p2;                                          /* L9 */
  char oprList[] = {'+', '-', '*', '/', '%', '^', '('};   /* L10 */
  int prioList[] = {0,0,1,1,2,3,4};                       /* L11 */
  if( oprStack == '(' )                                   /* L12 */
    return 0;                                             /* L13 */
  for(k = 0; k < 6; k ++) {                               /* L14 */
    if(opr == oprList[k])                                 /* L15 */
    p1 = prioList[k];                                     /* L16 */
  }                                                       /* L17 */
  for(k = 0; k < 6; k ++) {                               /* L18 */
    if(oprStack == oprList[k])                            /* L19 */
    p2 = prioList[k];                                     /* L20 */
  }                                                       /* L21 */
  if(p1 < p2)                                             /* L22 */
    return 1;                                             /* L23 */
  else                                                    /* L24 */
    return 0;                                             /* L25 */
}                                                         /* L26 */
                                                          /* BL */
void pushOpr(char opr)                                    /* L27 */
{                                                         /* L28 */
  if(intTop == 0) {                                       /* L29 */
    operatorStack[intTop] = opr;                          /* L30 */
    intTop++;                                             /* L31 */
  }                                                       /* L32 */
  else {                                                  /* L33 */
    if(opr != '(' ) {                                     /* L34 */
      while(lowPriority(opr, operatorStack[intTop-1]) ==
      1 && intTop > 0) {                                  /* L35 */
```

```
        postfixExp[j] = operatorStack[--intTop];        /* L36 */
        j++;                                             /* L37 */
      }                                                  /* L38 */
    }                                                    /* L39 */
    operatorStack[intTop] = opr;                         /* L40 */
    intTop++;                                            /* L41 */
  }                                                      /* L42 */
}                                                        /* L43 */
                                                         /* BL  */
void popOpr()                                            /* L44 */
{                                                        /* L45 */
  while(operatorStack[--intTop] != '(' ) {               /* L46 */
    postfixExp[j] = operatorStack[intTop];               /* L47 */
    j++;                                                 /* L48 */
  }                                                      /* L49 */
}                                                        /* L50 */
                                                         /* BL  */
void main()                                              /* L51 */
{                                                        /* L52 */
  char k;                                                /* L53 */
  printf("\n Enter Infix Expression : ");                /* L54 */
  gets(infixExp);                                        /* L55 */
  while( (k=infixExp[i++]) != '\0') { /* while statement begins. */  /* L56 */
    switch(k) {                     /* switch statement begins. */ /* L57 */
      case ' ' :                                         /* L58 */
                break;                                   /* L59 */
      case '(' :                                         /* L60 */
      case '+' :                                         /* L61 */
      case '-' :                                         /* L62 */
      case '*' :                                         /* L63 */
      case '/' :                                         /* L64 */
      case '^' :                                         /* L65 */
      case '%' :                                         /* L66 */
                pushOpr(k);                              /* L67 */
                break;                                   /* L68 */
      case ')' :                                         /* L69 */
                popOpr();                                /* L70 */
                break;                                   /* L71 */
       default :                                         /* L72 */
                postfixExp[j] = k;                       /* L73 */
                j++;                                     /* L74 */
    }                               /* switch statement ends. */ /* L75 */
  }                                 /* while state ment ends. */ /* L76 */
  while(intTop >= 0) {              /* while statement begins. */ /* L77 */
    postfixExp[j] = operatorStack[--intTop];             /* L78 */
    j++;                                                 /* L79 */
  }                                 /* while statement ends. */ /* L80 */
```

```
    postfixExp[j] = '\0';                                  /* L81 */
    printf("\n Infix Expression : %s ", infixExp);         /* L82 */
    printf("\n Postfix Expression : %s ", postfixExp);     /* L83 */
    printf("\n Thank you\n ");                             /* L84 */
}                                                          /* L85 */
```

Compile and execute this program. A few runs of this program are given here:
Here is the first run:

```
Enter Infix Expression: a+b     ↵

Infix Expression: a+b
Postfix Expression: ab+
Thank you
```

Here is the second run:

```
Enter Infix Expression: (a+b)*(c-d)     ↵

Infix Expression: (a+b)*(c-d)
Postfix Expression: ab+cd-*
Thank you
```

Here is the third run:

```
Enter Infix Expression: ((a+b)/(c-d))*((e-f)/(g+h))     ↵

Infix Expression: ((a+b)/(c-d))*((e-f)/(g+h))
Postfix Expression: ab+cd-/ef-gh/*
Thank you
```

How It Works

This program declares three functions: lowPriority(), pushOpr(), and popOpr(). LOCs 3 to 5 define the three arrays: postfixExp, infixExp, and operatorStack. LOC 6 declares the int variables i, j, and intTop. These items are declared outside of any function so that their scope is global. LOCs 7 to 26 define the function lowPriority(). The function lowPriority() assigns the appropriate priority value to every operator in the infix equation. The priority of various operators is as follows:

Operator	Priority or Precedence Values
{	4
(	3
^	2
*, /	1
+, -	0

266

LOCs 27 to 43 define the function pushOpr(). This function is responsible for pushing the element onto the stack. LOCs 44 to 50 define the function popOpr(). This function is responsible for popping the element from the stack. LOCs 51 to 85 consist of the code of the main() function. LOC 54 instructs the user to enter the infix equation. The equation entered by the user is read by the gets() function in LOC 55, and it is stored in the char array infixExp. LOCs 56 to 76 consist of a while loop. At the beginning of every iteration, elements in the array infixExp are read and assigned to the variable k. If the element is a null character, which signifies the end of the array, then the execution of the while loop terminates. The variable k is then passed to the switch statement. Depending upon the value of k, the appropriate case in the switch statement is executed.

8-4. Convert an Infix Expression to a Prefix Expression

Problem

You want to convert an infix expression into a prefix expression.

Solution

Write a C program that converts an infix expression into a prefix expression, with the following specifications:

- The program defines four functions: fillPre(), lowPriority(), pushOpr(), and popOpr(). The function fillPre() accepts a character as an input argument and places it as the first element in the array prefixExp. The function lowPriority() assigns an appropriate priority value to every operator in an infix equation. The function pushOpr() is invoked after pushing an operator into the stack. The function popOpr() is to be invoked after popping an operator from the stack.

- It is assumed that only one of the following operators is used in an expression: +, -, *, /, %, ^, (, and {.

The Code

The following is the code of the C program written with these specifications. Type the following C program in a text editor and save it in the folder C:\Code with the file name stack4.c:

```
/* This program converts infix expression into a prefix expression. */
                                                             /* BL */
# include <stdio.h>                                          /* L1 */
# include <string.h>                                         /* L2 */
                                                             /* BL */
```

```
char prefixExp[60];                                            /* L3 */
char infixExp[60];                                             /* L4 */
char operatorStack[60];                                        /* L5 */
int n=0, intTop=0;                                             /* L6 */
                                                               /* BL */
void fillPre(char let)                                         /* L7 */
{                                                              /* L8 */
  int m;                                                       /* L9 */
  if(n == 0)                                                   /* L10 */
    prefixExp[0] = let;                                        /* L11 */
  else {                                                       /* L12 */
    for(m = n + 1; m > 0; m--)                                 /* L13 */
    prefixExp[m] = prefixExp[m - 1];                           /* L14 */
    prefixExp[0] = let;                                        /* L15 */
  }                                                            /* L16 */
  n++;                                                         /* L17 */
}                                                              /* L18 */
                                                               /* BL */
int lowPriority(char opr, char oprStack)                       /* L19 */
{                                                              /* L20 */
  int k, p1, p2;                                               /* L21 */
  char oprList[] = {'+', '-', '*', '/', '%', '^', ')'};        /* L22 */
  int prioList[] = {0, 0, 1, 1, 2, 3, 4};                      /* L23 */
  if(oprStack == ')' )                                         /* L24 */
    return 0;                                                  /* L25 */
  for(k = 0; k < 6; k ++) {                                    /* L26 */
    if(opr == oprList[k])                                      /* L27 */
    p1 = prioList[k];                                          /* L28 */
  }                                                            /* L29 */
  for(k = 0; k < 6; k ++) {                                    /* L30 */
    if( oprStack == oprList[k] )                               /* L31 */
    p2 = prioList[k];                                          /* L32 */
  }                                                            /* L33 */
  if(p1 < p2)                                                  /* L34 */
    return 1;                                                  /* L35 */
  else                                                         /* L36 */
    return 0;                                                  /* L37 */
}                                                              /* L38 */
                                                               /* BL */
void pushOpr(char opr)                                         /* L39 */
{                                                              /* L40 */
  if(intTop == 0) {                                            /* L41 */
    operatorStack[intTop] = opr;                               /* L42 */
    intTop++;                                                  /* L43 */
  }                                                            /* L44 */
  else {                                                       /* L45 */
    if(opr != ')') {                                           /* L46 */
```

```
        while(lowPriority(opr, operatorStack[intTop-1]) ==                /* L47 */
1 && intTop > 0) {                                                         /* L47 */
            fillPre(operatorStack[--intTop]);                              /* L48 */
        }                                                                  /* L49 */
    }                                                                      /* L50 */
    operatorStack[intTop] = opr;                                           /* L51 */
    intTop++;                                                              /* L52 */
  }                                                                        /* L53 */
}                                                                          /* L54 */
                                                                           /* BL */
void popOpr()                                                              /* L55 */
{                                                                          /* L56 */
  while(operatorStack[--intTop] != ')')                                    /* L57 */
    fillPre(operatorStack[intTop]);                                        /* L58 */
}                                                                          /* L59 */
                                                                           /* BL */
void main()                                                                /* L60 */
{                                                                          /* L61 */
  char chrL;                                                               /* L62 */
  int length;                                                              /* L63 */
  printf("\n Enter Infix Expression : ");                                  /* L64 */
  gets(infixExp);                                                          /* L65 */
  length = strlen(infixExp);                                               /* L66 */
  while(length > 0) {              /* first while loop begins. */          /* L67 */
    chrL = infixExp[--length];                                             /* L68 */
    switch(chrL) {                 /* switch statement begins. */          /* L69 */
      case ' ' :                                                           /* L70 */
              break;                                                       /* L71 */
      case ')' :                                                           /* L72 */
      case '+' :                                                           /* L73 */
      case '-' :                                                           /* L74 */
      case '*' :                                                           /* L75 */
      case '/' :                                                           /* L76 */
      case '^' :                                                           /* L77 */
      case '%' :                                                           /* L78 */
              pushOpr(chrL);                                               /* L79 */
              break;                                                       /* L80 */
      case '(' :                                                           /* L81 */
              popOpr();                                                    /* L82 */
              break;                                                       /* L83 */
      default :                                                            /* L84 */
              fillPre(chrL);                                               /* L85 */
    }                              /* switch statement ends. */            /* L86 */
  }                                /* first while loop ends. */            /* L87 */
  while( intTop > 0 ) {            /* second while loop begins. */         /* L88 */
    fillPre( operatorStack[--intTop] );                                    /* L89 */
    n++;                                                                   /* L90 */
  }                                /* second while loop ends. */           /* L91 */
```

```
    prefixExp[n] = '\0';                                      /* L92 */
    printf("\n Infix Expression : %s ", infixExp);            /* L93 */
    printf("\n Prefix Expression : %s ", prefixExp);          /* L94 */
    printf("\n Thank you\n");                                 /* L95 */
}                                                             /* L96 */
```

Compile and execute this program. A few runs of this program are given here:
Here is the first run:

```
Enter Infix Expression: a+b    ↵

Infix Expression: a+b
Prefix Expression: +ab
Thank you
```

Here is the second run:

```
Enter Infix Expression: (a+b)*(c-d)    ↵

Infix Expression: (a+b)*(c-d)
Prefix Expression: *+ab-cd
Thank you
```

Here is the third run:

```
Enter Infix Expression: ((a+b)/(c-d))*((e-f)/(g+h))    ↵

Infix Expression: ((a+b)/(c-d))*((e-f)/(g+h))
Prefix Expression:  */+ab-cd/-ef+gh
Thank you
```

How It Works

This program consists of four functions: fillPre(), lowPriority(), pushOpr(), and popOpr(). LOCs 3 to 5 define the three arrays: prefixExp, infixExp, and operatorStack. LOC 6 declares the int variables n and intTop. These items are declared outside of any function so that their scope is global. LOCs 7 to 18 define the function fillPre(). LOCs 19 to 38 define the function lowPriority(). The function lowPriority() assigns the appropriate priority value to every operator in the infix equation. LOCs 39 to 54 define the function pushOpr(). This function is responsible for pushing the element onto the stack. LOCs 55 to 59 define the function popOpr(). This function is responsible for popping the element from the stack.

LOCs 60 to 96 consist of the code of the main() function. LOC 64 instructs the user to enter the infix equation. The equation entered by the user is read by the gets() function in LOC 65, and it is stored in the char array infixExp. The length of this infix equation is computed in LOC 66, and it is stored in the int variable length.

LOCs 67 to 87 consist of the first while loop, and LOCs 88 to 91 consist of the second while loop. In the first while loop, at the beginning of every iteration, elements in the array infixExp are read and assigned to the variable chrL. The execution of this loop terminates when all the elements in the array infixExp are read. This loop consists of a switch statement spanning LOCs 69 to 86. The variable chrL is passed to this switch statement. Depending upon the value of chrL, the appropriate case is executed. Particularly, the operators are pushed onto the stack using the function pushOpr(). In the second while loop, the function fillPre() is called repeatedly. Operators stored in the array operatorStack are passed to this function, one by one. Finally, in LOCs 93 and 94, the infix and prefix expressions are displayed on the screen.

8-5. Implement a Circular Queue as an Array
Problem

You want to implement a circular queue as an array.

Solution

Write a C program that implements a circular queue as an array, with the following specifications:

- The program defines four functions: insertCircQue(), deleteCircQue(), displayCircQue(), and displayMenu().

- The function insertCirQue() is called when an element is inserted in the circular queue. The function deleteCircQue() is called when an element from a circular queue is deleted. The function displayCircQue() is called when a circular queue is displayed on the screen. The function displayMenu() is called when the menu is displayed on the screen.

The Code

The following is the code of the C program written with these specifications. Type the following C program in a text editor and save it in the folder C:\Code with the file name stack5.c:

```
/* This program implments a circular queue. */
                                                   /* BL */
# include <stdio.h>                                /* L1 */
# define SIZE 8                                    /* L2 */
                                                   /* L3 */
                                                   /* BL */
int circQue[SIZE];                                 /* L4 */
int frontCell = 0;                                 /* L5 */
int rearCell = 0;                                  /* L6 */
int kount = 0;                                     /* L7 */
                                                   /* BL */
```

```
void insertCircQue()                                              /* L8  */
{                                                                 /* L9  */
 int num;                                                         /* L10 */
 if(kount == SIZE) {                                              /* L11 */
    printf("\nCircular Queue is Full. Enter Any
    Choice Except 1.\n ");                                        /* L12 */
 }                                                                /* L13 */
  else {                                                          /* L14 */
    printf("\nEnter data, i.e, a number N (0 <= N : 30000): ");   /* L15 */
    scanf("%d", &num);                                            /* L16 */
    circQue[rearCell] = num;                                      /* L17 */
    rearCell = (rearCell + 1) % SIZE;                             /* L18 */
    kount ++;                                                     /* L19 */
    printf("\nData Inserted in the Circular Queue. \n");          /* L20 */
 }                                                                /* L21 */
}                                                                 /* L22 */
                                                                  /* BL  */
void deleteCircQue()                                              /* L23 */
{                                                                 /* L24 */
  if(kount == 0) {                                                /* L25 */
    printf("\nCircular Queue is Exhausted!\n");                   /* L26 */
 }                                                                /* L27 */
  else {                                                          /* L28 */
    printf("\nElement Deleted from Cir Queue is %d \n",
    circQue[frontCell]);                                          /* L30 */
    frontCell = (frontCell + 1) % SIZE;                           /* L31 */
    kount --;                                                     /* L32 */
 }                                                                /* L33 */
}                                                                 /* L34 */
                                                                  /* BL  */
void displayCircQue()                                             /* L35 */
{                                                                 /* L36 */
  int i, j;                                                       /* L37 */
  if(kount == 0) {                                                /* L38 */
    printf("\nCircular Queue is Exhausted!\n ");                  /* L39 */
 }                                                                /* L40 */
  else {                                                          /* L41 */
    printf("\nElements in Circular Queue are given below: \n");   /* L42 */
    j = kount;                                                    /* L43 */
    for(i = frontCell; j != 0; j--) {                             /* L44 */
      printf("%d    ", circQue[i]);                               /* L45 */
      i = (i + 1) % SIZE;                                         /* L46 */
    }                                                             /* L47 */
    printf("\n");                                                 /* L48 */
 }                                                                /* L49 */
}                                                                 /* L50 */
                                                                  /* BL  */
```

```
int displayMenu()                                              /* L51 */
{                                                              /* L52 */
  int choice;                                                  /* L53 */
  printf("\nEnter 1 to Insert Data.");                         /* L54 */
  printf("\nEnter 2 to Delete Data.");                         /* L55 */
  printf("\nEnter 3 to Display Data.");                        /* L56 */
  printf("\nEnter 4 to Quit the Program. ");                   /* L57 */
  printf("\nEnter Your Choice: ");                             /* L58 */
  scanf("%d", &choice);                                        /* L59 */
  return choice;                                               /* L60 */
}                                                              /* L61 */
                                                               /* BL  */
void main()                                                    /* L62 */
{                                                              /* L63 */
  int choice;                                                  /* L64 */
  do {                            /* do-while loop begins. */  /* L65 */
    choice = displayMenu();                                    /* L66 */
    switch(choice) {              /* switch statement begins. */ /* L67 */
      case 1:                                                  /* L68 */
              insertCircQue();                                 /* L69 */
              break;                                           /* L70 */
      case 2:                                                  /* L71 */
              deleteCircQue();                                 /* L72 */
              break;                                           /* L73 */
      case 3:                                                  /* L74 */
              displayCircQue();                                /* L75 */
              break;                                           /* L76 */
      case 4:                                                  /* L77 */
              exit(0);                                         /* L78 */
      default:                                                 /* L79 */
              printf("\nInvalid Choice. Please enter again. \n "); /* L80 */
    }                            /* switch statement ends. */  /* L81 */
  } while(1);                     /* do-while loop ends. */     /* L82 */
}                                                              /* L83 */
```

Compile and execute this program. A run of this program is given here:

```
Enter 1 to Insert Data.
Enter 2 to Delete Data.
Enter 3 to Display Data.
Enter 4 to Quit the Program.
Enter Your Choice: 1   ↵

Entr data, i.e., a number N (0 <= N <= 30000): 222   ↵

Data Inserted in the Circular Queue.

Enter 1 to Insert Data.
Enter 2 to Delete Data.
```

```
Enter 3 to Display Data.
Enter 4 to Quit the Program.
Enter Your Choice: 1    ↵

Entr data, i.e., a number N (0 <= N <= 30000): 333    ↵

Data Inserted in the Circular Queue.

Enter 1 to Insert Data.
Enter 2 to Delete Data.
Enter 3 to Display Data.
Enter 4 to Quit the Program.
Enter Your Choice: 1    ↵
Entr data, i.e., a number N (0 <= N <= 30000): 444    ↵

Data Inserted in the Circular Queue.

Enter 1 to Insert Data.
Enter 2 to Delete Data.
Enter 3 to Display Data.
Enter 4 to Quit the Program.
Enter Your Choice: 3    ↵

Elements in the Circular Queue are given below:
222    333    444

Enter 1 to Insert Data.
Enter 2 to Delete Data.
Enter 3 to Display Data.
Enter 4 to Quit the Program.
Enter Your Choice: 2    ↵

Element Deleted from Cir Queue is 222

Enter 1 to Insert Data.
Enter 2 to Delete Data.
Enter 3 to Display Data.
Enter 4 to Quit the Program.
Enter Your Choice: 3    ↵

Elements in the Circular Queue are given below:
333    444

Enter 1 to Insert Data.
Enter 2 to Delete Data.
Enter 3 to Display Data.
Enter 4 to Quit the Program.
Enter Your Choice: 4    ↵
```

How It Works

In LOC 2, the size of the circular queue is limited to eight elements. LOC 4 defines an int type array called circQue to store the data elements in the array. LOCs 5 to 7 define three int variables: frontCell, rearCell, and kount. This array and the variables are defined outside of any function so that their scope is global. Initially, when the queue is empty, then the values of frontCell and rearCell are zero; i.e., both variables are pointing to the first cell in the array circQue.

Next, when the user inserts the first data element in the queue (say, 222), then the value of frontCell continues to be zero. However, the value of rearCell becomes 1 because [(rearCell + 1) % 8] = [(0 + 1) % 8] = 1. This means the variable frontCell is pointing to the first cell in the array, and the variable rearCell is pointing to the second element in the array.

Next, when the user inserts the second data element in the queue (say, 333), then the value of frontCell continues to be zero. However, the value of rearCell becomes 2 because [(rearCell + 1) % 8] = [(1 + 1) % 8] = 2. This means the variable frontCell is pointing to the first cell in the array, and the variable rearCell is pointing to the third element in the array.

Next, when the user inserts the third data element in the queue (say, 444), then the value of frontCell continues to be zero. However, the value of rearCell becomes 3 because [(rearCell + 1) % 8] = [(2 + 1) % 8] = 3. This means the variable frontCell is pointing to the first cell in the array, and the variable rearCell is pointing to the fourth element in the array.

Next, when the user deletes the data element in the queue (it is 222), then the value of rearCell continues to be 3. However, the value of frontCell becomes 1 because [(frontCell + 1) % 8] = [(0 + 1) % 8] = 1. This means the variable frontCell is pointing to the second cell in the array, and the variable rearCell is pointing to the fourth element in the array.

This program consists of four functions: insertCircQue(), deleteCircQue(), displayCircQue(), and displayMenu(). LOC 4 defines an int type array called circQue.

LOCs 8 to 22 define the function insertCircQue(). This function is called when an element is inserted in the circular queue. LOCs 23 to 34 define the function deleteCircQue(). This function is called when an element is deleted from the circular queue. LOCs 35 to 50 define the function displayCircQue(). This function is called when a circular queue is to be displayed on the screen. LOCs 51 to 61 define the function displayMenu(). This function is called when the user menu is to be displayed on the screen.

LOCs 62 to 83 consist of the main() function. In LOC 64, an int variable choice is declared in order to store the choice of the user. LOCs 65 to 82 consist of the do-while loop. This loop is executed repeatedly until the program is terminated by the user. This do-while loop consists of a switch statement on LOCs 67 to 81. When the user menu is displayed on the screen, the user enters his or her choice, and this choice is stored in the int variable called choice. This variable choice is passed to the switch statement. Depending upon the value of choice, an appropriate case is executed. If the value of choice is 1, then the function insertCircQue() is called. If the value of choice is 2, then the function deleteCircQue() is called. If the value of choice is 3, then the function displayCircQue() is called. If the value of choice is 4, then the program is terminated. If the value of choice is something else, then the default case is executed and the message "Invalid Choice. Please enter again." is displayed on the screen.

CHAPTER 9

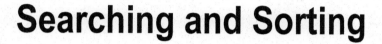

Searching and Sorting

The current English meaning of the terms "searching" and "sorting" also holds good in computer science. Sometimes, this is not the case. For example, the current English meaning of the terms "root," "garbage" or "tree" is very different from their meaning in computer science.

Note Searching is the process of finding the location of a desired element from a group of elements.

For searching, generally following methods are used:

- Linear search,
- Binary search,
- Interpolation search.

Note Sorting is the process of arranging the elements in desired order (e.g., ascending or descending, etc.), given a group of elements.

For sorting, generally following methods are used:

- Bubble sort,
- Inserting sort,
- Selection sort,
- Merge sort,
- Shell sort,
- Quick sort,

© Shirish Chavan 2017
S. Chavan, *C Recipes*, DOI 10.1007/978-1-4842-2967-5_9

9-1. Find a Data Element Using a Linear Search
Problem
You want to find a desired data element from an unordered list of data elements using a linear search.

Solution
Write a C program that finds a data element from an unordered list of data elements using a linear search, with the following specifications:

- Program defines int type array intStorage to store the list of numbers entered by user.

- Program defines the function searchData() that searches the desired data element in a given list of numbers using a linear or sequential search algorithm.

The Code
Code of C program written with these specifications is given below. Type the following C program in a text editor and save it in the folder C:\Code with the filename srch1.c:

```
/* This program performs linear search to find a desired data element from */
/* a set of given data elements. */
                                                                /* BL */
#include <stdio.h>                                              /* L1 */
                                                                /* BL */
int intStorage[50];                                             /* L2 */
int kount = 0;                                                  /* L3 */
                                                                /* BL */
int searchData(int intData)                                     /* L4 */
{                                                               /* L5 */
  int intCompare = 0;                                           /* L6 */
  int intNum = -1;                                              /* L7 */
  int i;                                                        /* L8 */
  for(i = 0; i < kount; i++) {                                  /* L9 */
    intCompare++;                                               /* L10 */
    if(intData == intStorage[i]){                               /* L11 */
      intNum = i;                                               /* L12 */
      break;                                                    /* L13 */
    }                                                           /* L14 */
  }                                                             /* L15 */
  printf("Total Number of Comparisons Made Are: %d", intCompare); /* L16 */
  return intNum;                                                /* L17 */
}                                                               /* L18 */
                                                                /* BL */
```

```
void main()                                                    /* L19 */
{                                                              /* L20 */
 int intPosition, intData, i;                                  /* L21 */
  printf("Enter the number of data elements N (2 <= N <= 50): ");  /* L22 */
  scanf("%d", &kount);                                         /* L23 */
  printf("Enter the %d integers I (0 <= I <= 30000) ", kount); /* L24 */
  printf("separated by white spaces: \n");                     /* L25 */
  for (i=0; i < kount; i++)                                    /* L26 */
    scanf("%d", &intStorage[i]);                               /* L27 */
  fflush(stdin);                                               /* L28 */
  printf("Enter the Data Element D to be Searched (0 <= D <= 30000): ");  /* L29 */
  scanf("%d", &intData);                                       /* L30 */
  intPosition = searchData(intData);                           /* L31 */
  if(intPosition != -1) {                                      /* L32 */
    printf("\nData Element Found at Position ");               /* L33 */
    printf("or Location: %d\n", (intPosition + 1));            /* L34 */
  }                                                            /* L35 */
  else                                                         /* L36 */
     printf("\nData Element Not Found.\n");                    /* L37 */
  printf("\nThank you.\n");                                    /* L38 */
}                                                              /* L39 */
```

Compile and execute this program. A couple of runs of this program are given below. First run:

```
Enter the number of data elements N (2 <= N <= 50): 8   ↵
Enter the 8 integers I (0 <= I <= 30000) separated by white spaces:
10 20 30 40 50 60 70 80   ↵
Enter the Data Element D to be Searched (0 <= D <= 30000): 60   ↵
Total Number of Comparisons Made Are: 6
Data Element Found at Position or Location: 6
Thank you.
```

Second run:

```
Enter the number of data elements N (2 <= N <= 50): 8   ↵
Enter the 8 integers I (0 <= I <= 30000) separated by white spaces:
10 20 30 40 50 60 70 80   ↵
Enter the Data Element D to be Searched (0 <= D <= 30000): 55   ↵
Total Number of Comparisons Made Are: 8
Data Element Not Found.
Thank you.
```

How It Works

In a linear or sequential search, every element in list is compared with the data element to be searched, until a match is found. This method is convenient when list contains a small number of data elements. The benefits of this method are: (a) you can use unordered list of numbers and (b) logic used in this program is very simple. Linear search has worst-case complexity of O(n), where n is the size of the list.

LOC 2 defines int type array intStorage to store the list of numbers entered by user. LOC 3 defines the int variable kount that represents the size of list of data elements. LOCs 4-18 define the function searchData() that finds the desired number (i.e., data element) in a given list. The number to be searched is passed to this function as an input argument. This number, i.e., intData, is compared with every number in the list intStorage using the for loop. When match is found, looping is terminated and result is returned. If no match is found then appropriate result is returned.

LOCs 19-39 consists of main() function. In LOC 22, user is asked to enter the size of list. The size of list should be in the range of 2 to 50. The size of list entered by user is stored in the int variable kount. In LOC 24 user is asked to enter the numbers to fill in the list. The numbers entered by user are stored in the array intStorage. In LOC 29, user is asked to enter the number to be searched. The number entered by user is stored in the int type variable intData. In LOC 31, function searchData() is called and variable intData is passed to this function as an input argument. The result returned by this function is stored in the int type variable intPosition. Then result is displayed on the screen.

9-2. Find a Data Element Using a Binary Search
Problem

You want to find a data element from an unordered list of data elements using a binary search.

Solution

Write a C program that finds a data element from an ordered list - in increasing order - of data elements using a binary search, with the following specifications:

- Program defines int type array intStorage to store the list of numbers entered by user.

- Program defines the function searchData() that searches the desired data element in a given list of numbers - in increasing order - using the binary search algorithm.

The Code

Code of C program written with these specifications is given below. Type the following C program in a text editor and save it in the folder C:\Code with the filename srch2.c:

```
/* This program performs a binary search to find a desired data element from */
/* an ordered set of given data elements. */
                                                                         /* BL */
#include <stdio.h>                                                       /* L1 */
                                                                         /* BL */
int intStorage[50];                                                      /* L2 */
int kount = 0;                                                           /* L3 */
                                                                         /* BL */
int searchData(int intData)                                             /* L4 */
{                                                                        /* L5 */
  int intLowBound = 0;                                                   /* L6 */
  int intUpBound = kount -1;                                             /* L7 */
  int intMidPoint = -1;                                                  /* L8 */
  int intCompare = 0;                                                    /* L9 */
  int intNum = -1;                                                       /* L10 */
  while(intLowBound <= intUpBound) {                                     /* L11 */
    intCompare++;                                                        /* L12 */
    intMidPoint = intLowBound + (intUpBound - intLowBound) / 2;          /* L13 */
    if(intStorage[intMidPoint] == intData) {                            /* L14 */
      intNum = intMidPoint;                                             /* L15 */
      break;                                                            /* L16 */
    }                                                                    /* L17 */
    else {                                                               /* L18 */
      if(intStorage[intMidPoint] < intData) {                          /* L19 */
        intLowBound = intMidPoint + 1;                                 /* L20 */
      }                                                                  /* L21 */
      else {                                                             /* L22 */
        intUpBound = intMidPoint -1;                                   /* L23 */
      }                                                                  /* L24 */
    }                                                                    /* L25 */
  }                                                                      /* L26 */
  printf("Total comparisons made: %d" , intCompare);                    /* L27 */
  return intNum;                                                        /* L28 */
}                                                                        /* L29 */
                                                                         /* BL */
void main()                                                             /* L30 */
{                                                                        /* L31 */
  int intPosition, intData, i;                                          /* L32 */
  printf("Enter the number of data elements N (2 <= N <= 50): ");       /* L33 */
  scanf("%d", &kount);                                                  /* L34 */
  printf("Enter the %d integers I (0 <= I <= 30000) ", kount);          /* L35 */
  printf("in increasing order, \nseparated by white spaces: ");         /* L36 */
  for (i=0; i < kount; i++)                                             /* L37 */
```

```
   scanf("%d", &intStorage[i]);                              /* L38 */
 fflush(stdin);                                              /* L39 */
 printf("Enter the Data Element D to be Searched (0 <= D <= 30000): "); /* L40 */
 scanf("%d", &intData);                                     /* L41 */
 intPosition = searchData(intData);                         /* L42 */
 if(intPosition != -1) {                                    /* L43 */
   printf("\nData Element Found at Position ");             /* L44 */
   printf("or Location: %d" ,(intPosition+1));              /* L45 */
 }                                                          /* L46 */
 else                                                       /* L47 */
   printf("\nData Element not found.");                     /* L48 */
 printf("\nThank you.\n");                                  /* L49 */
}                                                           /* L50 */
```

Compile and execute this program. A couple of runs of this program are given below. First run:

```
Enter the number of data elements N (2 <= N <= 50): 8    ⏎
Enter the 8 integers I (0 <= I <= 30000) in increasing order,
separated by white spaces: 10 20 30 40 50 60 70 80    ⏎
Enter the Data Element D to be Searched (0 <= D <= 30000): 50    ⏎
Total comparisons made: 3
Data Element Found at Position or Location: 5
Thank you.
```

Second run:

```
Enter the number of data elements N (2 <= N <= 50): 8    ⏎
Enter the 8 integers I (0 <= I <= 30000) in increasing order,
separated by white spaces: 10 20 30 40 50 60 70 80    ⏎
Enter the Data Element D to be Searched (0 <= D <= 30000): 65    ⏎
Total comparisons made: 3
Data Element Not Found.
Thank you.
```

How It Works

In a binary search, the list that contains data elements (i.e., integer numbers) must be an ordered list either in increasing or decreasing order. Here, in this program, a list sorted in increasing order is used. You are given a data element intData to be searched in this list. Firstly, a list is divided into two equal parts (say, upper part and lower part). Then it is found whether the intData lies in upper part or lower part. Suppose, it lies in upper part then lower part of the list is discarded and upper part of this list is again divided into two equal parts (say up part and low part). Once again it is found whether intData lies in up part or low part. Suppose, intData lies in low part. Then up part is discarded and low part is again divided into two parts. This procedure is repeated until a match for intData is found in the given list or it is confirmed that there is no match for intData in the given list. The benefit of this method is that it is more efficient compared to linear search method. You get the match for intData in less number of comparisons compared to linear search. When list is big and already ordered then it is advisable to use this method. Linear search has worst-case complexity of $O(n)$ whereas binary search has worst-case complexity of $O(\log n)$, where n is size of the list of numbers.

LOC 2 defines int type array intStorage to store the list of numbers entered by user. LOC 3 defines the int variable kount that represents the size of list of data elements. LOCs 4-34 define the function searchData() that finds the desired number (i.e., data element) in a given list of numbers using a binary search. The number to be searched is passed to this function as an input argument.

Five int type variables are declared in the LOCs 6-10. LOCs 11-26 consist of a while-loop. Binary search is performed in this loop. LOCs 30-50 consist of main() function. LOC 33 instructs the user to enter the size of the list in the range 2 to 50. The size entered by user is stored in the int variable kount. LOC 35 instructs the user to enter the list of integers in increasing order. The list of numbers entered by user is stored in int type array intStorage. LOC 40 instructs the user to enter the data element to be searched. The data element entered by user is stored in the int variable intData. LOC 42 calls the function searchData(). The variable intData is passed to function searchData() as an input argument. The function searchData() finds the match for intData in the list of numbers intStorage and returns it. The value returned by searchData() is assigned to int variable intPosition in the LOC 42. The result of search is then displayed on the screen in the LOCs 44, 45 and 48.

9-3. Sort a Given List of Numbers Using a Bubble Sort

Problem

You want to sort a given list of unordered numbers in an ascending (ie, increasing) order using a bubble sort.

Solution

Write a C program that sorts a given list of unordered numbers in an ascending (ie. increasing) order, with the following specifications:

- Program defines int type array intStorage to store the list of numbers entered by user.

- Program defines the function bubbleSort() that sorts the given list of unordered numbers in an asending (ie, increasing) order using the bubble sort algorithm.

The Code

Code of C program written with these specifications is given below. Type the following C program in a text editor and save it in the folder C:\Code with the filename sort1.c:

```
/* This program sorts a given list of integers in an increasing order
using bubble sort. */
                                                               /* BL */
#include <stdio.h>                                             /* L1 */
                                                               /* BL */
int intStorage[20];                                            /* L2 */
int kount = 0;                                                 /* L3 */
                                                               /* BL */
void bubbleSort()                                              /* L4 */
{                                                              /* L5 */
  int intTemp;                                                 /* L6 */
  int i,j;                                                     /* L7 */
  int intSwap = 0; /* 0-false & 1-true */                      /* L8 */
  for(i = 0; i < kount-1; i++) {       /* outer for loop begins */  /* L9 */
    intSwap = 0;                                               /* L10 */
    for(j = 0; j < kount-1-i; j++) { /* inner for loop begins */  /* L11 */
      if(intStorage[j] > intStorage[j+1]) { /* if statement begins */ /* L12 */
        intTemp = intStorage[j];                               /* L13 */
        intStorage[j] = intStorage[j+1];                       /* L14 */
        intStorage[j+1] = intTemp;                             /* L15 */
        intSwap = 1;                                           /* L16 */
      }                              /* if statement ends */   /* L17 */
    }                                /* inner for loop ends */ /* L18 */
    if(!intSwap) {                                             /* L19 */
      break;                                                   /* L20 */
    }                                                          /* L21 */
  }                                  /* outer for loop ends */ /* L22 */
}                                                              /* L23 */
                                                               /* BL */
void main()                                                    /* L24 */
{                                                              /* L25 */
  int i;                                                       /* L26 */
  printf("Enter the number of items in the list, N (2 <= N <= 20): "); /* L27 */
  scanf("%d", &kount);                                         /* L28 */
  printf("Enter the %d integers I (0 <= I <= 30000) ", kount); /* L29 */
  printf("separated by white spaces: \n");                     /* L30 */
  for (i=0; i < kount; i++)                                    /* L31 */
    scanf("%d", &intStorage[i]);                               /* L32 */
  fflush(stdin);                                               /* L33 */
  bubbleSort();                                                /* L34 */
  printf("Sorted List: ");                                     /* L35 */
  for(i = 0; i < kount; i++)                                   /* L36 */
```

```
    printf("%d ", intStorage[i]);                                      /* L37 */
  printf("\nThank you.\n");                                            /* L38 */
}                                                                      /* L39 */
```

Compile and execute this program. A run of this program is given below:

```
Enter the number of items in the list, N (2 <= N <= 20): 8  ↵
Enter the 8 integers I (0 <= I <= 30000) separated by white spaces:
30  80  20  70  40  10  60  90  ↵
Sorted List: 10  20  30  40  60  70  80  90
Thank you.
```

How It Works

Bubble sort is simple yet effective sorting algorithm and hence it is quite popular when lists to be ordered are not very big. In bubble sort two successive elements are compared and are swapped if first element is greater than the second one. If lists to be ordered are big then this method is not used because the worst case complexity for this method is $O(n^2)$ where n represents the number of items or elements in the list.

Suppose unordered list contains 4 numbers as follows:

17 19 16 14

To begin with, first number 17 is compared with 19. These numbers are already in ascending order hence no swapping is needed. Next, second number 19 is compared with third number 16. As these numbers are not in ascending order, swapping is needed. After swapping, the list of numbers looks as follows:

17 16 19 14

Next, third number 19 is compared with fourth number 14. As these numbers are not in ascending order, they are swapped. After swapping the list becomes as follows:

17 16 14 19

Next, first number 17 is compared with second number. As these numbers are not in ascending order, they are swapped. After swapping the list becomes as follows:

16 17 14 19

This process is repeated until the complete list is sorted in ascending order.

In this program, LOC 2 defines int type array intStorage to store the list of numbers entered by user. LOC 3 defines the int variable kount that represents the size of list of data elements.

LOCs 4-23 define the function bubbleSort() that sorts a list of unordered numbers in to a list of ascending numbers.

Four int type variables are declared in the LOCs 6-8. LOCs 9-22 consist of outer for loop and LOCs 11-18 consist of inner for loop.

LOCs 24-39 consists of main() function. LOC 27 asks the user to enter the size of list and this size of list is assigned to int variable kount. LOS 29 asks the user to populate the list. The elements of list are stored in the int array intStorage. LOC 34 calls the function bubbleSort() that sorts the numbers in the list. LOCs 36-37 consists of a for loop that displays the sorted list of numbers on the screen.

285

9-4. Sort a Given List of Numbers Using an Insertion Sort

Problem

You want to sort a given list of unordered numbers in an ascending (ie, increasing) order using an insertion sort.

Solution

Write a C program that sorts a given list of unordered numbers in an ascending (ie. increasing) order, with the following specifications:

- Program defines int type array intStorage to store the list of numbers entered by user.

- Program defines the function insertionSort() that sorts the given list of unordered numbers in an asending (ie, increasing) order using the insertion sort algorithm.

The Code

Code of C program written with these specifications is given below. Type the following C program in a text editor and save it in the folder C:\Code with the filename sort2.c:

```
/* This program sorts a given list of unordered integers in an
increasing order */
/* using an insertion sort. */
                                                            /* BL */
#include <stdio.h>                                          /* L1 */
                                                            /* BL */
int intStorage[20];                                         /* L2 */
int kount = 0;                                              /* L3 */
                                                            /* BL */
void insertionSort()                                        /* L4 */
{                                                           /* L5 */
  int intInsert;                                            /* L6 */
  int intVacancy;                                           /* L7 */
  int i;                                                    /* L8 */
  for(i = 1; i < kount; i++) {        /* for loop begins */ /* L9 */
    intInsert = intStorage[i];                              /* L10 */
    intVacancy = i;                                         /* L11 */
    while (intVacancy > 0 && intStorage[intVacancy-1] > intInsert) { /* L12 */
      intStorage[intVacancy] = intStorage[intVacancy-1];    /* L13 */
      intVacancy--;                                         /* L14 */
    }                                                       /* L15 */
```

```
    if(intVacancy != i) {        /* if statement begins */      /* L16 */
      intStorage[intVacancy] = intInsert;                       /* L17 */
    }                            /* if statement ends */        /* L18 */
  }                                 /* for loop ends */         /* L19 */
}                                                               /* L20 */
                                                                /* BL  */
void main()                                                     /* L21 */
{                                                               /* L22 */
  int i;                                                        /* L23 */
  printf("Enter the number of data elements N (2 <= N <= 20): ");  /* L24 */
  scanf("%d", &kount);                                          /* L25 */
  printf("Enter the %d integers I (0 <= I <= 30000) ", kount);  /* L26 */
  printf("separated by white spaces: \n");                      /* L27 */
  for (i=0; i < kount; i++)                                     /* L28 */
    scanf("%d", &intStorage[i]);                                /* L29 */
  fflush(stdin);                                                /* L30 */
  insertionSort();                                              /* L31 */
  printf("Sorted List: ");                                      /* L32 */
  for(i = 0; i < kount; i++)                                    /* L33 */
    printf("%d ",intStorage[i]);                                /* L34 */
  printf("\nThank you.\n");                                     /* L35 */
}                                                               /* L36 */
```

Compile and execute this program. A run of this program is given below:

```
Enter the number of items in the list, N (2 <= N <= 20): 8   ↵
Enter the 8 integers I (0 <= I <= 30000) separated by white spaces:
98  23  45  67  55  30  78  45  ↵
Sorted List:  23  30  45  45  55  67  78  98
Thank you.
```

How It Works

In insertion sort, the list is divided into two parts, lower part and upper part. The lower part is sorted and upper part is unsorted, in general. As sorting proceeds, the lower part grows in size and upper part shrinks in size. Ultimately, when upper part is reduced to zero, the list is completely sorted. Suppose the unsorted list consists of five numbers as follows:

> 8 6 3 1 7

To begin with, compare first number 8 with second number 6. These numbers are not in order, therefore, swap these numbers. After swapping, the list becomes as given below. Notice that first two numbers now form a lower part of the list that is completely sorted. Also, last three numbers form the upper part of the list that is unsorted:

> 6 8 3 1 7

Next, compare second number 8 with third number 3. These numbers are not in order, therefore swap these numbers. After swapping, the list becomes as given below:

    6 3 8 1 7

Next, compare first number 6 with second number 3. These numbers are not in order, therefore swap these numbers. After swapping, the list becomes as given below:

    3 6 8 1 7

Notice that lower part of the list now consist of three numbers (3, 6, and 8) and this sub-list is now completely sorted. Upper part of the list now consists of two numbers (1 and 7) and this sub-list is unsorted, in general.

Next, compare third number 8 with fourth number 1. These numbers are not in order, therefore swap these numbers. After swapping, the list becomes as given below:

    3 6 1 8 7

Next, there is comparison between 6 and 1. Proceeding in this manner, the complete list is sorted.

In this program, LOC 2 defines int type array intStorage to store the list of numbers entered by user. LOC 3 defines the int variable kount that represents the size of list of data elements. LOCs 4-20 define the function insertionSort() that sorts a list of unordered numbers in to a list of ascending numbers. Three int type variables are declared in the LOCs 6-8. LOCs 9-19 consist of a for loop. LOCs 12-15 consist of a while loop.

LOCs 21-36 consist of the main() function. LOC 24 asks the user to enter the size of list and this size of list is assigned to int variable kount. LOS 26 asks the user to populate the list. The elements of list are stored in the int array intStorage. LOC 31 calls the function insertionSort() that sorts the the unordered list. LOCs 33-34 consists of a for loop that displays the sorted list of numbers on the screen.

9-5. Sort a Given List of Numbers Using a Selection Sort

Problem

You want to sort a given list of unordered numbers in an ascending (ie, increasing) order using a selection sort.

Solution

Write a C program that sorts a given list of unordered numbers in an ascending (ie. increasing) order, with the following specifications:

- Program defines int type array intStorage to store the list of numbers entered by user.

- Program defines the function selectSort() that sorts the given list of unordered numbers in an asending (ie, increasing) order using the selection sort algorithm.

288

The Code

Code of C program written with these specifications is given below. Type the following C program in a text editor and save it in the folder C:\Code with the filename sort3.c:

```
/* This program sorts a given list of unordered integers in an increasing
order */
/* using a selection sort. */
                                                                  /* BL */
#include<stdio.h>                                                 /* L1 */
                                                                  /* BL */
int intStorage[20];                                               /* L2 */
int kount = 0;                                                    /* L3 */
                                                                  /* BL */
void selectSort()                                                 /* L4 */
{                                                                 /* L5 */
  int i, j, k, intTemp, intMin;                                   /* L6 */
  for(i=0; i < kount-1; i++) {      /* outer for loop begins */   /* L7 */
    intMin = intStorage[i];                                       /* L8 */
    k = i;                                                        /* L9 */
    for(j = i+1; j < kount; j++) {  /* inner for loop begins */   /* L10 */
      if(intMin > intStorage[j]) {  /* if statement begins */     /* L11 */
        intMin = intStorage[j];                                   /* L12 */
        k = j;                                                    /* L13 */
      }                             /* if statement ends */       /* L14 */
    }                               /* inner for loop end */      /* L15 */
    intTemp = intStorage[i];                                      /* L16 */
    intStorage[i] = intStorage[k];                                /* L17 */
    intStorage[k] = intTemp;                                      /* L18 */
  }                                 /* outer for loop end */      /* L19 */
}                                                                 /* L20 */
                                                                  /* BL */
void main()                                                       /* L21 */
{                                                                 /* L22 */
  int i;                                                          /* L23 */
  printf("Enter the number of data elements N (2 <= N <= 20): "); /* L24 */
  scanf("%d", &kount);                                            /* L25 */
  printf("Enter the %d integers I (0 <= I <= 30000) ", kount);    /* L26 */
  printf("separated by white spaces: \n");                        /* L27 */
  for (i=0; i < kount; i++)                                       /* L28 */
    scanf("%d", &intStorage[i]);                                  /* L29 */
  fflush(stdin);                                                  /* L30 */
  selectSort();                                                   /* L31 */
  printf("Sorted List: ");                                        /* L32 */
  for(i = 0; i < kount; i++)                                      /* L33 */
    printf("%d ",intStorage[i]);                                  /* L34 */
  printf("\nThank you.\n");                                       /* L35 */
}                                                                 /* L36 */
```

Compile and execute this program. A run of this program is given below:

```
Enter the number of items in the list, N (2 <= N <= 20): 8    ↵
Enter the 8 integers I (0 <= I <= 30000) separated by white spaces:
80  20  10  30  60  40  70  50    ↵
Sorted List: 10   20   30   40   50   60   70   80
Thank you.
```

How It Works

Like insertion sort, selection sort is also an in-place comparison-based sorting algorithm. In selection sort, list is divided into two parts: sorted part that lies to left end and unsorted part that lies to right end. The smallest number is selected from the unsorted list and it is interchanged with the first number (ie, leftmost number). Then next smallest number is selected from the unsorted list and it is swapped with second number. This process is repeated until the complete list is sorted. Selection sort has worst case complexity of $O(n^2)$ where n is the size of list.

Suppose the unsorted list is as given below:

90 30 50 10 20 80

The smallest number in this list is 10, interchange it with the first number 90. After interchange, the list becomes as follows:

10 30 50 90 20 80

Now, the first number 10 represents the sorted sub-list that lies to left-end and remaining four numbers represent the unsorted sub-list that lies to right-end. Next, the smallest number in the unsorted sub-list is 20. Interchange it with the first number in the unsorted sub-list, ie, with 30. After interchange the complete list becomes as follows:

10 20 50 90 30 80

Now the first two numbers 10 and 20 represent the sorted sub-list that lies to left-end and remaining three numbers represent the unsorted sub-list that lies to right-end. Next, the smallest number in the unsorted sub-list is 30. Interchange it with the first number in the unsorted sub-list, ie. with 50. After interchange the complete list becomes as follows:

10 20 30 90 50 80

Now the first three numbers 10, 20 and 30 represent the sorted sub-list that lies to left-end and remaining two numbers represent unsorted sub-list that lies to right-end. Proceeding in this manner, the complete list is sorted.

In this program, LOC 2 defines int type array intStorage to store the list of numbers entered by user. LOC 3 defines the int variable kount that represents the size of list of data elements. LOCs 4-20 define the function selectSort() that sorts a list of unordered numbers in to a list of ascending numbers. Five int type variables are declared in the LOC 6. LOCs 7-19 consist of an outer for loop and LOCs 10-15 consist of an inner for loop.

LOCs 21-36 consist of main() function. LOC 24 asks the user to enter the size of list and this size of list is assigned to int variable kount. LOS 26 asks the user to populate the list.

The elements of list are stored in the int array intStorage. LOC 31 calls the function selectSort() that sorts the the unordered list. LOCs 33-34 consists of a for loop that displays the sorted list of numbers on the screen.

9-6. Sort a Given List of Numbers Using a Merge Sort

Problem

You want to sort a given list of unordered numbers in an ascending (ie, increasing) order using a merge sort.

Solution

Write a C program that sorts a given list of unordered numbers in an ascending (ie. increasing) order, with the following specifications:

- Program defines int type array intStorage to store the list of numbers entered by user.

- Program defines the function mergeSort() that sorts the given list of unordered numbers in an asending (ie, increasing) order using the merge sort algorithm.

The Code

Code of C program written with these specifications is given below. Type the following C program in a text editor and save it in the folder C:\Code with the filename sort4.c:

```
/* This program sorts a given list of unordered integers in an increasing
order */
/* using a merge sort. */
                                                    /* BL */
#include<stdio.h>                                   /* L1 */
                                                    /* BL */
int intStorage[20];                                 /* L2 */
int kount = 0;                                       /* L3 */
                                                    /* BL */
void merge(int m1, int n1, int m2, int n2);         /* L4 */
                                                    /* BL */
void mergeSort(int m, int n)                        /* L5 */
{                                                    /* L6 */
    int intMid;                                     /* L7 */
    if(m < n)                                       /* L8 */
```

291

```
    {                                                      /* L9  */
        intMid = (m + n)/2;                                /* L10 */
        mergeSort(m, intMid);                              /* L11 */
        mergeSort(intMid + 1, n);                          /* L12 */
        merge(m, intMid, intMid + 1, n);                   /* L13 */
    }                                                      /* L14 */
}                                                          /* L15 */
                                                           /* BL  */
void merge(int m1, int n1, int m2, int n2)                 /* L16 */
{                                                          /* L17 */
    int tmpStorage[40];                                    /* L18 */
    int m, n, k;                                           /* L19 */
    m = m1;                                                /* L20 */
    n = m2;                                                /* L21 */
    k = 0;                                                 /* L22 */
    while(m <= n1 && n <= n2)                              /* L23 */
    {                                                      /* L24 */
        if(intStorage[m] < intStorage[n])                  /* L25 */
            tmpStorage[k++] = intStorage[m++];             /* L26 */
        else                                               /* L27 */
            tmpStorage[k++] = intStorage[n++];             /* L28 */
    }                                                      /* L29 */
    while(m <= n1)                                         /* L30 */
        tmpStorage[k++] = intStorage[m++];                 /* L31 */
    while(n <= n2)                                         /* L32 */
        tmpStorage[k++] = intStorage[n++];                 /* L33 */
    for(m = m1, n = 0; m <= n2; m++, n++)                  /* L34 */
        intStorage[m] = tmpStorage[n];                     /* L35 */
}                                                          /* L36 */
                                                           /* BL  */
void main()                                                /* L37 */
{                                                          /* L38 */
  int kount, i;                                            /* L39 */
  printf("Enter the number of data elements N (2 <= N <= 20): ");  /* L40 */
  scanf("%d", &kount);                                     /* L41 */
  printf("Enter the %d integers I (0 <= I <= 30000) ", kount);    /* L42 */
  printf("separated by white spaces: \n");                 /* L43 */
  for (i=0; i < kount; i++)                                /* L44 */
    scanf("%d", &intStorage[i]);                           /* L45 */
  fflush(stdin);                                           /* L46 */
  mergeSort(0, kount-1);                                   /* L47 */
  printf("Sorted List: ");                                 /* L48 */
  for(i = 0; i < kount; i++)                               /* L49 */
    printf("%d ",intStorage[i]);                           /* L50 */
  printf("\nThank you.\n");                                /* L51 */
}                                                          /* L52 */
```

Compile and execute this program. A run of this program is given below:

```
Enter the number of items in the list, N (2 <= N <= 20): 8  ↵
Enter the 8 integers I (0 <= I <= 30000) separated by white spaces:
80 70 60 50 40 30 60 10   ↵
Sorted List: 10  30  40  50  60  60  70  80
Thank you.
```

How It Works

Merge sort is an efficient algorithm and it can be used with large sized lists. Merge sort divides the array into two equal, or almost equal, halves. If list consists of eight elements, then it is divided into two sub-lists each containing four elements. If list consists of nine elements then it is divided into two sub-lists with four and five elements. These halves are again divided into equal, or almost equal, halves. This process is repeated untill each sub-list consists of only one element. A list that consists of only one element is already sorted. Then these sorted sublists are merged together in stepwise manner to form the completely sorted list. This process is implemented with the help of recursion. Mege sort has worst case complexity of O(n log n).

Suppose, the unsorted list is as given below:

83472165

This list consists of eight elements; therefore divide this list into two equal sub-lists, each containing four elements, as given below:

8347 2165

Again divide these sub-lists into still smaller sub-lists (total four sub-lists) as follows

83 47 21 65

Again divide these sub-lists into still smaller sub-lists (total eight sub-lists) as follows:

8 3 4 7 2 1 6 5

Now the process of merging the sub-lists begins. Consider first and second sub-lists (8 and 3). These are not in order, therefore, you need to swap these sub-lists. Consider third and fourth sub-lists (4 and 7). These are in order and hence no swapping is needed. Consider fifth and sixth sub-lists (2 and 1). These are not in order, therefore, you need to swap these sub-lists. Similarly, the seventh and eights sub-lists (6 and 5) are not in order and you need to interchange these sub-lists. Finally, you get the four sorted sub-lists as follows:

38 47 12 56

Next first and second sub-lists are merged together with sorting in mind. Also, third and fourth sub-lists are merged together. You get the following two sorted sub-lists:

3478 1256

Next, these two sub-lists are merged together with sorting in mind and you get the sorted list as follows:

12345678

In this program, LOC 2 defines int type array intStorage to store the list of numbers entered by user. LOC 3 defines the int variable kount that represents the size of list of data elements. LOCs 5-15 define the function mergeSort() that sorts a list of unordered numbers in to a list of ascending numbers. LOCs 16-36 define the function merge(). Function mergeSort() is called by the main() function and the function merge() is called by the function mergeSort(). Function mergeSort() also calls itself recursively.

LOCs 37-52 define the main() function. LOC 40 asks the user to enter the size of list and this size of list is assigned to int variable kount. LOS 42 asks the user to populate the list. The elements of list are stored in the int array intStorage. LOC 47 calls the function mergeSort() that sorts the the unordered list. LOCs 49-50 consists of a for loop that displays the sorted list of numbers on the screen.

9-7. Sort a Given List of Numbers Using a Shell Sort

Problem

You want to sort a given list of unordered numbers in an ascending (ie, increasing) order using a shell sort.

Solution

Write a C program that sorts a given list of unordered numbers in an ascending (ie. increasing) order, with the following specifications:

- Program defines int type array intStorage to store the list of numbers entered by user.

- Program defines the function shellSort() that sorts the given list of unordered numbers in an asending (ie, increasing) order using the shell sort algorithm.

The Code

Code of C program written with these specifications is given below. Type the following C program in a text editor and save it in the folder C:\Code with the filename sort5.c:

```
/* This program sorts a given list of unordered integers in an increasing
order */
/* using a shell sort. */
                                                           /* BL */
#include<stdio.h>                                          /* L1 */
                                                           /* BL */
int intStorage[20];                                        /* L2 */
int kount = 0;                                             /* L3 */
                                                           /* BL */
```

```
void shellSort()                                                  /* L4  */
{                                                                 /* L5  */
  int in, out;                                                    /* L6  */
  int insert;                                                     /* L7  */
  int gap = 1;                                                    /* L8  */
  int elements = kount;                                           /* L9  */
  int i = 0;                                                      /* L10 */
  while(gap <= elements/3)                                        /* L11 */
    gap = gap * 3 + 1;                                            /* L12 */
  while(gap > 0) {                                                /* L13 */
    for(out = gap; out < elements; out++) {                      /* L14 */
      insert = intStorage[out];                                  /* L15 */
      in = out;                                                  /* L16 */
      while(in > gap -1 && intStorage[in - gap] >= insert) {     /* L17 */
        intStorage[in] = intStorage[in - gap];                   /* L18 */
        in -= gap;                                               /* L19 */
      }                                                          /* L20 */
      intStorage[in] = insert;                                   /* L21 */
    }                                                            /* L22 */
    gap = (gap -1) /3;                                           /* L23 */
    i++;                                                         /* L24 */
  }                                                              /* L25 */
}                                                                /* L26 */
                                                                 /* BL  */
void main() {                                                    /* L27 */
  int i;                                                         /* L28 */
  printf("Enter the number of items in the list, N (2 <= N <= 20): ");  /* L29 */
  scanf("%d", &kount);                                           /* L30 */
  printf("Enter the %d integers I (0 <= I <= 30000) ", kount);   /* L31 */
  printf("separated by white spaces: \n");                       /* L32 */
  for (i=0; i < kount; i++)                                      /* L33 */
    scanf("%d", &intStorage[i]);                                 /* L34 */
  fflush(stdin);                                                 /* L35 */
  shellSort();                                                   /* L36 */
  printf("Sorted List: ");                                       /* L37 */
  for(i = 0; i < kount; i++)                                     /* L38 */
    printf("%d ", intStorage[i]);                                /* L39 */
  printf("\nThank you.\n");                                      /* L40 */
}                                                                /* L41 */
```

Compile and execute this program. A run of this program is given below:

```
Enter the number of items in the list, N (2 <= N <= 20): 8   ↵
Enter the 8 integers I (0 <= I <= 30000) separated by white spaces:
80 70 60 50 40 30 20 10   ↵
Sorted List: 10  20  30  40  50  60  70  80
Thank you.
```

How It Works

Shell sort is an efficient sorting method and it is based on insertion sort method. In this method, pairs of elements which are far apart from each other are sorted firstly, then the gap between the elements to be compared is reduced progressively. The gap between the elements is generally denoted by h and the process stated above is repeated by reducing the value of h until it becomes 1. In this program, however, int variable gap is used to denote the gap between the elements. Thus out-of-place elements are moved faster to their proper position compared to insertion sort. This method is developed by Donald Shell. Worst case complexity of shell sort is O(n) where n is size of the list.

In this program, LOC 2 defines int type array intStorage to store the list of numbers entered by user. LOC 3 defines the int variable kount that represents the size of list of data elements. LOCs 4-26 define the function shellSort() that sorts a list of unordered numbers in to a list of ascending numbers. LOCs 6-10 declare the five int type variables. LOCs 11-12 consist of a while-loop that sets the value of int variable gap. LOCs 13-25 consist of a while-loop that carries out the task of sorting the list of unordered numbers.

LOCs 27-41 define the main() function. LOC 29 asks the user to enter the size of list and this size of list is assigned to int variable kount. LOS 31 asks the user to populate the list. The elements of list are stored in the int type array intStorage. LOC 36 calls the function shellSort() that sorts the unordered list. LOCs 38-39 consists of a for loop that displays the sorted list of numbers on the screen.

9-8. Sort a Given List of Numbers Using a Quick Sort

Problem

You want to sort a given list of unordered numbers in an ascending (ie, increasing) order using a quick sort.

Solution

Write a C program that sorts a given list of unordered numbers in an ascending (ie. increasing) order, with the following specifications:

- Program defines int type array intStorage to store the list of numbers entered by user.

- Program defines the function quickSort() that sorts the given list of unordered numbers in an asending (ie, increasing) order using the quick sort algorithm.

The Code

Code of C program written with these specifications is given below. Type the following C program in a text editor and save it in the folder C:\Code with the filename sort6.c:

```
/* This program sorts a given list of unordered integers in an increasing      order */
/* using a quick sort. */
                                                                /* BL */
#include<stdio.h>                                               /* L1 */
                                                                /* BL */
int intStorage[20];                                             /* L2 */
int kount = 0;                                                  /* L3 */
                                                                /* BL */
void swap(int n1, int n2)                                       /* L4 */
{                                                               /* L5 */
  int intTemp = intStorage[n1];                                 /* L6 */
  intStorage[n1] = intStorage[n2];                              /* L7 */
  intStorage[n2] = intTemp;                                     /* L8 */
}                                                               /* L9 */
                                                                /* BL */
int partition(int left, int right, int pivot)                  /* L10 */
{                                                               /* L11 */
  int lPtr = left -1;                                           /* L12 */
  int rPtr = right;                                             /* L13 */
  while(1) {                                                    /* L14 */
    while(intStorage[++lPtr] < pivot) {                         /* L15 */
    }                                                           /* L16 */
    while(rPtr > 0 && intStorage[--rPtr] > pivot) {             /* L17 */
    }                                                           /* L18 */
    if(lPtr >= rPtr)                                            /* L19 */
      break;                                                    /* L20 */
    else                                                        /* L21 */
      swap(lPtr, rPtr);                                         /* L22 */
  }                                                             /* L23 */
  swap(lPtr,right);                                             /* L24 */
  return lPtr;                                                  /* L25 */
}                                                               /* L26 */
                                                                /* BL */
void quickSort(int left, int right)                            /* L27 */
{                                                               /* L28 */
  int pivot, partPt;                                            /* L29 */
  if(right - left <= 0) {                                       /* L30 */
    return;                                                     /* L31 */
  }                                                             /* L32 */
```

```
  else {                                              /* L33 */
    pivot = intStorage[right];                        /* L34 */
    partPt = partition(left, right, pivot);           /* L35 */
    quickSort(left, partPt - 1);                      /* L36 */
    quickSort(partPt + 1,right);                      /* L37 */
  }                                                   /* L38 */
}                                                     /* L39 */
                                                      /* BL  */
void main()                                           /* L40 */
{                                                     /* L41 */
  int i;                                              /* L42 */
  printf("Enter the number of items in the list, N (2 <= N <= 20): ");  /* L43 */
  scanf("%d", &kount);                                /* L44 */
  printf("Enter the %d integers I (0 <= I <= 30000) ", kount);  /* L45 */
  printf("separated by white spaces: \n");            /* L46 */
  for (i=0; i < kount; i++)                           /* L47 */
    scanf("%d", &intStorage[i]);                      /* L48 */
  fflush(stdin);                                      /* L49 */
  quickSort(0, kount - 1);                            /* L50 */
  printf("Sorted List: ");                            /* L51 */
   for(i = 0; i < kount; i++)                         /* L52 */
    printf("%d ", intStorage[i]);                     /* L53 */
  printf("\nThank you.\n");                           /* L54 */
}                                                     /* L55 */
```

Compile and execute this program. A run of this program is given below:

```
Enter the number of items in the list, N (2 <= N <= 20): 8    ↵
Enter the 8 integers I (0 <= I <= 30000) separated by white spaces:
80 70 60 50 40 30 20 10    ↵
Sorted List: 10  20  30  40  50  60  70  80
Thank you.
```

How It Works

Quick sort method is very efficient and can be used for sorting the large sized lists. In this method an array is partitioned into two arrays such that one array holds the values smaller than the pivot and other array holds the values greater than the pivot. Once a list is partitioned into two smaller sub-lists, the function that performs the sorting, calls itself recursively to sort the smaller sub-lists. The worst case complexity of this method is $O(n \log n)$ where n is the size of the list.

In this program, LOC 2 defines int type array intStorage to store the list of numbers entered by user. LOC 3 defines the int variable kount that represents the size of list of data elements.

LOCs 4-9 define the function swap() that simply swaps the numbers in the list. LOCs 10-26 define the function partition(). This function calls the function swap() as per requirement. LOCs 27-39 define the function quickSort(). This function calls the function partition() and it also calls itself recursively.

LOCs 40-55 define the function main(). LOC 43 asks the user to enter the size of list and this size of list is assigned to int variable kount. LOS 45 asks the user to populate the list. The elements of list are stored in the int array intStorage. LOC 50 calls the function quickSort() that sorts the the unordered list. LOCs 52-53 consists of a for loop that displays the sorted list of numbers on the screen.

CHAPTER 10

■ ■ ■

Cryptographic Systems

In this chapter we will deal with application programs related to cryptography. In love, war and business, we need to send the messages secretly. The art and science of keeping the messages secure is called cryptography. A message to be dispatched is also called as plaintext or cleartext. Encryption is the process of converting the plaintext into a scrambled, unreadable message. This message is called ciphertext. The process of converting the scrambled message back into plaintext is called decryption.

The various methods used for encryption/decryption of messages are as follows:

- Reverse cipher. In reverse cipher, the text is simply reversed in order to encrypt it. Unless the text is palindrome, the encrypted text is Greek to anyone. For example, the word "computer" is encrypted as "retupmoc" in reverse cipher. During decryption, ciphertext is reversed to retrieve plaintext.

- Caesar cipher. Caesar cipher was invented by Julius Caesar hence the name. If key = 2, then letters A, B, C,..., X, Y, Z in plaintext are replaced by the letters C, D, E,..., Z, A, B, respectively, to obtain the ciphertext. During decryption, the letters C, D, E,..., Z, A, B in ciphertext are replaced by the letters A, B, C,..., X, Y, Z, respectively, to retrieve the plaintext. In program, letters are first conveted to their ASCII code and then key is added (during encryption) and subtracted (during decryption) from the ASCII codes.

- Transposition cipher. In transposition cipher, firstly, plaintext is written in a 2-dimensional array, then dimensions of this 2-dimensional array are interchanged (ie, rows become columns and columns become rows), and then text is read from this modified 2-dimensional array which is nothing but ciphertext. See Figure 10-1.

© Shirish Chavan 2017
S. Chavan, *C Recipes*, DOI 10.1007/978-1-4842-2967-5_10

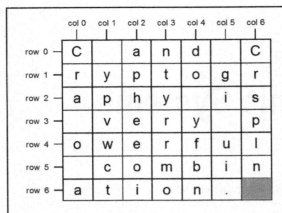

In order to read plaintext, simply read row after row, starting from row 0, followed by row 1, followed by row 2, and so on.

In order to read ciphertext, simply read column after column, starting from column 0, followed by column 1, followed by column 2, and so on.

Plaintext → C and Cryptography is very powerful combination.

Ciphertext → Cra o a ypvwctapheeointyrrmodo yfbn gi ui.Crspln

Figure 10-1. *Cryptography using Transposition cipher. Here, key is 7, hence number of columns are 7.*

- Multiplicative cipher. Multiplicative cipher is analogous to Caesar cipher. However, instead of addition/subtraction, multiplication/division is performed. During encryption, ASCII codes of letters in plaintext are multiplied by key to obtain ciphertext. During decryption, ASCII codes of letters in ciphertext are multiplied by an inverse function of the key to retrieve the plaintext.

- Affine cipher. Affine cipher is combination of Caesar cipher and Multiplicative cipher.

- Simple Substitution cipher. In Simple Substitution cipher, every letter in alphabet is randomly replaced by another letter to obtain the key. Thus key in this cipher is nothing but the string of 26 letters (alphabets) in random order. Using this key, encryption and decryption is performed.

- Vigenère cipher. Vigenère cipher is nothing but the Caesar cipher with multiple keys. As it uses multiple keys, it is called as "polyalphabetic substitution cipher." Let the word CAT be the Vigenere cipher text key (see Figure 10-2). Here, letter C means key is 2, letter A means key is 0, and letter T means key is 19. During encryption and decryption these keys are used in cyclical order. During encryption, first letter in plaintext is encrypted using the key = 2, second letter in plaintext is encrypted using the key = 0, third letter in plaintext is encrypted using the key = 19, fourth letter in plaintext is encrypted using the key = 2, and so on. During decryption also these keys are used in the same order.

A	B	C	D	E	F	G	H	I
0	1	2	3	4	5	6	7	8
J	K	L	M	N	O	P	Q	R
9	10	11	12	13	14	15	16	17
S	T	U	V	W	X	Y	Z	
18	19	20	21	22	23	24	25	

Figure 10-2. *Letters A to Z are serially numbered as 0 to 25 as shown here*

- One-Time Pad cipher. This cipher is impossible to crack but also inconvenient to use. It is nothing but a Vigenère cipher with the following additional features: (a) key is exactly as long as the plaintext message, (b) key is made up of randomly selected characters, and (c) the key once used is thrown away and never used again. Like many consumable items, this key also believes in the policy of "use and throw."

- RSA cipher. RSA cipher is named after its inventors Ron Rivest, Adi Shamir, and Leonard Adleman. This cipher uses two types of keys, namely, Public key and Private key. Public key is used for encryption of plaintext. Private key is used for decryption of ciphertext. This cipher derives its strenght from the fact that if two large prime numbers are multiplied then the resulting number is difficult to factorize.

10-1. Use the Reverse Cipher Method
Problem

You want to implement a cryptographic system using the Reverse cipher method.
  Merits:

- Easy to implement
- Quick execution of program
- Needs less memory

Demerits:

- Not very difficult to decipher
- Cannot be used in high-level applications

Solution

Write a C program that implements a cryptographic system using the Reverse cipher method, with the following specifications:

- Program defines the functions: (a) menu() to display menu for users on the screen, (b) encryptMsg() to encrypt the plaintext, and (c) decryptMsg() to decrypt the ciphertext.

- Function encryptMsg() simply reverses the plaintext in order to encrypt it. Function decryptMsg() simply reverses the encrypted text in order to restore the plaintext.

- Program also defines the char type arrays msgOriginal, msgEncrypt, and msgDecrypt to store the messages. Array should accommodate 100 characters.

The Code

Code of C program written with these specifications is given below. Type the following C program in a text editor and save it in the folder C:\Code with the filename crypt1.c:

```
/* This program implements cryptographic system using the Reverse cipher method. */  /* BL */
                                                                                     /* L1 */
#include <stdio.h>                                                                   /* L2 */
#include <string.h>                                                                  /* BL */
                                                                                     /* L3 */
char msgOriginal[100];                                                               /* L4 */
char msgEncrypt[100];                                                                /* L5 */
char msgDecrypt[100];                                                                /* L6 */
int intChoice, length;                                                               /* BL */
                                                                                     /* L7 */
void menu()                                                                          /* L8 */
{                                                                                    /* L9 */
  printf("\nEnter 1 to Encrypt a Message.");                                         /* L10 */
  printf("\nEnter 2 to Decrypt an Encrypted Message.");                              /* L11 */
  printf("\nEnter 3 to Stop the Execution of Program.");                             /* L12 */
  printf("\nNow Enter Your Choice (1, 2 or 3) and Strike Enter Key: ");              /* L13 */
  scanf("%d", &intChoice);                                                           /* L14 */
}                                                                                    /* BL */
                                                                                     /* L15 */
void encryptMsg()                                                                    /* L16 */
{                                                                                    /* L17 */
  int i, j;                                                                          /* L18 */
  fflush(stdin);                                                                     /* L19 */
  printf("Enter the Message to be Encrypted (upto 100 characters): \n");             /* L20 */
  gets(msgOriginal);                                                                 /* L21 */
  length = strlen(msgOriginal);
```

```
  j = length - 1;                                                  /* L22 */
  for (i = 0; i < length; i++) {                                   /* L23 */
    msgEncrypt[j] = msgOriginal[i] ;                               /* L24 */
    j--;                                                           /* L25 */
  }                                                                /* L26 */
  msgEncrypt[length] = '\0';                                       /* L27 */
  printf("\nEncrypted Message: %s", msgEncrypt);                   /* L28 */
}                                                                  /* L29 */
                                                                   /* BL   */
void decryptMsg()                                                  /* L30 */
{                                                                  /* L31 */
  int i, j;                                                        /* L32 */
  fflush(stdin);                                                   /* L33 */
  printf("Enter the Message to be Decrypted (upto 100 characters): \n"); /* L34 */
  gets(msgEncrypt);                                                /* L35 */
  length = strlen(msgEncrypt);                                     /* L36 */
  j = length - 1;                                                  /* L37 */
  for (i = 0; i < length; i++) {                                   /* L38 */
    msgDecrypt[j] = msgEncrypt[i] ;                                /* L39 */
    j--;                                                           /* L40 */
  }                                                                /* L41 */
  msgDecrypt[length] = '\0';                                       /* L42 */
  printf("\nDecrypted Message: %s", msgDecrypt);                   /* L43 */
}                                                                  /* L44 */
                                                                   /* BL   */
void main()                                                        /* L45 */
{                                                                  /* L46 */
  do {                                                             /* L47 */
    menu();                                                        /* L48 */
    switch (intChoice) {                                           /* L49 */
      case 1:                                                      /* L50 */
              encryptMsg();                                        /* L51 */
              break;                                               /* L52 */
      case 2:                                                      /* L53 */
              decryptMsg();                                        /* L54 */
              break;                                               /* L55 */
      default:                                                     /* L56 */
              printf("\nThank you.\n");                            /* L57 */
              exit(0);                                             /* L58 */
    }                                                              /* L59 */
  } while (1);                                                     /* L60 */
}                                                                  /* L61 */
```

Compile and execute this program. A run of this program is given below:

```
Enter 1 to Encrypt a Message.
Enter 2 to Decrypt an Encrypted Message.
Enter 3 to Stop the Execution of Program.
Now Enter Your Choice (1, 2, or 3) and Strike Enter Key: 1  ↵
Enter the Message to be Encrypted (upto 100 characters):
C and Cryptography is very powerful combination.  ↵

Encrypted Message: .noitanibmoc lufrewop yrev si yhpargotpyrC dna C
Enter 1 to Encrypt a Message.
Enter 2 to Decrypt an Encrypted Message.
Enter 3 to Stop the Execution of Program.
Now Enter Your Choice (1, 2, or 3) and Strike Enter Key: 2  ↵
Enter the Message to be Decrypted (upto 100 characters):
.noitanibmoc lufrewop yrev si yhpargotpyrC dna C  ↵

Decrypted Message: C and Cryptography is very powerful combination.
Enter 1 to Encrypt a Message.
Enter 2 to Decrypt an Encrypted Message.
Enter 3 to Stop the Execution of Program.
Now Enter Your Choice (1, 2, or 3) and Strike Enter Key: 3  ↵
Thank you.
```

How It Works

Reverse cipher is a simple method to cipher the plaintext. In this method, the plaintext to be encrypted is simply reversed. For example, if plaintext is "computer" then encrypted text according to Reverse cipher is "retupmoc." This method can be implemented using recursion. However, in this program, recursion is avoided to keep the logic simple.

In the LOCs 3-5, three char type arrays are declared namely, msgOriginal, msgEncrypt, and msgDecrypt. LOCs 7-14 consist of definition of function menu(). This function displays menu for users on the screen so that various options in this program can be used conveniently. LOCs 9-12 ask the user to enter an appropriate choice and also describe the various options available to user. LOC 13 reads the choice entered by user and stores this choice in the int variable intChoice.

LOCs 15-29 consist of definition of the function encryptMsg(). This function simply reverses the plaintext and stores the encrypted text in the array msgEncrypt. LOC 19 asks the user to enter the plaintext. The plaintext entered by user is stored in the variable msgOriginal. LOCs 23-26 consist of a for loop which reverses the plaintext stored in the msgOriginal and processed text is stored in the variable msgEncrypt.

LOCs 30-44 consist of definition of the function decryptMsg(). This function again reverses the ciphertext stored in the array msgEncrypt and stores the processed text in the array msgDecrypt.

LOCs 45-61 consist of definition of the function `main()`. LOCs 47-61 consist of a `do-while` loop. This seems to be an infinite loop, however, function `exit()` in the LOC 58 effectively stops the execution of this loop. LOC 48 calls the function `menu()` which displays the menu for users on the screen. The choice entered by user is stored in the `int` variable `intChoice`. LOCs 49-59 consist of `switch` statement. Value stored in `intChoice` is passsed to this statement. If value of `intChoice` is 1 then function `encryptMsg()` is called. If value of `intChoice` is 2 then function `decryptMsg()` is called. If value of `intChoice` is else then function `exit()` is called which terminates the execution of `do-while` loop and also terminates the execution of this program.

10-2. Use the Caesar Cipher Method
Problem

You want to implement a cryptographic system using the `Caesar cipher` method. Merits:

- Based on simple logic

- Historically important

- Can be modified to make the deciphering of ciphertext difficult

- Economical to implement

Demerits:

- Ciphertext can be deciphered using brute-force techniques

- Cannot be used in high-level applications without modifications

- Transportation of key securely is difficult

Solution

Write a C program that implements a cryptographic system using the `Caesar cipher` method, with the following specifications:

- Program defines the functions: (a) `menu()` to display menu for users on the screen, (b) `encryptMsg()` to encrypt the plaintext, and (c) `decryptMsg()` to decrypt the ciphertext.

- Assume the suitable value for KEY. Function `encryptMsg()` encrypts the plaintext simply by adding the KEY to ASCII values of letters. Function `decryptMsg()` decrypts the ciphertext simply by subtracting the KEY from the ASCII values of letters.

- Program also defines the char type arrays `msgOriginal`, `msgEncrypt`, and `msgDecrypt` to store the messages. Array should accommodate 100 characters.

The Code

Code of C program written with these specifications is given below. Type the following C program in a text editor and save it in the folder C:\Code with the filename crypt2.c:

```
/* This program implements a cryptographic system using Caesar cipher method. */
                                                                    /* BL */
#include <stdio.h>                                                  /* L1 */
#include <string.h>                                                 /* L2 */
                                                                    /* BL */
#define  KEY  5                                                     /* L3 */
                                                                    /* BL */
char msgOriginal[100];                                              /* L4 */
char msgEncrypt[100];                                              /* L5 */
char msgDecrypt[100];                                              /* L6 */
int intChoice, length;                                             /* L7 */
                                                                    /* BL */
void menu()                                                        /* L8 */
{                                                                   /* L9 */
  printf("\nEnter 1 to Encrypt a Message.");                       /* L10 */
  printf("\nEnter 2 to Decrypt an Encrypted Message.");            /* L11 */
  printf("\nEnter 3 to Stop the Execution of Program.");           /* L12 */
  printf("\nNow Enter Your Choice (1, 2 or 3) and Strike Enter Key: ");  /* L13 */
  scanf("%d", &intChoice);                                          /* L14 */
}                                                                   /* L15 */
                                                                    /* BL */
void encryptMsg()                                                  /* L16 */
{                                                                   /* L17 */
  int i, ch;                                                        /* L18 */
  fflush(stdin);                                                    /* L19 */
  printf("Enter the Message to Encrypt, Do Not Include Spaces and \n");  /* L20 */
  printf("Punctuation Symbols (upto 100 alphabets): \n");          /* L21 */
  gets(msgOriginal);                                                /* L22 */
  length = strlen(msgOriginal);                                     /* L23 */
    for(i = 0; i < length; i++) {                                   /* L24 */
      ch = msgOriginal[i];                                          /* L25 */
      if(ch >= 'a' && ch <= 'z') {                                  /* L26 */
        ch = ch + KEY;                                              /* L27 */
        if(ch > 'z')                                                /* L28 */
          ch = ch - 'z' + 'a' - 1;                                  /* L29 */
        msgEncrypt[i] = ch;                                         /* L30 */
      }                                                             /* L31 */
      else if(ch >= 'A' && ch <= 'Z'){                              /* L32 */
        ch = ch + KEY;                                              /* L33 */
        if(ch > 'Z')                                                /* L34 */
          ch = ch - 'Z' + 'A' - 1;                                  /* L35 */
        msgEncrypt[i] = ch;                                         /* L36 */
      }                                                             /* L37 */
    }                                                               /* L38 */
```

```
  msgEncrypt[length] = '\0';                                      /* L39 */
  printf("\nEncrypted Message: %s", msgEncrypt);                  /* L40 */
}                                                                 /* L41 */
                                                                  /* BL  */
void decryptMsg()                                                 /* L42 */
{                                                                 /* L43 */
  int i, ch;                                                      /* L44 */
  fflush(stdin);                                                  /* L45 */
  printf("Enter the Message to Decrypt (upto 100 alphabets):\n"); /* L46 */
  gets(msgEncrypt);                                               /* L47 */
  length = strlen(msgEncrypt);                                    /* L48 */
  for(i = 0; i < length; i++) {                                   /* L49 */
    ch = msgEncrypt[i];                                           /* L50 */
    if(ch >= 'a' && ch <= 'z') {                                  /* L51 */
      ch = ch - KEY;                                              /* L52 */
      if(ch < 'a')                                                /* L53 */
        ch = ch + 'z' - 'a' + 1;                                  /* L54 */
      msgDecrypt[i] = ch;                                         /* L55 */
    }                                                             /* L56 */
    else if(ch >= 'A' && ch <= 'Z'){                              /* L57 */
      ch = ch - KEY;                                              /* L58 */
      if(ch < 'A')                                                /* L59 */
        ch = ch + 'Z' - 'A' + 1;                                  /* L60 */
      msgDecrypt[i] = ch;                                         /* L61 */
    }                                                             /* L62 */
  }                                                               /* L63 */
  msgDecrypt[length] = '\0';                                      /* L64 */
  printf("\nDecrypted Message: %s", msgDecrypt);                  /* L65 */
}                                                                 /* L66 */
                                                                  /* BL  */
void main()                                                       /* L67 */
{                                                                 /* L68 */
  do {                                                            /* L69 */
    menu();                                                       /* L70 */
    switch (intChoice) {                                          /* L71 */
      case 1:                                                     /* L72 */
              encryptMsg();                                       /* L73 */
              break;                                              /* L74 */
      case 2:                                                     /* L75 */
              decryptMsg();                                       /* L76 */
              break;                                              /* L77 */
      default:                                                    /* L78 */
              printf("\nThank you.\n");                           /* L79 */
              exit(0);                                            /* L80 */
    }                                                             /* L81 */
  } while (1);                                                    /* L82 */
}                                                                 /* L83 */
```

Compile and execute this program. A run of this program is given below:

```
Enter 1 to Encrypt a Message.
Enter 2 to Decrypt an Encrypted Message.
Enter 3 to Stop the Execution of Program.
Now Enter Your Choice (1, 2, or 3) and Strike Enter Key: 1  ↵
Enter the Message to Encrypt, Do Not Include Spaces and
Punctuation Symbols (upto 100 alphabets):
CandCryptographyIsVeryPowerfulCombination  ↵

Encrypted Message: HfsiHwduytlwfumdNxAjwdUtbjwkzqHtrgnfynts
Enter 1 to Encrypt a Message.
Enter 2 to Decrypt an Encrypted Message.
Enter 3 to Stop the Execution of Program.
Now Enter Your Choice (1, 2, or 3) and Strike Enter Key: 2  ↵
Enter the Message to Decrypt (upto 100 alphabets):
HfsiHwduytlwfumdNxAjwdUtbjwkzqHtrgnfynts  ↵

Decrypted Message: CandCryptographyIsVeryPowerfulCombination
Enter 1 to Encrypt a Message.
Enter 2 to Decrypt an Encrypted Message.
Enter 3 to Stop the Execution of Program.
Now Enter Your Choice (1, 2, or 3) and Strike Enter Key: 3  ↵
Thank you.
```

How It Works

Caesar cipher was invented by Julius Caesar. In this cipher, during encryption, key is added to ASCII values of letters in plaintext in order to obtain the ciphertext. Also, during decryption, key is subtracted from the ASCII values of letters in ciphertext in order to retrieve the plaintext.

For example, if value of key is 3 then during encryption, A would be ciphered to D, B would be ciphered to E, …, W would be ciphered to Z, X would be ciphered to A, Y would be ciphered to B, and Z would be ciphered to C. Ditto for lowercase letters. During decryption, the procedure is reverted.

In LOC 3, the value of KEY is set to be 5. In the LOCs 4-6, three char type arrays are declared namely, msgOriginal, msgEncrypt, and msgDecrypt. LOCs 8-15 consist of definition of function menu(). This function displays menu for users on the screen so that various options in this program can be used conveniently. LOCs 10-13 ask the user to enter an appropriate choice and also describe the various options available to user. LOC 14 reads the choice entered by user and stores this choice in the int variable intChoice.

LOCs 16-41 consist of definition of the function encryptMsg(). This function converts the plaintext into ciphertext. LOCs 20-21 ask the user to enter plaintext. LOC 22 reads this plaintext and stores it in the variable msgOriginal. LOCs 24-38 consist of a for loop. In this for loop the plaintext is converted into ciphertext using the Caesar cipher method. Ciphertext is stored in the variable msgEncrypt. LOC 40 displays the ciphertext on the screen.

LOCs 42-66 consist of definition of the function decryptMsg(). This function retrieves the plaintext from the ciphertext. LOC 46 asks the user to enter the ciphertext. The ciphertext entered by user is read and stored in the variable msgEncrypt in LOC 47. LOCs 49-63 consist of a for loop. In this for loop, the ciphertext is decrypted into a plaintext and is stored in the variable msgDecrypt. LOC 65 displays this decrypted text on the screen.

LOCs 67-83 consist of definition of the function main(). LOCs 69-82 consist of a do-while loop. This seems to be an infinite loop, however, function exit() in the LOC 80 effectively stops the execution of this loop. LOC 70 calls the function menu() which displays the menu for users on the screen. The choice entered by user is stored in the int variable intChoice. LOCs 71-81 consist of a switch statement. Value stored in intChoice is passsed to this statement. If value of intChoice is 1 then function encryptMsg() is called. If value of intChoice is 2 then function decryptMsg() is called. If value of intChoice is else then function exit() is called which terminates the execution of do-while loop and also terminates the execution of this program.

10-3. Use the Transposition Cipher Method
Problem

You want to implement a cryptographic system using the Transposition cipher method.
Merits:

- More secure compared to Caesar cipher

- Can be modified to make the deciphering of ciphertext difficult

- Different versions of transposition cipher are available and we have a choice to select a suitable method that serves the problem best

Demerits:

- Logic is not simple and hence program is somewhat difficult to debug

- Level of security offered is moderate

- Not very effective for small messages

- Transportation of keys securely is difficult

Solution

Write a C program that implements a cryptographic system using the Transposition cipher method, with the following specifications:

- Program defines the functions: (a) menu() to display menu for users on the screen, (b) encryptMsg() to encrypt the plaintext, and (c) decryptMsg() to decrypt the ciphertext.

- Program also defines the char type arrays msgOriginal, msgEncrypt, and msgDecrypt to store the messages. Array should accommodate 100 characters.

The Code

Code of C program written with these specifications is given below. Type the following C program in a text editor and save it in the folder C:\Code with the filename crypt3.c:

```
/* This program implements a cryptographic system using the Transposition   /* BL */
cipher method. */
#include <stdio.h>                                                          /* L1 */
#include <string.h>                                                         /* L2 */
                                                                            /* BL */
#define  KEY  7                                                             /* L3 */
                                                                            /* BL */
char msgToEncrypt[110];                                                     /* L4 */
char msgToDecrypt[110];                                                     /* L5 */
char msgEncrypt[20][KEY];                                                   /* L6 */
char msgDecrypt[20][KEY];                                                   /* L7 */
int intChoice, length;                                                      /* L8 */
                                                                            /* BL */
void menu()                                                                 /* L9 */
{                                                                           /* L10 */
  printf("\nEnter 1 to Encrypt a Message.");                                /* L11 */
  printf("\nEnter 2 to Decrypt an Encrypted Message.");                     /* L12 */
  printf("\nEnter 3 to Stop the Execution of Program.");                    /* L13 */
  printf("\nNow Enter Your Choice (1, 2 or 3) and Strike Enter Key: ");     /* L14 */
  scanf("%d", &intChoice);                                                  /* L15 */
}                                                                           /* L16 */
                                                                            /* BL */
void encryptMsg()                                                           /* L17 */
{                                                                           /* L18 */
  int row, col, rows, cilr, length, k = 0;                                  /* L19 */
  printf("Enter the Message (20 to 110 letters) to be Encrypted: \n");      /* L20 */
  fflush(stdin);                                                            /* L21 */
  gets(msgToEncrypt);                                                       /* L22 */
  length = strlen(msgToEncrypt);                                            /* L23 */
  rows = (length/KEY) + 1 ;                                                 /* L24 */
  cilr = length % KEY; /* cilr - characters in last row */                  /* L25 */
  for(row = 0; row < rows; row++) {                                         /* L26 */
   for(col = 0; col < KEY; col++) {                                         /* L27 */
    msgEncrypt[row][col] = msgToEncrypt[k++];                               /* L28 */
    if (k == length) break;                                                 /* L29 */
   }                                                                        /* L30 */
  }                                                                         /* L31 */
 printf("\nEncrypted Message: \n");                                         /* L32 */
  for(col = 0; col < KEY; col++) {                                          /* L33 */
   for(row = 0; row < rows; row++) {                                        /* L34 */
    if ((col >= cilr) && (row == (rows-1)))                                 /* L35 */
       continue;                                                            /* L36 */
```

```
      printf("%c", msgEncrypt[row][col]);               /* L37 */
    }                                                    /* L38 */
  }                                                      /* L39 */
}                                                        /* L41 */
                                                         /* BL  */
void decryptMsg()                                        /* L42 */
{                                                        /* L43 */
  int row, col, rows, cilr, length, k = 0;               /* L44 */
  printf("Enter the Message (20 to 110 letters) to be Decrypted: \n"); /* L45 */
  fflush(stdin);                                         /* L46 */
  gets(msgToDecrypt);                                    /* L47 */
  length = strlen(msgToDecrypt);                         /* L48 */
  rows = (length/KEY) + 1 ;                              /* L49 */
  cilr = length % KEY;     /* cilr - characters in last row */  /* L50 */
  for(col = 0; col < KEY; col++) {                       /* L51 */
   for(row = 0; row < rows; row++) {                     /* L52 */
     if ((col >= cilr) && (row == (rows-1)))             /* L53 */
       continue;                                         /* L54 */
     msgDecrypt[row][col] = msgToDecrypt[k++];           /* L55 */
     if (k == length) break;                             /* L56 */
   }                                                     /* L57 */
  }                                                      /* L58 */
  printf("\nDecrypted Message: \n");                     /* L59 */
  for(row = 0; row < rows; row++) {                      /* L60 */
   for(col = 0; col < KEY; col++) {                      /* L61 */
     printf("%c", msgDecrypt[row][col]);                 /* L62 */
   }                                                     /* L63 */
  }                                                      /* L64 */
}                                                        /* L65 */
                                                         /* BL  */
void main()                                              /* L66 */
{                                                        /* L67 */
  do {                                                   /* L68 */
    menu();                                              /* L69 */
    switch (intChoice) {                                 /* L70 */
      case 1:                                            /* L71 */
              encryptMsg();                              /* L72 */
              break;                                     /* L73 */
      case 2:                                            /* L74 */
              decryptMsg();                              /* L75 */
              break;                                     /* L76 */
      default:                                           /* L77 */
              printf("\nThank you.\n");                  /* L78 */
              exit(0);                                   /* L79 */
    }                                                    /* L80 */
  } while (1);                                           /* L81 */
}                                                        /* L82 */
```

Compile and execute this program. A run of this program is given below:

```
Enter 1 to Encrypt a Message.
Enter 2 to Decrypt an Encrypted Message.
Enter 3 to Stop the Execution of Program.
Now Enter Your Choice (1, 2, or 3) and Strike Enter Key: 1    ⏎
Enter the Message (20 to 110 letters) to be Encrypted:
C and Cryptography is very powerful combination.    ⏎

Encrypted Message:
Cra o a ypvwctapheeointyrrmodo yfbn gi ui.Crspln
Enter 1 to Encrypt a Message.
Enter 2 to Decrypt an Encrypted Message.
Enter 3 to Stop the Execution of Program.
Now Enter Your Choice (1, 2, or 3) and Strike Enter Key: 2    ⏎
Enter the Message (20 to 110 letters) to be Decrypted:
Cra o a ypvwctapheeointyrrmodo yfbn gi ui.Crspln    ⏎

Decrypted Message:
C and Cryptography is very powerful combination.
Enter 1 to Encrypt a Message.
Enter 2 to Decrypt an Encrypted Message.
Enter 3 to Stop the Execution of Program.
Now Enter Your Choice (1, 2, or 3) and Strike Enter Key: 3    ⏎
Thank you.
```

How It Works

Firstly, let us discuss the working of Transposition cipher. Transposition cipher is illustrated in figure 10-1. Draw the table as shown in figure. Number of columns in this table should be equal to key. Here, key is 7, hence number of columns is also 7. Now write the plaintext in this table as follows: Write the first 7 (because key is 7) characters in the first row (i.e., row 0), then write the next 7 characters in the second row (i.e., row 1), and so on. The last cell in the last row is unoccupied hence it is shown shaded. Now plaintext is encrypted as follows: Firstly, write the characters in the first column (i.e., col 0), then write the characters in the second column (i.e., col 1), and so on. In this manner you get the encrypted text. Decryption is simply reverse of the encryption.

Now let us discuss the working of this program. In LOC 3, the value of KEY is set to be 7. LOCs 4-8 consist of variable declaration. In LOCs 4-5 two 1-dimensional char type arrays are declared, namely, msgToEncrypt and msgToDecrypt. In LOCs 6-7 two 2-dimensional char type arrays are declared, namely, msgEncrypt and msgDecrypt.

LOCs 9-16 consist of definition of function menu(). This function displays menu for users on the screen so that various options in this program can be used conveniently. LOCs 11-14 ask the user to enter an appropriate choice and also describe the various options available to user. LOC 15 reads the choice entered by user and stores this choice in the int variable intChoice.

LOCs 17-41 consist of definition of the function encryptMsg(). This function converts the plaintext into ciphertext. LOC 20 asks the user to enter plaintext. LOC 22 reads this plaintext and stores it in the variable msgToEncrypt. LOC 24 computes the number of row required for the storage of message. LOC 25 computes the cilr, i.e., characters in last row. Here, cilr is 6 and hence one cell in the last row is empty and it is shown shaded. LOCs 26-31 consist of nested for loops. In this nested for loops, message is encrypted and stored in the variable msgEncrypt. LOCs 32-39 display the encrypted message on the screen.

LOCs 42-65 consist of definition of the function decryptMsg(). This function retrieves the plaintext from the ciphertext. LOC 45 asks the user to enter the ciphertext. The ciphertext entered by user is read and stored in the variable msgToDecrypt in LOC 47. LOC 49 calculates number of rows required. LOC 50 calculates cilr, i.e., characters in the last row. LOCs 51-58 consist of nested for loops. In these nested loops, plaintext is retrieved from the ciphertext. LOCs 59-64 display the decrypted message on the screen.

LOCs 66-82 consist of definition of the function main(). LOCs 68-81 consist of a do-while loop. This seems to be an infinite loop, however, function exit() in the LOC 79 effectively stops the execution of this loop. LOC 69 calls the function menu() which displays the menu for users on the screen. The choice entered by user is stored in the int variable intChoice. LOCs 70-80 consist of a switch statement. Value stored in intChoice is passsed to this statement. If value of intChoice is 1 then function encryptMsg() is called. If value of intChoice is 2 then function decryptMsg() is called. If value of intChoice is else then function exit() is called which terminates the execution of do-while loop and also terminates the execution of this program.

10-4. Use the Multiplicative Cipher Method
Problem

You want to implement a cryptographic system using the Multiplicative cipher method.
   Merits:

- Level of security offered is good

- System requirements are not very high

Demerits:

- Logic is not simple and hence program is somewhat difficult to implement and debug

- Letter A in plaintext always encrypts to A

- Ciphertext can be deciphered using brute force techniques with a very high speed computer

- Transportation of keys securely is difficult

Solution

Write a C program that implements a cryptographic system using the Multiplicative cipher method, with the following specifications:

- Program defines the functions: (a) menu() to display menu for users on the screen, (b) encryptMsg() to encrypt the plaintext, and (c) decryptMsg() to decrypt the ciphertext.

- Program also defines the char type arrays msgOriginal, msgEncrypt, and msgDecrypt to store the messages. Array should accommodate 100 characters.

The Code

Code of C program written with these specifications is given below. Type the following C program in a text editor and save it in the folder C:\Code with the filename crypt4.c:

```
/* This program implements a cryptographic system using the Multiplicative
cipher method. */
                                                               /* BL */
#include <stdio.h>                                             /* L1 */
#include <string.h>                                            /* L2 */
                                                               /* BL */
char msgOriginal[100];                                         /* L3 */
char msgEncrypt[100];                                          /* L4 */
char msgDecrypt[100];                                          /* L5 */
int length, intChoice, a = 3;    /* a is the KEY */            /* L6 */
                                                               /* BL */
void menu()                                                    /* L7 */
{                                                              /* L8 */
  printf("\nEnter 1 to Encrypt a Message.");                   /* L9 */
  printf("\nEnter 2 to Decrypt an Encrypted Message.");        /* L10 */
  printf("\nEnter 3 to Stop the Execution of Program.");       /* L11 */
  printf("\nNow Enter Your Choice (1, 2 or 3) and Strike Enter Key: "); /* L12 */
  scanf("%d", &intChoice);                                     /* L13 */
}                                                              /* L14 */
                                                               /* BL  */
void encryptMsg()                                              /* L15 */
{                                                              /* L16 */
  int i ;                                                      /* L17 */
  printf("Enter the Message to Encrypt in FULL CAPS, Do Not Include \n"); /* L18 */
  printf("Spaces and Punctuation Symbols (upto 100 characters): \n"); /* L19 */
  fflush(stdin);                                               /* L20 */
  gets(msgOriginal);                                           /* L21 */
  length = strlen(msgOriginal);                                /* L22 */
  for (i = 0; i < length; i++)                                 /* L23 */
    msgEncrypt[i] = (((a * msgOriginal[i]) % 26) + 65);        /* L24 */
```

```
  msgEncrypt[length] = '\0';                                    /* L25 */
  printf("\nEncrypted Message: %s", msgEncrypt);                /* L26 */
}                                                               /* L27 */
                                                                /* BL  */
void decryptMsg()                                               /* L28 */
{                                                               /* L29 */
  int i;                                                        /* L30 */
  int aInv = 0;                                                 /* L31 */
  int flag = 0;                                                 /* L32 */
  printf("Enter the Message to Decrypt (upto 100 characters): \n"); /* L33 */
  fflush(stdin);                                                /* L34 */
  gets(msgEncrypt);                                             /* L35 */
  length = strlen(msgEncrypt);                                  /* L36 */
   for (i = 0; i < 26; i++) {                                   /* L37 */
     flag = (a * i) % 26;                                       /* L38 */
             if (flag == 1)                                     /* L39 */
                 aInv = i;                                      /* L40 */
   }                                                            /* L41 */
   for (i = 0; i < length; i++)                                 /* L42 */
      msgDecrypt[i] = (((aInv * msgEncrypt[i]) % 26) + 65);     /* L43 */
   msgDecrypt[length] = '\0';                                   /* L44 */
   printf("\nDecrypted Message: %s", msgDecrypt);               /* L45 */
}                                                               /* L46 */
                                                                /* BL  */
void main()                                                     /* L47 */
{                                                               /* L48 */
  do {                                                          /* L49 */
    menu();                                                     /* L50 */
    switch (intChoice) {                                        /* L51 */
      case 1:                                                   /* L52 */
               encryptMsg();                                    /* L53 */
               break;                                           /* L54 */
      case 2:                                                   /* L55 */
               decryptMsg();                                    /* L56 */
               break;                                           /* L57 */
      default:                                                  /* L58 */
               printf("\nThank you.\n");                        /* L59 */
               exit(0);                                         /* L60 */
    }                                                           /* L61 */
  } while (1);                                                  /* L62 */
}                                                               /* L63 */
```

Compile and execute this program. A run of this program is given below:

```
Enter 1 to Encrypt a Message.
Enter 2 to Decrypt an Encrypted Message.
Enter 3 to Stop the Execution of Program.
Now Enter Your Choice (1, 2, or 3) and Strike Enter Key: 1    ↵
Enter the Message to Encryptin FULL CAPS, Do Not Include
Spaces and Punctuation Symbols (upto 100 characters):
CANDCRYPTOGRAPHYISVERYPOWERFULCOMBINATION    ↵

Encrypted Message: TNAWTMHGSDFMNGIHLPYZMHGDBZMCVUTDXQLANSLDA
Enter 1 to Encrypt a Message.
Enter 2 to Decrypt an Encrypted Message.
Enter 3 to Stop the Execution of Program.
Now Enter Your Choice (1, 2, or 3) and Strike Enter Key: 2    ↵
Enter the Message to Decrypt (upto 100 characters):
TNAWTMHGSDFMNGIHLPYZMHGDBZMCVUTDXQLANSLDA    ↵

Decrypted Message: CANDCRYPTOGRAPHYISVERYPOWERFULCOMBINATION
Enter 1 to Encrypt a Message.
Enter 2 to Decrypt an Encrypted Message.
Enter 3 to Stop the Execution of Program.
Now Enter Your Choice (1, 2, or 3) and Strike Enter Key: 3    ↵
Thank you.
```

How It Works

Firstly, let us discuss the working of Multiplicative cipher. In Caesar cipher, key is added to serial number of letters in plaintext. In Multiplicative cipher, key is multiplied to serial number of letters in plaintext in order to encrypt it. During decryption, serial numbers of letters in ciphertext are multiplied by an inverse function of the key to retrieve the plaintext. To keep the things simple, let us consider only capital alphabets. Hence, the symbol set consists of only 26 characters. The serial number of capital alphabets are as follows: A → 0, B → 1, C → 2, ..., I → 8, ..., K → 10, ..., U → 20, ..., X → 23, Y → 24, Z → 25. Suppose the key is 3. With this key, letter A (whose serial number is 0) would be encrypted as follows:

```
A would be encrypted to → (serial no. of A x key) = 0 x 3 = 0  = A
```

With the same key, letter B (whose serial number is 1) would be encrypted as follows:

```
B would be encrypted to → (serial no. of B x key) = 1 x 3 = 3 = D
```

With the same key, letter C (whose serial number is 2) would be encyrpted as follows:

```
C would be encrypted to → (serial no. of C x key) = 2 x 3 = 6 = G
```

With the same key, letter K (whose serial number is 10) would be encrypted as follows:

K would be encrypted to → (serial no. of D x key) = 10 x 3 = 30 = 30 - 26 = 4 = E

With the same key, letter U (whose serial number is 20) would be encrypted as follows:

U would be encrypted to → (serial no. of U x key) = 20 x 3 = 60 = 60 - 26 - 26 = 8 = I

If the product (serial no. × key) exceeds 25 we subtract 26 from it repeatedly till the result is less than 26. In program this is done using the modulus operator %. Notice the LOC 24 given below:

```
msgEncrypt[i] = (((a * msgOriginal[i]) % 26) + 65);          /* L24 */
```

In this LOC a is key and its value is set to 3 in LOC 6. The msgOriginal[i] is nothing but ASCII value of (i+1)th letter in the plaintext. Also, 65 are added to result in order to convert serial number of letter to its ASCII value as ASCII value of letter A is 65.

LOC 43 is mainly responsible for decryption of ciphertext and it is reproduced below for your quick reference:

```
msgDecrypt[i] = (((aInv * msgEncrypt[i]) % 26) + 65);        /* L43 */
```

Here, aInv is modular inverse of (a % 26) and msgEncrypt[i] is nothing but the ASCII value of (i+1)th letter in the ciphertext. Also, 26 is the size of symbol set. Only capital alphabets are used to form the plaintext hence symbol set consists of only 26 characters. Modular inverse is computed using the following formula. Let i be the modular inverse of (a % m) then following relation holds good:

```
(a * i) % m = 1
```

LOCs 37-41 consist of a for loop which computes the aInv, the modular inverse of (a % 26) where a is the key and 26 is the size of symbol set.

In this program, the key is 7. Generally, the key is kept very large in order to make its hacking with brute-force technique very difficult. Keys with 7 or 8 digits are not uncommon in Multiplicative cipher. But unlike in Caesar cipher, you just cannot take any intger as a key in Multiplicative cipher. For example, if you choose the key = 8. Then both B and O encrypt to the same letter I. Also, both C and P encrypt to the same letter Q. Certainly, this key is useless. Ideally, every letter in alphabet A to Z must encrypt to a unique letter in alphabet A to Z, otherwise the cipher would not work. The useful key in Multiplicative cipher is selected using the following formula:

■ **Note** Key and size of symbol set must be relatively prime to each other. Numbers m and n are relatively prime to each other when their gcd ("greatest common divisor" also called "greatest common factor") is 1.

There is Euclid's algorithm to find the gcd of two positive numbers m and n, given below:

```
Step 1: Divide m by n and let r be the remainder.
Step 2: If r is 0, n is the answer; if r is not 0, go to step 3.
Step 3: Set m = n and n = r. Go back to step 1.
```

In this program key is 3 and size of symbol set is 26. As these numbers are small, it is immediately clear that their gcd is 1 and these numbers are realtivley prime. However, if numbers are large, then you are required to use Euclid's algorithm to verify the usefulness of key.

Now let us discuss the working of this program. LOCs 3-6 consist of variable declaration. In LOCs 3-5 three char type arrays are declared, namely, msgOriginal, msgEncrypt, and msgDecrypt. In LOC 6, the value of variable a is set to 3.

LOCs 7-14 consist of definition of function menu(). This function displays menu for users on the screen so that various options in this program can be used conveniently. LOCs 9-12 ask the user to enter an appropriate choice and also describe the various options available to user. LOC 13 reads the choice entered by user and stores this choice in the int variable intChoice.

LOCs 15-27 consist of definition of the function encryptMsg(). This function converts the plaintext into ciphertext. LOCs 18-19 ask the user to enter plaintext. LOC 21 reads this plaintext and stores it in the variable msgOriginal. LOCs 23-24 consist of a for loop. In this for loop the plaintext is converted into a ciphertext according to multiplicative cipher logic. LOC 26 displays the encrypted message on the screen.

LOCs 28-46 consist of definition of the function decryptMsg(). This function retrieves the plaintext from the ciphertext. LOC 33 asks the user to enter the ciphertext. The ciphertext entered by user is read and stored in the variable msgEncrypt in LOC 35. LOCs 37-43 consist of two for loops in consecution. In these for loops the plaintext is retrieved from the ciphertext. In LOC 45, the decrypted message is displayed on the screen.

LOCs 47-63 consist of definition of the function main(). LOCs 49-62 consist of a do-while loop. This seems to be an infinite loop, however, function exit() in the LOC 60 effectively stops the execution of this loop. LOC 50 calls the function menu() which displays the menu for users on the screen. The choice entered by user is stored in the int variable intChoice. LOCs 51-61 consist of a switch statement. Value stored in intChoice is passsed to this statement. If value of intChoice is 1 then function encryptMsg() is called. If value of intChoice is 2 then function decryptMsg() is called. If value of intChoice is else then function exit() is called which terminates the execution of do-while loop and also terminates the execution of this program.

10-5. Use the Affine Cipher Method
Problem

You want to implement a cryptographic system using the Affine cipher method.
  Merits:

- Level of security offered is better than multiplicative cipher

- System requirements are not very high

- Utilizes the benefits of Caesar cipher and multiplicative cipher

Demerits:

- Logic is not simple and hence program is somewhat difficult to implement and debug

- Ciphertext can be deciphered using brute force technique with a very high speed computer

- Transportation of keys securely is difficult

Solution

Write a C program that implements a cryptographic system using the Affine cipher method, with the following specifications:

- Program defines the functions: (a) menu() to display menu for users on the screen, (b) encryptMsg() to encrypt the plaintext, and (c) decryptMsg() to decrypt the ciphertext.

- Program also defines the char type arrays msgOriginal, msgEncrypt, and msgDecrypt to store the messages. Array should accommodate 100 characters.

The Code

Code of C program written with these specifications is given below. Type the following C program in a text editor and save it in the folder C:\Code with the filename crypt5.c:

```c
/* This program implements a cryptographic system using the Affine cipher
method. */                                                      /* BL */
                                                                /* L1 */
#include <stdio.h>                                              /* L1 */
#include <string.h>                                             /* L2 */
                                                                /* BL */
char msgOriginal[100];                                          /* L3 */
char msgEncrypt[100];                                           /* L4 */
char msgDecrypt[100];                                           /* L5 */
int intChoice, length, a = 3, b = 5;                            /* L6 */
                                                                /* BL */
void menu()                                                     /* L7 */
{                                                               /* L8 */
  printf("\nEnter 1 to Encrypt a Message.");                    /* L9 */
  printf("\nEnter 2 to Decrypt an Encrypted Message.");         /* L10 */
  printf("\nEnter 3 to Stop the Execution of Program.");        /* L11 */
  printf("\nNow Enter Your Choice (1, 2 or 3) and Strike Enter Key: "); /* L12 */
  scanf("%d", &intChoice);                                      /* L13 */
}                                                               /* L14 */
                                                                /* BL */
void encryptMsg()                                               /* L15 */
{                                                               /* L16 */
```

```c
  int i;                                                           /* L17 */
  printf("Enter the Message to Encrypt in FULL CAPS, Do Not Include \n"); /* L18 */
  printf("Spaces and Punctuation Symbols (upto 100 characters): \n"); /* L19 */
  fflush(stdin);                                                   /* L20 */
  gets(msgOriginal);                                               /* L21 */
  length = strlen(msgOriginal);                                    /* L22 */
  for (i = 0; i < length; i++)                                     /* L23 */
    msgEncrypt[i] = ((((a * msgOriginal[i]) + b) % 26) + 65);      /* L24 */
  msgEncrypt[length] = '\0';                                       /* L25 */
  printf("\nEncrypted Message: %s", msgEncrypt);                   /* L26 */
}                                                                  /* L27 */
                                                                   /* BL */
void decryptMsg()                                                  /* L28 */
{                                                                  /* L29 */
 int i;                                                            /* L30 */
  int aInv = 0;                                                    /* L31 */
  int flag = 0;                                                    /* L32 */
  printf("Enter the Message to Decrypt (upto 100 chars): \n");     /* L33 */
  fflush(stdin);                                                   /* L34 */
  gets(msgEncrypt);                                                /* L35 */
  length = strlen(msgEncrypt);                                     /* L36 */
  for (i = 0; i < 26; i++) {                                       /* L37 */
    flag = (a * i) % 26;                                           /* L38 */
    if (flag == 1)                                                 /* L39 */
        aInv = i;                                                  /* L40 */
  }                                                                /* L41 */
  for (i = 0; i < length; i++)                                     /* L42 */
      msgDecrypt[i] = (((aInv * ((msgEncrypt[i] - b)) % 26)) + 65); /* L43 */
  msgDecrypt[length] = '\0';                                       /* L44 */
  printf("\nDecrypted Message: %s", msgDecrypt);                   /* L45 */
}                                                                  /* L46 */
                                                                   /* BL  */
void main()                                                        /* L47 */
{                                                                  /* L48 */
  do {                                                             /* L49 */
    menu();                                                        /* L50 */
    switch (intChoice) {                                           /* L51 */
    case 1:                                                        /* L52 */
            encryptMsg();                                          /* L53 */
            break;                                                 /* L54 */
    case 2:                                                        /* L55 */
            decryptMsg();                                          /* L56 */
            break;                                                 /* L57 */
    default:                                                       /* L58 */
            printf("\nThank you.\n");                              /* L59 */
            exit(0);                                               /* L60 */
    }                                                              /* L61 */
  } while (1);                                                     /* L62 */
}                                                                  /* L63 */
```

Compile and execute this program. A run of this program is given below:

```
Enter 1 to Encrypt a Message.
Enter 2 to Decrypt an Encrypted Message.
Enter 3 to Stop the Execution of Program.
Now Enter Your Choice (1, 2, or 3) and Strike Enter Key: 1    ↵
Enter the Message to Encrypt in FULL CAPS, Do Not Include
Spaces and Punctuation Symbols (upto 100 characters):
CANDCRYPTOGRAPHYISVERYPOWERFULCOMBINATION    ↵

Encrypted Message: YSFBYRMLXIKRSLNMQUDERMLIGERHAZYICVQFSXQIF
Enter 1 to Encrypt a Message.
Enter 2 to Decrypt an Encrypted Message.
Enter 3 to Stop the Execution of Program.
Now Enter Your Choice (1, 2, or 3) and Strike Enter Key: 2    ↵
Enter the Message to Decrypt (upto 100 characters):
YSFBYRMLXIKRSLNMQUDERMLIGERHAZYICVQFSXQIF    ↵

Decrypted Message: CANDCRYPTOGRAPHYISVERYPOWERFULCOMBINATION
Enter 1 to Encrypt a Message.
Enter 2 to Decrypt an Encrypted Message.
Enter 3 to Stop the Execution of Program.
Now Enter Your Choice (1, 2, or 3) and Strike Enter Key: 3    ↵
Thank you.
```

How It Works

Firstly, let us discuss the working of Affine cipher. A notable drawback of Multiplicative cipher is that letter A in plaintext always encrypts to A. This is a sort of loop hole. In order to deal with this drawback, Multiplicative cipher is modified to Affine cipher. Affice cipher is combination of Multiplicative cipher and Caesar cipher. Consequently, there are two keys in Affine cipher, namely, key_A and key_B; and in this program, these keys are represented by the variables a and b, respectively. Also, their values are set to 3 (for a) and 5 (for b) in LOC 6. First key, key_A is used for Multiplicative component of Affine cipher and second key, key_B is used for Caesar component of Affine cipher. The restrictions on the selection of key_A in Affine cipher are same as that of in Multiplicative cipher. Like in Caesar cipher, there are almost no restrictions on the selection key_B.

LOC 24 mainly encrypts the plaintext into ciphertext and it is reproduced below for your quick reference:

```
msgEncrypt[i] = ((((a * msgOriginal[i]) + b) % 26) + 65);     /* L24 */
```

Here, msgOriginal[i] represents the ASCII value of (i+1)th character in plaintext. Also, a and b are first and second keys, respectively. Key a is meant for Multiplicative component and key b is meant for Ceasar component. 26 is the size of the symbol set as only capital alphabets A..Z are used for forming the plaintext. Finally, integer 65 is ASCII value of letter A.

LOC 43 mainly decrypts the ciphertext to retrieve the plaintext and it is reproduced below for your quick reference:

```
msgDecrypt[i] = (((aInv * ((msgEncrypt[i] - b)) % 26)) + 65);      /* L43 */
```

Here, aInv is modular inverse of (a % 26), b is second key meant for Caesar component, msgEncrypt[i] is ASCII value of (i+1)th character in ciphertext, 26 is size of symbol set, and 65 is ASCII value of A.

Now let us discuss the working of this program. LOCs 3-6 consist of variable declaration. In LOCs 3-5 three char type arrays are declared, namely, msgOriginal, msgEncrypt, and msgDecrypt. In LOC 6, the value of variable a is set to 3 and value of variable b is set to 5.

LOCs 7-14 consist of definition of function menu(). This function displays menu for users on the screen so that various options in this program can be used conveniently. LOCs 9-12 ask the user to enter an appropriate choice and also describe the various options available to user. LOC 13 reads the choice entered by user and stores this choice in the int variable intChoice.

LOCs 15-27 consist of definition of the function encryptMsg(). This function converts the plaintext into ciphertext. LOCs 18-19 ask the user to enter plaintext. LOC 21 reads this plaintext and stores it in the variable msgOriginal. LOCs 23-24 consist of a for loop. In this for loop the plaintext is converted into a ciphertext according to affine cipher logic. LOC 26 displays the encrypted message on the screen.

LOCs 28-46 consist of definition of the function decryptMsg(). This function retrieves the plaintext from the ciphertext. LOC 33 asks the user to enter the ciphertext. The ciphertext entered by user is read and stored in the variable msgEncrypt in LOC 35. LOCs 37-43 consist of two for loops in consecution. In these for loops the plaintext is retrieved from the ciphertext. In LOC 45, the decrypted message is displayed on the screen.

LOCs 47-63 consist of definition of the function main(). LOCs 49-62 consist of a do-while loop. This seems to be an infinite loop, however, function exit() in the LOC 60 effectively stops the execution of this loop. LOC 50 calls the function menu() which displays the menu for users on the screen. The choice entered by user is stored in the int variable intChoice. LOCs 51-61 consist of a switch statement. Value stored in intChoice is passsed to this statement. If value of intChoice is 1 then function encryptMsg() is called. If value of intChoice is 2 then function decryptMsg() is called. If value of intChoice is else then function exit() is called which terminates the execution of do-while loop and also terminates the execution of this program.

10-6. Use the Simple Substitution Cipher Method
Problem

You want to implement a cryptographic system using the Simple Substitution cipher method.
   Merits:

- Level of security offered is good

- System requirements are not very high

- Logic used is simple to implement

Demerits:

- Execution of program is not very fast
- Ciphertext can be deciphered using brute force technique with a very high speed computer
- Transportation of keys securely is difficult

Solution

Write a C program that implements a cryptographic system using the Simple Substitution cipher method, with the following specifications:

- Program defines the functions: (a) generateKey() to generate the encrypt key and decrypt key, (b) menu() to display menu for users on the screen, (c) encryptMsg() to encrypt the plaintext, and (d) decryptMsg() to decrypt the ciphertext.
- Program also defines the char type arrays msgOriginal, msgEncrypt, and msgDecrypt to store the messages. Array should accommodate 100 characters.

The Code

Code of C program written with these specifications is given below. Type the following C program in a text editor and save it in the folder C:\Code with the filename crypt6.c:

```
/* This program implements a cryptographic system using the Simple Substitution */
/* cipher method. */
                                                        /* BL */
#include <stdio.h>                                      /* L1 */
#include <stdlib.h>                                     /* L2 */
#include <string.h>                                     /* L3 */
                                                        /* BL */
char msgOriginal[100];                                  /* L4 */
char msgEncrypt[100];                                   /* L5 */
char msgDecrypt[100];                                   /* L6 */
int intEncryptKey[26], intDecryptKey[26];               /* L7 */
int intChoice, i, j, seed, length, randNum, num, flag = 1, tag = 0; /* L8 */
                                                        /* BL */
void generateKey()                                      /* L9 */
{                                                       /* L10 */
  printf("\nEnter seed S (1 <= S <= 30000): ");         /* L11 */
  scanf("%d", &seed);                                   /* L12 */
  srand(seed);                                          /* L13 */
  for(i=0; i < 26; i++)                                 /* L14 */
    intEncryptKey[i] = -1;                              /* L15 */
  for(i=0; i < 26; i++) {                               /* L16 */
```

```
    do {                                                   /* L17 */
      randNum = rand();                                    /* L18 */
      num = randNum % 26;                                  /* L19 */
      flag = 1;                                            /* L20 */
      for(j = 0; j < 26; j++)                              /* L21 */
        if (intEncryptKey[j] == num)                       /* L22 */
          flag = 0;                                        /* L23 */
        if (flag == 1){                                    /* L24 */
          intEncryptKey[i] = num;                          /* L25 */
          tag = tag + 1;                                   /* L26 */
        }                                                  /* L27 */
    } while ((!flag) && (tag < 26 ));                      /* L28 */
  }                                                        /* L29 */
  printf("\nEncryption KEY = ");                           /* L30 */
  for(i=0; i < 26; i++)                                    /* L31 */
    printf("%c", intEncryptKey[i] + 65);                   /* L32 */
  for(i = 0; i < 26; i++) {                                /* L33 */
    for(j = 0; j < 26; j++) {                              /* L34 */
      if(i  == intEncryptKey[j]) {                         /* L35 */
        intDecryptKey[i] = j ;                             /* L36 */
        break;                                             /* L37 */
      }                                                    /* L38 */
    }                                                      /* L39 */
  }                                                        /* L40 */
  printf("\nDecryption KEY = ");                           /* L41 */
  for(i=0; i < 26; i++)                                    /* L42 */
    printf("%c", intDecryptKey[i] + 65);                   /* L43 */
}                                                          /* L44 */
                                                           /* BL  */
void menu()                                                /* L45 */
{                                                          /* L46 */
  printf("\nEnter 1 to Encrypt a Message.");               /* L47 */
  printf("\nEnter 2 to Decrypt an Encrypted Message.");    /* L48 */
  printf("\nEnter 3 to Stop the Execution of Program.");   /* L49 */
  printf("\nNow Enter Your Choice (1, 2 or 3) and Strike Enter Key: "); /* L50 */
  scanf("%d", &intChoice);                                 /* L51 */
}                                                          /* L52 */
                                                           /* BL  */
void encryptMsg()                                          /* L53 */
{                                                          /* L54 */
  printf("Enter the Message to Encrypt in FULL CAPS, Do Not Include \n"); /* L55 */
  printf("Spaces and Punctuation Symbols (upto 100 characters): \n"); /* L56 */
  fflush(stdin);                                           /* L57 */
  gets(msgOriginal);                                       /* L58 */
  length = strlen(msgOriginal);                            /* L59 */
  for (i = 0; i < length; i++)                             /* L60 */
    msgEncrypt[i] = (intEncryptKey[(msgOriginal[i]) - 65]) + 65; /* L61 */
  msgEncrypt[length] = '\0';                               /* L62 */
```

```
  printf("\nEncrypted Message: %s", msgEncrypt);          /* L63 */
}                                                          /* L64 */
                                                           /* BL */
void decryptMsg()                                          /* L65 */
{                                                          /* L66 */
  printf("Enter the Message to Decrypt (upto 100 chars): \n");   /* L67 */
  fflush(stdin);                                           /* L68 */
  gets(msgEncrypt);                                        /* L69 */
  length = strlen(msgEncrypt);                             /* L70 */
  for (i = 0; i < length; i++)                             /* L71 */
   msgDecrypt[i] = (intDecryptKey[(msgEncrypt[i]) - 65]) + 65;   /* L72 */
   msgDecrypt[length] = '\0';                              /* L73 */
   printf("\nDecrypted Message: %s", msgDecrypt);          /* L74 */
}                                                          /* L75 */
                                                           /* BL */
void main()                                                /* L76 */
{                                                          /* L77 */
  generateKey();                                           /* L78 */
  do {                                                     /* L79 */
    menu();                                                /* L80 */
    switch (intChoice) {                                   /* L81 */
      case 1:                                              /* L82 */
              encryptMsg();                                /* L83 */
              break;                                       /* L84 */
      case 2:                                              /* L85 */
              decryptMsg();                                /* L86 */
              break;                                       /* L87 */
      default:                                             /* L88 */
              printf("\nThank you.\n");                    /* L89 */
              exit(0);                                     /* L90 */
    }                                                      /* L91 */
  } while (1);                                             /* L92 */
}                                                          /* L93 */
```

Compile and execute this program. A run of this program is given below:

```
Enter seed S (1 <= S <= 30000): 2000   ↵

Encryption KEY = KJVWBAIZRUHNFXGDMTLPOQSCEY
Decryption KEY = FEXPYMOKGBASQLUTVIWRJCDNZH

Enter 1 to Encrypt a Message.
Enter 2 to Decrypt an Encrypted Message.
Enter 3 to Stop the Execution of Program.
Now Enter Your Choice (1, 2, or 3) and Strike Enter Key: 1   ↵
Enter the Message to Encrypt in FULL CAPS, Do Not Include
Spaces and Punctuation Symbols (upto 100 characters):
CANDCRYPTOGRAPHYISVERYPOWERFULCOMBINATION   ↵
```

327

```
Encrypted Message: VKXWVTEDPGITKDDZERLQBTEDGSBTAONVGFJRXKPRGX
Enter 1 to Encrypt a Message.
Enter 2 to Decrypt an Encrypted Message.
Enter 3 to Stop the Execution of Program.
Now Enter Your Choice (1, 2, or 3) and Strike Enter Key: 2   ↵
Enter the Message to Decrypt (upto 100 characters):
VKXWVTEDPGITKDDZERLQBTEDGSBTAONVGFJRXKPRGX   ↵

Decrypted Message: CANDCRYPTOGRAPHYISVERYPOWERFULCOMBINATION
Enter 1 to Encrypt a Message.
Enter 2 to Decrypt an Encrypted Message.
Enter 3 to Stop the Execution of Program.
Now Enter Your Choice (1, 2, or 3) and Strike Enter Key: 3   ↵
Thank you.
```

How It Works

Firstly, let us discuss the working of Simple Substitution cipher. In Simple Substitution cipher both encryption and decryption keys are 26 letters long. Here, to keep the things simple, plaintext will be formed using only capital alphabets A..Z. In order to create encryption key, simply place all the 26 capital alphabets in random order, one by one, and you get encryption key. The encryption key generated in a sample run of this program is given below:

```
Encryption KEY = KJVWBAIZRUHNFXGDMTLPOQSCEY
```

There are whopping 403,291,461,126,605,635,584,000,000 number of encryption keys possible for Simple Substitution cipher. This rules out the chances of hacking the ciphertext created under Simple Substitution cipher. Even if you employ a computer that would try out a billion keys every second, it would take about twelve billion years to try out all the possible keys.

Suppose your plaintext is CAT. Let us encrypt it. Encryption key is reproduced below alongwith standard alphabet for quick comparison:

```
Standard Alphabet = ABCDEFGHIJKLMNOPQRSTUVWXYZ
Encryption KEY    = KJVWBAIZRUHNFXGDMTLPOQSCEY
```

Letter C (which is third letter in standard alphabet) would encrypt to letter V because third letter in encryption key is V. Letter A (which is first letter in standard alphabet) would encrypt to letter K because first letter in encryption key is K. Letter T (which is twentieth letter in standard alphabet) would encrypt to letter P because twentieth letter in encryption key is P. Thus ciphertext is VKP.

Now let us decrypt this ciphertext. The decryption key corresponding to this encryption key is given below along with standard alphabet for quick comparison:

```
Standard Alphabet = ABCDEFGHIJKLMNOPQRSTUVWXYZ
Decryption KEY    = FEXPYMOKGBASQLUTVIWRJCDNZH
```

Ciphertext is VKP. Letter V would decrypt to letter C because twenty second letter in decryption key is C. Letter K would decrypt to letter A because eleventh letter in decryption key is A. Letter P would decrypt to letter T because sixteenth letter in decryption key is T. Thus plaintext retrieved from ciphertext is CAT, as expected.

Encryption key is generated by placing the 26 alphabets randomly, one by one. However, generation of decryption key is dependent on encryption key. Let us see how this, above given, decryption key is generated.

First letter in decryption key is F because in encryption key A is the sixth letter and sixth letter in standard alphabet is F. Second letter in decryption key is E because in encryption key B is the fifth letter and fifth letter in standard alphabet is E. Third letter in decryption key is X because in encryption key C is the twenty fourth letter and twenty fourth letter in standard alphabet is X. And so on.

While generating the encryption key in this program, random numbers are generated using the function rand(). Random number generation in computers is not truly random. However, in this program, provision is made to enter the "seed" (an integer) that can push the random number generation in computers close to true random number generation. User can type different seed everytime he/she runs a program and get a different encryption key.

Now let us discuss the working of this program. LOCs 4-8 consist of variable declaration. In LOCs 4-6 three char type arrays are declared, namely, msgOriginal, msgEncrypt, and msgDecrypt. The size of these char arrays is 100. In LOC 7, two int type arrays are declared, namely, intEncryptKey and intDecryptKey. The size of these int arrays is 26. In LOC 8, few int type variables are declared.

LOCs 9-44 consist of definition of the function generateKey(). This function generates two keys, namely, encrypt key and decrypt key. LOC 11 asks the user to enter the "seed" which is nothing but an integer in the range 1 to 30,000. The "seed" entered by user is read and stored in the variable seed in the LOC 12. This "seed" is used for generating a random number. LOCs 14-15 consist of a for loop which places the number -1 in every cell of the array intEncryptKey. Number -1 in any cell indicates that proper key is not yet placed in that cell. LOCs 16-29 consist of a for loop. In this for loop encrypt key is generated, i.e., 26 capital letters are filled in the array intEncryptKey at random. This encrypt key is displayed on the screen in the LOCs 30-32. LOCs 31-40 again consist of a for loop. In this for loop decrypt key is generated. This decrypt is, however, dependent on encrypt key and it is displayed on the screen in the LOCs 41-43.

LOCs 45-52 consist of definition of function menu(). This function displays menu for users on the screen so that various options in this program can be used conveniently. LOCs 47-50 ask the user to enter an appropriate choice and also describe the various options available to user. LOC 51 reads the choice entered by user and stores this choice in the int variable intChoice.

LOCs 53-64 consist of definition of the function encryptMsg(). This function converts the plaintext into ciphertext. LOCs 55-56 ask the user to enter plaintext. LOC 58 reads this plaintext and stores it in the variable msgOriginal. LOCs 60-61 consist of a for loop. In this for loop the plaintext is converted into a ciphertext according to simple substitution cipher logic. LOC 63 displays the encrypted message on the screen.

LOCs 65-75 consist of definition of the function decryptMsg(). This function retrieves the plaintext from the ciphertext. LOC 67 asks the user to enter the ciphertext. The ciphertext entered by user is read and stored in the variable msgEncrypt in LOC 69. LOCs 71-72 consist of a for loop which retrieves the plaintext from the ciphertext and stores it in msgDecrypt. In LOC 74, the decrypted message is displayed on the screen.

LOCs 76-93 consist of definition of the function main(). LOC 78 consists of a call to the function generateKey(). LOCs 79-92 consist of a do-while loop. This seems to be an infinite loop, however, function exit() in the LOC 90 effectively stops the execution of this loop. LOC 80 calls the function menu() which displays the menu for users on the screen. The choice entered by user is stored in the int variable intChoice. LOCs 81-91 consist of a switch statement. Value stored in intChoice is passsed to this statement. If value of intChoice is 1 then function encryptMsg() is called. If value of intChoice is 2 then function decryptMsg() is called. If value of intChoice is else then function exit() is called which terminates the execution of do-while loop and also terminates the execution of this program.

10-7. Use the Vigenère Cipher Method
Problem

You want to implement a cryptographic system using the Vigenère cipher method.
  Merits:

- Level of security offered is better than Caesar cipher method. For about 300 years, this cipher was believed to be unbreakable, however, Charles Babbage and Friedrich Kasiski independently invented a method of breaking it in the middle of the nineteenth century

- Not very difficult to implement and debug

- Combines the benefits of Caesar cipher method and multiple keys

Demerits:

- Logic used is not very simple

- Ciphertext can be deciphered using brute force technique with a very high speed computer

- Transportation of keys securely is difficult

Solution

Write a C program that implements a cryptographic system using the Vigenère cipher method, with the following specifications:

- Program defines the functions: (a) getKey() to accept text key from user, (b) menu() to display menu for users on the screen, (c) encryptMsg() to encrypt the plaintext, and (d) decryptMsg() to decrypt the ciphertext.

- Program also defines the char type arrays msgOriginal, msgEncrypt, and msgDecrypt to store the messages. Array should accommodate 100 characters.

The Code

Code of C program written with these specifications is given below. Type the following C program in a text editor and save it in the folder C:\Code with the filename crypt7.c:

```
/* This program implements a cryptographic system using the Vigenere cipher
method. */
                                                                       /* BL */
#include<stdio.h>                                                      /* L1 */
#include <string.h>                                                    /* L2 */
                                                                       /* BL */
char msgOriginal[100];                                                 /* L3 */
char msgEncrypt[100];                                                  /* L4 */
char msgDecrypt[100];                                                  /* L5 */
char msgKey[15];                                                       /* L6 */
int intChoice, lenKey, lenMsg, intKey[15];                             /* L7 */
                                                                       /* BL */
void getKey()                                                          /* L8 */
{                                                                      /* L9 */
  int i, j;                                                            /* L10 */
  fflush(stdin);                                                       /* L11 */
  printf("\nEnter TEXT KEY in FULL CAPS, Do Not Include Spaces and \n"); /* L12 */
  printf("Punctuation Symbols (upto 15 characters): \n");             /* L13 */
  gets(msgKey);                                                        /* L14 */
  lenKey = strlen(msgKey);                                             /* L15 */
  for(i = 0; i < lenKey; i++)                                          /* L16 */
      intKey[i] = msgKey[i] - 65;                                      /* L17 */
}                                                                      /* L18 */
                                                                       /* BL */
void menu()                                                            /* L19 */
{                                                                      /* L20 */
  printf("\nEnter 1 to Encrypt a Message.");                           /* L21 */
  printf("\nEnter 2 to Decrypt an Encrypted Message.");                /* L22 */
  printf("\nEnter 3 to Stop the Execution of Program.");               /* L23 */
  printf("\nNow Enter Your Choice (1, 2 or 3) and Strike Enter Key: "); /* L24 */
  scanf("%d", &intChoice);                                             /* L25 */
}                                                                      /* L26 */
                                                                       /* BL */
void encryptMsg()                                                      /* L27 */
{                                                                      /* L28 */
  int i, j, ch;                                                        /* L29 */
  fflush(stdin);                                                       /* L30 */
  printf("Enter the Message to be Encrypted (upto 100 alphabets), "); /* L31 */
  printf("do not include \nspaces and punctuation symbols:\n");        /* L32 */
  gets(msgOriginal);                                                   /* L33 */
  lenMsg = strlen(msgOriginal);                                        /* L34 */
    for(i = 0; i < lenMsg; i++) {                                      /* L35 */
      j = i % lenKey;                                                  /* L36 */
```

```
      ch = msgOriginal[i];                                       /* L37 */
      if(ch >= 'a' && ch <= 'z') {                               /* L38 */
        ch = ch + intKey[j];                                     /* L39 */
        if(ch > 'z')                                             /* L40 */
          ch = ch - 'z' + 'a' - 1;                               /* L41 */
        msgEncrypt[i] = ch;                                      /* L42 */
      }                                                          /* L43 */
      else if(ch >= 'A' && ch <= 'Z'){                           /* L44 */
        ch = ch + intKey[j];                                     /* L45 */
        if(ch > 'Z')                                             /* L46 */
          ch = ch - 'Z' + 'A' - 1;                               /* L47 */
        msgEncrypt[i] = ch;                                      /* L48 */
      }                                                          /* L49 */
    }                                                            /* L50 */
  msgEncrypt[lenMsg] = '\0';                                     /* L51 */
  printf("\nEncrypted Message: %s", msgEncrypt);                 /* L52 */
}                                                                /* L53 */
                                                                 /* BL  */
void decryptMsg()                                                /* L54 */
{                                                                /* L55 */
  int i, j, ch;                                                  /* L56 */
  fflush(stdin);                                                 /* L57 */
  printf("Enter the Message to be Decrypted (upto 100 alphabets):\n"); /* L58 */
  gets(msgEncrypt);                                              /* L59 */
  lenMsg = strlen(msgEncrypt);                                   /* L60 */
  for(i = 0; i < lenMsg; i++) {                                  /* L61 */
    j = i % lenKey;                                              /* L62 */
    ch = msgEncrypt[i];                                          /* L63 */
    if(ch >= 'a' && ch <= 'z') {                                 /* L64 */
      ch = ch - intKey[j];                                       /* L65 */
      if(ch < 'a')                                               /* L66 */
        ch = ch + 'z' - 'a' + 1;                                 /* L67 */
      msgDecrypt[i] = ch;                                        /* L68 */
    }                                                            /* L69 */
    else if(ch >= 'A' && ch <= 'Z'){                             /* L70 */
      ch = ch - intKey[j];                                       /* L71 */
      if(ch < 'A')                                               /* L72 */
        ch = ch + 'Z' - 'A' + 1;                                 /* L73 */
      msgDecrypt[i] = ch;                                        /* L74 */
    }                                                            /* L75 */
  }                                                              /* L76 */
  msgDecrypt[lenMsg] = '\0';                                     /* L77 */
  printf("\nDecrypted Message: %s", msgDecrypt);                 /* L78 */
}                                                                /* L79 */
                                                                 /* BL  */
void main()                                                      /* L80 */
{                                                                /* L81 */
  getKey();                                                      /* L82 */
```

```
do {                                              /* L83 */
   menu();                                        /* L84 */
   switch (intChoice) {                           /* L85 */
      case 1:                                     /* L86 */
              encryptMsg();                       /* L87 */
              break;                              /* L88 */
      case 2:                                     /* L89 */
              decryptMsg();                       /* L90 */
              break;                              /* L91 */
      default:                                    /* L92 */
              printf("\nThank you.\n");           /* L93 */
              exit(0);                            /* L94 */
   }                                              /* L95 */
} while (1);                                       /* L96 */
}                                                 /* L97 */
```

Compile and execute this program. A run of this program is given below:

```
Enter TEXT KEY in FULL CAPS, Do Not Include Spaces and
Punctuation Symbols (upto 15 characters):
WORLDPEACE   ↵

Enter 1 to Encrypt a Message.
Enter 2 to Decrypt an Encrypted Message.
Enter 3 to Stop the Execution of Program.
Now Enter Your Choice (1, 2, or 3) and Strike Enter Key: 1   ↵
Enter the Message to be Encrypted (upto 100 alphabets), do not include
Spaces and punctuation symbols:
CandCryptographyIsVeryPowerfulCombination   ↵

Encrypted Message: YoeoFgcpvscfraknMsXinmGzztvfwpYcdmlcetksj
Enter 1 to Encrypt a Message.
Enter 2 to Decrypt an Encrypted Message.
Enter 3 to Stop the Execution of Program.
Now Enter Your Choice (1, 2, or 3) and Strike Enter Key: 2   ↵
Enter the Message to be Decrypted (upto 100 alphabets):
YoeoFgcpvscfraknMsXinmGzztvfwpYcdmlcetksj   ↵

Decrypted Message: CandCryptographyIsVeryPowerfulCombination
Enter 1 to Encrypt a Message.
Enter 2 to Decrypt an Encrypted Message.
Enter 3 to Stop the Execution of Program.
Now Enter Your Choice (1, 2, or 3) and Strike Enter Key: 3   ↵
Thank you.
```

How It Works

Firstly, let us discuss the working of Vigenère cipher. Vigenère cipher is nothing but the Caesar cipher with multiple keys. It carries the name of Italian cryptographer Blaise de Vigenère. However, most possibly, it was inveted by another Italian cryptographer Giovan Battista Bellaso. As it uses multiple keys, it is also called Polyalphabetic Substitution cipher. Let the word CAT be the Vigenere cipher key. The letters in A to Z are serially numbered as 0 to 25, respectively, as shown in figure 10-2. Here, letter C means key is 2, letter A means key 0, and letter T means key is 19. During encryption and decryption these keys are used in cyclical order. During encryption, first letter in plaintext is encrypted using the key = 2, second letter in plaintext is encrypted using the key = 0, third letter in plaintext is encrypted using the key = 19, fourth letter in plaintext is encrypted using the key = 2, and so on. During decryption also these keys are used in the same order.

For simplicity, let us form a sample plaintext using only capital alphabets. In program, however, provision is made for both upper and lower case letters. Suppose plaintext is COMPUTER and let us encrypt it using the key CAT. The keys will be used in the following order:

Plaintext	=	C	O	M	P	U	T	E	R
Keys	=	2	0	19	2	0	19	2	0
Ciphertext	=	E	O	F	R	U	M	G	R

The first letter in plaintext is C and its serial number is 2, also key is 2, therefore it encrypts to (serial number of C + key = 2 + 2 = 4 =) E. Second letter in plaintext is O and its serial number is 14, also key is 0, therefore and it encrypts to (serial number of O + key = 14 + 0 = 14 =) O. Third letter in plaintext is M and its serial number is 12, also key is 19, therefore it encrypts to (serial number of M + key = 12 + 19 = 31 = 31 - 26 = 5 =) F. Fourth letter in plaintext is P and its serial number is 15, also key is 2, therefore it encrypts to (serial number of P + key = 15 + 2 = 17 =) R. Proceeding in this manner, we get the ciphertext EOFRUMGR. You can retrieve the plaintext from ciphertext simply by proceeding in the reverse manner.

Now let us discuss the working of this program. LOCs 3-7 consist of variable declaration. In LOCs 3-6 four char type arrays are declared, namely, msgOriginal, msgEncrypt, msgDecrypt, and msgKey. The size of first three char arrays is 100 and that of fourth array is 15. In LOC 7, an int type array intKey of size 15 is declared. Also, in LOC 7, few int type variables are declared.

LOCs 8-18 consist of definition of the function getKey(). This function accepts text key from user. LOCs 12-13 ask the user to enter the text key in upper case. Text key entered by user is read in LOC 14 and stored in the variable msgKey. LOCs 16-17 consist of a for loops and in this loop serial numbers of letters in msgKey are filled in the array intKey.

LOCs 19-26 consist of definition of function menu(). This function displays menu for users on the screen so that various options in this program can be used conveniently. LOCs 21-24 ask the user to enter an appropriate choice and also describe the various options available to user. LOC 25 reads the choice entered by user and stores this choice in the int variable intChoice.

LOCs 27-53 consist of definition of the function `encryptMsg()`. This function converts the plaintext into ciphertext. LOCs 31-32 ask the user to enter plaintext. LOC 33 reads this plaintext and stores it in the variable `msgOriginal`. LOCs 35-50 consist of a `for` loop. In this `for` loop the plaintext is converted into a ciphertext according to Vigenere cipher logic. LOC 52 displays the encrypted message on the screen.

LOCs 54-79 consist of definition of the function `decryptMsg()`. This function retrieves the plaintext from the ciphertext. LOC 58 asks the user to enter the ciphertext. The ciphertext entered by user is read and stored in the variable `msgEncrypt` in LOC 59. LOCs 61-76 consist of a `for` loop which retrieves the plaintext from the ciphertext and stores it in `msgDecrypt`. In LOC 78, the decrypted message is displayed on the screen.

LOCs 80-97 consist of definition of the function `main()`. LOC 82 consists of a call to the function `getKey()`. LOCs 83-96 consist of a `do-while` loop. This seems to be an infinite loop, however, function `exit()` in the LOC 94 effectively stops the execution of this loop. LOC 84 calls the function `menu()` which displays the menu for users on the screen. The choice entered by user is stored in the `int` variable `intChoice`. LOCs 85-95 consist of a `switch` statement. Value stored in `intChoice` is passsed to this statement. If value of `intChoice` is 1 then function `encryptMsg()` is called. If value of `intChoice` is 2 then function `decryptMsg()` is called. If value of `intChoice` is else then function `exit()` is called which terminates the execution of `do-while` loop and also terminates the execution of this program.

10-8. Use the One-Time Pad Cipher Method
Problem

You want to implement a cryptographic system using the One-Time Pad cipher method.
Merits:

- Almost unbreakable cipher; breaks only if key is compromised otherwise it is unbreakable

- Based on simple logic

- System requirement is not very high

Demerits:

- Key is as long as plaintext hence generation of key is time consuming if message is very long

- Key needs to be generated on the "use and throw" basis

- Due to abnormal size of key, handling and storage of key is troublesome

- Transportation of key securely is very difficult compared to other methods

Solution

Write a C program that implements a cryptographic system using the One-Time Pad cipher method, with the following specifications:

- Program defines the functions: (a) generateKey() to generate the key, (b) menu() to display menu for users on the screen, (c) encryptMsg() to encrypt the plaintext, and (d) decryptMsg() to decrypt the ciphertext.

- Program also defines the char type arrays msgOriginal, msgEncrypt, and msgDecrypt to store the messages. Array should accommodate 100 characters.

The Code

Code of C program written with these specifications is given below. Type the following C program in a text editor and save it in the folder C:\Code with the filename crypt8.c:

```
/* This program implements a cryptographic system using the One-Time Pad
cipher method. */
                                                           /* BL */
#include <stdio.h>                                         /* L1 */
#include<string.h>                                         /* L2 */
                                                           /* BL */
char msgOriginal[100];                                     /* L3 */
char msgEncrypt[100];                                      /* L4 */
char msgDecrypt[100];                                      /* L5 */
char msgKey[100];                                          /* L6 */
int intChoice, lenKey, lenMsg, intKey[100];                /* L7 */
                                                           /* BL */
void generateKey()                                         /* L8 */
{                                                          /* L9 */
  int i, randNum, num, seed;                               /* L10 */
  lenKey = lenMsg;                                         /* L11 */
  printf("\nEnter seed S (1 <= S <= 30000): ");            /* L12 */
  scanf("%d", &seed);                                      /* L13 */
  srand(seed);                                             /* L14 */
  for(i = 0; i < lenKey; i++) {                            /* L15 */
      randNum = rand();                                    /* L16 */
      num = randNum % 26;                                  /* L17 */
      msgKey[i] = num + 65;                                /* L18 */
      intKey[i] = num;                                     /* L19 */
  }                                                        /* L20 */
  msgKey[lenKey] = '\0';                                   /* L21 */
  printf("\nKey: %s", msgKey);                             /* L22 */
}                                                          /* L23 */
                                                           /* BL */
```

```
void menu()                                                        /* L24 */
{                                                                  /* L25 */
  printf("\nEnter 1 to Encrypt a Message.");                       /* L26 */
  printf("\nEnter 2 to Stop the Execution of Program.");           /* L27 */
  printf("\nNow Enter Your Choice (1 or 2) and Strike Enter Key: "); /* L28 */
  scanf("%d", &intChoice);                                         /* L29 */
}                                                                  /* L30 */
                                                                   /* BL  */
void encryptMsg()                                                  /* L31 */
{                                                                  /* L32 */
  int i, j, ch;                                                    /* L33 */
  fflush(stdin);                                                   /* L34 */
  printf("Enter the Message to be Encrypted (upto 100 alphabets), "); /* L35 */
  printf("Do Not Include \nSpaces and Punctuation Symbols:\n");    /* L36 */
  gets(msgOriginal);                                               /* L37 */
  lenMsg = strlen(msgOriginal);                                    /* L38 */
  generateKey();                                                   /* L39 */
    for(i = 0; i < lenMsg; i++) {                                  /* L40 */
      ch = msgOriginal[i];                                         /* L41 */
      if(ch >= 'a' && ch <= 'z') {                                 /* L42 */
        ch = ch + intKey[i];                                       /* L43 */
        if(ch > 'z')                                               /* L44 */
          ch = ch - 'z' + 'a' - 1;                                 /* L45 */
        msgEncrypt[i] = ch;                                        /* L46 */
      }                                                            /* L47 */
      else if(ch >= 'A' && ch <= 'Z'){                             /* L48 */
        ch = ch + intKey[i];                                       /* L49 */
        if(ch > 'Z')                                               /* L50 */
          ch = ch - 'Z' + 'A' - 1;                                 /* L51 */
        msgEncrypt[i] = ch;                                        /* L52 */
      }                                                            /* L53 */
    }                                                              /* L54 */
  msgEncrypt[lenMsg] = '\0';                                       /* L55 */
  printf("\nEncrypted Message: %s", msgEncrypt);                   /* L56 */
}                                                                  /* L57 */
                                                                   /* BL  */
void decryptMsg()                                                  /* L58 */
{                                                                  /* L59 */
  int i, j, ch;                                                    /* L60 */
  fflush(stdin);                                                   /* L61 */
  printf("\nEnter the Message to be Decrypted (upto 100 alphabets):\n"); /* L62 */
  gets(msgEncrypt);                                                /* L63 */
  lenMsg = strlen(msgEncrypt);                                     /* L64 */
  for(i = 0; i < lenMsg; i++) {                                    /* L65 */
    ch = msgEncrypt[i];                                            /* L66 */
    if(ch >= 'a' && ch <= 'z') {                                   /* L67 */
      ch = ch - intKey[i];                                         /* L68 */
      if(ch < 'a')                                                 /* L69 */
```

```
      ch = ch + 'z' - 'a' + 1;                              /* L70 */
      msgDecrypt[i] = ch;                                   /* L71 */
    }                                                       /* L72 */
    else if(ch >= 'A' && ch <= 'Z'){                        /* L73 */
      ch = ch - intKey[i];                                  /* L74 */
      if(ch < 'A')                                          /* L75 */
        ch = ch + 'Z' - 'A' + 1;                            /* L76 */
      msgDecrypt[i] = ch;                                   /* L77 */
    }                                                       /* L78 */
  }                                                         /* L79 */
  msgDecrypt[lenMsg] = '\0';                                /* L80 */
  printf("\nDecrypted Message: %s", msgDecrypt);            /* L81 */
}                                                           /* L82 */
                                                            /* BL  */
void main()                                                 /* L83 */
{                                                           /* L84 */
  do {                                                      /* L85 */
    menu();                                                 /* L86 */
    switch (intChoice) {                                    /* L87 */
      case 1:                                               /* L88 */
              encryptMsg();                                 /* L89 */
              decryptMsg();                                 /* L90 */
              break;                                        /* L91 */
      default:                                              /* L92 */
              printf("\nThank you.\n");                     /* L93 */
              exit(0);                                      /* L94 */
    }                                                       /* L95 */
  } while (1);                                              /* L96 */
}                                                           /* L97 */
```

Compile and execute this program. A run of this program is given below:

```
Enter 1 to Encrypt a Message.
Enter 2 to Stop the Execution of Program.
Now Enter Your Choice (1 or 2) and Strike Enter Key: 1    ↵
Enter the Message to be Encrypted (upto 100 alphabets), Do Not Include
Spaces and Punctuation Symbols:
CandCryptographyIsVeryPowerfulCombination    ↵

Enter seed S (1 <= S <= 30000): 2000

Key: KJVWBAIZRUHRKNAFFHRBXNKUGHDMJHTDKLRWTZVMZ
Encrypted Message: MjizDrgokinikchdNzMfolZiclurdsVrwmzjtsdam

Enter the Message to be Decrypted (upto 100 alphabets):
MjizDrgokinikchdNzMfolZiclurdsVrwmzjtsdam    ↵
```

```
Decrypted Message: CandCryptographyIsVeryPowerfulCombination
Enter 1 to Encrypt a Message.
Enter 2 to Stop the Execution of Program.
Now Enter Your Choice (1 or 2) and Strike Enter Key: 2   ↵
Thank you.
```

How It Works

Firstly, let us discuss the working of One-Time Pad cipher. One-Time Pad cipher is impossible to crack. It is a Vigenère cipher with the following modifications:

- The text key is exactly as long as the plaintext.

- The text key is made simply by placing the randomly picked characters, one by one.

- The text key is generated on "use and throw" basis. The key once used is never used again.

Suppose, the plaintext is COMPUTER. Now to encrypt this plaintext you are required to generate the key that is eight characters long and it consists of randomly picked characters. Let the text key be BDLVACFX. The keys corresponding to these letters are given below (see also Figure 10-2):

```
Letters in Text Key  =   B    D    L    V    A    C    F    X
Keys                 =   1    3    11   21   0    2    5    23
```

Using these keys, the plaintext COMPUTER is encrypted as follows:

```
Plaintext    =   C    O    M    P    U    T    E    R
Keys         =   1    3    11   21   0    2    5    23
Ciphertext   =   D    R    X    K    U    V    J    O
```

The plaintext COMPUTER is encrypted to DRXKUVJO. Decryption is simply reverse of the encryption.

Now let us discuss the working of this program. LOCs 3-7 consist of variable declaration. In LOCs 3-6 four char type arrays, each of size 100, are declared, namely, msgOriginal, msgEncrypt, msgDecrypt, and msgKey. In LOC 7, an int type array intKey of size 100 is declared. Also, in LOC 7, few int type variables are declared.

LOCs 8-23 consist of definition of the function generateKey(). This function generates the key. The length of key is same as that of plaintext, i.e., msgOriginal. LOC 12 asks the user to enter the "seed" which is nothing but an integer in the range 1 to 30,000. The "seed" entered by user is read in the LOC 13 and stored in the int variable seed. LOCs 15-20 consist of a for loop in which the key is generated and stored in the variable msgKey. The key consist of only upper case letters. LOC 22 displays the key on the screen.

LOCs 24-30 consist of definition of function menu(). This function displays menu for users on the screen so that various options in this program can be used conveniently. LOCs 26-28 ask the user to enter an appropriate choice and also describe the various options available to user. LOC 29 reads the choice entered by user and stores this choice in the int variable intChoice.

LOCs 31-57 consist of definition of the function encryptMsg(). This function converts the plaintext into ciphertext. LOCs 35-36 ask the user to enter plaintext. LOC 37 reads this plaintext and stores it in the variable msgOriginal. LOC 38 computes the length of msgOriginal. LOC 39 calls the function generateKey(). LOCs 40-54 consist of a for loop. In this for loop the plaintext is converted into a ciphertext according to One-Time Pad cipher logic. LOC 56 displays the encrypted message on the screen.

LOCs 58-82 consist of definition of the function decryptMsg(). This function retrieves the plaintext from the ciphertext. LOC 62 asks the user to enter the ciphertext. The ciphertext entered by user is read and stored in the variable msgEncrypt in LOC 63. LOCs 65-79 consist of a for loop which retrieves the plaintext from the ciphertext and stores it in msgDecrypt. In LOC 81, the decrypted message is displayed on the screen.

LOCs 83-97 consist of definition of the function main(). LOCs 85-96 consist of a do-while loop. This seems to be an infinite loop, however, function exit() in the LOC 94 effectively stops the execution of this loop. LOC 86 calls the function menu() which displays the menu for users on the screen. The choice entered by user is stored in the int variable intChoice. LOCs 87-95 consist of a switch statement. Value stored in intChoice is passsed to this statement. If value of intChoice is 1 then case 1 is activated and functions encryptMsg() and decryptMsg() are called in succession. If value of intChoice is else then function exit() is called which terminates the execution of do-while loop and also terminates the execution of this program.

10-9. Use the RSA Cipher Method
Problem

You want to implement a cryptographic system using the RSA cipher method.
   Merits:

- Almost unbreakable cipher

- Being public key cryptographic system, problem of transportation of key securely is done away with

- This cipher - or any public key cipher - provides digital signatures that cannot be repudiated

Demerits:

- Uses complex arithmetic and hence difficult to implement and debug

- System requirement is high

- Implementation of this cipher may not be economical

- Program execution is slow

Solution

Write a C program that implements a cryptographic system using the RSA cipher method, with the following specifications:

- Program defines the functions prime(), findPrime(), computeKeys(), cd(), encryptMsg(), and decryptMsg(). Function prime() detects whether a given integer is prime or not. Function findPrime() finds the nth prime number. Functions cd() and computeKeys() together find the permissible values of d and e. Function encryptMsg() converts the plaintext into ciphertext. Function decryptMsg() retrieves the plaintext from ciphertext.

- Program defines the char type array msgOriginal, and int type arrays d, e, temp, msgEncrypt, and msgDecrypt. Size of all arrays should be 100.

The Code

Code of C program written with these specifications is given below. Type the following C program in a text editor and save it in the folder C:\Code with the filename crypt9.c:

```
/* This program implements a cryptographic system using the RSA cipher method. */
                                                                  /* BL */
#include <stdio.h>                                                /* L1 */
#include <math.h>                                                 /* L2 */
#include <string.h>                                               /* L3 */
                                                                  /* BL */
long int i, j, p, q, n, t, flag;                                  /* L4 */
long int e[100], d[100], temp[100], msgDecrypt[100], msgEncrypt[100]; /* L5 */
char msgOriginal[100];                                            /* L6 */
int prime(long int);                                              /* L7 */
int findPrime(long int s);                                        /* L8 */
void computeKeys();                                               /* L9 */
long int cd(long int);                                            /* L10 */
void encryptMsg();                                                /* L11 */
void decryptMsg();                                                /* L12 */
                                                                  /* BL */
void main() {                                                     /* L13 */
  long int s;                                                     /* L14 */
  do{                                                             /* L15 */
    printf("Enter the serial number S of 1st prime number (10 <= S <= 40): "); /* L16 */
    scanf("%ld", &s) ;                                            /* L17 */
  } while ((s < 10) || (s > 40));                                 /* L18 */
  p = findPrime(s);                                               /* L19 */
  printf("First prime number p is: %d \n", p) ;                   /* L20 */
  do{                                                             /* L21 */
    printf("Enter the serial number S of 2nd prime number (10 <= S <= 40):"); /* L22 */
    scanf("%ld", &s) ;                                            /* L23 */
```

```
  } while ((s < 10) || (s > 40));                                      /* L24 */
  q = findPrime(s);                                                    /* L25 */
  printf("Second prime number q is: %d \n", q) ;                       /* L26 */
  printf("\nEnter the Message to be Encrypted, Do Not Include Spaces:\n"); /* L27 */
  fflush(stdin);                                                       /* L28 */
  scanf("%s",msgOriginal);                                             /* L29 */
  for (i = 0; msgOriginal[i] != NULL; i++)                             /* L30 */
    msgDecrypt[i] = msgOriginal[i];                                    /* L31 */
  n = p * q;                                                           /* L32 */
  t = (p - 1) * (q - 1);                                               /* L33 */
  computeKeys();                                                       /* L34 */
  printf("\nPossible Values of e and d Are:\n");                       /* L35 */
  for (i = 0; i < j - 1; i++)                                          /* L36 */
    printf("\n %ld \t %ld", e[i], d[i]);                               /* L37 */
  printf("\nSample Public Key: (%ld,  %ld)", n, e[i-1]);               /* L38 */
  printf("\nSample Private Key: (%ld,  %ld)", n, d[i-1]);              /* L39 */
  encryptMsg();                                                        /* L40 */
  decryptMsg();                                                        /* L41 */
}                                                                      /* L42 */
                                                                       /* BL  */

int findPrime(long int s)                                              /* L43 */
{                                                                      /* L44 */
  int f, d, tag;                                                       /* L45 */
  f = 2;                                                               /* L46 */
  i = 1;                                                               /* L47 */
  while(i <= s){                                                       /* L48 */
    tag = 1;                                                           /* L49 */
    for(d = 2 ; d <= f-1 ; d++){                                       /* L50 */
      if(f % d == 0) {                                                 /* L51 */
        tag = 0;                                                       /* L52 */
        break ;                                                        /* L53 */
      }                                                                /* L54 */
    }                                                                  /* L55 */
    if(tag == 1) {                                                     /* L56 */
      if (i == s)                                                      /* L57 */
        return(f);                                                     /* L58 */
      i++ ;                                                            /* L59 */
    }                                                                  /* L60 */
    f++ ;                                                              /* L61 */
  }                                                                    /* L62 */
  return(0);                                                           /* L63 */
}                                                                      /* L64 */
                                                                       /* BL  */

int prime(long int pr)                                                 /* L65 */
{                                                                      /* L66 */
  int i;                                                               /* L67 */
  j=sqrt(pr);                                                          /* L68 */
  for (i = 2; i <= j; i++) {                                           /* L69 */
```

```
    if(pr % i == 0)                                    /* L70 */
       return 0;                                        /* L71 */
  }                                                     /* L72 */
  return 1;                                             /* L73 */
}                                                       /* L74 */
                                                        /* BL  */
void computeKeys()                                      /* L75 */
{                                                       /* L76 */
  int k;                                                /* L77 */
  k = 0;                                                /* L78 */
  for (i = 2; i < t; i++) {                             /* L79 */
    if(t % i == 0)                                      /* L80 */
      continue;                                         /* L81 */
    flag = prime(i);                                    /* L82 */
    if(flag == 1 && i != p && i != q) {                 /* L83 */
      e[k] = i;                                         /* L84 */
      flag = cd(e[k]);                                  /* L85 */
        if(flag > 0) {                                  /* L86 */
          d[k] = flag;                                  /* L87 */
          k++;                                          /* L88 */
        }                                               /* L89 */
        if(k == 99)                                     /* L90 */
        break;                                          /* L91 */
    }                                                   /* L92 */
  }                                                     /* L93 */
}                                                       /* L94 */
                                                        /* BL  */
long int cd(long int x)                                 /* L95 */
{                                                       /* L96 */
  long int k = 1;                                       /* L97 */
  while(1) {                                            /* L98 */
    k = k + t;                                          /* L99 */
    if(k % x == 0)                                      /* L100 */
      return(k/x);                                      /* L101 */
  }                                                     /* L102 */
}                                                       /* L103 */
                                                        /* BL   */
void encryptMsg()                                       /* L104 */
{                                                       /* L105 */
  long int pt, ct, key = e[0], k, length;               /* L106 */
  i = 0;                                                /* L107 */
  length = strlen(msgOriginal);                         /* L108 */
  while(i != length) {                                  /* L109 */
    pt = msgDecrypt[i];                                 /* L110 */
    pt = pt-96;                                         /* L111 */
    k = 1;                                              /* L112 */
    for (j = 0; j < key; j++) {                         /* L113 */
      k = k * pt;                                       /* L114 */
```

```
      k = k % n;                                 /* L115 */
    }                                            /* L116 */
    temp[i] = k;                                 /* L117 */
    ct = k + 96;                                 /* L118 */
    msgEncrypt[i] = ct;                          /* L119 */
    i++;                                         /* L120 */
  }                                              /* L121 */
  msgEncrypt[i] =- 1;                            /* L122 */
  printf("\nThe Encrypted Message:\n");          /* L123 */
  for (i = 0; msgEncrypt[i] != -1; i++)          /* L124 */
    printf("%c", msgEncrypt[i]);                 /* L125 */
}                                                /* L126 */
                                                 /* BL   */
void decryptMsg()                                /* L127 */
{                                                /* L128 */
  long int pt, ct, key = d[0], k;                /* L129 */
  i = 0;                                         /* L130 */
  while(msgEncrypt[i] != -1) {                   /* L131 */
    ct = temp[i];                                /* L132 */
    k = 1;                                       /* L133 */
    for (j = 0; j < key; j++) {                  /* L134 */
      k = k * ct;                                /* L135 */
      k = k % n;                                 /* L136 */
    }                                            /* L137 */
    pt = k + 96;                                 /* L138 */
    msgDecrypt[i] = pt;                          /* L139 */
    i++;                                         /* L140 */
  }                                              /* L141 */
  msgDecrypt[i] =- 1;                            /* L142 */
  printf("\nThe Decrypted Message:\n");          /* L143 */
  for (i = 0; msgDecrypt[i] != -1; i++)          /* L144 */
    printf("%c", msgDecrypt[i]);                 /* L145 */
  printf("\nThank you. \n ");                    /* L146 */
}                                                /* L147 */
```

Compile and execute this program. A run of this program is shown in Figure 10-3.

```
Enter the serial number S of 1st prime number (10 <= S <= 40): 12
First prime number p is: 37
Enter the serial number S of 2nd prime number (10 <= S <= 40): 34
Second prime number q is: 139

Enter the Message to be Encrypted, Do Not Include Spaces:
CandCryptographyIsVeryPowerfulCombination!!!

Possible Values of e and d Are:
 89       2177
 97       3073
 101      4181
Sample Public Key: (5143,  101)
Sample Private Key: (5143,  4181)
The Encrypted Message:
 aΣ` ç╙#~z┬Sa#╓╙╫luòç╙¥z≥òç┌Å► zEÇ♀Σa~♀zΣ↓↓↓
The Decrypted Message:
CandCryptographyIsVeryPowerfulCombination!!!
Thank you.
```

Figure 10-3. *A sample run of the program crypt9. A part of the output is cropped out to save the space.*

How It Works

Firstly, let us discuss the working of `RSA cipher`. All the preceding cryptographic systems are known as private key cryptographic systems. In private key cryptogaphy, you are required to send to receiver of message: (a) ciphertext and (b) secret key. But when you send ciphertext alongwith a secret key then very purpose of ciphering is challenged. Because anyone with a key can decrypt the ciphertext. In practice, when when both parties (sender and receiver) agree to use private key cryptography then they personally meet to share the secret key, and then only ciphertext is sent to receiving party, time to time.

The problem of sharing the secret key is solved by public key cryptographic systems. The very first such system is called RSA cipher. It is also most popular cryptographic system. It was first described by Ron Rivest, Adi Shamir and Leonard Adleman in 1977, hence the name RSA (R for Ron, S for Shamir and A for Adleman).

Public key cipher has two keys, one for encryption and other for decryption. Private key cipher has only one key that is used for encryption as well as decryption. All the preceding cryptographic systems are private key cryptographic systems. In some of the preceding programs, there is mention of two keys, one for encryption and another for decryption (for example, Recipe 10.6, Simple Substitution cipher). But actually it is only one key and decryption key is nothing but encryption key in another suitable form.

`Private Key cipher` is also called as `Symmetric cipher` and `Public Key cipher` is also called as `Asymmetric cipher`. In `Public Key cipher`, encryption key is called public key and decryption key is called private key. Public key is shared with all, however, private key is secret and it is in possession of the receiver (of the message) only. Thus public key is used for encryption and private key is used for decryption.

In RSA cipher, the generic procedure of encryption and decryption is as follows:

- Create two very large prime numbers randomly. These numbers are called p and q.

- Multiply p by q and the result is called n. Therefore, n = p * q.

- Calculate the product (p - 1) * (q - 1) and call it t. Therefore, t = (p - 1) * (q - 1).

- Create a random number e such that e is relatively prime with t. Also, 1 < e < t.

- Calculate the modular inverse of (e % t) and call it d. It means, find the value d such that (d * e) % t = 1. Also d < t.

- Public key is (e, n) and private key is (d, n).

- Let letter M from plaintext is encrypted to letter C. It is done as follows: $C = M^e \% n$.

- Letter C from ciphertext is decrypted back to M. It is done as follows: $M = C^d \% n$.

The RSA cipher derives its strenght from the fact that if two large prime numbers are multiplied then the resulting number is difficult to factorize.

Now let us discuss the working of this program. LOCs 4-6 consist of variable declaration. LOC 4 declares few long int type variables. LOC 5 declares five long int type arrays. LOC 6 declares a char type array msgOriginal. The size of all arrays is 100. LOCs 7-12 consist of six function prototypes.

LOCs 13-42 consist of definition of the function main(). LOCs 15-18 consist of a do-while loop. This loop asks the user to enter the serial number S of the first prime number where S is an integer in the range 10 to 40. The number entered by user is read in the LOC 17 and is stored in the variable s. In LOC 19, call is made to function findPrime() and s is passed to it as an input argument. Function findPrime() finds the sth prime number and returns it and returned value is assigned to variable p. In LOC 20, the value of first prime number p is displayed on the screen. LOCs 21-26 contain the code that is similar to code in the LOCs 15-20. Only difference is that code in the LOCs 15-20 is related to first prime number p and code in the LOCs 21-26 is related to the second prime number q. LOC 27 asks the user to enter the plaintext. The plaintext entered by user is read in the LOC 28 and is assigned to the variable msgOriginal. LOCs 30-31 consist of a for loop that copies the array msgOriginal to array msgDecrypt. This is done to facilitate some computations in the function encryptMsg(). In function decryptMsg(), however, the contents of msgDecrypt are overwritten.

In LOC 32, value of n is computed. In LOC 33, value of t is computed. In LOC 34, function computeKeys() is called. Permissible values of e and d are displayed on the screen in the LOCs 35-37. Sample public key and sample private key are displayed on the screen in the LOCs 38-39. In the LOC 40, function encryptMsg() is called that converts plaintext into ciphertext. In the LOC 41, function decryptMsg() is called that retrieves the plaintext from the ciphertext.

LOCs 43-64 consist of definition of the function findPrime(). This function finds the sth prime number and s is passed to it as an input argument. First prime number is 2, second prime number is 3, third prime number is 5, and so on. This function starts with integer 2 (see LOC 46, variable f is used for this integer) and then goes to check every next integer for its primeness. If that integer is prime and its serial number is s then it is returned (see LOC 58).

LOCs 65-74 consist of definition of the function prime(). Long integer variable pr is passed to this function as an input argument. This function checks whether pr is prime number or not; if pr is prime number then it returns 1 (see LOC 73), otherwise it returns 0 (see LOC 71).

LOCs 75-94 consist of definition of the function computeKeys(). LOCs 95-103 consist of definition of the function cd(). These two functions together compute the permissible values of d and e using the standard formulae in RSA cipher method.

LOCs 104-126 consist of definition of the function encryptMsg(). This function converts the plaintext into ciphertext. In this function plaintext is converted into ciphertext using the standard formulae in RSA cipher method. Ciphertext is stored in the variable msgEncrypt. Encrypted message is displayed on the screen in the LOCs 123-125.

LOCs 127-147 consist of definition of the function decryptMsg(). This function retrieves the plaintext from the ciphertext using the standard formulae in RSA cipher method. Retrieved plaintext (i.e., decrypted message) is stored in variable msgDecrypt. Decrypted message is displayed on the screen in the LOCs 143-145.

CHAPTER 11

■ ■ ■

Numerical Methods

We use numerical methods to solve the equations and integrations for which exact solutions are not possible. Using numerical methods we find approximate solutions to these problems. Most of the real life problems fall in this category. While solving a problem using numerical methods, one has to perform a large number of computations by hand. Fortunately, computers are number crunchers, and hence, since the arrival of computers, this task has been mostly done by the computers. In this chapter, few numerical methods - listed below - are discussed in the context of C programming.

- Bisection Method to find the roots of an equation.

- Regula Falsi Method to find the roots of an equation.

- Muller's Method to find the roots of an equation.

- Newton Raphson Method to find the roots of an equation.

- Newton's Forward Method of interpolation to construct the new data points.

- Newton's Backward Method of interpolation to construct the new data points.

- Gauss's Forward Method of interpolation to construct the new data points.

- Gauss's Backward Method of interpolation to construct the new data points.

- Stirling's Method of interpolation to construct the new data points.

- Bessel's Method of interpolation to construct the new data points.

- Laplace Everett's Method of interpolation to construct the new data points.

- Lagrange's Method of interpolation to construct the new data points.

- Trapezoidal Method to compute the value of integration.

- Simpson's 3/8th Method to compute the value of integration.

© Shirish Chavan 2017
S. Chavan, *C Recipes*, DOI 10.1007/978-1-4842-2967-5_11

- Simpson's 1/3rd Method to compute the value of integration.

- Modified Euler's Method to solve a differential equation.

- Runge Kutta Method to solve a differential equation.

11-1. To Find the Roots of an Equation Using the Bisection Method

Problem

You want to find the roots of an equation using the Bisection Method.
Merits:

- It is always convergent.

- The root bracket gets halved with each iteration and this is guarenteed.

Demerits:

- Convergence is slow

- If one of the initial guesses is close to the root, the convergence is slower.

Solution

Write a C program that finds the roots of an equation using the Bisection Method, with the following specifications:

- Program defines the function bisect() that computes the roots of equation.

- Set the value of EPS (epsilon) to 0.00001.

The Code

Code of C program written with these specifications is given below. Type the following C program in a text editor and save it in the folder C:\Code with the filename numrc1.c:

```
/* This program implements a Bisection method to find the roots of
an equation. */
                                                        /* BL */
#include <stdio.h>                                      /* L1 */
#include <math.h>                                       /* L2 */
                                                        /* BL */
#define EPS 0.00001                                     /* L3 */
```

```
#define F(x) (5*x*x) * log10(x) - 5.3              /* L4 */
                                                   /* BL */
void bisect();                                     /* L5 */
                                                   /* BL */
int kount = 1, intN;                               /* L6 */
float root = 1;                                    /* L7 */
                                                   /* BL */
void main()                                        /* L8 */
{                                                  /* L9 */
  printf("\nSolution of Equation by Bisection Method. ");  /* L10 */
  printf("\nEquation: ");                          /* L11 */
  printf("   (5*x*x) * log10(x) - 5.3 = 0");       /* L12 */
  printf("\nEnter the number of iterations: ");    /* L13 */
  scanf("%d", &intN);                              /* L14 */
  bisect();                                        /* L15 */
}                                                  /* L16 */
                                                   /* BL  */
void bisect()                                      /* L17 */
{                                                  /* L18 */
  float x1, x2, x3, func1, func2, func3;           /* L19 */
  x3 = 1;                                          /* L20 */
  do{                                              /* L21 */
    func3 = F(x3);                                 /* L22 */
    if (func3 > 0) {                               /* L23 */
      break;                                       /* L24 */
    }                                              /* L25 */
    x3++;                                          /* L26 */
  } while(1);                                      /* L27 */
  x2 = x3 - 1;                                     /* L28 */
  do{                                              /* L29 */
    func2 = F(x2);                                 /* L30 */
    if(func2 < 0) {                                /* L31 */
      break;                                       /* L32 */
    }                                              /* L33 */
    x3--;                                          /* L34 */
  } while(1);                                      /* L35 */
  while (kount <= intN) {                          /* L36 */
    x1 = (x2 + x3) / 2.0;                          /* L37 */
    func1 = F(x1);                                 /* L38 */
    if(func1 == 0) {                               /* L39 */
      root = x1;                                   /* L40 */
    }                                              /* L41 */
    if(func1 * func2  <0) {                        /* L42 */
      x3 = x1;                                     /* L43 */
    }                                              /* L44 */
    else {                                         /* L45 */
      x2 = x1;                                     /* L46 */
```

```
    func2 = func1;                                              /* L47 */
  }                                                             /* L48 */
  printf("\nIteration No. %d", kount);                          /* L49 */
  printf("     :      Root, x = %f",x1);                        /* L50 */
  if(fabs((x2 - x3) / x2) < EPS) {                              /* L51 */
    printf("\n\nTotal No. of Iterations:  %d", kount);          /* L52 */
    printf("\nRoot, x = %f", x1);                               /* L53 */
    printf("\n\nThank you.\n");                                 /* L54 */
    exit(0) ;                                                   /* L55 */
  }                                                             /* L56 */
  kount++;                                                      /* L57 */
}                                                               /* L58 */
printf("\n\nTotal No. of Iterations = %d", kount-1);            /* L59 */
printf("\nRoot, x = %8.6f", x1);                                /* L60 */
printf("\n\nThank you.\n");                                     /* L61 */
}                                                               /* L62 */
```

Compile and execute this program. A run of this program is given below:

```
Solution of Equation by Bisection Method.
Equation:  (5*x*x) * log10(x) - 5.3 = 0
Enter the number of iterations: 40   ⏎

Iteration No. 1     :     Root, x = 1.500000
Iteration No. 2     :     Root, x = 1.750000
---------------------------------------------
---------------------------------------------
Iteration No. 15    :     Root, x = 1.928131
Iteration No. 16    :     Root, x = 1.928116

Total No. of Iterations:  16
Root, x = 1.928116
Thank you.
```

How It Works

Let the equation of curve be $y = f(x)$. The problem is to find the value of x for which y is zero and this value of x is termed as root. In Bisection Method intermediate value property is repeatedly applied till the root is found. Let $f(x)$ be continuous function between a and b where a and b define the boundary values for x. Value of x is to be found for which y is zero. Let $f(a)$ and $f(b)$ be values of y for $x = a$ and $x = b$, respectively. For definiteness, let us assume that $f(a)$ is negative and $f(b)$ is positive. If both $f(a)$ and $f(b)$ are either positive or negative then root doesn't exist in the interval a to b.

Now the first approximation to the root is x1 = 1/2(a+b). Next, three cases arise as follows:

> Case (a): if f(x1) = 0 then x1 is the root.
>
> Case (b): if f(x1) is positive then root lies between a and x1.
>
> Case (c): if f(x1) is negative then root lies between x1 and b.

If case (a) occurs then we repeat this process (of bisecting the interval) with the new boundaries a and x1. If case (b) occurs then we repeat this process (of bisecting the interval) with the new boundaries x1 and b.

And the process is repeated till the root is found. Benefit of bisection method is that in iterative process convergence is guarenteed. The order of convergence of the Bisection Method is 0.5.

In the LOCs 3-4 the values of EPS and F(x) are defined. In the LOC 5, function bisect() is declared. In the LOCs 6-7, few variables are declared. LOCs 8-16 consist of definition of the main() function. LOCs 17-62 consist of definition of the bisect() function.

In the main() function LOCs 10-12 display the equation. In LOC 13 user is asked to enter the number of iterations. The number entered by user is read in the LOC 14 and stored in the int variable intN. In LOC 16 function bisect() is called. This function computes the roots of the given equation using the procedure stated above. LOCs 49-54 and LOCs 59-61 display the results on the screen.

11-2. To Find the Roots of an Equation Using the Regula Falsi Method
Problem

You want to find the roots of an equation using the Regula Falsi (False Position) Method.
  Merits:

- Bound to converge, like Bisection method

- As the interval becomes small, the interior point is generally becomes much closer to root.

- Faster convergence than bisection.

Demerits:

- It can not predict number of iterations to reach a given precision.

- It can be less precise than bisection. No strict precision is guaranteed.

Solution

Write a C program that finds the roots of an equation using the Regula Falsi (Falose Position) Method, with the following specifications:

- Program defines the function falsePosition() that computes the roots of equation.

- Set the value of EPS to 0.00001.

The Code

Code of C program written with these specifications is given below. Type the following C program in a text editor and save it in the folder C:\Code with the filename numrc2.c:

```
/* This program implements the Regula Falsi method to find the roots of an
equation. */
                                                        /* BL */

#include<stdio.h>                                       /* L1 */
#include<math.h>                                        /* L2 */
                                                        /* BL */
#define EPS 0.00001                                     /* L3 */
#define f(x) 3*x*x*x + 5*x*x + 4*cos(x) - 2*exp(x)      /* L4 */
                                                        /* BL */
void falsePosition();                                   /* L5 */
                                                        /* BL */
void main()                                             /* L6 */
{                                                       /* L7 */
  printf("\nSolution of Equation by False Position Method\n");  /* L8 */
  printf("\nEquation :    ");                           /* L9 */
  printf("3*x*x*x + 5*x*x + 4*cos(x) - 2*exp(x) = 0");  /* L10 */
  falsePosition();                                      /* L11 */
}                                                       /* L12 */
                                                        /* BL */
void falsePosition()                                    /* L13 */
{                                                       /* L14 */
  float fun1, fun2, fun3;                               /* L15 */
  float x1, x2, x3;                                     /* L16 */
  int iterations;                                       /* L17 */
  int i;                                                /* L18 */
  printf("\nEnter the Number of Iterations: ");         /* L19 */
  scanf("%d", &iterations);                             /* L20 */
  x2 = 0.0;                                             /* L21 */
  do {                                                  /* L22 */
    fun2 = f(x2);                                       /* L23 */
    if(fun2 > 0) {                                      /* L24 */
      break;                                            /* L25 */
    }                                                   /* L26 */
```

```
    else {                                                          /* L27 */
      x2 = x2 + 0.1;                                                /* L28 */
    }                                                               /* L29 */
  } while(1);                                                       /* L30 */
  x1 = x2 - 0.1;                                                    /* L31 */
  fun1 = f(x1);                                                     /* L32 */
  printf("\nIteration No.\t\tx\t\tF(x)\n");                         /* L33 */
  i = 0;                                                            /* L34 */
  while (i < iterations) {                                          /* L35 */
    x3 = x1 - ((x2 - x1) / (fun2 - fun1)) * fun1;                   /* L36 */
    fun3 = f(x3);                                                   /* L37 */
    if(fun1 * fun3 > 0) {                                           /* L38 */
      x2 = x3;                                                      /* L39 */
      fun2 = fun3;                                                  /* L40 */
    }                                                               /* L41 */
    else {                                                          /* L42 */
      x1 = x3;                                                      /* L43 */
      fun1 = fun3;                                                  /* L44 */
    }                                                               /* L45 */
    printf("\n%d\t\t\t%f\t%f\n", i+1, x3, fun3);                    /* L46 */
    if (fabs(fun3) <= EPS)                                          /* L47 */
      break;                                                       /* L48 */
    i++;                                                            /* L49 */
  }                                                                 /* L50 */
  printf("\n\nTotal No. of Iterations:  %d", i+1);                  /* L51 */
  printf("\nRoot, x = %8.6f \n", x3);                               /* L52 */
  printf("\nThank you.\n");                                         /* L53 */
}                                                                   /* L54 */
```

Compile and execute this program. A run of this program is given below:

```
Solution by False Position Method

Equation :    3*x*x*x + 5*x*x + 4*cos(x) - 2*exp(x) = 0
Enter the Number of Iterations: 30  ←

Iteration No.                  x             F(x)
1                       0.920209        3.974567
2                      -1.387344        1.843082
------------------------------------------------
------------------------------------------------
12                     -1.599190        0.000014
13                     -1.599192       -0.000004

Total No. of Iterations: 15
Root, x = -1.599192

Thank you.
```

How It Works

Let the equation of curve be $y = f(x)$. The problem is to find the value of x for which y is zero and this value of x is termed as root. In the preceding recipe, the bisection method is discussed. The convergence process in the bisection method is very slow. It depends on the choice of boundaries a and b. Let the midpoint of a and b be c. Then $f(x)$ has no role in determining the point c. Refula Falsi Method represents an improvemet in the bisection method in this matter.

Let a and b be the boundaries of initial interval. Let $f(a)$ be positive and $f(b)$ be negative. Let $(a, f(a))$ be point A and $(b, f(b))$ be point B. The graph $y = f(x)$ is actually a curve between the points A and B and cutting the X-axis somewhere between the points a and b. The essence of this method is to consider the chord AB instead of curve AB and then to take the point of intersection of the chord with the X-axis as an approximation to root. The equation of chord is given by the following expression:

$$y - f(a) = (f(b) - f(a)) * (x-a) / (b-a)$$

Putting $y = 0$ in this expression we get the point where chord cuts the X-axis and this point represents the first approximation to the root. Let c be the x-coordinate of this point and it is given by:

$$c = a - ((b - a) * (f(a))) / (f(b) - f(a))$$

The next smaller interval which contains the root can be obtained by inspecting the value of $f(a)*f(b)$. Now the three cases arise as follows:

Case (a): If $f(a)*f(b) = 0$ then c is the root.

Case (b): If $f(a)*f(b)$ is negative then root lies between a and c.

Case (c): If $f(a)*f(b)$ is positive then root lies between b and c.

And the process is repeated till the root is found. Benefit of bisection method is that in iterative process convergence is guarenteed. The order of convergence of the Regula Falsi method is 1.618.

In the LOCs 3-4 the values of EPS and $f(x)$ are defined. In the LOC 5, function falsePosition() is declared. LOCs 6-12 consist of definition of the main() function. LOCs 13-54 consist of definition of the falsePosition() function.

Inside the main() function LOCs 8-10 display the equation. LOC 11 calls the function falsePosition().

Inside the falsePosition() function, in the LOCs 15-18 few variables are declared. LOC 19 asks the user to enter the number of iterations. The number entered by user is read in the LOC 20 and stored in the int variable iterations. Results are computed using the standard formulae of Regula Falsi method stated above. LOCs 33, 46, 51-53 display the results on the screen.

11-3. To Find the Roots of an Equation Using Muller's Method

Problem

You want to find the roots of an equation using Muller's Method.

Merits:

- This method can find imaginary roots

- In this method, there is no need to use derivatives.

Demerits:

- Lengthy computations. Troublesome to implement and debug.

- Extraneous roots can be found.

Solution

Write a C program that finds the roots of an equation using Muller's Method, with the following specifications:

- Program defines the function f() that computes the value of equation.

- Set the value of EPS to 0.00001.

The Code

Code of C program written with these specifications is given below. Type the following C program in a text editor and save it in the folder C:\Code with the filename numrc3.c:

```
/* This program implements Muller's method to find the roots of an equation. */
                                                            /* BL */
#include<stdio.h>                                           /* L1 */
#include<math.h>                                            /* L2 */
                                                            /* BL */
#define EPS   0.00001                                       /* L3 */
                                                            /* BL */
float f(float x)                                            /* L4 */
{                                                           /* L5 */
  return (x*x*x)-(2*x)-5;                                   /* L6 */
}                                                           /* L7 */
                                                            /* BL */
main ()                                                     /* L8 */
{                                                           /* L9 */
  int i, itr, maxItr;                                       /* L10 */
```

```
float x[4], m, n, p, q, r;                                              /* L11 */
printf("\nSolution of Equation by Muller's Method.");                   /* L12 */
printf("\nEquation: x*x*x - 2*x - 5 = 0  \n");                          /* L13 */
printf("\n\n Enter the first initial guess: ");                         /* L14 */
scanf("%f", &x[0]);                                                     /* L15 */
printf("\nEnter the second initial guess: ");                           /* L16 */
scanf("%f", &x[1]);                                                     /* L17 */
printf("\nEnter the third initial guess: ");                            /* L18 */
scanf("%f", &x[2]) ;                                                    /* L19 */
printf("\nEnter the maximum number of iterations: ");                   /* L20 */
scanf("%d", &maxItr);                                                   /* L21 */
for (itr = 1; itr <= maxItr; itr++)     {                               /* L22 */
  m = (x[2] - x[1]) / (x[1] - x[0]);                                    /* L23 */
  n = (x[2] - x[0]) / (x[1] - x[0]);                                    /* L24 */
  p = f(x[0])*m*m - f(x[1])*n*n + f(x[2])*(n+m);                        /* L25 */
  q = sqrt ((p*p - 4*f(x[2])*n*m*(f(x[0])*m - f(x[1])*n + f(x[2])))); /* L26 */
  if (p < 0)                                                            /* L27 */
    r = (2*f(x[2])*n)/(-p+q);                                           /* L28 */
  else                                                                  /* L29 */
    r = (2*f(x[2])*n)/(-p-q);                                           /* L30 */
  x[3] = x[2] + r*(x[2] - x[1]);                                        /* L31 */
  printf("Iteration No. : %d,      x = %8.6f\n", itr, x[3]);            /* L32 */
  if (fabs (x[3] - x[2]) < EPS) {                                       /* L33 */
    printf("\nTotal No. of Iterations: %d\n", itr);                     /* L34 */
    printf("\Root, x = %8.6f\n", x[3]);                                 /* L35 */
    printf("Thank you.\n");                                             /* L36 */
    return 0;                                                           /* L37 */
  }                                                                     /* L38 */
    for (i=0; i<3; i++)                                                 /* L39 */
        x[i] = x[i+1];                                                  /* L40 */
}                                                                       /* L41 */
printf("\nSolution Doesn't Converge or Iterations are Insufficient.\n"); /* L42 */
printf("Thank you.\n");                                                 /* L43 */
return(1);                                                              /* L44 */
}                                                                       /* L45 */
```

Compile and execute this program. A run of this program is given below:

```
Solution of Equation by Muller's Method.
Equation:  x*x*x - 2*x - 5 = 0
Enter the first initial guess: 1     ↵
Enter the second initial guess: 2    ↵
Enter the third initial guess: 3     ↵
Enter the maximum number of iterations: 30    ↵
Iteration No. : 1,      x = 2.086800
Iteration No. : 2,      x = 2.094492
Iteration No. : 3,      x = 2.094552
```

```
Iteration No. : 4,      x = 2.094552
Total No. of Iterations: 4
Root, x = 2.094552
Thank you.
```

How It Works

Let the equation of curve be y = f(x). The problem is to find the value of x for which y is zero and this value of x is termed as root. Muller's Method is based on secant method. In secant method two points on the curve y = f(x) are picked as initial approximations to the root which may or may not bracket the root. However, these approximations should be reasonably close to the root. A chord is constructed through these two points. Then with every iteration, next approximation moves closer to the root.

In Muller's Method, instead of two points, three points on the curve y = f(x) are picked as initial approximations to the root. Then, instead of a chord, a parabola is constructed passing through these three points. Next, intersection of this parabola with the X-axis is taken as the next approximation.

Let (x1, y1), (x2, y2) and (x3, y3) be the three distinct points as initial approximations to root. The approximation to next point x4 is given by the following expression:

$$x4 - x3 = \frac{-B \pm \sqrt{B^2 - 4*A*y3}}{2*A}$$

Here, A and B are given by the following expressions:

$$A = \frac{(x1-x3)*(y2-y3)-(x2-x3)*(y1-y3)}{(x2-x1)*(x2-x2)*(x1-x3)}$$

and

$$B = \frac{(x1-x3)^2*(y2-y3)-(x2-x3)^2*(y1-y3)}{(x1-x2)*(x2-x3)*(x1-x3)}$$

The order of convergence of Muller's Method is approximately 1.84.

In the LOC 3 the value of EPS is defined. LOCs 4-7 define the function f(). LOCs 8-45 define the function main(). Inside the main() function, in LOCs 10-11, few variables are declared. LOC 13 displays the equation. LOCs 14, 16 and 18 ask the user to enter the first, second and third intial guess respectively. The guesses entered by user are stored in the array x.

LOC 20 asks the user to enter the maximum number of iterations. The numbered entered by user is stored in the variable maxItr. LOCs 22-41 consist of a for loop and results are computed in this for loop using the standard formuale for Muller's Method stated above. LOCs 34-35 and 42-43 display the results on the screen.

11-4. To Find the Roots of an Equation Using the Newton Raphson Method

Problem

You want to find the roots of an equation using the Newton Raphson Method.
   Merits:

- One of the fastest convergences to the root.

- Converges on the root quadratially.

- Easy to convert to multiple dimensions.

Demerits:

- Derivative of function f(x) is needed.

- Poor global convergence properties.

- Computation is dependent on initial guess.

Solution

Write a C program that finds the roots of an equation using the Newton Raphson Method, with the following specifications:

- Program defines the function newtonRaphson() that computes the roots of equation.

- Set the value of EPS to 0.00001.

The Code

Code of C program written with these specifications is given below. Type the following C program in a text editor and save it in the folder C:\Code with the filename numrc4.c:

```
/* This program implements Newton Raphson method to find the roots of an
equation. */
                                                        /* BL */
#include<stdio.h>                                       /* L1 */
#include<math.h>                                        /* L2 */
                                                        /* BL */
#define EPS  0.00001                                    /* L3 */
#define f(x) 17*x*x*x - 13*x*x - 7*x - 2973             /* L4 */
#define df(x) 51*x*x - 26*x - 7                         /* L5 */
                                                        /* BL */
void newtonRaphson();                                   /* L6 */
                                                        /* BL */
```

```
void main()                                                          /* L7 */
{                                                                    /* L8 */
  printf ("\nSolution of Equation by Newton Raphson method.\n");     /* L9 */
  printf ("\nEquation is: 17*x*x*x - 13*x*x - 7*x - 2973 = 0 \n\n"); /* L10 */
  newtonRaphson();                                                   /* L11 */
}                                                                    /* L12 */
                                                                     /* BL  */
void newtonRaphson()                                                 /* L13 */
{                                                                    /* L14 */
  long float x1, x2, f1, f2, df;                                     /* L15 */
  int i=1, iterations;                                               /* L16 */
  float error;                                                       /* L17 */
  x2 = 0;                                                            /* L18 */
  do {                                                               /* L19 */
    f2 = f(x2);                                                      /* L20 */
    if (f2 > 0)                                                      /* L21 */
      break;                                                         /* L22 */
    x2 += 0.01;                                                      /* L23 */
  } while (1);                                                       /* L24 */
  x1 = x2 - 0.01;                                                    /* L25 */
  f1 = f(x1);                                                        /* L26 */
  printf("Enter the number of iterations: ");                       /* L27 */
  scanf(" %d",&iterations);                                          /* L28 */
  x1 = (x1 + x2) / 2;                                                /* L29 */
  while (i <= iterations) {                                          /* L30 */
    f1 = f(x1);                                                      /* L31 */
    df = df(x1);                                                     /* L32 */
    x2 = x1 - (f1/df);                                               /* L33 */
    printf("\nThe %d th approximation, x = %f", i, x2);              /* L34 */
    error = fabs(x2 - x1);                                           /* L35 */
    if(error < EPS)                                                  /* L36 */
      break;                                                         /* L37 */
    x1 = x2;                                                         /* L38 */
    i++;                                                             /* L39 */
  }                                                                  /* L40 */
  if(error > EPS)                                                    /* L41 */
    printf("Solution Doesn't Converge or No. of Iterations Insufficient."); /* L42 */
  printf("\nRoot,  x = %8.6f ", x2);                                 /* L43 */
  printf("\nThank you.\n");                                          /* L44 */
}                                                                    /* L45 */
```

Compile and execute this program. A run of this program is given below:

```
Solution of Equation by Newton Raphson Method.
Equation is: 17*x*x*x - 13*x*x - 7*x - 2973 = 0

Enter the number of iterations: 10  ↵

The 1 th approximation, x = 5.884717
The 2 th approximation, x = 5.884717
Root, x = 5.884717
Thank you.
```

How It Works

Let the equation of curve be y = f(x). The problem is to find the value of x for which y is zero and this value of x is termed as root. In Newton Raphson Method, a single point (say, x0, y0) is picked as an initial approximation to the root. At this point (x0, y0) a tangent to curve is drawn. The point at which this tangent line crosses the X-axis represents a better estimate of root than x0. Let this point be (x1, 0). Draw a tangent to curve at (x1, y1). Let this tangent crosses the X-axis at point x2. Now, x2 represents the better estimate of root than x1. Draw a tangent to curve at (x2, y2), and so on. This procedure need to be repeated till a root is found. If xn is known then next value of x, say x(n+1), can be computed using following formula:

x(n+1) = xn - f(xn)/f'(xn)

where f'(xn) is nothing but derivative of f(xn). The order of convergence of Newton Raphson Method is 2. However, there is no guranteed convergence in case of Newton Raphon Method.

In the LOC 3 the value of EPS is defined. In LOC 4, the equation f(x) is defined. In LOC 5, the derivative of f(x), df(x) is defined. LOC 6 consists of declaration of the function newtonRaphson(). LOCs 7-12 consist of the definition of the function main(). LOCs 13-45 consist of the definition of the function newtonRaphson(). Inside the main() function, in the LOCs 9-10, equation f(x) = 0 is displayed on the screen. In the LOC 11, function newtonRaphson() is called.

Inside the function newtonRaphson(), in the LOCs 15-17, few variables are declared. In the LOC 27, user is asked to enter the number of iterations. The number entered by user is read in the LOC 28 and stored in the variable iterations.

Results are computed in this function using the standard procedure and formula of the Newton Raphson Method, stated above. Finally, results are displayed on the screen in the LOCs 34, 42-44.

11-5. To Construct the New Data Points Using Newton's Forward Method of Interpolation

Problem

You want to construct the new data points using Newton's Forward Method of Interpolation.

Merits:

- Particularly useful for interpolating the values of f(x) near the beginning of the set of values given.

- Newton forward method of interpolation is more efficient than Lagrange method of interpolation and is easily implemented.

Demerits:

- Method has a constraint that function f(x) must be continuous and differentiable.

Solution

Write a C program that constructs the new data points using Newton's Forward Method of Interpolation, with the following specifications:

- Let the maximum number of terms be 20.

- Accept the values of x upto 2 decimal point accurate.

- Accept the values of y upto 4 decimal point accurate.

The Code

Code of C program written with these specifications is given below. Type the following C program in a text editor and save it in the folder C:\Code with the filename numrc5.c:

```
/* This program implements Newton's Forward Method of Interpoloation. */
                                                              /* BL */
#include<stdio.h>                                             /* L1 */
                                                              /* BL */
#define MAX 20                                                /* L2 */
                                                              /* BL */
void main()                                                   /* L3 */
{                                                             /* L4 */
  float ax[MAX], ay[MAX], diff[MAX][5];                       /* L5 */
  float nr = 1.0, dr=1.0, x, p, h, yp;                        /* L6 */
  int terms, i, j, k;                                         /* L7 */
  printf("\nInterpolation by Newton's Forward Method.");      /* L8 */
  printf("\nEnter the number of terms (Maximum 20): ");       /* L9 */
```

363

```
  scanf("%d", &terms);                                      /* L10 */
  printf("\nEnter the values of x upto 2 decimal points.\n");  /* L11 */
  for (i=0; i<terms; i++) {                                 /* L12 */
    printf("Enter the value of x%d: ", i+1);                /* L13 */
    scanf("%f",&ax[i]);                                     /* L14 */
  }                                                         /* L15 */
  printf("\nNow enter the values of y upto 4 decimal points.\n"); /* L16 */
  for (i=0; i<terms; i++) {                                 /* L17 */
    printf("Enter the value of y%d: ", i+1);                /* L18 */
    scanf("%f", &ay[i]);                                    /* L19 */
  }                                                         /* L20 */
  printf("\nEnter the value of x for which the value of y is wanted: "); /* L21 */
  scanf("%f", &x);                                          /* L22 */
  h = ax[1] - ax[0];                                        /* L23 */
  for (i = 0; i < terms-1; i++)                             /* L24 */
    diff[i][1] = ay[i+1] - ay[i];                           /* L25 */
  for (j=2; j<=4; j++)                                      /* L26 */
    for(i=0; i<=terms-j; i++)                               /* L27 */
      diff[i][j] = diff[i+1][j-1] - diff[i][j-1];           /* L28 */
  i=0;                                                      /* L29 */
  do {                                                      /* L30 */
    i++;                                                    /* L31 */
  } while (ax[i] < x);                                      /* L32 */
  i--;                                                      /* L33 */
  p = (x - ax[i]) / h;                                      /* L34 */
  yp = ay[i];                                               /* L35 */
  for (k=1; k <= 4; k++)     {                              /* L36 */
    nr *= p - k + 1;                                        /* L37 */
    dr *= k;                                                /* L38 */
    yp += (nr/dr) * diff[i][k];                             /* L39 */
  }                                                         /* L40 */
  printf("\nFor x = %6.2f,    y = %6.4f",x,yp);             /* L41 */
  printf("\nThank you.\n");                                 /* L42 */
}                                                           /* L43 */
```

Compile and execute this program. A run of this program is given below:

```
Interpolation by Newton's Forward Method.
Enter the number of terms (Maximum 20): 5  ⏎

Enter the values of x upto 2 decimal points.
Enter the value of x1: 10.11  ⏎
Enter the value of x2: 20.22  ⏎
Enter the value of x3: 30.33  ⏎
Enter the value of x4: 40.44  ⏎
Enter the value of x5: 50.55  ⏎
```

```
Now enter the values of y upto 4 decimal points.
Enter the value of y1: 35.3535    ↵
Enter the value of y2: 45.4545    ↵
Enter the value of y3: 55.5555    ↵
Enter the value of y4: 65.6565    ↵
Enter the value of y5: 75.7575    ↵

Enter the value of x for which the value of y is wanted: 36.67

For x = 36.67,   y = 61.3494
Thank you.
```

How It Works

In interpolation, instead of an equation of type y = f(x), a set of few data points is provided and using this set you are required to construct the new data points. Suppose the following five data points are provided: (x1, y1), (x2, y2), (x3, y3), (x4, y4), and (x5, y5). Using these data points you are required to create the new data points (xi, yi) such that (x1 < xi < x5) and (y1 < yi < y5).

In Newton's Forward Method of Interpolation, the formula shown in Figure 11-1 is used to construct the new data points. Here f(x) is polynomial of the nth degree. This formula is particularly useful when f(x) is required near the beginning of the table of data points.

$$f(a+hu) = f(a) + u\,\Delta f(a) + \frac{u\,(u-1)}{2!}\,\Delta^2 f(a) + \dots$$
$$+ \frac{u\,(u-1)\,(u-2)\dots(u-n+1)}{n!}\,\Delta^n f(a)$$

where $y = f(x)$ is a function of x which assumes the values $f(a)$, $f(a+h)$, $f(a+2h)$, ..., $f(a+nh)$ for $(n+1)$ equidistant values a, $a+h$, $a+2h$, ..., $a+nh$ of the independent variable x. Also, $f(a+h) - f(a) = \Delta f(a)$ and $u = (x-a)/h$.

Figure 11-1. *Formula for Newton's Forward Method of interpolation*

LOC 2 defines the symbolic constant MAX with the value of 20. LOCs 3-43 define the function main(). In LOCs 5-7 few variables are declared. LOC 9 asks the user to enter the number of terms. The number entered by user is read in the LOC 10 and it is stored in the variable terms. LOC 11 asks the user to enter the values of x. The values entered by user are read in the for loop spanning the LOCs 12-15. LOC 16 asks the user to enter the values of y. The values entered by user are read in the for loop spanning the LOCs 17-20.

LOC 21 asks the user to enter the value of x for which the value of y is wanted. The value - a floating point number - entered by user is read in the LOC 22 and stored in the variable x. In the LOCs 23-40, the corresponding value of y is computed. Thus (x, y) represents the newly constructed data point. The result is displayed on the screen in the LOC 41.

11-6. To Construct the New Data Points Using Newton's Backward Method of Interpolation

Problem

You want to construct the new data points using Newton's Backward Method of Interpolation.

Merits:

- Particularly useful for interpolating the values of f(x) near the end of the set of values given.

- Newton backward method of interpolation is more efficient than Lagrange method of interpolation and is easily implemented.

Demerits:

- Method has a constraint that function f(x) must be continuous and differentiable.

Solution

Write a C program that constructs the new data points using Newton's Backward Method of Interpolation, with the following specifications:

- Let the maximum number of terms be 20.

- Accept the values of x upto 2 decimal point accurate.

- Accept the values of y upto 4 decimal point accurate.

The Code

Code of C program written with these specifications is given below. Type the following C program in a text editor and save it in the folder C:\Code with the filename numrc6.c:

```
/* This program implements Newton's Backward Method of Interpoloation. */
                                                              /* BL */
# include <stdio.h>                                           /* L1 */
# include <ma th.h>                                           /* L2 */
                                                              /* BL */
# define MA X 20                                              /* L3 */
                                                              /* BL */
void main ()                                                  /* L4 */
{                                                             /* L5 */
  int i, j, k, terms;                                         /* L6 */
  float ax[MAX], ay[MAX], x, x0 = 0, y0, sum, h, store, p;    /* L7 */
  float diff[MAX][5], y1, y2, y3, y4;                         /* L8 */
  printf("\nInterpolation by Newton's Backward Method.");     /* L9 */
```

```
    printf("\nEnter the number of terms (Maximum 20): ");          /* L10 */
    scanf("%d", &terms) ;                                          /* L11 */
    printf("\nEnter the values of x upto 2 decimal points.\n");    /* L12 */
    for (i=0; i<terms; i++) {                                      /* L13 */
      printf("Enter the value of x%d: ", i+1);                     /* L14 */
      scanf("%f",&ax[i]);                                          /* L15 */
    }                                                              /* L16 */
    printf("\nNow enter the values of y upto 4 decimal points.\n"); /* L17 */
    for (i=0; i < terms; i++) {                                    /* L18 */
      printf("Enter the value of y%d: ", i+1);                     /* L19 */
      scanf("%f", &ay[i]);                                         /* L20 */
    }                                                              /* L21 */
    printf("\nEnter the value of x for which the value of y is wanted: "); /* L22 */
    scanf("%f", &x);                                               /* L23 */
    h = ax[1] - ax[0];                                             /* L24 */
    for(i=0; i < terms-1; i++) {                                   /* L25 */
      diff[i][1] = ay[i+1] - ay[i];                                /* L26 */
    }                                                              /* L27 */
    for (j=2; j<=4; j++) {                                         /* L28 */
      for (i=0; i<terms-j; i++) {                                  /* L29 */
        diff[i][j] = diff[i+1][j-1] - diff[i][j-1];                /* L30 */
      }                                                            /* L31 */
    }                                                              /* L32 */
    i=0;                                                           /* L33 */
    while(!ax[i] > x) {                                            /* L34 */
      i++;                                                         /* L35 */
    }                                                              /* L36 */
    x0 = ax[i];                                                    /* L37 */
    sum = 0;                                                       /* L38 */
    y0 = ay[i];                                                    /* L39 */
    store = 1;                                                     /* L40 */
    p = (x - x0) / h;                                              /* L41 */
    sum = y0;                                                      /* L42 */
    for (k=1; k <= 4; k++) {                                       /* L43 */
      store = (store * (p-(k-1)))/k;                               /* L44 */
      sum = sum + store * diff[i][k];                              /* L45 */
    }                                                              /* L46 */
    printf ("\nFor x = %6.2f,    y = %6.4f", x, sum);              /* L47 */
    printf("\nThank you.\n");                                      /* L48 */
}                                                                  /* L50 */
```

Compile and execute this program. A run of this program is given below:

```
Interpolation by Newton's Backward Method.
Enter the number of terms (Maximum 20): 5   ↵
```

```
Enter the values of x upto 2 decimal points.
Enter the value of x1: 10.11    ↵
Enter the value of x2: 20.22    ↵
Enter the value of x3: 30.33    ↵
Enter the value of x4: 40.44    ↵
Enter the value of x5: 50.55    ↵

Now enter the values of y upto 4 decimal points.
Enter the value of y1: 35.3535    ↵
Enter the value of y2: 45.4545    ↵
Enter the value of y3: 55.5555    ↵
Enter the value of y4: 65.6565    ↵
Enter the value of y5: 75.7575    ↵

Enter the value of x for which the value of y is wanted: 46.82

For x = 46.82,   y = 72.0308
Thank you.
```

How It Works

In interpolation, instead of an equation of type y = f(x), a set of few data points is provided and using this set you are required to construct the new data points. Suppose the following five data points are provided: (x1, y1), (x2, y2), (x3, y3), (x4, y4), and (x5, y5). Using these data points you are required to create the new data points (xi, yi) such that (x1 < xi < x5) and (y1 < yi < y5).

In Newton's Backward Method of Interpolation, the formula shown in Figure 11-2 is used to construct the new data points. Here f(x) is polynomial of the nth degree. This formula is particularly useful when f(x) is required near the end of the table.

$$f(a + nh + uh) = f(a + nh) + u\,\Delta f(a + nh) + \frac{u(u+1)}{2!}\,\Delta^2 f(a + nh) + \dots$$

$$+ \frac{u(u+1)\dots(u+n-1)}{n!}\,\Delta^n f(a + nh)$$

where $y = f(x)$ is a function of x which assumes the values $f(a)$, $f(a+h)$, $f(a+2h)$, ..., $f(a+nh)$ for $(n+1)$ equidistant values a, a + h, a + 2h, ..., a + nh of the independent variable x. Also, $f(a+h) - f(a) = \Delta f(a)$ and $u = (x - a)/h$.

Figure 11-2. Formula for Newton's Backward Method of interpolation

LOC 3 defines the symbolic constant MAX with the value of 20. LOCs 4-50 define the function main(). In LOCs 6-8 few variables are declared. LOC 10 asks the user to enter the number of terms. The number entered by user is read in the LOC 11 and it is stored in the variable terms. LOC 12 asks the user to enter the values of x. The values entered by user are read in the for loop spanning the LOCs 13-16. LOC 17 asks the user to enter the values of y. The values entered by user are read in the for loop spanning the LOCs 18-21.

LOC 22 asks the user to enter the value of x for which the value of y is wanted. The value - a floating point number - entered by user is read in the LOC 23 and stored in the variable x. In the LOCs 24-46, the corresponding value of y is computed using the standard formula for Newton's Backward Method of Interpolation stated above. Thus (x, y) represents the newly constructed data point. The result is displayed on the screen in the LOC 47.

11-7. To Construct the New Data Points Using Gauss's Forward Method of Interpolation
Problem

You want to construct the new data points using Gauss's Forward Method of Interpolation.

Merits:

- This formula is particulary useful when u lies between 0 and 0.5.

- This formula is suited for interpolation near the middle of the set of values given.

Demerits:

- Lengthy computations. Troublesome to implement and debug.

- Not much useful when u is less than zero or greater than 0.5.

Solution

Write a C program that constructs the new data points using Gauss's Forward Method of Interpolation, with the following specifications:

- Let the maximum number of terms be 20.

- Accept the values of x upto 2 decimal point accurate.

- Accept the values of y upto 4 decimal point accurate.

The Code

Code of C program written with these specifications is given below. Type the following C program in a text editor and save it in the folder C:\Code with the filename numrc7.c:

```
/* This program implements Gauss's Forward Method of Interpoloation. */
                                                                /* BL */
# include <stdio.h>                                             /* L1 */
                                                                /* BL */
# define MAX 20                                                 /* L2 */
                                                                /* BL */
void main()                                                     /* L3 */
{                                                               /* L4 */
  int i, j, terms;                                              /* L5 */
  float ax[MAX], ay[MAX], x, y = 0, h, p;                       /* L6 */
  float diff[MAX][5], y1, y2, y3, y4;                           /* L7 */
  printf("\nInterpolation by Gauss's Forward Method.");         /* L8 */
  printf("\nEnter the number of terms (Maximum 20): ");         /* L9 */
  scanf("%d", &terms);                                          /* L10 */
  printf("\nEnter the values of x upto 2 decimal points.\n");   /* L11 */
  for (i=0; i<terms; i++) {                                     /* L12 */
    printf("Enter the value of x%d: ", i+1);                    /* L13 */
    scanf("%f",&ax[i]);                                         /* L14 */
  }                                                             /* L15 */
  printf("\nNow enter the values of y upto 4 decimal points.\n"); /* L16 */
  for (i=0; i < terms; i++) {                                   /* L17 */
    printf("Enter the value of y%d: ", i+1);                    /* L18 */
    scanf("%f", &ay[i]);                                        /* L19 */
  }                                                             /* L20 */
  printf("\nEnter the value of x for which the value of y is wanted:"); /* L21 */
  scanf("%f", &x);                                              /* L22 */
  h = ax[1] - ax[0];                                            /* L23 */
  for(i=0; i < terms-1; i++)                                    /* L24 */
    diff[i][1] = ay[i+1] - ay[i];                               /* L25 */
  for(j=2; j <= 4; j++)                                         /* L26 */
    for(i=0; i < terms-j; i++)                                  /* L27 */
      diff[i][j] = diff[i+1][j-1] - diff[i][j-1];               /* L28 */
  i = 0;                                                        /* L29 */
  do {                                                          /* L30 */
    i++;                                                        /* L31 */
  } while(ax[i] < x);                                           /* L32 */
  i--;                                                          /* L33 */
  p = (x - ax[i]) / h;                                          /* L34 */
  y1 = p * diff[i][1] ;                                         /* L35 */
  y2 = p * (p - 1) * diff[i - 1][2] / 2;                        /* L36 */
  y3 = (p + 1) * p * (p - 1) * diff[i - 2][3] / 6;              /* L37 */
```

```
y4 = (p + 1) * p * (p - 1) * (p - 2) * diff[i - 3][4] / 24;    /* L38 */
y = ay[i] + y1 + y2 + y3 + y4;                                 /* L39 */
printf("\nFor x = %6.2f,    y = %6.4f ", x, y);                /* L40 */
printf("\nThank you.\n");                                      /* L41 */
}                                                              /* L42 */
```

Compile and execute this program. A run of this program is given below:

```
Interpolation by Gauss's Forward Method.
Enter the number of terms (Maximum 20): 7    ↵

Enter the values of x upto 2 decimal points.
Enter the value of x1: 1.22    ↵
Enter the value of x2: 2.33    ↵
Enter the value of x3: 3.44    ↵
Enter the value of x4: 4.55    ↵
Enter the value of x5: 5.66    ↵
Enter the value of x6: 6.77    ↵
Enter the value of x7: 7.88    ↵

Now enter the values of y upto 4 decimal points.
Enter the value of y1: 100.1111    ↵
Enter the value of y2: 200.2222    ↵
Enter the value of y3: 300.3333    ↵
Enter the value of y4: 400.4444    ↵
Enter the value of y5: 500.5555    ↵
Enter the value of y6: 600.6666    ↵
Enter the value of y7: 700.7777    ↵

Enter the value of x for which the value of y is wanted: 6.12

For x = 6.12,    y = 542.0430
Thank you.
```

How It Works

In interpolation, instead of an equation of type y = f(x), a set of few data points is provided and using this set you are required to construct the new data points. Suppose the following five data points are provided: (x1, y1), (x2, y2), (x3, y3), (x4, y4), and (x5, y5). Using these data points you are required to create the new data points (xi, yi) such that (x1 < xi < x5) and (y1 < yi < y5).

In Gauss's Forward Method of Interpolation, the formula shown in Figure 11-3 is used to construct the new data points. Here f(x) is polynomial of the nth degree. This formula is useful when u is between 0 and 1/2.

371

$$f(u) = f(0) + u \, \Delta f(0) + \frac{u(u-1)}{2!} \, \Delta^2 f(-1) + \frac{(u+1)u(u-1)}{3!} \, \Delta^3 f(-1) +$$

$$+ \frac{(u+1)u(u-1)(u-2)}{4!} \, \Delta^4 f(-2) + \ldots.$$

where $y = f(x)$ is a function of x which assumes the values $f(a)$, $f(a+h)$, $f(a+2h)$, ..., $f(a+nh)$ for $(n+1)$ equidistant values a, $a+h$, $a+2h$, ..., $a+nh$ of the independent variable x. Also, $f(a+h) - f(a) = \Delta f(a)$ and $u = (x-a)/h$.

Figure 11-3. Formula for Gauss's Forward Method of interpolation

LOC 2 defines the symbolic constant MAX with the value of 20. LOCs 3-42 define the function main(). In LOCs 5-7 few variables are declared. LOC 9 asks the user to enter the number of terms. The number entered by user is read in the LOC 10 and it is stored in the variable terms. LOC 11 asks the user to enter the values of x. The values entered by user are read in the for loop spanning the LOCs 12-15. LOC 16 asks the user to enter the values of y. The values entered by user are read in the for loop spanning the LOCs 17-20.

LOC 21 asks the user to enter the value of x for which the value of y is wanted. The value - a floating point number - entered by user is read in the LOC 22 and stored in the variable x. In the LOCs 23-39, the corresponding value of y is computed using the standard formula for Gauss's Forward Method of Interpolation stated above. Thus (x, y) represents the newly constructed data point. The result is displayed on the screen in the LOC 40.

11-8. To Construct the New Data Points Using Gauss's Backward Method of Interpolation
Problem

You want to construct the new data points using Gauss's Backward Method of Interpolation.

Merits:

- This formula is particularly useful when u lies between -0.5 and 0.

- This formula is suited for interpolation near the middle of the set of values given.

Demerits:

- Lengthy computations. Troublesome to implement and debug.

- Not much useful when u is less than -0.5 or greater than zero.

CHAPTER 11 ▪ NUMERICAL METHODS

Solution

Write a C program that constructs the new data points using Gauss's Backward Method of Interpolation, with the following specifications:

- Let the maximum number of terms be 20.
- Accept the values of x upto 2 decimal point accurate.
- Accept the values of y upto 4 decimal point accurate.

The Code

Code of C program written with these specifications is given below. Type the following C program in a text editor and save it in the folder C:\Code with the filename numrc8.c:

```
/* This program implements Gauss's Backward Method of Interpoloation. */
                                                                  /* BL */
# include <stdio.h>                                               /* L1 */
                                                                  /* BL */
# define MAX 20                                                   /* L2 */
                                                                  /* BL */
void main()                                                       /* L3 */
{                                                                 /* L4 */
  int i, j, terms;                                                /* L5 */
  float ax[MAX], ay[MAX], x, y = 0, h, p;                         /* L6 */
  float diff[MAX][5], y1, y2, y3, y4;                             /* L7 */
  printf("\nInterpolation by Gauss's Backward Method.");          /* L8 */
  printf("\nEnter the number of terms (Maximum 20): ");           /* L9 */
  scanf("%d", &terms);                                            /* L10 */
  printf("\nEnter the values of x upto 2 decimal points.\n");     /* L11 */
  for (i=0; i<terms; i++) {                                       /* L12 */
    printf("Enter the value of x%d: ", i+1);                      /* L13 */
    scanf("%f",&ax[i]);                                           /* L14 */
  }                                                               /* L15 */
  printf("\nNow enter the values of y upto 4 decimal points.\n"); /* L16 */
  for (i=0; i < terms; i++) {                                     /* L17 */
    printf("Enter the value of y%d: ", i+1);                      /* L18 */
    scanf("%f", &ay[i]);                                          /* L19 */
  }                                                               /* L20 */
  printf("\nEnter the value of x for which the value of y is wanted: "); /* L21 */
  scanf("%f", &x);                                                /* L22 */
  h = ax[1] - ax[0];                                              /* L23 */
  for(i=0; i < terms-1; i++)                                      /* L24 */
    diff[i][1] = ay[i+1] - ay[i];                                 /* L25 */
  for(j=2; j <= 4; j++)                                           /* L26 */
    for(i=0; i < terms-j; i++)                                    /* L27 */
      diff[i][j] = diff[i+1][j-1] - diff[i][j-1];                 /* L28 */
```

373

```
i = 0;                                                      /* L29 */
do {                                                        /* L30 */
  i++;                                                      /* L31 */
} while (ax[i] < x);                                        /* L32 */
i--;                                                        /* L33 */
p = (x - ax[i]) / h;                                        /* L34 */
y1 = p * diff[i-1][1];                                      /* L35 */
y2 = p *(p+1) * diff[i-1][2]/2;                             /* L36 */
y3 = (p+1) * p * (p-1) * diff[i-2][3]/6;                    /* L37 */
y4 = (p+2) * (p+1) * p * (p-1) * diff[i-3][4]/24;           /* L38 */
y = ay[i] + y1 + y2 + y3 + y4;                              /* L39 */
printf("\nFor x = %6.2f,      y = %6.4f ", x, y);           /* L40 */
printf("\nThank you.\n");                                   /* L41 */
}                                                           /* L42 */
```

Compile and execute this program. A run of this program is given below:

```
Interpolation by Gauss's Backward Method.
Enter the number of terms (Maximum 20): 7    ↩

Enter the values of x upto 2 decimal points.
Enter the value of x1: 1.22    ↩
Enter the value of x2: 2.33    ↩
Enter the value of x3: 3.44    ↩
Enter the value of x4: 4.55    ↩
Enter the value of x5: 5.66    ↩
Enter the value of x6: 6.77    ↩
Enter the value of x7: 7.88    ↩

Now enter the values of y upto 4 decimal points.
Enter the value of y1: 100.1111    ↩
Enter the value of y2: 200.2222    ↩
Enter the value of y3: 300.3333    ↩
Enter the value of y4: 400.4444    ↩
Enter the value of y5: 500.5555    ↩
Enter the value of y6: 600.6666    ↩
Enter the value of y7: 700.7777    ↩

Enter the value of x for which the value of y is wanted: 7.16

For x = 7.16,   y = 635.8408
Thank you.
```

How It Works

In interpolation, instead of an equation of type y = f(x), a set of few data points is provided and using this set you are required to construct the new data points. Suppose the following five data points are provided: (x1, y1), (x2, y2), (x3, y3), (x4, y4), and (x5, y5). Using these data points you are required to create the new data points (xi, yi) such that (x1 < xi < x5) and (y1 < yi < y5).

In Gauss's Backward Method of Interpolation, the formula shown in Figure 11-4 is used to construct the new data points. Here f(x) is polynomial of the nth degree. This formula is useful when u is between -1/2 and 0.

$$f(u) = f(0) + u\,\Delta f(-1) + \frac{(u+1)u}{2!}\,\Delta^2 f(-1) + \frac{(u+1)u(u-1)}{3!}\,\Delta^3 f(-2) +$$

$$+ \frac{(u+2)(u+1)(u-1)}{4!}\,\Delta^4 f(-2) + \ldots$$

where y = f(x) is a function of x which assumes the values f(a), f(a + h), f(a + 2h), ..., f(a + nh) for (n + 1) equidistant values a, a + h, a + 2h, ..., a + nh of the independent variable x. Also, f(a + h) − f(a) = Δf(a) and u = (x − a) / h.

Figure 11-4. Formula for Gauss's Backward Method of interpolation

LOC 2 defines the symbolic constant MAX with the value of 20. LOCs 3-42 define the function main(). In LOCs 5-7 few variables are declared. LOC 9 asks the user to enter the number of terms. The number entered by user is read in the LOC 10 and it is stored in the variable terms. LOC 11 asks the user to enter the values of x. The values entered by user are read in the for loop spanning the LOCs 12-15. LOC 16 asks the user to enter the values of y. The values entered by user are read in the for loop spanning the LOCs 17-20.

LOC 21 asks the user to enter the value of x for which the value of y is wanted. The value - a floating point number - entered by user is read in the LOC 22 and stored in the variable x. In the LOCs 23-39, the corresponding value of y is computed using the standard formula for Gauss's Backward Method of Interpolation stated above. Thus (x, y) represents the newly constructed data point. The result is displayed on the screen in the LOC 40.

11-9. To Construct the New Data Points Using Stirling's Method of Interpolation

Problem

You want to construct the new data points using Stirling's Method of Interpolation.
Merits:

- Forward or backward difference formulae use the oneside information of the function where as Stirling's formula uses the function values on both sides of f(x).

- Gives the best estimate when -0.25 < u < 0.25

Demerits:

- Formula is not much useful when u is less than -0.5 or greater than 0.5.

Solution

Write a C program that constructs the new data points using Stirling's Method of Interpolation, with the following specifications:

- Let the maximum number of terms be 20.

- Accept the values of x upto 2 decimal point accurate.

- Accept the values of y upto 4 decimal point accurate.

The Code

Code of C program written with these specifications is given below. Type the following C program in a text editor and save it in the folder C:\Code with the filename numrc9.c:

```
/* This program implements Stirling's Method of Interpoloation. */
                                                        /* BL */
#include<stdio.h>                                       /* L1 */
                                                        /* BL */
# define MAX 20                                         /* L2 */
                                                        /* BL */
void main()                                             /* L3 */
{                                                       /* L4 */
  int i, j, terms;                                      /* L5 */
  float ax[MAX], ay[MAX], x, y, h, p;                   /* L6 */
  float diff[MAX][5], y1, y2, y3, y4;                   /* L7 */
  printf("\nInterpolation by Stirling Method.");        /* L8 */
  printf("\nEnter the number of terms (Maximum 20): "); /* L9 */
```

```
    scanf("%d", &terms);                                        /* L10 */
    printf("\nEnter the values of x upto 2 decimal points.\n");  /* L11 */
    for (i=0; i<terms; i++) {                                   /* L12 */
      printf("Enter the value of x%d: ", i+1);                  /* L13 */
      scanf("%f",&ax[i]);                                       /* L14 */
    }                                                           /* L15 */
    printf("\nNow enter the values of y upto 4 decimal points.\n"); /* L16 */
    for (i=0; i < terms; i++) {                                 /* L17 */
      printf("Enter the value of y%d: ", i+1);                  /* L18 */
      scanf("%f", &ay[i]);                                      /* L19 */
    }                                                           /* L20 */
    printf("\nEnter the value of x for which the value of y is wanted: "); /* L21 */
    scanf("%f", &x);                                            /* L22 */
    h = ax[1] - ax[0];                                          /* L23 */
    for(i=0; i < terms-1; i++)                                  /* L24 */
      diff[i][1] = ay[i+1] - ay[i];                             /* L25 */
    for(j=2; j <= 4; j++)                                       /* L26 */
      for(i=0; i < terms-j; i++)                                /* L27 */
        diff[i][j] = diff[i+1][j-1] - diff[i][j-1];             /* L28 */
    i = 0;                                                      /* L29 */
    do {                                                        /* L30 */
      i++;                                                      /* L31 */
    } while(ax[i] < x);                                         /* L32 */
    i--;                                                        /* L33 */
    p = (x - ax[i])/h;                                          /* L34 */
    y1 = p * (diff[i][1] + diff[i-1][1])/2;                     /* L35 */
    y2 = p * p * diff[i-1][2]/2;                                /* L36 */
    y3 = p * (p*p-1) * (diff[i-1][3] + diff[i-2][3])/6;         /* L37 */
    y4 = p * p * (p*p-1) * diff[i-2][4]/24;                     /* L38 */
    y = ay[i] + y1 + y2 + y3 + y4;                              /* L39 */
    printf("\n\nFor x = %6.2f,     y = %6.4f", x, y);           /* L40 */
    printf("\nThank you. \n);                                   /* L41 */
}                                                               /* L42 */
```

Compile and execute this program. A run of this program is given below:

```
Interpolation by Stirling Method.
Enter the number of terms (Maximum 20): 5   ↵

Enter the values of x upto 2 decimal points.
Enter the value of x1: 1.22   ↵
Enter the value of x2: 2.33   ↵
Enter the value of x3: 3.44   ↵
Enter the value of x4: 4.55   ↵
Enter the value of x5: 5.66   ↵
```

Now enter the values of y upto 4 decimal points.
Enter the value of y1: 100.1111 ↵
Enter the value of y2: 200.2222 ↵
Enter the value of y3: 300.3333 ↵
Enter the value of y4: 400.4444 ↵
Enter the value of y5: 500.5555 ↵

Enter the value of x for which the value of y is wanted: 3.87

For x = 3.87,   y = 339.1151
Thank you.

How It Works

In interpolation, instead of an equation of type y = f(x), a set of few data points is provided and using this set you are required to construct the new data points. Suppose the following five data points are provided: (x1, y1), (x2, y2), (x3, y3), (x4, y4), and (x5, y5). Using these data points you are required to create the new data points (xi, yi) such that (x1 < xi < x5) and (y1 < yi < y5).

In Stirling's Method of Interpolation, the formula shown in Figure 11-5 is used to construct the new data points. Here f(x) is polynomial of the nth degree. This formula is useful when -0.5 < u < 0.5. It gives quite accurate results when -0.25 < u < 0.25.

$$f(u) = f(0) + u \left\{ \frac{\Delta f(0) + \Delta f(-1)}{2} \right\} + \frac{u^2}{2!} \Delta^2 f(-1)$$

$$+ \frac{(u+1)u(u-1)}{3!} \left\{ \frac{\Delta^3 f(-1) + \Delta^3 f(-2)}{2} \right\} + \frac{u^2(u^2-1)}{4!} \Delta^4 f(-2) + ...$$

where $y = f(x)$ is a function of x which assumes the values $f(a)$, $f(a+h)$, $f(a+2h)$, ..., $f(a+nh)$ for $(n+1)$ equidistant values a, a+h, a+2h, ..., a+nh of the independent variable x. Also, $f(a+h) - f(a) = \Delta f(a)$ and $u = (x-a)/h$.

Figure 11-5. Formula for Stirling's Method of interpolation

LOC 2 defines the symbolic constant MAX with the value of 20. LOCs 3-41 define the function main(). In LOCs 5-7 few variables are declared. LOC 9 asks the user to enter the number of terms. The number entered by user is read in the LOC 10 and it is stored in the variable terms. LOC 11 asks the user to enter the values of x. The values entered by user are read in the for loop spanning the LOCs 12-15. LOC 16 asks the user to enter the values of y. The values entered by user are read in the for loop spanning the LOCs 17-20.

LOC 21 asks the user to enter the value of x for which the value of y is wanted. The value - a floating point number - entered by user is read in the LOC 22 and stored in the variable x. In the LOCs 23-39, the corresponding value of y is computed using the standard formula for Gauss's Backward Method of Interpolation stated above. Thus (x, y) represents the newly constructed data point. The result is displayed on the screen in the LOC 40.

11-10. To Construct the New Data Points Using Bessel's Method of Interpolation
Problem

You want to construct the new data points using Bessel's Method of Interpolation.
   Merits:

- It is most useful when u = 0.5.

- It is used mainly to compute entry against any argument between 0 and 1.

Demerits:

- Not much useful when u is less than 0.25 or greater than 0.75.

Solution

Write a C program that constructs the new data points using Bessel's Method of Interpolation, with the following specifications:

- Let the maximum number of terms be 20.

- Accept the values of x upto 2 decimal point accurate.

- Accept the values of y upto 4 decimal point accurate.

The Code

Code of C program written with these specifications is given below. Type the following C program in a text editor and save it in the folder C:\Code with the filename numrc10.c:

```
/* This program implements Bessel's Method of Interpoloation. */
                                                      /* BL */
#include<stdio.h>                                     /* L1 */
                                                      /* BL */
# define MAX 20                                       /* L2 */
                                                      /* BL */
void main()                                           /* L3 */
{                                                     /* L4 */
```

```
int i, j, terms;                                              /* L5 */
float ax[MAX], ay[MAX], x, y, h, p;                           /* L6 */
float diff[MAX][5], y1, y2, y3, y4;                           /* L7 */
printf("\nImplementation of Interpolation by Bessel's Method.");  /* L8 */
printf("\nEnter the number of terms (Maximum 20): ");         /* L9 */
scanf("%d", &terms);                                          /* L10 */
printf("\nEnter the values of x upto 2 decimal points.\n");   /* L11 */
for (i=0; i<terms; i++) {                                     /* L12 */
  printf("Enter the value of x%d: ", i+1);                    /* L13 */
  scanf("%f",&ax[i]);                                         /* L14 */
}                                                             /* L15 */
printf("\nNow enter the values of y upto 4 decimal points.\n"); /* L16 */
for (i=0; i < terms; i++) {                                   /* L17 */
  printf("Enter the value of y%d: ", i+1);                    /* L18 */
  scanf("%f", &ay[i]);                                        /* L19 */
}                                                             /* L20 */
printf("\nEnter the value of x for which the value of y is wanted: "); /* L21 */
scanf("%f", &x);                                              /* L22 */
h = ax[1] - ax[0];                                            /* L23 */
for(i=0; i < terms-1; i++)                                    /* L24 */
  diff[i][1] = ay[i+1] - ay[i];                               /* L25 */
for(j=2; j <= 4; j++)                                         /* L26 */
  for(i=0; i < terms-j; i++)                                  /* L27 */
    diff[i][j] = diff[i+1][j-1] - diff[i][j-1];               /* L28 */
i = 0;                                                        /* L29 */
do {                                                          /* L30 */
  i++;                                                        /* L31 */
} while (ax[i] < x);                                          /* L32 */
i--;                                                          /* L33 */
p = (x-ax[i])/h;                                              /* L34 */
y1 = p * (diff[i][1]);                                        /* L35 */
y2 = p * (p-1) * (diff[i][2] + diff[i-1][2])/4;               /* L36 */
y3 = p * (p-1) * (p-0.5) * (diff[i-1][3])/6;                  /* L37 */
y4 = (p+1) * p * (p-1) * (p-2) * (diff[i-2][4] + diff[i-1][4])/48; /* L38 */
y = ay[i] + y1 + y2 + y3 + y4;                                /* L39 */
printf("\For x = %6.2f,     y = %6.4f ", x, y);               /* L40 */
printf("\nThank you.\n");                                     /* L41 */
}                                                             /* L42 */
```

Compile and execute this program. A run of this program is given below:

```
Implementation of Interpolation by Bessel's Method.
Enter the number of terms (Maximum 20): 5    ↵

Enter the values of x upto 2 decimal points.
Enter the value of x1: 1.22    ↵
Enter the value of x2: 2.33    ↵
Enter the value of x3: 3.44    ↵
```

```
Enter the value of x4: 4.55    ↵
Enter the value of x5: 5.66    ↵

Now enter the values of y upto 4 decimal points.
Enter the value of y1: 100.1111   ↵
Enter the value of y2: 200.2222   ↵
Enter the value of y3: 300.3333   ↵
Enter the value of y4: 400.4444   ↵
Enter the value of y5: 500.5555   ↵

Enter the value of x for which the value of y is wanted: 4.87

For x = 4.87,    y = 429.3052
Thank you.
```

How It Works

In interpolation, instead of an equation of type y = f(x), a set of few data points is provided and using this set you are required to construct the new data points. Suppose the following five data points are provided: (x1, y1), (x2, y2), (x3, y3), (x4, y4), and (x5, y5). Using these data points you are required to create the new data points (xi, yi) such that (x1 < xi < x5) and (y1 < yi < y5).

In Bessel's Method of Interpolation, the formula shown in Figure 11-6 is used to construct the new data points. Here f(x) is polynomial of the nth degree. This formula is most useful when u = 0.5. It gives quite accurate results when 0.25 < u < 0.75.

$$f(u) = \left\{ \frac{f(0) + f(1)}{2} \right\} + (u - 0.5)\,\Delta f(0) + \frac{u\,(u-1)}{2!} \left\{ \frac{\Delta^2 f(-1) + \Delta^2 f(0)}{2} \right\}$$

$$+ \frac{(u-1)\,(u-0.5)\,u}{3!}\,\Delta^3 f(-1)$$

$$+ \frac{(u+1)\,u\,(u-1)\,(u-2)}{4!} \left\{ \frac{\Delta^4 f(-2) + \Delta^4 f(-1)}{2} \right\} + \dots$$

where $y = f(x)$ is a function of x which assumes the values $f(a)$, $f(a+h)$, $f(a+2h)$, ..., $f(a+nh)$ for $(n+1)$ equidistant values a, $a+h$, $a+2h$, ..., $a+nh$ of the independent variable x. Also, $f(a+h) - f(a) = \Delta f(a)$ and $u = (x-a)/h$.

Figure 11-6. Formula for Bessel's Method of interpolation

LOC 2 defines the symbolic constant MAX with the value of 20. LOCs 3-42 define the function main(). In LOCs 5-7 few variables are declared. LOC 9 asks the user to enter the number of terms. The number entered by user is read in the LOC 10 and it is stored in the variable terms. LOC 11 asks the user to enter the values of x. The values entered by user are read in the for loop spanning the LOCs 12-15. LOC 16 asks the user to enter the values of y. The values entered by user are read in the for loop spanning the LOCs 17-20.

LOC 21 asks the user to enter the value of x for which the value of y is wanted. The value - a floating point number - entered by user is read in the LOC 22 and stored in the variable x. In the LOCs 23-39, the corresponding value of y is computed using the standard formula for Bessel's Method of Interpolation stated above. Thus (x, y) represents the newly constructed data point. The result is displayed on the screen in the LOC 40.

11-11. To Construct the New Data Points Using Laplace Everett's Method of Interpolation

Problem

You want to construct the new data points using Laplace Everett's Method of Interpolation.

Merits:

- It gives the good estimate when u > 0.5.

- It is used to compute any entry against any argument between 0 and 1.

- It is useful when intervening values in successive intervals are required.

Demerits:

- Not much useful when u is less than 0.5.

Solution

Write a C program that constructs the new data points using Laplace Everett's Method of Interpolation, with the following specifications:

- Let the maximum number of terms be 20.

- Accept the values of x upto 2 decimal point accurate.

- Accept the values of y upto 4 decimal point accurate.

The Code

Code of C program written with these specifications is given below. Type the following C program in a text editor and save it in the folder C:\Code with the filename numrc11.c:

```
/* This program implements Laplace Everett's Method of Interpoloation.  */
                                                                  /* BL */
# include <stdio.h>                                               /* L1 */
                                                                  /* BL */
# define MAX 20                                                   /* L2 */
                                                                  /* BL */
void main()                                                       /* L3 */
{                                                                 /* L4 */
  int i, j, terms;                                                /* L5 */
  float ax[MAX], ay[MAX], x, y = 0, h, p, q;                      /* L6 */
  float diff[MAX][5], y1, y2, y3, y4, py1, py2, py3, py4;         /* L7 */
  printf("\nInterpolation by Laplace Everett's Method.");         /* L8 */
  printf("\nEnter the number of terms (Maximum 20): ");           /* L9 */
  scanf("%d", &terms);                                            /* L10 */
  printf("\nEnter the values of x upto 2 decimal points.\n");     /* L11 */
  for (i=0; i<terms; i++) {                                       /* L12 */
    printf("Enter the value of x%d: ", i+1);                      /* L13 */
    scanf("%f",&ax[i]);                                           /* L14 */
  }                                                               /* L15 */
  printf("\nNow enter the values of y upto 4 decimal points.\n"); /* L16 */
  for (i=0; i < terms; i++) {                                     /* L17 */
    printf("Enter the value of y%d: ", i+1);                      /* L18 */
    scanf("%f", &ay[i]);                                          /* L19 */
  }                                                               /* L20 */
  printf("\nEnter the value of x for which the value of y is wanted: "); /* L21 */
  scanf("%f", &x);                                                /* L22 */
  h = ax[1] - ax[0];                                              /* L23 */
  for(i=0; i < terms-1; i++)                                      /* L24 */
    diff[i][1] = ay[i+1] - ay[i];                                 /* L25 */
  for(j=2; j <= 4; j++)                                           /* L26 */
    for(i=0; i < terms-j; i++)                                    /* L27 */
      diff[i][j] = diff[i+1][j-1] - diff[i][j-1];                 /* L28 */
  i = 0;                                                          /* L29 */
  do {                                                            /* L30 */
    i++;                                                          /* L31 */
  } while(ax[i] < x);                                             /* L32 */
  i--;                                                            /* L33 */
  p = (x - ax[i])/h;                                              /* L34 */
  q = 1 - p;                                                      /* L35 */
  y1 = q * (ay[i]);                                               /* L36 */
  y2 = q * (q*q-1) * diff[i-1][2]/6;                              /* L37 */
  y3 = q * (q*q-1) * (q*q-4) * (diff[i-2][4])/120;                /* L38 */
  py1 = p * ay[i+1];                                              /* L39 */
```

```
    py2 = p * (p*p-1) * diff[i][2]/6;                          /* L40 */
    py3 = p * (p*p-1) * (p*p-4) * (diff[i-1][4])/120;          /* L41 */
    y = y1 + y2 + y3 + y4 + py1 + py2 + py3;                   /* L42 */
    printf("\nFor x = %6.2f,      y = %6.4f ", x, y);          /* L43 */
    printf("\nThank you.\n");                                  /* L44 */
}                                                              /* L45 */
```

Compile and execute this program. A run of this program is given below:

```
Interpolation by Laplace Everett's Method.
Enter the number of terms (Maximum 20): 5      ↵

Enter the values of x upto 2 decimal points.
Enter the value of x1: 1.22    ↵
Enter the value of x2: 2.33    ↵
Enter the value of x3: 3.44    ↵
Enter the value of x4: 4.55    ↵
Enter the value of x5: 5.66    ↵

Now enter the values of y upto 4 decimal points.
Enter the value of y1: 100.1111    ↵
Enter the value of y2: 200.2222    ↵
Enter the value of y3: 300.3333    ↵
Enter the value of y4: 400.4444    ↵
Enter the value of y5: 500.5555    ↵

Enter the value of x for which the value of y is wanted: 3.89

For x = 3.89,    y = 340.9189
Thank you.
```

How It Works

In interpolation, instead of an equation of type y = f(x), a set of few data points is provided and using this set you are required to construct the new data points. Suppose the following five data points are provided: (x1, y1), (x2, y2), (x3, y3), (x4, y4), and (x5, y5). Using these data points you are required to create the new data points (xi, yi) such that (x1 < xi < x5) and (y1 < yi < y5).

In Laplace Everett's Method of Interpolation, the formula shown in Figure 11-7 is used to construct the new data points. Here f(x) is polynomial of the nth degree. It gives quite accurate results when u > 0.5.

$$f(u) = \left\{ \begin{array}{l} u\,f(1) + \dfrac{(u+1)\,u\,(u-1)}{3!}\ \Delta^2 f(0) \\[2ex] \end{array} \right.$$

$$+\ \dfrac{(u+2)\,(u+1)\,u\,(u-1)\,(u-2)}{5!}\ \Delta^4 f(-1) + \ldots \left. \right\}$$

$$+ \left\{ \begin{array}{l} w\,f(0) + \dfrac{(w+1)\,w\,(w-1)}{3!}\ \Delta^2 f(-1) \\[2ex] \end{array} \right.$$

$$+\ \dfrac{(w+2)\,(w+1)\,w\,(w-1)\,(w-2)}{5!}\ \Delta^4 f(-2) + \ldots \left. \right\}$$

where $y = f(x)$ is a function of x which assumes the values $f(a)$, $f(a+h)$, $f(a+2h)$, ..., $f(a+nh)$ for $(n+1)$ equidistant values a, $a+h$, $a+2h$, ..., $a+nh$ of the independent variable x. Also, $f(a+h) - f(a) = \Delta f(a)$, $u = (x-a)/h$, and $w = 1 - u$.

Figure 11-7. *Formula for Laplace Everett's Method of interpolation*

LOC 2 defines the symbolic constant MAX with the value of 20. LOCs 3-45 define the function main(). In LOCs 5-7 few variables are declared. LOC 9 asks the user to enter the number of terms. The number entered by user is read in the LOC 10 and it is stored in the variable terms. LOC 11 asks the user to enter the values of x. The values entered by user are read in the for loop spanning the LOCs 12-15. LOC 16 asks the user to enter the values of y. The values entered by user are read in the for loop spanning the LOCs 17-20.

LOC 21 asks the user to enter the value of x for which the value of y is wanted. The value - a floating point number - entered by user is read in the LOC 22 and stored in the variable x. In the LOCs 23-42, the corresponding value of y is computed using the standard formula for Laplace Everett's Method of Interpolation stated above. Thus (x, y) represents the newly constructed data point. The result is displayed on the screen in the LOC 43.

11-12. To Construct the New Data Points Using Lagrange's Method of Interpolation
Problem

You want to construct the new data points using Lagrange's Method of Interpolation.
    Merits:

- Does not require function values at equal intervals.

Demerits:

- Degree of the approximating polynomial must be chosen at the outset.

Solution

Write a C program that constructs the new data points using Lagrange's Method of Interpolation, with the following specifications:

- Let the maximum number of terms be 20.
- Accept the values of x upto 2 decimal point accurate.
- Accept the values of y upto 4 decimal point accurate.

The Code

Code of C program written with these specifications is given below. Type the following C program in a text editor and save it in the folder C:\Code with the filename numrc12.c:

```
/* This program implements Lagrange's Method of Interpoloation. */
                                                                    /* BL */
#include<stdio.h>                                                   /* L1 */
                                                                    /* BL */
# define MAX 20                                                     /* L2 */
                                                                    /* BL */
void main()                                                         /* L3 */
{                                                                   /* L4 */
  int i, j, terms;                                                  /* L5 */
  float ax[MAX], ay[MAX], nr, dr, x, y = 0;                         /* L6 */
  printf("\nImplementation of Interpolation by Lagrange's Method."); /* L7 */
  printf("\nEnter the number of terms (Maximum 20): ");             /* L8 */
  scanf("%d", &terms);                                              /* L9 */
  printf("\nEnter the values of x upto 2 decimal points.\n");       /* L10 */
  for (i=0; i < terms; i++) {                                       /* L11 */
    printf("Enter the value of x%d: ", i+1);                        /* L12 */
    scanf("%f", &ax[i]);                                            /* L13 */
  }                                                                 /* L14 */
  printf("\nNow enter the values of y upto 4 decimal points.\n");   /* L15 */
  for (i=0; i < terms; i++) {                                       /* L16 */
    printf("Enter the value of y%d: ", i+1);                        /* L17 */
    scanf("%f", &ay[i]);                                            /* L18 */
  }                                                                 /* L19 */
  printf("\nEnter the value of x for which the value of y is wanted: "); /* L20 */
  scanf("%f", &x);                                                  /* L21 */
  for(i=0; i < terms; i++) {                                        /* L22 */
    nr = 1;                                                         /* L23 */
    dr = 1;                                                         /* L24 */
    for(j=0; j < terms; j++) {                                      /* L25 */
      if(j != i) {                                                  /* L26 */
        nr = nr * (x - ax[j]);                                      /* L27 */
        dr = dr * (ax[i] - ax[j]);                                  /* L28 */
```

```
    }                                               /* L29 */
  }                                                 /* L30 */
  y = y + ((nr/dr) * ay[i]);                        /* L31 */
  }                                                 /* L32 */
  printf("\nFor x = %6.2f,    y = %6.4f", x, y);    /* L33 */
  printf("\nThank you.\n");                         /* L34 */
}                                                   /* L35 */
```

Compile and execute this program. A run of this program is given below:

```
Interpolation by Lagrange's Method.
Enter the number of terms (Maximum 20): 5   ↵

Enter the values of x upto 2 decimal points.
Enter the value of x1: 1.22   ↵
Enter the value of x2: 2.33   ↵
Enter the value of x3: 3.44   ↵
Enter the value of x4: 4.55   ↵
Enter the value of x5: 5.66   ↵

Now enter the values of y upto 4 decimal points.
Enter the value of y1: 100.1111   ↵
Enter the value of y2: 200.2222   ↵
Enter the value of y3: 300.3333   ↵
Enter the value of y4: 400.4444   ↵
Enter the value of y5: 500.5555   ↵

Enter the value of x for which the value of y is wanted: 1.98

For x = 1.98,    y = 168.6557
Thank you.
```

How It Works

In interpolation, instead of an equation of type $y = f(x)$, a set of few data points is provided and using this set you are required to construct the new data points. Suppose the following five data points are provided: $(x1, y1)$, $(x2, y2)$, $(x3, y3)$, $(x4, y4)$, and $(x5, y5)$. Using these data points you are required to create the new data points (xi, yi) such that $(x1 < xi < x5)$ and $(y1 < yi < y5)$.

In Lagrange's Method of Interpolation, the formula shown in Figure 11-8 is used to construct the new data points. Here $f(x)$ is polynomial of the nth degree.

$$f(x) = \frac{(x - x_1)\,(x - x_2)\,....\,(x - x_n)}{(x_0 - x_1)\,(x_0 - x_2)\,....\,(x_0 - x_n)}\; f(x_0)$$

$$+\; \frac{(x - x_0)\,(x - x_2)\,....\,(x - x_n)}{(x_1 - x_0)\,(x_1 - x_2)\,....\,(x_1 - x_n)}\; f(x_1)$$

$$+\; ....\; +\; \frac{(x - x_0)\,(x - x_1)\,....\,(x - x_{n-1})}{(x_n - x_0)\,(x_n - x_1)\,....\,(x_n - x_{n-1})}\; f(x_n)$$

where $f(x_0), f(x_1), ..., f(x_n)$ be (n+1) entries of a function $y = f(x)$, where $f(x)$ is a polynomial of corresponding to arguments $x_0, x_1, x_2, ..., x_n$.

Figure 11-8. Formula for Lagrange's Method of interpolation

LOC 2 defines the symbolic constant MAX with the value of 20. LOCs 3-35 define the function main(). In LOCs 5-6 few variables are declared. LOC 8 asks the user to enter the number of terms. The number entered by user is read in the LOC 9 and it is stored in the variable terms. LOC 10 asks the user to enter the values of x. The values entered by user are read in the for loop spanning the LOCs 11-14. LOC 15 asks the user to enter the values of y. The values entered by user are read in the for loop spanning the LOCs 16-19.

LOC 20 asks the user to enter the value of x for which the value of y is wanted. The value - a floating point number - entered by user is read in the LOC 21 and stored in the variable x. LOCs 22-32 consist of a for loop. In this for loop the corresponding value of y is computed using the standard formula for Lagrange's Method of Interpolation stated above. Thus (x, y) represents the newly constructed data point. The result is displayed on the screen in the LOC 33.

11-13. To Compute the Value of Integration Using Trapezoidal Method of Numerical Integration
Problem

You want to compute the value of integration using Trapezoidal Method of Numerical Integration.

Merits:

- Based on simple logic. Easy to implement.

- Gives accurate results for piecewise linear function.

Demerits:

- Not as accurate as Simpson's method when the underlying function is smooth.

- Convergence is slow compared to Simpson's method.

Solution

Write a C program that computes the value of integration using Trapezoidal Method of Numerical Integration, with the following specifications:

- Program defines the function trapezoid() that computes the value of f(x).

- Width of trapezium should be such that maximum number of subintervals be 50.

The Code

Code of C program written with these specifications is given below. Type the following C program in a text editor and save it in the folder C:\Code with the filename numrc13.c:

```
/* This program implements Trapezoidal Method of Numerical Integration. */
                                                                   /* BL */
#include<stdio.h>                                                  /* L1 */
                                                                   /* BL */
# define MAX 50                                                    /* L2 */
                                                                   /* BL */
float trapezoid(float x)                                           /* L3 */
{                                                                  /* L4 */
    return (1/(1+x*x));                                            /* L5 */
}                                                                  /* L6 */
                                                                   /* BL */
void main()                                                        /* L7 */
{                                                                  /* L8 */
  int i, num;                                                      /* L9 */
  float a, b, h, x[MAX], y[MAX], sumOdd, sumEven, result;          /* L10 */
  printf("\nTrapezoidal Method of Numerical Integration.");        /* L11 */
  printf("\nIntegrand:  f(x) = 1/(1+x*x) \n");                     /* L12 */
  printf("\nEnter the lower limit of integration, a :  ");         /* L13 */
  scanf("%f", &a);                                                 /* L14 */
  printf("Enter the upper limit of integration, b :  ");           /* L15 */
  scanf("%f", &b);                                                 /* L16 */
  printf("Enter the width of trapezium, h :  ");                   /* L17 */
  scanf("%f", &h);                                                 /* L18 */
  num = (b - a) / h;                                               /* L19 */
  if(num%2 == 1)                                                   /* L20 */
    num = num + 1;                                                 /* L21 */
  h = (b - a) / num;                                               /* L22 */
  printf("Refined value of h, the width of trapezium : %5.3f", h); /* L23 */
  printf("\nRefined value of num, the number of trapaziums : %d\n", num); /* L24 */
  for(i=0; i <= num; i++) {                                        /* L25 */
    x[i] = a + i * h;                                              /* L26 */
    y[i] = trapezoid(x[i]);                                        /* L27 */
  }                                                                /* L28 */
```

```
  sumOdd = 0;                                                    /* L29 */
  sumEven = 0;                                                   /* L30 */
  for(i=1; i < num; i++) {                                       /* L31 */
    if(i%2 == 1)                                                 /* L32 */
      sumOdd = sumOdd + y[i];                                    /* L33 */
    else                                                         /* L34 */
      sumEven = sumEven + y[i];                                  /* L35 */
  }                                                              /* L36 */
  result = h / 3 * (y[0] + y[num] + 4 * sumOdd + 2 * sumEven);   /* L37 */
  printf("\nValue of Integration : %5.3f", result);             /* L38 */
  printf("\nThank you.\n");                                      /* L39 */
}                                                                /* L40 */
```

Compile and execute this program. A run of this program is given below:

```
Trapezoidal Method of Numerical Integration.
Integrand:  f(x) = a/(1+x*x)

Enter the lower limit of integration, a : 1   ⏎
Enter the upper limit of integration, b : 4   ⏎
Enter the width of trapezium, h : 0.1   ⏎
Refined value of h, the width of trapezium : 0.100
Refined value of num, the number of trapeziums : 30

Value of Integration : 0.540
Thank you.
```

How It Works

In numerical integration, you are given a set of tabulated values of the integrand $f(x)$ and you are required to compute the value of $\int f(x)\,dx$. Geometrically, integration can be represented as area enclosed between the curve $y = f(x)$, the X-axis, and the lines $y = a$ and $y = b$ where a and b are lower and upper limits of integration respectively. This area is divided into n number of strips parallel to Y-axis and width of each strip is h. Figure 11-9 shows the formula for Trapezoidal Method of Numerical Integration.

$$\int_{x_0}^{x_0+nh} f(x)\,dx = \frac{h}{2}\,[\,(y_0 + y_n) + 2\,(y_1 + y_2 + \ldots + y_{n-1})\,]$$

The limits of integration 'a' and 'b' are typically written as $a = x_0$ and $b = x_0 + nh$. The 'h' represents the width of strip and the 'n' represents the number of strips. Area of first strip is $x_1 * y_1$, area of second strip is $x_2 * y_2$, ..., and area of nth strip is $x_n * y_n$. Also, $x_1 = x_0 + h$, $x_2 = x_0 + 2h$, ..., $x_n = x_0 + nh$.

Figure 11-9. *Formula for Trapezoidal Method of numerical integration*

In LOC 2, the symbolic constant MAX is defined with the value of 50. LOCs 3-6 consist of definition of the function trapezoid(). LOCs 7-40 consist of definition of the function main(). In LOCs 9-10 few variables are declared. LOC 13 asks the user to enter the lower limit of integration. The number entered by user is stored in the float variable a, in the LOC 14. LOC 15 asks the user to enter the upper limit of integration. The number entered by user is stored in the float variable b, in the LOC 16.

LOC 17 asks the user to enter the width of trapezium. The number entered by user is stored in the float variable h, in the LOC 18. In the LOCs 19-37, the result is computed using the standard formula for Trepezoidal Method of Numerical Integration, stated above. LOC 38 displays the result on the screen.

11-14. To Compute the Value of Integration Using Simpson's 3/8th Method of Numerical Integration
Problem

You want to compute the value of integration using Simpson's 3/8th Method of Numerical Integration.

Merits:

- Accuracy is good compared to other methods.

Demerits:

- Works under the constraint that the given interval of integratin must be divided into sub-intervals whose number n is mutliple of 3.

Solution

Write a C program that computes the value of integration using Simpson's 3/8th Method of Numerical Integration, with the following specifications:

- Program defines the function simpson() that computes the value of f(x).

- Let the maximum number of subintervals be 50.

The Code

Code of C program written with these specifications is given below. Type the following C program in a text editor and save it in the folder C:\Code with the filename numrc14.c:

```
/* This program implements Simpson's 3/8th Method of Numerical Integration. */
                                                              /* BL */
#include<stdio.h>                                             /* L1 */
                                                              /* BL */
# define MAX 50                                               /* L2 */
```

391

```
                                                                   /* BL */
float simpson(float x)                                             /* L3 */
{                                                                  /* L4 */
    return (1/(1+x*x));                                            /* L5 */
}                                                                  /* L6 */
                                                                   /* BL */
void main()                                                        /* L7 */
{                                                                  /* L8 */
  int i, j, num;                                                   /* L9 */
  float a, b, h, x[MAX], y[MAX], sum, result = 1;                  /* L10 */
  printf("\nSimpson's 3/8th Method of Computation of Integral.");  /* L11 */
  printf("\nIntegrand:  f(x) = 1/(1+x*x) \n");                     /* L12 */
  printf("\nEnter the lower limit of integration, a :  ");         /* L13 */
  scanf("%f", &a);                                                 /* L14 */
  printf("Enter the upper limit of integration, b :  ");           /* L15 */
  scanf("%f", &b);                                                 /* L16 */
  printf("Enter the number of subintervals, num :  ");             /* L17 */
  scanf("%d" ,&num);                                               /* L18 */
  h = (b - a)/num;                                                 /* L19 */
  sum = 0;                                                         /* L20 */
  sum = simpson(a) + simpson(b);                                   /* L21 */
  for(i=1; i < num; i++) {                                         /* L22 */
    if(i%3 == 0) {                                                 /* L23 */
      sum += 2*simpson(a + i*h);                                   /* L24 */
    }                                                              /* L25 */
    else {                                                         /* L26 */
      sum += 3*simpson(a + i*h);                                   /* L27 */
    }                                                              /* L28 */
  }                                                                /* L29 */
  result = sum * 3 * h / 8;                                        /* L30 */
  printf("\nValue of Integration : %5.3f", result);               /* L31 */
  printf("\nThank you.\n");                                        /* L32 */
}                                                                  /* L33 */
```

Compile and execute this program. A run of this program is given below:

```
Simpson's 3/8th Method of Computation of Integral.
Integrand:  f(x) = 1/(1+x*x)

Enter the lower limit of integration, a : 1    ↵
Enter the upper limit of integration, b : 4    ↵
Enter the number of subintervals, num : 50    ↵

Value of Integration : 0.540
Thank you.
```

How It Works

In numerical integration, you are given a set of tabulated values of the integrand $f(x)$ and you are required to compute the value of $\int f(x)dx$. Geometrically, integration can be represented as area enclosed between the curve $y = f(x)$, the X-axis, and the lines $y = a$ and $y = b$ where a and b are lower and upper limits of integration respectively. This area is divided into n number of strips parallel to Y-axis and width of each strip is h. Figure 11-10 shows the formula for Simpson's 3/8th Method of Numerical Integration.

$$\int_{x_0}^{x_0+nh} f(x)\, dx = \frac{3h}{8}\, [\, (y_0 + y_n) + 3\, (y_1 + y_2 + y_4 + y_5 + \dots + y_{n-2} + y_{n-1})$$

$$+\, 2\, (y_3 + y_6 + \dots + y_{n-3})\,]$$

The limits of integration 'a' and 'b' are typically written as $a = x_0$ and $b = x_0 + nh$. The 'h' represents the width of strip and the 'n' represents the number of strips. Area of first strip is $x_1 * y_1$, area of second strip is $x_2 * y_2$, ..., and area of nth strip is $x_n * y_n$. Also, $x_1 = x_0 + h$, $x_2 = x_0 + 2h$, ..., $x_n = x_0 + nh$.

Figure 11-10. *Formula for Simpson's 3/8th Method of numerical integration*

In LOC 2, the symbolic constant MAX is defined with the value of 50. LOCs 3-6 consist of definition of the function simpson(). LOCs 7-33 consist of definition of the function main(). In LOCs 9-10 few variables are declared. LOC 13 asks the user to enter the lower limit of integration. The number entered by user is stored in the float variable a, in the LOC 14. LOC 15 asks the user to enter the upper limit of integration. The number entered by user is stored in the float variable b, in the LOC 16.

LOC 17 asks the user to enter the number of subintervals. The number entered by user is stored in the int variable num, in the LOC 18. In the LOCs 19-30, the result is computed using the standard formula for Simpson's 3/8th Method of Numerical Integration, stated above. LOC 31 displays the result on the screen.

11-15. To Compute the Value of Integration Using Simpson's 1/3rd Method of Numerical Integration
Problem

You want to compute the value of integration using Simpson's 1/3rd Method of Numerical Integration.

Merits:

- Computations are less cumbersome compared to other methods.

Demerits:

- Works under the constraint that the given interval of integration must be divided into sub-intervals whose number n is even.

Solution

Write a C program that computes the value of integration using Simpson's 1/3rd Method of Numerical Integration, with the following specifications:

- Program defines the function simpson() that computes the value of f(x).

- Let the maximum number of subintervals be 50.

The Code

Code of C program written with these specifications is given below. Type the following C program in a text editor and save it in the folder C:\Code with the filename numrc15.c:

```
/* This program implements Simpson's 1/3rd Method of Numerical Integration. */
                                                              /* BL */
#include<stdio.h>                                             /* L1 */
                                                              /* BL */
# define MAX 50                                               /* L2 */
                                                              /* BL */
float simpson(float x)                                        /* L3 */
{                                                             /* L4 */
    return (1/(1+x*x));                                       /* L5 */
}                                                             /* L6 */
                                                              /* BL */
void main()                                                   /* L7 */
{                                                             /* L8 */
  int i, j, num;                                              /* L9 */
  float a, b, h, x[MAX], y[MAX], sum, result = 1;             /* L10 */
  printf("\nSimpson's 1/3rd Method of Computation of Integral."); /* L11 */
  printf("\nIntegrand:  f(x) = 1/(1+x*x) \n");                /* L12 */
  printf("\nEnter the lower limit of integration, a :  ");    /* L13 */
  scanf("%f", &a);                                            /* L14 */
  printf("Enter the upper limit of integration, b :  ");      /* L15 */
  scanf("%f", &b);                                            /* L16 */
  printf("Enter the number of subintervals, num :  ");        /* L17 */
  scanf("%d" ,&num);                                          /* L18 */
  h = (b - a)/num;                                            /* L19 */
  sum = 0;                                                    /* L20 */
  sum = simpson(a) + 4 * simpson(a + h) + simpson(b);         /* L21 */
  for(i=3; i < num; i+=2) {                                   /* L22 */
```

```
    sum += 2 * simpson(a + (i-1) * h) + 4 * simpson(a + i * h);    /* L23 */
    }                                                              /* L24 */
    result = sum * h / 3;                                          /* L25 */
    printf("\nValue of Integration : %5.3f", result);             /* L26 */
    printf("\nThank you.\n");                                      /* L27 */
}                                                                  /* L28 */
```

Compile and execute this program. A run of this program is given below:

```
Simpson's 1/3rd Method of Computation of Integral.
Integrand:  f(x) = 1/(1+x*x)

Enter the lower limit of integration, a : 1    ↵
Enter the upper limit of integration, b : 4    ↵
Enter the number of subintervals, num : 50     ↵

Value of Integration : 0.540
Thank you.
```

How It Works

In numerical integration, you are given a set of tabulated values of the integrand $f(x)$ and you are required to compute the value of $\int f(x)\,dx$. Geometrically, integration can be represented as area enclosed between the curve $y = f(x)$, the X-axis, and the lines $y = a$ and $y = b$ where a and b are lower and upper limits of integration respectively. This area is divided into n number of strips parallel to Y-axis and width of each strip is h. Figure 11-11 shows the formula for Simpson's 1/3rd Method of Numerical Integration.

$$\int_{x_0}^{x_0+nh} f(x)\,dx = \frac{h}{3}\,[\,(y_0 + y_n) + 4\,(y_1 + y_3 + \dots + y_{n-1}) + 2\,(y_2 + y_4 + \dots + y_{n-2})\,]$$

The limits of integration 'a' and 'b' are typically written as $a = x_0$ and $b = x_0 + nh$. The 'h' represents the width of strip and the 'n' represents the number of strips. Area of first strip is $x_1 * y_1$, area of second strip is $x_2 * y_2$, ..., and area of nth strip is $x_n * y_n$. Also, $x_1 = x_0 + h$, $x_2 = x_0 + 2h$, ..., $x_n = x_0 + nh$.

Figure 11-11. *Formula for Simpson's 1/3rd Method of numerical integration*

In LOC 2, the symbolic constant MAX is defined with the value of 50. LOCs 3-6 consist of definition of the function simpson(). LOCs 7-28 consist of definition of the function main(). In LOCs 9-10 few variables are declared. LOC 13 asks the user to enter the lower limit of integration. The number entered by user is stored in the float variable a, in the LOC 14. LOC 15 asks the user to enter the upper limit of integration. The number entered by user is stored in the float variable b, in the LOC 16.

LOC 17 asks the user to enter the number of subintervals. The number entered by user is stored in the int variable num, in the LOC 18. In the LOCs 19-25, the result is computed using the standard formula for Simpson's 1/3rd Method of Numerical Integration, stated above. LOC 26 displays the result on the screen.

11-16. To Solve a Differential Equation Using Modified Euler's Method

Problem

You want to solve a differential equation using Modified Euler's Method.
   Merits:

- Improved Accuarcy. Error is of the order of h*3.

   Demerits:

- Needs to perform more computations compared to other methods.

Solution

Write a C program that solves a differential equation using Modified Euler's Method, with the following specifications:

- Value of subinterval should be such that maximum number of subintervals be 50.

- Result should consist of at least three pairs of values of x and y.

The Code

Code of C program written with these specifications is given below. Type the following C program in a text editor and save it in the folder C:\Code with the filename numrc16.c:

```
/* This program implements Modified Euler's Method to Solve a Differential Equation. */
                                                              /* BL */
#include<stdio.h>                                             /* L1 */
                                                              /* BL */
# define MAX 50                                               /* L2 */
                                                              /* BL */
```

```
float euler(float p, float q)                                    /* L3 */
{                                                                /* L4 */
  float r;                                                       /* L5 */
  r = p * p + q;                                                 /* L6 */
  return(r);                                                     /* L7 */
}                                                                /* L8 */
                                                                 /* BL */
void main()                                                      /* L9 */
{                                                                /* L10 */
  int i = 1, j, k;                                               /* L11 */
  float x[MAX], y[MAX], store1[MAX], store2[MAX];                /* L12 */
  float b, h, u, v, w;                                           /* L13 */
  printf("\nModified Euler's Method to Solve a Differential Equation. "); /* L14 */
  printf("\nFunction for calculation of slope: y' = x * x + y\n"); /* L15 */
  printf("Enter the initial value of the variable x, x0: ");     /* L16 */
  scanf("%f", &x[0]);                                            /* L17 */
  printf("Enter the final value of the variable x, xn: ");       /* L18 */
  scanf("%f", &b);                                               /* L19 */
  printf("Enter the initial value of the variable y, y0: ");     /* L20 */
  scanf("%f", &y[0]);                                            /* L21 */
  printf("Enter the value of subinterval, h: ");                 /* L22 */
  scanf("%f", &h);                                               /* L23 */
  store2[0] = y[0];                                              /* L24 */
  while(x[i-1] < b) {                                            /* L25 */
    w = 100.0;                                                   /* L26 */
    x[i] = x[i-1] + h;                                           /* L27 */
    store1[i] = euler(x[i-1], y[i-1]);                           /* L28 */
    k = 0;                                                       /* L29 */
    while(w > 0.0001) {                                          /* L30 */
      u = euler(x[i], store2[k]);                                /* L31 */
      v = (store1[i] + u)/2;                                     /* L32 */
      store2[k+1] = y[i-1] + v * h;                              /* L33 */
      w = store2[k] - store2[k+1];                               /* L34 */
      w = fabs(w);                                               /* L35 */
      k = k + 1;                                                 /* L36 */
    }                                                            /* L37 */
    y[i] = store2[k];                                            /* L38 */
    i = i + 1;                                                   /* L39 */
  }                                                              /* L40 */
  printf("\nThe Values of X and Y are: \n");                     /* L41 */
  printf("\nX-values        Y-values\n");                        /* L42 */
  for(j=0; j < i; j++) {                                         /* L43 */
    printf("%f        %f\n", x[j], y[j]);                        /* L44 */
  }                                                              /* L45 */
  printf("\nThank you.\n");                                      /* L46 */
}                                                                /* L47 */
```

Compile and execute this program. A run of this program is given below:

```
Modified Euler's Method to Solve a Differential Equation.
Function for calculation of slope: y' = x * x + y
Enter the initial value of the variable x, x0: 0     ↵
Enter the final value of the variable x, xn: 0.1     ↵
Enter the initial value of the variable y, y0: 1     ↵
Enter the value of subinterval, h: 0.025     ↵

The Values of X and Y are:

X-values          Y-values
0.000000          1.000000
0.025000          1.025008
0.050000          1.050359
0.075000          1.076091
0.100000          1.102237

Thank you.
```

How It Works

Formula for Modified Euler's Method is given below:

$$y \ (x + h) = y(x) + h * f(x + h/2, \ y + hf/2)$$

where,

$$dy/dx = f(x,y)$$

is the differential equation to be solved subjected to the boundary condition:

$$y(x0) = y0$$

Also, h is nothing but the small increment in x. In this recipe, the differential equation to be solved is:

$$dy/dx = x * x + y$$

In LOC 2, the symbolic constant MAX is defined with the value of 50. LOCs 3-8 consist of definition of the function euler(). LOCs 9-47 consist of definition of the function main(). In LOCs 11-13 few variables are declared.

LOC 16 asks the user to enter the initial value of x. The number entered by user is stored in the first cell of float type array x, i.e., in x[0], in LOC 17. LOC 18 asks the user to enter the final value of x. The number entered by user is stored in the float variable b, in LOC 19. In LOC 20, user is asked to enter the initial value of y. The number entered by user is stored in the first cell of float type array y, i.e., in y[0], in LOC 21. LOC 22 asks the user to enter the value of subinterval. The number entered by user is stored in the float variable h, in LOC 23.

In the LOCs 24-40, the results are computed using the standard formulae for Modified Euler's Method to solve a differential equation. In the LOCs 41-45, the results are displayed on the screen.

11-17. To Solve a Differential Equation Using Runge Kutta Method

Problem

You want to solve a differential equation using Runge Kutta Method.
Merits:

- One step method. Global error is of the same order as local order.

- Derivative of f(x) is not needed

Demerits:

- Method does not contain in itself any simple means for estimating the error or for detecting computation mistakes.

- Each step requires four susbstitutions into the differential equation. For the complicated equations, this demands excessive amount of computations.

Solution

Write a C program that solves a differential equation using Runge Kutta Method, with the following specifications:

- Value of subinterval should be accurate upto 2 decimal points.

- Result should consist of at least three pairs of values of x and y.

The Code

Code of C program written with these specifications is given below. Type the following C program in a text editor and save it in the folder C:\Code with the filename numrc17.c:

```
/* This program implements Runge Kutta Method to Solve a Differential
Equation. */
                                                            /* BL */
#include<stdio.h>                                           /* L1 */
                                                            /* BL */
#define F(x,y) (2*x-y)/(x+y)                                /* L2 */
                                                            /* BL */
void main()                                                 /* L3 */
{                                                           /* L4 */
  int i, n;                                                 /* L5 */
  float x0, y0, h, xn, k1, k2, k3, k4, x, y, k;             /* L6 */
  printf("\nRunge Kutta Method to Solve a Differential Equation."); /* L7 */
  printf("\nEquation: y' = (2*x-y)/(x+y) ");                /* L8 */
  printf("\nEnter initial value of the variable x, x0: ");  /* L9 */
```

```
  scanf("%f", &x0);                                        /* L10 */
  printf("Enter initial value of the variable y, y0: ");   /* L11 */
  scanf("%f", &y0);                                        /* L12 */
  printf("Enter final value of the variable x, xn: ");     /* L13 */
  scanf("%f", &xn);                                        /* L14 */
  printf("Enter the subinterval, h: ");                    /* L15 */
  scanf("%f", &h);                                         /* L16 */
  n = (xn - x0)/h;                                         /* L17 */
  x = x0;                                                  /* L18 */
  y = y0;                                                  /* L19 */
  i = 0;                                                   /* L20 */
  while (i <= n) {                                         /* L21 */
    k1 = h * F(x,y);                                       /* L22 */
    k2 = h * F(x+h/2.0, y+k1/2.0);                         /* L23 */
    k3 = h * F(x+h/2.0, y+k2/2.0);                         /* L24 */
    k4 = h * F(x+h, y+k3);                                 /* L25 */
    k = (k1 + (k2+k3) * 2.0 + k4) / 6.0;                   /* L26 */
    printf("\nX = %f  Y = %f", x, y);                      /* L27 */
    x = x + h;                                             /* L28 */
    y = y + k;                                             /* L29 */
    i = i + 1;                                             /* L30 */
  }                                                        /* L31 */
  printf("\n\nThank you.\n");                              /* L32 */
}                                                          /* L33 */
```

Compile and execute this program. A run of this program is given below:

```
Runge Kutta Method to Solve a Differential Equation.
Equation: y' = (2*x-y)/(x+y)
Enter initial value of x, x0: 0      ↵
Enter initial value of y, y0: 1      ↵
Enter final value of x, xn: 0.25     ↵
Enter the subinterval, h: 0.05       ↵


X = 0.000000  Y = 1.000000
X = 0.050000  Y = 0.950000
X = 0.100000  Y = 0.907856
X = 0.150000  Y = 0.873379
X = 0.200000  Y = 0.846212

Thank you.
```

How It Works

Formula for Runge Kutta Method is given below:

y (x + h) = y(x) + h * f(x, y)

where,

dy/dx = f(x,y)

is the differential equation to be solved subjected to the boundary condition:

y(x0) = y0

Also, h is nothing but the small increment in x. In this recipe, the differential equation to be solved is:

dy/dx = (2*x-y)/(x+y)

LOC 2 defines the symbolic constant F(x, y). LOCs 3-33 consist of definition of the function main(). In the LOCs 5-6 few variables are declared. LOC 9 asks the user to enter the initial value of x. The number entered by user is stored in the float variable x0, in LOC 10. LOC 11 asks the user to enter the initial value of y. The number entered by user is stored in the float variable y, in LOC 12. LOC 13 asks the user to enter the final value of x. The number entered by user is stored in the float variable xn, in LOC 14.

LOC 15 asks the user to enter the value of subinterval. The number entered by user is stored in the float variable h, in LOC 16. The results are computed in the LOCs 17-31 using the standard formulae of Runge Kutta Method to solve a differential equation. The results are displayed on the screen in the LOC 27.

APPENDIX A

■ ■ ■

Reference Tables

Table A-1. *Escape Sequences in C*

Character	Escape Sequence	ASCII value
bell (alert)	\a	007
backspace	\b	008
tab	\t	009
newline (line feed)	\n	010
form feed	\f	012
carriage return	\r	013
double quote, inserts a double quote	\"	034
single quote, inserts a single quote	\'	039
question mark, inserts a question mark	\?	063
backslash, inserts a backslash	\\	092
null	\0	000

Table A-2. *Basic Data Types in C*

Basic Data Type	Size in Bits	Range of Values
char	8	-128 to 127
int	16	-32,768 to 32,767
float	32	-3.4e-38 to -3.4e+38, 0, 3.4e-38 to 3.4e+38
double	64	-1.7e-307 to -1.7e+308, 0, 1.7e-307 to 1.7e+308

© Shirish Chavan 2017
S. Chavan, *C Recipes*, DOI 10.1007/978-1-4842-2967-5

Table A-3. *Qualified Basic Data Types in C*

Basic Data Type	Size in Bits	Range of Values
signed char	8	-128 to 127
unsigned char	8	0 to 255
signed int	16	-32,768 to 32,767
unsigned int	16	0 to 65,535
short int or signed short int	8	-128 to 127
unsigned short int	8	0 to 255
long int or signed long int	32	-2,147,483,648 to 2,147,483,647
unsigned long int	32	0 to 4,294,967,295
long double	80	-3.4e-4932 to -1.1e+4932, 0, 3.4e-4932 to 1.1e+4932

Table A-4. *Additional Basic Data Types in C*

Additional Basic Data Type	Size in Bits	Range of Values
Void	0	No value
Enum	16	-32,768 to 32,767

Table A-5. *Number of Digits and Digits in the Various Number Systems*

System	No. of Digits	Digits
Binary	2	0, 1
Octal	8	0, 1, 2, 3, 4, 5, 6, 7
Decimal	10	0, 1, 2, 3, 4, 5, 6, 7, 8, 9
Hexadecimal	16	0, 1, 2, 3, 4, 5, 6, 7, 8, 9, A, B, C, D, E, F

Table A-6. *Prefixes for Variable Names in C as per Hungarian Naming Convention*

Data Type / Qualifiers	Prefix
char	chr
int	int
float	flt
double	dbl
unsigned	un
signed	sgn
short	sht
long	lng

Table A-7. *Arithmetic Operators in C*

No.	Operator	Meaning	Example	Result
1	+	Addition	5 + 3	8
2	–	1) Subtraction	5 – 3	2
		2) Unary minus	– (6)	–6
			– (–8)	8
3	*	Multiplication	5 * 3	15
4	/	1) Integer Division	5 / 3	1
		2) Floating Point Division	5.0 / 3.0	1.67
5	%	Modulus	5 % 3	2

Table A-8. *Precedence and Associativity of Operators in C*

Operators	Associativity
( ) [ ] -> .	left to right
! ~ ++ -- + - * & (type) sizeof	right to left
* / %	left to right
+ -	left to right
<< >>	left to right
< <= > >=	left to right
== !=	left to right
&	left to right
^	left to right
|	left to right
&&	left to right
||	left to right
?:	right to left
= += -= *= /= %= &= ^= |= <<= >>=	right to left
,	left to right

Table A-9. *Relational and Equality Operators in C*

Operator	Name	Example	Result	Meaning
>	Greater than	9 > 1	1	True
		2 > 9	0	false
>=	Greater than or equal to	8 >= 8	1	True
		6 >= 1	1	true
		2 >= 9	0	false
<	Less than	1 < 9	1	True
		8 < 3	0	false
<=	Less than or equal to	1 <= 1	1	true
		2 <= 9	1	true
		7 <= 2	0	false
==	Equal to	4 == 4	1	true
		5 == 9	0	false
!=	Not equal to	3 != 8	1	true
		7 != 7	0	false

Table A-10. *Logical Operators in C*

Operator	Name	Example	Result	Meaning
&&	logical AND	1 && 1	1	True
		1 && 0	0	False
		0 && 1	0	False
		0 && 0	0	False
||	logical OR	1 || 1	1	True
		1 || 0	1	true
		0 || 1	1	true
		0 || 0	0	false
!	logical NOT	!1	0	false
		!0	1	true

Table A-11. *Truth Table Used in Logic*

Operation	Result
true AND true	true
true AND false	false
false AND true	false
false AND false	false
true OR true	true
true OR false	true
false OR true	true
false OR false	false
NOT true	false
NOT false	true

Table A-12. *Bitwise Operators in C*

Operator	Name	Description
~	Bitwise unary NOT	It inverts the value of bit
&	Bitwise AND	Result is 1 if both bits are 1, otherwise result is 0.
|	Bitwise OR	Result is 0 if both bits are 0, otherwise result is 1.
^	Bitwise XOR	Result is 1 if one bit is 1 and other bit is 0, otherwise result is 0
<<	Left shift	Shift the bits to left and fill the vacated bits with 0.
>>	Right shift	Shift the bits to right and : (a) in case of unsigned quantity fills the vacated bits with 0, and (b) in case of signed quantity fills the vacated bits with 0 (logical shift) on some machines and with sign bits (arithmetic shift) on other machines.

Table A-13. *Bitwise Operations Using the Operators ~, &, |, and ^*

M	N	~M	M & N	M | N	M ^ N
1	1	0	1	1	0
0	0	1	0	0	0
1	0	0	0	1	1
0	1	1	0	1	1

Table A-14. *Assignment Operators in C*

Operator	Example	Expanded Version, if any
=	var = expr	No expansion
+=	var += expr	var = var + expr
-=	var -= expr	var = var - expr
*=	var *= expr	var = var * expr
/=	var /= expr	var = var / expr
%=	var %= expr	var = var % expr
&=	var &= expr	var = var & expr
|=	var |= expr	var = var | expr
^=	var ^= expr	var = var ^ expr
>>=	var >>= expr	var = var >> expr
<<=	var <<= expr	var = var << expr

Table A-15. *Permissible sizes of one-dimensional arrays for various basic types*

Type	Range
char	$1 <= N <= 65535$
int	$1 <= N <= 32767$
float	$1 <= N <= 16383$
double	$1 <= N <= 8191$

Table A-16. *Table of Standard Input and Ouput Functions*

Function	Formatted/Unformatted	Purpose
scanf()	formatted	input of all types
printf()	formatted	output of all types
getchar()	unformatted	for char type input
gets()	unformatted	for string input
putchar()	unformatted	for char type output
puts()	unformatted	for string output

Table A-17. *Conversion Specifications (C.S.) for function scanf()*

C. S.	Input Data and Supported Types
%c	character. The default width of input field is 1. White space characters are also treated as data by this conversion specification. Types: char.
%d	decimal integer. Types: short int, int, signed int, signed short int, unsigned short int.
%hd	decimal integer. Types: short int, signed short int, unsigned short int.
%ld	decimal integer. Types: long int, signed long int.
%i	integer. The integer may be octal (leading 0) or hexadecimal (leading 0x or 0X). Types: short int, int, signed int, signed short int, unsigned short int.
%li	integer. The integer may be octal (leading 0) or hexadecimal (leading 0x or 0X). Types: long int, signed long int.
%o	octal integer, with or without leading zero. Types: unsigned short int, unsigned int.
%lo	octal integer, with or without leading zero. Types: unsigned long int.
%u	unsigned decimal integer. Types: unsigned int.
%lu	decimal integer. Types: unsigned long int.
%x	hexadecimal integer, with or without leading 0x or 0X. unsigned short int, unsigned int.

(continued)

409

Table A-17. (*continued*)

C. S.	Input Data and Supported Types
%lx	hexadecimal integer, with or without leading 0x or 0X. unsigned long int.
%s	string of non-white space characters which is not delimited by double quotes.
%f	floating-point number. Accepts number in standard form. Types: float.
%e	floating-point number. Accepts number in exponent form. Types: float.
%g	floating-point number. Accepts number in exponent form. Types: float.
%lf	floating-point number. Accepts number in standard form. Types: double.
%le	floating-point number. Accepts number in exponent form. Types: double.
%lg	floating-point number. Accepts number in exponent form. Types: double.
%Lf	floating-point number. Accepts number in standard form. Types: long double.
%Le	floating-point number. Accepts number in exponent form. Types: long double.
%Lg	floating-point number. Accepts number in exponent form. Types: long double.
%p	pointer value as printed by printf("%p");
%n	writes into the argument the number of characters read so far by this call.
%[...]	matches the longest non-empty string of input characters from the set between square brackets.
%[^...]	matches the longest non-empty string of input characters not from the set between square brackets.

Table A-18. *Conversion Specifications (C.S.) for function printf()*

C. S.	Output Data and Supported Types
%c	character. Types: char.
%d	decimal integer. Types: short int, int, signed int, signed short int, unsigned short int.
%hd	decimal integer. Types: short int, signed short int, unsigned short int.
%ld	decimal integer. Types: long int, signed long int.
%i	octal, hexadecimal, or decimal integer. Types: short int, int, signed int, signed short int, unsigned short int.
%li	octal, hexedecimal, or decimal integer. Types: long int, signed long int.
%o	octal integer. Types: unsigned short int, unsigned int.
%lo	octal integer. Types: unsigned long int.
%u	unsigned decimal integer. Types: unsigned int.
%lu	decimal integer. Types: unsigned long int.

(*continued*)

Table A-18. *(continued)*

C. S.	Output Data and Supported Types
%x	hexadecimal integer. unsigned short int, unsigned int.
%lx	hexadecimal integer. unsigned long int.
%s	string of non-white space characters which is not delimted by double quotes.
%f	floating-point number. Displays number in standard form. Types: float.
%e	floating-point number. Displays number in exponent form. Types: float.
%g	floating-point number. Displays number in exponent form. Suppresses trailing zeros after decimal point. Types: float.
%lf	floating-point number. Displays number in standard form. Types: double.
%le	floating-point number. Displays number in exponent form. Types: double.
%lg	floating-point number. Displays number in exponent form. Suppresses trailing zeros after decimal point. Types: double.
%Lf	floating-point number. Displays number in standard form. Types: long double.
%Le	floating-point number. Displays number in exponent form. Types: long double.
%Lg	floating-point number. Displays number in exponent form. Suppresses trailing zeros after decimal point. Types: long double.

Table A-19. *Flags used in conversion specifications in function printf()*

Flag	Meaning
- (hyphen)	It causes the data to be displayed be left justified within its field. Spaces are postfixed to data.
+	It causes a positive or negative sign to be prefixed to a numeric datum. Without this flag, only negative datums are prefixed with sign.
0 (zero)	It causes leading zeros to appear instead of leading blanks to fill the extra space. Applies only to numeric datums which are right justified.
' ' (blank space)	It causes a blank space to be prefixed to a positive numeric datum. This flag is overridden by + flag, if both flags are present.
#	When used with conversion specifications %o and %x, it causes the octal and hexadecimal datums to be preceded by 0 and 0x respectively.
#	When used with conversion specifications %f, %e, and %g, it causes a decimal point to be present in all floating-point datums, even if datum is a whole number. It also prevents the truncation of trailing zeros after decimal point in conversion specification %g.

Table A-20. *Various File Opening Modes in C*

Mode string	Description
"r"	Existing text file is opened for reading only. If specified text file doesn't exist then error is reported.
"rb"	Existing binary file is opened for reading only. If specified binary file doesn't exist then error is reported.
"rt"	Same as "r".
"r+"	Existing text file is opened for reading as well as writing. If specified text file doesn't exist then error is reported.
"r+b"	Existing binary file is opened for reading as well as writing. If specified binary file doesn't exist then error is reported.
"r+t"	Same as "r+".
"w"	Contents of specified text file are deleted and then it is opened for writing. If specified text file doesn't exist then it is created.
"wb"	Contents of specified binary file are deleted and then it is opened for writing. If specified binary file doesn't exist then it is created.
"wt"	Same as "w".
"w+"	Contents of specified text file are deleted and then it is opened for writing as well as reading. If specified text file doesn't exist then it is created.
"w+b"	Contents of specified binary file are deleted and then it is opened for writing as well as reading. If specified binary file doesn't exist then it is created.
"w+t"	Same as "w+".
"a"	Specified text file is opened for writing at the end of file (i.e., appending). If specified text file doesn't exist then it is created.
"ab"	Specified binary file is opened for writing at the end of file (i.e., appending). If specified binary file doesn't exist then it is created.
"at"	Same as mode "a".
"a+"	Specified text file is opened for reading as well as writing at the end of file (i.e., appending). If specified text file doesn't exist then it is created.
"a+b"	Specified binary file is opened for reading as well as writing at the end of file (i.e., appending). If specified binary file doesn't exist then it is created.
"a+t"	Same as "a+".

412

Table A-21. *Predefined Pointers to FILE Constants for Device Files in C*

Pointer to FILE Constants	Device File
stdin	keyboard
stdout	monitor
stderr	monitor

Note: The header file <stdio.h> consists of the declaration of FILE structure as shown below:

```
typedef struct  {
        int             level;      /* fill/empty level of buffer */
        unsigned        flags;      /* File status flags          */
        char            fd;         /* File descriptor            */
        unsigned char   hold;       /* Ungetc char if no buffer   */
        int             bsize;      /* Buffer size                */
        unsigned char   *buffer;    /* Data transfer buffer       */
        unsigned char   *curp;      /* Current active pointer      */
        unsigned        istemp;     /* Temporary file indicator   */
        short           token;      /* Used for validity checking */
}       FILE;                       /* This is the FILE object    */
```

Table A-22. *Table of Trigraph Sequences and Equivalent Characters in C*

Trigraph Sequence	Equivalent Character
??=	#
??/	\
??'	^
??(	[
??)	]
??!	|
??<	{
??>	}
??-	~

413

■ ■ ■

Library Functions

In this appendix, we have included the library functions falling under the catetories:

- Character testing and processing functions,
- String processing functions,
- Mathematical functions, and
- Utility functions

Character Testing and Processing Functions

In order to use any of these functions you are required to #include the file <ctype.h>. For each function, an argument is int and return type is also int. Argument represents a character or EOF, if underlying condition is satisfied then function returns nonzero (true) value, otherwise it returns zero (false) value. The names of these functions and underlying conditions are listed below:

Name of function	Underlying condition
isupper(ch)	ch should represent upper case letter
islower(ch)	ch should represent lower case letter.
isalpha(ch)	ch should represent upper or lower case letter.
isdigit(ch)	ch should represent a decimal digit (0, 1, 2, 4, 5, 6, 7, 8, or 9).
isalnum(ch)	ch should represent upper case letter, lower case letter or decimal digit.
iscntrl(ch)	ch should represent a control character. Notice that characters with ASCII values 0 to 31 are treated as control characters.
isgraph(ch)	ch should represent a printing character except space.
isprint(ch)	ch should represent a printing character including space.
ispunct(ch)	ch should represent a printing character except space, letter, or digit.
isspace(ch)	ch should represent a space, formfeed, newline, carriage return, tab, or vertical tab.
isxdigit(ch)	ch should represent a hexadecimal digit.

© Shirish Chavan 2017
S. Chavan, *C Recipes*, DOI 10.1007/978-1-4842-2967-5

Also, there are two character processing functions that convert the case of letters, as follows:

Name of function	Underlying condition
int tolower(int ch)	If ch represent uppercase letter then it is converted to lowercase, otherwise it is returned without any change.
int toupper(int ch)	If ch represents lowercase letter then it is converted to uppercase, otherwise it is returned without any change.

String Processing Functions

The string processing functions are listed below along with their description. In order to use these functions you are required to #include the header file <string.h>. It is assumed that s and t are of type char *; cs and ct are of type const char *; n is of type int; and c is of type int, however, it is converted to char when passed as an argument to function.

Function name	Description
char *strcpy (s, ct)	String ct is copied to string s including terminating null character. Return value is s.
char *strncpy (s, ct, n)	At most n characters are copied from string ct to string s. Return value is s.
char *strcat (s, ct)	String ct is appended (concatenated) to string s. Return value is s.
char *strncat (s, ct, n)	At most n characters are appended (concatenated) from string ct to string s. Return value is s.
int strcmp (cs, ct)	String cs is compared to string ct. Return value is negative if cs < ct, return value is zero if cs == ct, return value is positive if cs > ct.
int strncmp (cs, ct, n)	At most n characters from string ct are compared to string cs. Return value is: negative if cs < ct, zero if cs == ct, and positive if cs > ct.
char *strchr (cs, c)	String cs is searched for the occurrence of c. Return value is pointer to first occurrence of c in cs or NULL value if c is not found in cs.
char *strrchr (cs, c)	String cs is searched for the occurrence of c. Return value is pointer to last occurrence of c in cs or NULL value if c is not found in cs.
int strspn (cs, ct)	String cs is searched for any of the characters not available in string ct. Return value is the index of the first character in cs which is not available in ct.

(continued)

Function name	Description
`int strcspn (cs, ct)`	String cs is searched for the occurrence of any of the characters in string ct. Return value is the index of the first character in cs which is also available in ct.
`char *strpbrk (cs, ct)`	String cs is searched for the occurrence of any of the characters in string ct. Return value is pointer to first occurrence of any character of ct in cs, or NULL if no character of ct is found in cs.
`char *strstr (cs, ct)`	String cs is searched for the occurrence of string ct. Return value is pointer to first occurrence of ct in cs, or NULL if ct not found in cs.
`int strlen (cs)`	Length of string cs is computed and it is returned.

Mathematical Functions

The mathematical functions are listed below along with their description. The header file `<math.h>` contains the declarations of mathematical functions and macros, and needs to be #included in the source code. In order to catch the errors, the header file `<errno.h>` should also be #included. Two types of errors occur in these functions: (a) domain error and (b) range error. Domain error occurs if an argument is out of range. Range error occurs if result of the function cannot be expressed as double type value. Macros EDOM and ERANGE are used to signal domain and range errors respectively. If result overflows then return value is HUGE_VAL with appropriate sign. If the result underflows then return value is zero. HUGE_VAL is a macro and it represents a double, positive value.

It is assumed that u and v are expressions that evaluate to double type constant, m is an expression that evaluates to int type constant. Return type of all these functions is double. Unit of angles is radians.

Function name	Description
`sin(u)`	Computes the sine of u and returns it. Here, u is angle in radians.
`cos(u)`	Computes the cosine of u and returns it. Here, u is angle in radians.
`tan(u)`	Computers the tangent of u and returns it. Here, u is angle in radians.
`asin(u)`	Computes the arcsine of u and returns it. Here, u is sine value between -1.0 and +1.0. Return value is angle between $-\pi/2$ and $+\pi/2$ radians. If domain error is detected, value 0.0 is returned.
`acos(u)`	Computes the arccosine of u and returns it. Here, u is cosine value between -1.0 and +1.0. Return value is angle between 0 and π radians. If domain error is detected, value 0.0 is returned.
`atan(u)`	Computes the arctangent of u and returns it. Here, u is signed tangent value. Return value is angle between $-\pi/2$ and $+\pi/2$ radians.

(continued)

417

Function name	Description
atan2(u, v)	Computes the arctangent of u/v. Here, u and v represent any signed values. Return value is angle between $-\pi$ and $+\pi$ radians whose tangent value is u/v.
sinh(u)	Computes the hyperbolic sine of u and returns it. Here, u is angle in radians. If an overflow occurs then value of $\pm$(HUGE_VAL) is returned.
cosh(u)	Computes the hyperbolic cosine of u and returns it. Here, u is an angle in radians. If an overflow occurs then value of $\pm$(HUGE_VAL) is returned.
tanh(u)	Computes the hyperbolic tangent of u and returns it. Here, u is an angle in radians.
exp(u)	Computes the e^u where e = 2.7182818. It is called exponential function. Here, u represents any signed value. Return value is exponential of u. If an underflow occurs then a value of 0.0 is returned. If an overflow occurs then a value of HUGE_VAL is returned.
log(u)	Computes the natural logarithm of u. Here, u represents a positive floating point value. Return value is natural or base-e logarithm of u. If argument u is zero or negative, then a value of -(HUGE_VAL) is returned.
log10(u)	Computes the base 10 logarithm of u. Here, u represents a positive floating point value. Return value is base-10 logarithm of u. If argument u is zero or negative, then a value of -(HUGE_VAL) is returned.
pow(u, v)	Computes the u^v. Domain error occurs if u == 0 and v <= 0, or if u < 0 and v is not an integer. Here, u represents a nonzero floating point value; and v represents a signed, floating point power of u up to 264. Returned value is u^v. If both u and v are 0.0, then returned value is also 0.0. If u is nonzero and v is 0.0, then 1.0 is returned. If u is negative and v is not integral then 0.0 is returned. If u is 0.0 and v is negative, then 0.0 is returned. If an overflow occurs, then value of $\pm$(HUGE_VAL) is returned.
sqrt(u)	Computes the square root of u. Here, u is nonnegative number (u >= 0). Return value is square root of u. If u is negative then zero is returned.
ceil(u)	Computes the smallest integer that is greater than or equal to u. Return value is the smallest integer that is greater than or equal to u.
floor(u)	Computes the largest integer that is smaller than or equal to u. Return value is the largest integer that is smaller than or equal to u.
fabs(u)	Computes the absolute value of u, i.e.,	u |. Return value is the absolute value of u.
ldexp(u, m)	Computes u $\times$ 2^m. Here, u is any signed value (usually between 0.5 and 1.0). As told earlier, m is an expression that evaluates to int type constant. Return value is u $\times$ 2^m and its type is double. If overflow occurs then return value is $\pm$(HUGE_VAL).
fmod(u, v)	Computes the remainder of u/v. Return value is remainder of u/v. If value v is 0.0 then return value is also 0.0.

Utility Functions

The various utility functions available in C are listed below along with their description. The header file `<stdlib.h>` contains the declarations of these utility functions, and needs to be #included in the source code.

Function name	Description
`double atof (const char *str)`	Converts string `str` to a number of type double and returns it. For example, string `"24.36"` is converted to number `24.36` and then this number is returned.
`int atoi (const char *str)`	Converts string `str` to a number of type int and returns it. For example, string `"2537"` is converted to number 2537 and then this number is returned.
`long atol (const char *str)`	Converts string `str` to a number of type long and returns it. For example, string `"123456"` is converted to number 123456 and then this number is returned.
`int rand (void)`	Returns a pseudorandom integer in the range 0 to RAND_MAX. The value of constant RAND_MAX is at least 32,767.
`void srand (unsigned int seed)`	Uses seed (this seed is nothing but an integer) as a seed for generating new random numbers by function rand().
`void abort (void)`	Causes the abnormal termination of program.
`void exit (int status)`	Causes normal termination of program. Integer status is passed to this function to indicate the status of program. For example, integer 0 is passed to indicate the successful termination of program. Predefined constants EXIT_SUCCESS and EXIT_FAILURE are also passed to this function to indicate success and failure of program respectively.
`int abs (int num)`	Returns the absolute value of int argument num, i.e., | num |.
`long labs (long num)`	Returns the absolute value of long argument num, i.e., | num |.

APPENDIX C

C Idioms

Some statements in C are quite popular among the programmers and are respectfully referred to as C idioms. In this appendix you will find a good collection of C idioms.

C Idiom No. 1. This C idiom, given below, copies input to output:

```
int ch;
ch = getchar();
while(ch != EOF) {
  putchar(ch);
  ch = getchar();
}
```

C Idiom No. 2. This C idiom also, given below, copies input to output:

```
int ch;
while((ch = getchar()) != EOF)
    putchar(ch);
```

C Idiom No. 3. This C idiom, given below, counts number of characters in input:

```
long count = 0;
while(getchar() != EOF)
    ++count;
printf("%ld\n", count);
```

C Idiom No. 4. This C idiom also, given below, counts number of characters in input:

```
double count;
for(count = 0; getchar() != EOF; ++count)
    ;                                            /* null statement */
printf("%.0f\n", count);
```

© Shirish Chavan 2017
S. Chavan, *C Recipes*, DOI 10.1007/978-1-4842-2967-5

C Idiom No. 5. This C idiom, given below, counts number of lines in input:

```
int ch, count = 0;
while((ch = getchar()) != EOF)
   if(ch == '\n')
       ++count;
printf("%d\n", count);
```

C Idiom No. 6. This C idiom, given below, counts number of lines, words, and characters in input:

```
define IN  1                            /* inside a word */
define OUT 0                            /* outside a word */
int ch, lines, words, chars, state;
state = OUT;
lines = words = chars = 0;
while ((ch = getchar()) != EOF) {
  ++chars;
  if (ch == '\n')
    ++lines;
  if (ch == ' ' || ch == '\n' || ch == '\t')
    state = OUT;
  else if (state == OUT) {
    state = IN;
    ++words;
  }
}
printf("%d %d %d\n", lines, words, chars);
```

C Idiom No. 7. This C idiom, given below, represented as function, raises base to nth power where n is greater than or equal to zero:

```
int power(int base, int n)
{
  int po;
  for(po = 1; n > 0; --n)
    po = po * base;
  return(po);
}
```

C Idiom No. 8. This C idiom, given below, represented as function, reads a line of text into a char array q and returns its length:

```
int getline(char q[], int limit)
{
 int ch, j;
 for(j=0; j<limit-1 && (ch=getchar())!=EOF && ch!='\n'; ++j)
   q[j] = ch;
 if(ch == '\n'){
```

```
    q[j] = ch;
    ++j;
  }
  q[j] = '\0';
  return j;
}
```

C Idiom No. 9. This C idiom, given below, represented as function, copies char array source to char array target:

```
void copy(char target[], char source[])
{
  int j = 0;
  while((target[j] source[j]) != '\0')
    ++j;
}
```

C Idiom No. 10. This C idiom, given below, represented as function, returns a length of the string str:

```
int strlen(char str[])
{
  int j = 0;
  while(str[j] != '\0')
    ++j;
  return j;
}
```

C Idiom No. 11. This C idiom, given below, represented as function, converts a string of digits str into an equivalent integer:

```
int atoi(char str[])
{
  int j, n = 0;
  for(j=0; str[j] >= '0' && str[j] <= '9'; ++j)
    n = 10 * n + (str[j] - '0');
  return n;
}
```

C Idiom No. 12. This C idiom, given below, represented as function, converts an upper case letter into a lower case letter, and leaves lower case letter unchanged:

```
int lower(int ch)
{
  if (ch >= 'A' && ch <= 'Z')
    return ch + 'a' - 'A';
  else
    return ch;
}
```

C Idiom No. 13. This C idiom, given below, represented as function, removes all occurrences of the character ch from the string str:

```c
void remove(char str[], int ch)
{
  int j, k;
  for(j = k = 0; str[j] != '\0'; j++)
    if(str[j] != ch)
        str[k++] = str[j];
  str[k] = '\0';
}
```

C Idiom No. 14. This C idiom, given below, represented as function, concatenates string str2 to end of string str1; string str1 must be big enough so as to accommodate the string str2:

```c
void strcat(char str1[], str2[])
{
  int j = k = 0;
  while(str1[j] != '\0')              /* find end of str1 */
    j++;
  while((str1[j++] = str2[k++]) != '\0')   /* copy str2 to str1 */
    ;                                 /* null statement */
}
```

C Idiom No. 15. This C idiom, given below, represented as function, counts the number of 1-bits in its integer argument:

```c
int bitcounter(unsigned int y)
{
  int g;
  for(g = 0; y != 0; y >>= 1)
    if(y & 01)
        g++;
  return g;
}
```

C Idiom No. 16. This C idiom, given below, represented as function, performs binary search and finds integer y in int array w such that array is sorted and its elements consist of int values in increasing order:

```c
int binsearch(int y, int w[], int p)
{
  int low = 0, high, mid;
  high = p - 1;
  while(low <= high){
    mid = (low + high) / 2;
    if(y < w[mid])
```

```
      high = mid - 1;
    else if (y > w[mid])
      low = mid + 1;
    else
        return mid;
  }
  return -1;
}
```

C Idiom No. 17. This C idiom, given below, represented as function, converts a string of digits str into an equivalent integer. This version is more generic than C Idiom No. 11, in that now optional white spaces and optional + or - sign is taken into account. You are also required to #include the file <cype.h>:

```
int atoi(char str[])
{
  int j, p, sign;
  for(j = 0; isspace(str[j]); j++)
    ;                                          /* null statement */
  sign = (str[j] == '-') ? -1 : 1;
  if(str[j] == '+' || str[j] == '-')
    j++;
  for(p = 0; isdigit(str[j]); j++)
    p = 10 * p + (str[j] - '0');
  return sign * p;
}
```

C Idiom No. 18. This C idiom, given below, represented as function, sorts an int array into increasing order. This method is known as shellsort as it is invented by D. L. Shell in 1959:

```
void shellsort(int w[], int p)
{
  int gap, j, k, temp;
  for(gap = p/2; gap > 0; gap /= 2)
    for(j = gap; j < p; j++)
      for(k = j - gap; k >= 0 && w[k] > w[k + gap]; k -= gap) {
        temp = w[k];
        w[k] = w[k + gap];
        w[k + gap] = temp;
      }
}
```

C Idiom No. 19. This C idiom, given below, represented as function, reverses the contents of string str.

```
void reverse(char str[])
{
  int ch, j, k;
```

425

```
  for(j = 0, k = strlen(str) - 1; j < k; j++, k--){
    ch = str[j];
    str[j] = str[k];
    str[k] = ch;
  }
}
```

C Idiom No. 20. This C idiom also, given below, represented as function, reverses the contents of string str. You are required to #include the header file <string.h>.

```
void reverse(char str[])
{
  int ch, j, k;
  for(j = 0, k = strlen(str) - 1; j < k; j++, k--)
    ch = str[j], str[j] = str[k], str[k] = ch;
```

C Idiom No. 21. This C idiom, given below, represented as function, converts an integer into a string of digits:

```
void itoa(int p, char str[])
{
  int j, sign;
  if((sign = p) < 0)
    p = -p;
  j = 0;
  do{
    str[j++] = p % 10 + '0';
  }while((p /= 10) > 0);
  if(sign < 0)
    str[j++] = '-';
  str[j] = '\0';
  reverse(str);
}
```

C Idiom No. 22. This C idiom, given below, represented as function, removes trailing blanks, tabs, and newlines from string str:

```
int trim(char str[])
{
  int p;
  for(p = strlen(str) - 1; p >= 0; p--)
    if(str[p] != ' ' && str[p] != '\t' && str[p] != '\n')
      break;
  str[p + 1] = '\0';
  return p;
}
```

C Idiom No. 23. This C idiom, given below, represented as function, returns index of string s2 in string s1 and returns -1 if no substring s2 is found in s1.

```c
int strindex(char s1[], char s2[])
{
  int j, k, m;
  for(j = 0; s1[j] != '\0'; j++){
    for(k = j, m = 0; s2[m] != '\0' && s1[k] == s1[m]; k++, m++)
      ;                                              /* null statement */
    if(m > 0 && s2[m] == '\0')
      return j;
  }
  return -1;
}
```

C Idiom No. 24. This C idiom, given below, represented as function, converts a string of digits into a double type number. You are required to #include the header file <ctype.h>:

```c
double atof(char str[])
{
  double value, power;
  int j, sign;
  for(j = 0; isspace(str[j]); j++)
    ;                                              /* null statement */
  sign = (str[j] == '-') ? -1 : 1;
  if(str[j] == '+' || str[j] == '-')
    j++;
  for(value = 0.0; isdigit(str[j]); j++)
    value = 10.0 * value + (str[j] - '0');
  if(str[j] == '.')
    j++;
  for(power = 1.0; isdigit(str[j]); j++){
    value = 10.0 * value + (str[j] - '0');
    power = power * 10.0;
  }
  return sign * value / power;
}
```

C Idiom No. 25. This C idiom, given below, represented as function, sorts an int array into an increasing order using the method quicksort invented by C. A. R. Hoare in 1962:

```c
void qsort(int w[], int left, int right)
{
  int j, last;
  void swap(int w[], int j, int k);
  if(left >= right)
```

```
    return;
  swap(w, left, (left + right)/2);
  last = left;
  for(j = left + 1; j <= right; j++)
    if(w[j] < w[left])
      swap(w, ++last, j);
  swap(w, left, last);
  qsort(w, left, last - 1);
  qsort(w, last+1, right);
}
void swap(int w[], int j, int k)
{
  int temp;
  temp = w[j];
  w[j] = w[k];
  w[k] = temp;
}
```

C Idiom No. 26. This C idiom, given below, represented as function, computes the length of string str. This is pointer based version:

```
int strlen(char *str)
{
  int p;
  for(p = 0; *str != '\0'; str++)
    p++;
  return p;
}
```

C Idiom No. 27. This C idiom, given below, represented as function, copies string source to string target. This is an array subscript based version:

```
void strcpy(char *target, char *source)
{
  int j = 0;
  while((target[j] = source[j]) != '\0')
    j++;
}
```

C Idiom No. 28. This C idiom also, given below, represented as function, copies string source to string target. This is pointer based version:

```
void strcpy(char *target, char *source)
{
  while((*target = *source) != '\0'){
    target++;
    source++;
  }
}
```

C Idiom No. 29. This C idiom also, given below, represented as function, copies string source to string target. This is pointer based another version:

```
void strcpy(char *target, char *source)
{
  while((*target++ = *source++) != '\0')
    ;                                        /* null statement */
}
```

C Idiom No. 30. This C idiom also, given below, represented as function, copies string source to string target. This is pointer based still another version:

```
void strcpy(char *target, char *source)
{
  while(*target++ = *source++)
    ;                                        /* null statement */
}
```

C Idiom No. 31. This C idiom, given below, represented as function, compares character strings str1 and str2, and returns negative, zero, or positive if str1 is lexicographically less than, equal to, or greater than str2, respectively:

```
int strcomp(char *str1, char *str2)
{
  int j;
  for(j = 0; str1[j] == str2[j]; j++)
    if(str1[j] == '\0')
      return 0;
  return str1[j] - str2[j];
}
```

C Idiom No. 32. This C idiom also, given below, represented as function, compares character strings str1 and str2, and returns negative, zero, or positive if str1 is lexicographically less than, equal to, or greater than str2, respectively. This is pointer based version:

```
int strcomp(char *str1, char *str2)
{
  for( ; *str1 == *str2; str1++, str2++)
    if(*str1 == *str2)
      return 0;
  return *str1 - *str2;
}
```

APPENDIX D

Glossary of Terms

Activity diagram: A flowchart as per the specifications of Unified Modelling Language.

Address operator: It is used to retrieve the address of a variable. It is denoted by &.

Array: A list of items of same data type and name, but different subscripts or indices. A derived data type.

Argument: Datum that is passed to function through function-call.

Assembler: An assembler is a program or software that translates an assembly language program into a machine language program.

Assembly language: An assembly language is a low-level computer language one step above the machine language. In assembly language the phrases (such as ADD, SUB, MUL, etc.) are provided as synonyms of sequences of 1s and 0s (such as 10101, 10001, etc.). A typical instruction in assembly language may look something like shown below:

```
ADD NUM1, NUM2
```

Assignment operator: An operator used in assignment expression. It is denoted by =.

Associativity of operator: Associativity of operator is either from left to right or from right to left. Associativity of operators decide in which direction a given expression is to be evaluated – whether from left to right or from right to left.

Automatic type conversion: See implicit type conversion.

Automatic variable: A variable that is declared inside a block without any storage class specifier or with storage class specifier auto.

Basic type: A type that is fundamental. Basic types in C are: char, int, enum, float, double, and void.

Batch program: In batch program, user doesn't interfere with program during its execution. Batch program executes from start to finish without expecting any intervention from user.

Binary operator: An operator which operates on two operands is called as binary operator.

© Shirish Chavan 2017
S. Chavan, *C Recipes*, DOI 10.1007/978-1-4842-2967-5

Bit-field: A set of adjacent bits within a single storage unit.

Bitwise logical operator: An operator which operates on individual bits and performs logical operation in a given number.

Bitwise shift operator: An operator which shifts the individual bits – either to left or to right – in a given number.

Block: A group of statements grouped together inside a pair of curly braces. A block may contain another block.

Called function: If function A calls function B then function B is called function.

Caller function: If function A calls function B then function A is caller function.

Cast: An operator used in casting.

Casting: Explicit type conversion.

Code: Program. To code means to write a program. Coding is the process of writing a program according to some design.

Coercion: Coercion is nothing but explicit type conversion.

Compiler: A compiler is a program or software that translates a high-level language program into a machine language program.

Compound statement: See block.

Computer: A computer is a device that accepts the input data, processes it, and then returns the processed data as output.

Constant: Constant is a named item that retains a consistent value throughout the execution of a program, as opposed to a variable, which can have its value changed during the execution of a program.

Constant expression: An expression that is combination of constants only. A variable cannot be included in a constant expression. Constant expression is evaluated at compile-time.

Control string for function printf(): A string of characters that is passed to function printf and it may contain ordinary characters, escape sequences, and conversion specifications.

Control string for function scanf(): A string of characters that is passed to function scanf and it may contain white spaces, ordinary characters, and conversion specifications.

Conversion specification for function printf(): It consists of a percent symbol %, followed by an optional flag, followed by an optional minimum field width specifier which is nothing but an unsigned integral number, followed by a dot, followed by an optional precision specifier which is nothing but an unsigned integral number, followed by an optional target width specifier, followed by a conversion character.

Conversion specification for function scanf(): It consists of a percent symbol %, followed by an optional assignment suppression character *, followed by an optional maximum field width specifier which is nothing but an unsigned integral number, followed by an optional target width specifier which is nothing but h, l, or L, followed by a conversion character.

C's model of a file: A file is a transmitter or receiver of stream of characters (or bytes) to or from the central processing unit, respectively.

Decrement operator: An operator which decreases the value of numeric variable by 1. It is denoted by --.

Dereferencing operator: See indirection operator.

Derived type: A type that is derived from basic type(s). Derived types in C are: arrays, functions, pointers, structures, and unions.

Destination type: In type conversion, type of l value is called destination type.

Device-file: Keyboard and monitor are device files.

Disk-file: A collection of data that is named and saved on the secondary storage.

Documentation: Documentation is the collection of organized and stored records that describe the purpose, use, structure, details, and operational requirements of a program, for the purpose of making this information easily available to user.

Dynamic memory allocation: Process of allocation of contiguous block of memory to program for data storage during run-time.

Explicit type conversion: When type conversion is performed using cast then it is called explicit type conversion. Also called casting or coercion.

Expression: Any combination of variables and/or constants that evaluates to a constant, after assigning suitable values to variables.

Expression statement: An expression postfixed with semicolon.

External variable: A variable that is defined outside of any function and without any storage class specifier.

False value: If result of relational expression is 0 then it is treated as false value.

File: See disk-file, device-file, and C's model of file.

Flowchart: A graphical representation of all possible paths of computer control.

Function: A subprogram delimited by braces.

Function-definition: Return type, function-name, comma separated list of arguments, and body of function constitute function-definition.

Function-prototype: A statement which is placed before main() function and which informs the compiler that definition of this function is included in this program.

Global variable: See external variable.

GUI: The GUI stands for Graphical User Interface. It is an operating system that makes liberal use of graphics.

Hardware: The physical, tangible, and permanent components of a computer.

Header file: It contains prototypes of functions, macro definitions, and type definitions. It has extension .h.

High-level language: A language in which each instruction or statement correspond to several machine language instructions. For example, FORTRAN, Pascal, C, C++, and Java are high-level languages.

Identifier: Identifier means nothing but a name.

Implicit type conversion: When type conversion occurs automatically - i.e., without using cast - it is called implicit type conversion.

Increment operator: An operator which increases the value of numeric variable by 1. It is denoted by ++.

Indirection operator: An operator which is required while declaring pointer variable and also while retrieving the value of variable to which pointer variable is pointing. It is denoted by *.

Infinite loop: A loop that iterates indefinitely as there is no provision for termination of loop.

Initializer: A datum that is used to initialize a variable.

Interactive program: In interactive program, intervention of user is expected during the execution of former.

Internal variable: A variable that is created inside of some function. Generally speaking internal variable denotes automatic variable, register variable, or static automatic variable. Some writers equate internal variable with automatic variable only.

Interpreter: An interpreter is a program or software that translates and executes each source program statement before proceeding to the next one.

Iteration statement: A statement used to execute a group of statements repeatedly, finite number of times.

Jump statement: A statement used to jump from one statement to another by overriding linear flow of computer-control.

Keyword: Keyword is a reserved word having some predefined meaning. As it is reserved word, it cannot be used as user-defined identifier.

l value: l value is defined as the term that appears on left side in an assignment statement.

Labelled statement: A named statement.

Library function: A precompiled function that comes with compiler. There are standard and non-standard library functions.

Lifetime of a variable: It refers to the period from its creation to destruction during the execution of program.

Literal: Literal is a value, used in a program, that is expressed as itself rather than as a variable's value or the result of an expression.

LOC: Line Of Code. A single line of code in a source program.

Local variable: See automatic variable.

Logical expression: An expression that involves one of the three logical operators, namely && (AND), || (OR), and ! (NOT).

Low-level language: A low-level language is a computer language consisting of mnemonics that directly correspond to machine language instructions. For example, assembly language is a low-level language.

Machine language: The machine language is a language that consists of only two alphabets: 0 and 1. Also, a program in machine language can be readily executed by a computer. A typical instruction in machine language may look something like shown below:

11001101010101001

Macro: See macro name.

Macro name: A user-defined identifier that appears in macro expansion directive which in turn begins with preprocessor directive #define.

Main function: A function that is named main. It is coded by user. Every C program consists of one and only one main function. Execution of C program is nothing but execution of main function.

Maintenance: Program maintenance means: (i) fixing the errors in a program during its lifetime and (ii) modifying a program so as to expand its capability.

Narrowing type conversion: If range of destination type is narrower than range of source type then this type of type conversion is called narrowing type conversion.

Non-standard library function: A library function that is not supported by ANSI or ISO standard.

Operating system: An operating system is a set of programs that is responsible for handling the components of computer, so that user can use the computer efficiently. Also called as an executive system or a monitor system.

Parameter: It appears in function-definition and informs about the datum that will be passed to function in function-call.

Pdl: See Program design language.

Platform: A machine loaded with some operating system is termed as platform. If there are two IBM PCs, one loaded with LINUX and another loaded with Windows, then you are having two different platforms.

Pointer variable: A sort of variable that stores address of ordinary variable. Pointer variable is said to point to ordinary variable whose address it stores.

435

Population sequence: Population sequence begins with 1 and 2, and every successive term is a product of the two preceding terms. By definition, first term is 1 and second term is 2. Third term is 2. Fourth term is 4. Fifth term is 8. And so on. See page 193.

Portability: Portability is a property of a computer program to run on different platforms.

Precedence of operator: Precedence and priority are synonyms. Precedence of operator tells us which operation in a given expression is to be performed first and which one later. Suppose a given expression consists of two operators: operator A with precedence 1 and operator B with precedence 2 then operation involving operator A should be performed first, and so on.

Preprocessor: Preprocessor converts source code file with extension .c (say, hello.c) to intermediate file with extension .i (say, hello.i), which in turn is fed to compiler to convert it into an executable file with extension .exe (say, hello.exe).

Priority of operator: See precedence of operator.

Program: A program (i.e., computer-program) is a set of instructions which tells the computer what to do. Alternatively, Niklaus Wirth has defined a program as follows:

```
algorithm + data structures = program.
```

(Throughout this book we use the term "program" as a synonym of "computer-program.")

Program design language: A language developed as an aid in designing programming systems. It is mix of plain English and standard control structures.

Programmer: A programmer is a person who writes a program.

Programming language: The language used by a programmer to write a program for a computer.

r value: r value is defined as the term that appears on right side in an assignment statement.

Recursion: A process in which function calls itself either directly or indirectly through some other function.

Register variable: A variable that is declared inside some block and with storage class specifier register.

Relational expression: An expression that involves one of the six relational operators, namely > (greater than), >= (greater than or equal to), < (less than), <= (less than or equal to), == (equal to), and != (not equal to).

Scope of variable: It refers to the parts of a program in which that variable is accessible.

Selection statement: A statement used to choose one of the several flows of computer-control.

Self-referential structure: A structure in which one of its members is a pointer to that structure itself.

Software: Software is defined as follows:

```
Software = program + portability + documentation + maintenance.
```

Alternatively, Joseph Fox has defined software as a set of programs that interact with each other.

Source program: A source program is a program written by a programmer on paper. It can be entered in a computer using a suitable text editor.

Source type: In type conversion, type of r value is called source type.

Standard input device: Keyboard.

Standard output device: Monitor.

Standard library function: A library function that is supported by ANSI or ISO standard.

Static variable: A variable that is declared with storage class specifier static.

Static external variable: See static global variable.

Static global variable: A variable that is declared outside of any function and with storage class specfier static.

Static automatic variable: See static local variable.

Static internal variable: See static local variable.

Static local variable: A variable that is declared inside of some block and with storage class specifier static.

Storage class: An attribute of a variable (or function) which decides scope and lifetime of variable (or function).

String constant: A char type array that is terminated with null character '\0'.

Strongly typed language: Language that does not allow the mixing of different types at all is called a strongly typed language or language with strong typing.

Structure: A collection of one or more variables of different data types, in general, grouped together under a single name for convenient handling. A derived data type.

Ternary operator: An operator which operates on three operands is called as ternary operator.

Token: Tokens are basic elements of a program. What bricks are to a wall, tokens are to a program.

True value: If result of relational expression is 1 then it is interpreted as true value.

Two's complement: A method used to represent the negative numbers in some machines.

Type checking: When compiler compiles assignment statement, it checks the types of both sides of assignment statement for equality. This duty of compiler is termed as type checking.

Type conversion: Type conversion occurs in an assignment statement if types of r value and l value are not same. In type conversion, type of value of right side is changed to that of left side before assignment.

UML: See Unified Modelling Language.

Unary operator: An operator which operates on only one operand is called as unary operator.

Unified Modelling Language: A language developed by computer scientists – mainly by Grady Booch, James Rumbaugh, and Ivar Jacobson – to construct the models of programming systems.

Union: A derived data type which resembles structure. However, unlike structure, all members of union share same memory segment.

User-defined function: A function that is coded and named by user (here, user means programmer).

User-defined identifier: User-defined identifier is nothing but a specific term that is used to denote variable name, constant name, function name, or label name, provided that these items (e.g., variable, constant, label, etc.) are created by a user (programmer).

Variable: Variable is nothing but a named location in memory and when you assign some value to that variable, that value is stored in that memory location.

Variable declaration: In the context of internal variables (i.e., automatic, register, and static local), variable declaration consists of creation of a variable. In the context of external and static global variables, variable declaration consists of announcement that this variable exists and it is defined elsewhere.

Variable definition: In the context of internal variables (i.e., automatic, register, and static local), this term is not used. In the context of external variables, variable declaration consists of creation of a variable.

Weakly typed language: Language that freely allows the mixing of different types without any restriction is called a weakly typed language or language with weak typing.

Widening type conversion: If range of destination type is wider than range of source type then this type of type conversion is called widening type conversion.

Index

445

Get the eBook for only $5!

Why limit yourself?

With most of our titles available in both PDF and ePUB format, you can access your content wherever and however you wish—on your PC, phone, tablet, or reader.

Since you've purchased this print book, we are happy to offer you the eBook for just $5.

To learn more, go to http://www.apress.com/companion or contact support@apress.com.

Apress®

CPSIA information can be obtained
at www.ICGtesting.com
Printed in the USA
LVOW13s1538130218
566429LV00003B/106/P